Critiques of Theology

SUNY series in Contemporary Jewish Thought

Richard A. Cohen, editor

Critiques of Theology

German-Jewish Intellectuals
and the Religious Sources of Secular Thought

YOTAM HOTAM

Gesetz (Law, 1938) by Paul Klee. Gouache on newsprint laid down by the artist on thin card. Wikimedia Commons

Published by State University of New York Press, Albany

© 2023 State University of New York

All rights reserved

Printed in the United States of America

No part of this book may be used or reproduced in any manner whatsoever without written permission. No part of this book may be stored in a retrieval system or transmitted in any form or by any means including electronic, electrostatic, magnetic tape, mechanical, photocopying, recording, or otherwise without the prior permission in writing of the publisher.

For information, contact State University of New York Press, Albany, NY
www.sunypress.edu

Library of Congress Cataloging-in-Publication Data

Name: Hotam, Yotam, 1968– author.
Title: Critiques of theology : German-Jewish intellectuals and the religious sources of secular thought / Yotam Hotam.
Description: Albany : State University of New York Press, [2023] | Series: SUNY series in contemporary Jewish thought | Includes bibliographical references and index.
Identifiers: LCCN 2022053723 | ISBN 9781438494364 (hardcover : alk. paper) | ISBN 9781438494371 (ebook) | ISBN 9781438494388 (pbk. : alk. paper)
Subjects: LCSH: Theology—Study and teaching. | Judaism and culture. | Christianity and culture. | Secularism.
Classification: LCC BV4022 .H683 2023 | DDC 230.071—dc23/eng/20230515
LC record available at https://lccn.loc.gov/2022053723

10 9 8 7 6 5 4 3 2 1

To my mother

Contents

Acknowledgments ix

Introduction: A Handmaid's Tale 1

Chapter 1 Wit and Law 17

Chapter 2 A Theory of Youth 55

Chapter 3 Education Ex Machina 89

Chapter 4 Tradition 125

Epilogue: The World in Which We Live 161

Notes 169

Bibliography 213

Index 237

Acknowledgments

A book is not created in a vacuum, and even if penned by a single author, it could not have been completed without the discussions, disputes, shared thoughts, challenged ideas, and moments of inspiration—or frustration—that shape our intellectual association with others. I began formulating this book while serving as visiting professor in Yale University's Judaic Studies Program during the winter of 2015. I thank Steven Fraade, the head of the program, as well as Christine Hayes and Renee Reed, for granting me the space and conditions to undertake the first steps of my journey. During that time, I enjoyed deep, enriching, and occasionally challenging discussions with wonderful colleagues to whom I am greatly indebted. Hannan Hever was an ideal partner for discussions on topics related to political theology, and he is undoubtedly one of the most generous, sincere, and compassionate people I have met in the academic world. Yishai Kiel was an endless fountain of rare historical knowledge of Halakhic thought and a welcome source of assistance for the elucidation of Mishnaic and Talmudic topics. Kirk Wetters's brilliant observations regarding modern German thought provided me with new perspectives on secularization, theology, religion, and political theory, and every encounter with him was more enriching than the previous one. Paul North excelled at challenging my claims regarding modern German-Jewish thought, and his sharp remarks on a draft of the second chapter of this book were extremely helpful. Paul Franks called my attention to the relationship between German idealism and Jewish thought. David Sorkin offered an abundance of insights into the complex relationships between the Enlightenment and religious traditions, and in his quiet manner provided a source of encouragement and support when I most needed it.

I wish to thank the Bucerius Institute for Research of Contemporary German History and Society at the University of Haifa, and its head, Cedric Cohen Skalli. The institute became my intellectual home while writing the book, and it supported all stages of its composition most generously. During the various stages of my work, I received the assistance of colleagues and friends. I owe a great debt to Suzanne Schneider for her keen suggestions, which induced me to rethink and rearticulate some of my main arguments. Dirk Moses, Lior Libman, and Ofer Nur were their usual generous and patient selves, and their comments on earlier drafts were very helpful. Paul Mendes-Flohr offered valuable assistance and Pinhas Luzon helped me decipher some Talmudic discussions. Over the years, I had the privilege of enjoying fruitful discussions with Itzhak Benyamini, Dana Amir, Michal Ben-Naftali, Adi Efal, Philip Wexler, Avihu Shoshana, Ayman Agbaria, and Shakhar Rahav on a wide range of subjects that directly and indirectly touched upon the materials that went into this book—from concrete discussions of psychoanalysis and social thought, love and evil, dualism and dialectics, to wider questions regarding modern thought, critical theories, religion, secularization, and the world we live in. I owe a special thanks to Joshua Amaru and Jemma Dunhill for "Englishing my English"—as Hannah Arendt put it—as well as to the publishing house and the anonymous readers. Finally, I wish to thank my dear wife and beloved children, who serve as a daily reminder of what is truly important in this world. The book is dedicated to my loving mother who passed away during the last stages of copyediting and could not see this book completed.

Yotam Hotam
Haifa, December 2022

*An earlier version of the second chapter of this book appeared as "Eternal, Transcendent, and Divine: Walter Benjamin's Theory of Youth," *Sophia* 58.2 (2019): 175–95, and is reprinted with permission from Springer Nature.

Introduction

A Handmaid's Tale

Between Critique and Theology

It is hard to imagine a concept more significant to modern Western thought than that of "critique." Foucault, for example, argued that there was "in the modern West (dating, roughly, from the fifteenth to the sixteenth centuries) a certain manner of thinking, of speaking, likewise of acting, and a certain relation to what exists, to what one knows, to what one does, as well as a relation to society, to culture, to others, and all this one might name 'the critical attitude.'"[1] Particularly in the wake of the Enlightenment, a "critical attitude" became associated with a set of practices and ideas: a method of scientific investigation; a form of understanding social constructs and historical processes; an analysis of the scope and validity of concepts, theories, fields of knowledge, and mental states; an ethical approach; and the basis for optimism about human development.[2]

Yet, when characterizing critique as a fundamental concept "in the history of Western culture," Foucault, among others, also likened it to a secular worldview.[3] At the heart of the prevailing argument that "critique is, in short, secular" is the notion that the bedrock of a critical approach is human reason, its primary objective being to break free from deduction based on faith—or revelation.[4] On this basis, secularism appears "as the opposite of religion" and critique is held to be "the opposite of orthodoxy, dogmatism, or fundamentalism."[5] In practice, then, critique is conceived of as the torchbearer of secular ideology, signifying a binary opposition between "the secular" and its religious "other," while comprising the lens through which this "other" is framed and interpreted. Critique thus represents—in Talal Asad's compelling words—"the essence of secular heroism," propelling forward modernity's promise of human progress driven by rational inquiry and scientific development.[6]

Based on a close reading of selected and previously less discussed writings of four giants of twentieth-century thought—Sigmund Freud (1856–1939), Walter Benjamin (1892–1940), Theodor Adorno (1903–1969), and Hannah Arendt (1906–1975)—this book aims at reversing this understanding of critique. These leading German-Jewish intellectuals played a decisive role in the formation of twentieth-century social sciences, generating or deeply influencing diverse disciplines and scientific traditions (psychoanalysis, critical theory, and political science), with a resounding scholarly impact that is still felt today.[7] Decidedly secular thinkers, not one of them was in any way religious, nor even sympathetic to religious ways of life. Nonetheless, in bringing these four prominent thinkers together, the book shows how in their writings critique emerges from religious traditions and can in many ways be traced back to them. By drawing on the Enlightenment, they indeed saw critique as epitomizing the "essence of secular heroism," and this features in their work in two main ways: first, as an analysis of concepts, and second, as a means of interpreting and thus examining social, historical, and political questions so as to offer critical accounts of modernity "that address general human as well as specifically Jewish concerns."[8] At the same time, however, critique operates in their work in a way that is conscious of theology (pertaining to matters like transcendence, divine law, revelation, redemption, and God), often finding its expression within a predominantly religious frame of reference. The concept of theology is not identical with a specific academic discipline, with a methodology to substantiate the existence of God, nor is it synonymous with religious practices. It refers, rather, to a range of concepts, terms, and ideas carried over from religious thought, toward which it is always turned. In this sense, Kafka's remark that theology "was the main resource for our conceptual commitments" is largely applicable to these scholars.[9] As a resource for constructing new answers to ongoing questions, theology mainly depends on its use and function and resembles to some extent what Hans Blumenberg called a discourse of legitimation (which is not based on any level of accomplishment in making a certain argument or in proving a set of claims, but points to their necessity in responding to an intellectual call in the context of a specific historical exigency).[10] What is emphasized here, then, is not a sociological argument but a conceptual gesture, and this is central to their writings.

This is not to disregard the significant generational, historical, and disciplinary differences between the four selected thinkers. Indeed, these differences are important because they highlight the variety of profound and creative ways in which Jewish and Christian elements are in dialogue with modern conceptualizations of critique in the spotlight of this study.[11] I do not aim, however, to demonstrate cross-generational collaborations, nor to provide new data concerning personal or conceptual ties between these scholars (even if some of these ties and cross-references will be duly noted throughout the book). Rather, I highlight the shared dependency of their conceptions of critique on theology and the significance this carries. In particular, I wish to examine selected topics and texts (elaborated more closely below) spanning a century, across different fields of study, for I aim to show how—to use a musical metaphor—we are dealing here with a great intellectual symphony on the critique of a modern secular world, whose overtones have always resonated with religion and theology. Touching upon Jewish and Christian theological traditions, twentieth-century modern and secular critique seems to present a much richer, and perhaps more composite phenomenon than previously assumed.

With these thinkers, then, our view of critical thinking is reversed: contrary to the common separation between critique and its religious "other," this book traces the connection between them. Thus, despite the secular emphasis on critique, theological concerns lose neither their place nor their influence. In lieu of treating critique as a testament to the disengagement of modern thinking from religion, this book seeks to identify how the works of prominent modern German-Jewish intellectuals, although widely divergent, give expression to the religious sources of secular thought.

This argument is the core of the book. It points to a continual misreading of critique and draws our attention to something both fundamental and yet often unsaid: the mechanism that gives impetus to secular thinking is not secular. Moreover, and however counterintuitive it might seem, I argue that religious modes of critique power critique's secular distancing from religion. In this sense, modern critique is a form of immanent critique, which does not come from outside of religion to build a new world of ideas, but redeploys those already present within its constellation of theological considerations.

Within this conceptual framework, the book asks several key questions. What does critique mean for each of the thinkers in question? What theological traditions inform each thinker's thought? And in what ways do critique and theology interconnect? Each of the four chapters of the book is therefore dedicated to one thinker, focusing either on one particular text or on a selection of works and offering an analysis of how the thinker in question identified manifold interrelations between critique and theology.

Given today's increasing attention to the relation between politics and religion, faith and political action, and the "religious" and the "secular," there is also growing interest in the different ways in which these relationships unfold. Nonetheless, most of the scholarly investigations that underline the intricate links between secularism and religion tend to stop short of thinking about the mechanism of critique itself as being born out of theology.[12] This is also true in relation to the ongoing production of scholarly works dedicated to the role of religion and theology in the writings of twentieth-century German-Jewish thinkers.[13] The assertion that the "Western academy is still governed by the presumptive secularism of critique" seems to be valid even now.[14] This book's main argument, conversely, seeks to abandon our fixation on the secular character of critique in favor of a much broader and more compound understanding of its relation to theology. If critique is not secular, what does it look like? And what might its modern modes of expression tell us about the world in which we live? Answering these questions is important because it allows us to uncover points of connection between modern secular thought and religious traditions that have been hitherto neglected.

It is for this purpose that I draw upon the concept of a "critique of theology"; not only to present the critical positions of these thinkers regarding religion and theology, but also to capture a critique that is dependent on theology and that surfaces in different forms, within different intellectual disciplines and different sociopolitical contexts of the first and latter halves of the twentieth century. Critique of theology thus differs from the frequently used concept of "political theology." Unlike the focus on the emergence of modern political concepts, I wish to engage somewhat more broadly with what emerges from the interaction between the concepts of critique and theology, which may extend to, but is not limited to, political categories. I also suggest a shift in scholarly attention from the "political theological predicament" (a concept that relates to a modern diagnosis of the relation between politics and theology as much as to its reconstruction) to a "critical theological predicament" (denoting a modern analysis that acknowledges the dependency of critique on theology). A critique of theology, however, is also distinct from "critical theology."[15] Such a connotation usually indicates the manifestations of critical mechanisms in theological thinking.[16] It thus refers, for example, to religious thinking that makes use of analytical tools or logic-based argumentation to validate God's existence or to formulate principles of faith.[17] My purpose, however, is in many ways diametrically opposite. I wish to bring to light the ways in which theological concepts are manifested in critical thinking. The emphasis is on a modern critique that draws on the theological canon, and the complex interrelations formed as a result.

The Critical Path

I started with a prevailing view of secular critique and its vital role in the Enlightenment. Foucault, for example, suggested that in Kant's philosophy, in particular, we see an interlocking of the two concepts.[18] Kant's philosophical endeavors are indeed regarded as an attempt to secure the notion that critique "is secular." Contesting this particular issue seems to be important at this point because, as suggested above, not only critique but also its relation to theology in the writings of modern Jewish thinkers is intimately linked to the legacy of the Enlightenment, and specifically to Kant's "critical path" (*der kritische Weg*).[19]

There is, I believe, clear agreement as to the nature of this path. For Kant, the objective of critique is to "purify" concepts of fallacies. In the strict Kantian sense, therefore, critique means a form of analysis of certain content or of an object of study that includes charting its sources (*Quellen*), scope (*Umfang*), and boundaries (*Grenzen*).[20] In taking the faculty of reason as its object of study, for example, critique aims to "remove all errors" (*Abstellung aller Irrungen*) in our understanding of this faculty based on "principles" (*Prinzipien*) that are "independent of all experience" (*unabhängig von aller Erfahrung*).[21] This approach to critique implies the purification (*reinigen*) of "a ground that was completely overgrown."[22] These grounds also relate to theological claims and in such a way Kant seems to propose a clear differentiation between the dictate of reason and the guidance of an "other" (*Die Leitung eines Anderen*). True to this approach, and yet also critical of it, Heinrich Heine wrote in the epilogue to his last collection of poems that it is as if "one has to choose between religion and philosophy, between the dogma of the revelation of faith and the ultimate conclusion of systematic thought, between the biblical God and atheism."[23] A century later, Leo Strauss argued that the main choice faced by mankind, which leaves no middle ground, is between "human guidance" and "divine guidance." That is: "whether men can acquire knowledge of the good, without which they cannot guide their lives individually and collectively, by the unaided efforts of their reason, or whether they are dependent for that knowledge on divine revelation."[24]

Yet, the precise relation between this path of critique and theology appears to be disputed. Paul Franks, for example, makes a clear case not only for the importance of theology to Kant's epistemology and ethics, but particularly for his affinity to Jewish religious notions such as the "prohibition on representing God" and "the concept of law."[25] Through the Jewish notion of law, according to Franks, "Kant unites epistemology and ethics."[26] In such a way, Kant's critiques are indeed presented as relating to former theological categories. Specifically within the sphere of moral reason, we can observe that the theological concepts of God—intrinsic and vital to Kant's critical endeavors—and of an eternal soul (immortality) are postulated, along with free will, as conditions for the possibility of human morality.[27] We need theology, says Kant, "for religion, i.e., for the practical—specifically, the moral—use of reason."[28] Here, in our "inner religion" we are obligated by our practical reason as if it were a divine command, and thus: "So far as practical reason has the right to lead us, we will not hold actions to be obligatory because they are God's commands, but will rather regard them as divine commands because we are internally obligated to them."[29]

This reading of Kant may include his discussion of progress in the sphere of metaphysics. Kant posits that after the first, theoretical-dogmatic stage and the second, skeptical stage, comes a third, theological stage with all the a priori cognition that leads to it and makes it necessary.[30] Theology here appears (somewhat different from its definition in the *Critique of Judgment*) as knowledge "of the inscrutable determining ground of our willing, which we find, in ourselves alone" and which assumes its final end in "the supreme being above us."[31] This notion of theology is applicable "provided that it stays within the bounds of bare reason."[32] But Kant seems to advocate a theology of reason (associated with an ideal "invisible church" of rational morality) even if at odds with a theology of revelation and with the historical church, which he rejects.[33]

In *The Conflict of the Faculties*, "old Kant," as Hans Jonas rather amiably called him, appears to go further still.[34] While he articulates a clear structural distinction between the "lower" philosophical faculty (responsible for critical thinking and the pursuit of truth) and the "higher" theological faculty (which Kant associates primarily with biblical theology), he nevertheless explicitly contemplates the interaction between the two: "We can also grant the theology faculty's proud claim that the philosophy faculty is its handmaid (*Magd*) though the question remains, whether the servant is the mistress's *torchbearer (Fackel vorträger)* or *trainbearer (Schleppe nachträger)*, provided it is not driven away or silenced."³⁵

By using the handmaid's metaphor, Kant reformulates Thomas Aquinas's assertion about the servitude of philosophy with respect to theology. Kant's intention, however, was not to subjugate philosophical critique to theology; on the contrary, he attempted to challenge this hierarchy and to liberate critique within what he considered to be an unfavorable political constellation. Nevertheless, Kant's marvelous, somewhat Promethean imagery affirms the existence of a relation between critique and theology, even if the nature of this interconnection is open for discussion. Indeed, the manner in which the two are related seems to remain unresolved in Kant's self-coined metaphor. Since the conception of critique as handmaid of theology points to a rather more intricate narrative than the utter separation of the two, we may see in our moral interpretation of religion "an authentic one—that is, one that is given by the God within us (*der Gott in uns*)." It is, then, "only by concepts of *our* reason, in so far as they are pure moral concepts and hence infallible, that we recognize the divinity (*die Göttlichkeit*) of a teaching promulgated to us."³⁶

The handmaid's tale (to play on Kant's metaphor) could be read as an indicator of what Paul Franks sees as the dependency of Kant's critique on theological notions. David Sorkin's argument that "the Enlightenment was not only compatible with religious belief but conducive to it" may then be extended to include one of its central figures.³⁷ What is important to stress here, however, is that this line of reasoning may also encompass the twentieth-century modern Jewish intellectual legacy that is represented in this book. As suggested above, in drawing on the Enlightenment—and specifically on Kant—Freud, Benjamin, Adorno, and Arendt take up two main "secular" forms of critique: first, as a method of analysis, and second as a means of interpreting society, history, and politics. Seyla Benhabib, for example, demonstrated how the first form relates to critique as a rationalistic technique of scientific analysis, while the second applies critique as a kind of uncovering procedure that addresses the "*normative* dimension."³⁸ A far cry from simple skepticism, critique represents for these scholars these main forms of systematic investigation, based on human reason, beyond the sway of any faith-based deduction. Yet, in taking up, modifying, or developing these forms of critique, these thinkers also demonstrate a sensitivity not only to the synergy between critique and theology (taking into consideration Jewish religious themes), but also to the importance of preserving, or even, in some cases, rescuing this exchange. They present a critique that is constantly defined by its ongoing dialogue with theological legacies and it is for this reason that the positions they uphold are not in defiance of the Enlightenment inheritance, but rather convey a type of genealogical thinking that does it justice.[39]

To some extent, this last point also aims to challenge conventional wisdom concerning the critical path taken by each of the four thinkers. Indeed, these highly renowned and influential German-Jewish intellectuals invite particular attention because there appears to be a vibrant debate surrounding their relationships to everything theological. Freud's animosity toward religion, which he regarded as a delusion, is well-known. Equally famous is his self-perception as an "infidel Jew" (*ungläubiger Jude*), which has faced considerable scholarly scrutiny (particularly the element of "infidel"—not least thanks to Peter Gay's biography).[40] Attempts by scholars such as Yosef Hayim Yerushalmi and Eric Santner to offer an alternative view have been widely contested, mostly because Freud was remarkably consistent in his critical stance toward religion.[41] Similarly, Hannah Arendt is regarded by many as the "most secular" thinker of her generation. Peter Gordon, for example, underscores a dissimilarity between Arendt's "non-metaphysical account of the public world" and the common view of her contemporaries, for whom the "political theological predicament" was paramount.[42] In the same vein, Micha Brumlik distinguishes between modern Jewish thought, which secularizes theological concepts, and Arendt's political (by which he means strictly secular) analysis of the "Jewish fate" (*das jüdische Schicksal*).[43] These are but two examples of what may be regarded as the prevalent scholarly view.[44]

Somewhat differently, one may point to contemporary debates surrounding "critical theory" thinkers (a group that includes Benjamin and more prominently features Adorno). The progressive-enlightened-secular project that was associated with critical theory (also appearing as an antidote of sorts to the dangers of political theology) receives more and more attention today in terms of a growing scholarly focus on the theory's embedded theology.[45] For example, discussions on how best to interpret Benjamin's works reflect profound disagreement regarding the significance he attributes to concepts such as messianism, salvation, divinity, or mysticism.[46] A trace of the initial dispute between Adorno and Gershom Scholem—"the one a Marxist, the other a Zionist," according to Arendt's sharp-tongued description—seems to have resonated in every discussion of how to read Benjamin's corpus ever since.[47] Nevertheless, the disagreement between Adorno and Scholem sheds light on the complexity this book wishes to address. On the one hand, Adorno dismissed any extra-philosophical reading of Benjamin as a "sort of cliché" (pertinent to readings of Adorno himself); and in contrast, Scholem placed emphasis on Benjamin's messianic elements and his rootedness in the Jewish canon, which many scholars tended to dismiss.[48] On the other hand, both scholars agreed that "the 'transformation' of Benjamin from his early theological speculation to his later 'Materialisms' does not denote the 'disappearance' (*Verschwindung*) of the theological categories but rather their concealment (*Verschweigen*)."[49] One may further argue that this reading of Benjamin should also color interpretations of Adorno, who was himself in search of "religion's critical promise."[50] The question that merits attention here seems to relate to the type of relation between such a "promise" and its religious sources, and this question may apply to all four German-Jewish intellectuals at the center of this book.

Fingerprints of a Dynamic Spirit

To make the book's claim accessible, I have selected texts that, to paraphrase Adorno, reveal the "fingerprints" of these thinkers' "dynamic spirit."[51] Specifically, I focus on Sigmund Freud's work *Jokes and Their Relation to the Unconscious* (*Der Witz und seine Beziehung zum Unbewussten*) published in 1905; Walter Benjamin's early writings on youth (*Jugend*), composed between 1910 and 1917; Theodor Adorno's published texts and public lectures on education in the decade spanning 1959–1969; and Hannah Arendt's political writings from the 1960s, in which she developed the concept of tradition. These texts lie to some extent beyond what is considered the "classical writings" of these thinkers. They have thus remained less central in other scholarly investigations, with the additional implication that none of them have, to date, been read alongside one another. Compared to the vast scholarship on Freud's ideas about dreams, sexuality, civilizational discontent, totemism, or Moses and monotheism, his study of jokes—written in parallel to and sometimes simultaneously with his theories on sexuality—has remained relatively marginal. The theme was for a long time mainly regarded as a "Jewish" side issue with limited ties to Freud's psychoanalytic theory or metapsychological views on culture, society, and history.[52] Similarly, youth as formulated in Benjamin's early thought, before and during the First World War, has not attracted much scholarly attention.[53] In the same vein, interest in the role of education in Adorno's postwar thought has remained minimal in research, even though he repeatedly addressed the topic in a range of published texts and public lectures in the postwar context. This also seems to be true of Arendt's treatment of tradition, which has been understudied in other scholarly works that focus on her political writings from the 1960s, especially when compared to scholarly interest in her philosophical ideas like will, thinking, judgment, and action.[54]

Nonetheless, these texts and issues were selected because they were central to the thought of each of the four intellectuals in their day. Freud, for example, sought to make "contributions to the psychology of religion" in his study of jokes, which he certainly regarded as being much more than a minor "side issue."[55] Youth was, without doubt, the dominant concept with which Benjamin grappled at the beginning of his career.[56] Adorno's intellectual position—one could, perhaps, more fairly say self-positioning—in postwar Germany prompted him to seriously reflect on education as a central social and philosophical theme, even if he did so through a wide range of seemingly unrelated public lectures and written texts.[57] Arendt's political writings, as Dana Villa rightly argued, primarily exemplified her move "from totalitarianism to the tradition" that dominated her thinking at that time.[58] Thanks to these characteristics, the selected texts and themes (Freud's analysis of jokes, Benjamin's concept of youth, Adorno's interest in education, and Arendt's reading of tradition) not only expand our canon of literature. They lead us to some of these authors' central theoretical concerns—ranging from overarching arguments about history, politics, and society to views on specific matters like freedom, transgression, violence, or evil, and illuminating fundamental topics such as Freud's engagement with law and "lawgiving," Benjamin's social criticism, Adorno's negative dialectics, and Arendt's definition of a modern secular "new order of the world." These writings also show, more importantly, how these central issues bring into relief the relation between critique and theology. They represent different textual "sites" (to use Michel de Certeau's terminology) that may "bring into view" the variety of critiques of theology that the selected theorists produced, including the ways in which they introduced divergent theoretical frameworks (for example, psychoanalysis) into the "Western" concept of critique and to its dialogue with theology.[59]

Chapter 1 demonstrates how Freud defines jokes as a mechanism of social critique and how such a view of jokes is informed by theology.

First, the chapter shows that the common denominator of all jokes (*Witze*, which is for Freud analogous to "wit") is that they offer social critique. Such a critique, I argue, attests to Freud's recourse to a broad notion of law. Corresponding to a normative world in which we live, the concept of law for Freud is much broader than just a legal system of rules, and he explicitly highlights its role in Judaism. This ties in with what Eric Santner termed a "new awareness of the theological dimensions of Freudian thought" that relates mainly to the Jewish heritage in which he was raised.[60] Second, and in building on Freud's focus on Judaism, I suggest that Freud's study of jokes points to his critical engagement with the notion of law and lawgiving ascribed by a religious tradition and I examine how Jewish religious modes of critique fuel Freud's association between social critique and law in his theory of jokes. Discussions on Jewish religious law (Halakhah) are presented here as a main resource for Freud's understanding of critique. I do not argue that Freud was thoroughly familiar with Jewish rabbinic tradition—although he certainly was aware of it. But Freud does attach new, modern meaning to a fundamental dilemma relating to laws and their transgression, as featured in Jewish thought and pertaining to questions of living by the creed. Finally, I underline the dependency of Freud's concept of critique on this religious tradition and explain how this dependency feeds into Freud's critique of theology. With respect to this last point, the final section of this chapter explores how in Freud's case the social critique inherent in joking equates to a secular critique that redeploys the theological concepts on which it is based.

In chapter 2, I present Walter Benjamin's theory of youth as a form of critique of theology in that it offers social criticism of mystical lore. Here, in contrast to Freud, I do not focus on one main text but on a selection of philosophical writings, essays, fragmented texts and notes written between 1910 and 1917. These include the compositions "Socrates," "The Metaphysics of Youth," "On Language as Such and on the Language of Man," "The Life of Students"—some of which were published in contemporary periodicals and student journals—as well as "Dostoyevsky's *The Idiot*" from 1917, which may be regarded as Benjamin's last text dealing explicitly with youth. This selection reflects the evolution of Benjamin's theory of youth, which he developed before and during the First World War.

Following a short overview of the centrality of youth for the young Benjamin, I look at how he presents in these texts "youth" as the divine, eternal, and transcendent element of the human being and how such a theological vocabulary gives expression to Christian mysticism, such as the spirituality of Meister Eckhart. In relating particularly to divine "nothingness," central to the mystical tradition, Benjamin articulates youth mystically, evoking the potential for redemption that lies beyond human reach and historical realization, even though it is embedded, he says, in every present moment. I then trace the manner in which Benjamin's mystical articulation of youth informs his social criticism in these early years. Youth for Benjamin is not only a theological concept but also stands for a critique of social domination. I suggest that such a combination of mysticism and social criticism points to the dependency of his critique on theology. Finally, I examine the manner in which this form of critique that reiterates theological concepts could be considered secular, for Benjamin reframes transcendence within independent human experience of the world. I point to some of the main political implications of this theory, including Benjamin's explicit rejection of Jewish assimilation and Zionism.

While Freud and Benjamin's works showcase an interplay between critique and theology at the beginning of the twentieth century, the works of Theodor Adorno and Hannah Arendt from the 1960s reflect continued interest in this interrelation, decades later, within a different social and political context, which Adorno famously coined "after Auschwitz."[61] These two intellectuals may have displayed mutual personal antipathy (which they maintained with zeal, for reasons only they could perhaps understand); but they also manifested, each in his or her own way, a shared critical-theological legacy, reflected in a type of thinking that was "adequate to the disaster."[62]

Chapter 3 is dedicated to Adorno's postwar perspectives on education—which he regarded broadly, and somewhat loosely, as the arena for cultivating human beings. Between 1959 and 1969 Adorno's most evocative reflections on education are apparent, first and foremost, in his public lectures and talks, broadcast mainly (but not exclusively) by the Public Radio services of Hessen (Hessischer Rundfunk), which addressed the wider German audience and dealt, mostly explicitly, with educational themes.[63] In his endeavor to address the wider public of the new Federal Republic, Adorno turned rather surprisingly to radio, a medium he himself pejoratively described as the "progressive latecomer of mass culture" and "the voice of the nation" where "a recommendation becomes an order."[64] Second, he developed his ideas on education in some of his published works from that time, the most representative of which is his extensive paper *Theorie der Halbbildung*.[65] Third, in his university lectures that anticipated his *Negative Dialectics* he openly raised questions about the education of the young generation of an emerging Federal Republic.[66] In this range of engagements with education (in his popular public lectures, in his writings, or in the classroom) a "radical Adorno"—to use Russell Berman's words—is at work, one who presents some of his most intimate and fundamental standpoints on contemporary society and politics.

I first explicate how in these postwar addresses on and within the context of education, Adorno explicitly associates critique with metaphysical inquiry. He speaks of the "reconceptualization" of lost theological concepts that is intended to "rescue" them. This, I argue, is what critique of theology means for Adorno: critique both depends on and saves theology, after its disappearance. The chapter then traces Adorno's detailed attention to the transformation of the modern German cultural and educational tradition of *Bildung* into *Halbbildung* (a term that may be understood to mean "pseudoculture" and "pseudo-education"), which epitomizes for him a distortion of the "rescue" mission of critique. This distortion relates to the "entrapment" of human beings in existing, overwhelmingly oppressive, modern, social and, for Adorno, mechanized conditions, which provide the precondition for Auschwitz. I discuss how Adorno responds to this difficulty by calling for an education for "critical self-reflection," designed to reengage with the mission of saving theology that is not available anymore. It is this reengagement with a lost object (theology) that enables critique to resist entrapment by liberating the human being *ex machine,* an image that stands for resisting modern mechanisms of domination and control. Especially in the field of education, and because of its specific mission, Adorno seems to articulate critical theory as a critique of theology. I conclude by exploring the relationships between the critical-theological mission of education, negative theology, messianism, and the notion of divine love, explicitly evoked by Adorno in this context.

Following this discussion, chapter 4 underlines Arendt's critique of modernity that is rooted in the Roman religious tradition. Perhaps somewhat of an outlier for the discussion in this book, Arendt nonetheless makes a unique contribution to the relation between critique and theology in her political writings from the 1960s.[67] Typically made up of different chapters approaching an array of theoretical issues alongside "mundane" topics (some of which were published in the press beforehand), these writings notably include *On Revolution, Men in Dark Times, On Violence, Crises of the Republic,* and *Between Past and Future.*[68] The latter is central to this chapter because it contains much of Arendt's unfinished project on "Marx and the Great Traditions" and represented in her view "the best of her books."[69]

I first explore how Arendt defines tradition as a Roman religious concept, pertaining to the intergenerational transference of a sacred testament originating in a mythical past. As such, tradition is based on the Roman tripartite theology (constituting a three-part division between political theology, physical or philosophical theology, and mythical theology). Here, I suggest, Arendt's discussion draws mainly on her 1928 study of Saint Augustine's concept of love, to which she returned in her meticulous editing of its various English translations, a project she never completed.[70] Thus, it is the Roman tripartite theological tradition that, according to Arendt, Augustine absorbed into his Christian order of love, even if this was "against his wishes." Augustine is relevant to the attempt to understand the "crisis" of modernity because his reasoning represents a "fundamental chord which sounds in its endless modulations through the whole history of Western thought."[71] I then show that Arendt evokes this particular engagement with Augustine's theology as a basis for her critical analysis of modernity, with its "break" in tradition (namely the "disappearance" of the Roman religious tradition). I demonstrate the extent to which Arendt constructs a unique form of immanent critique in which Roman "traditional concepts" provide the foundation not only for her argument regarding what modernity has lost, but more profoundly for her critical analysis of this loss. For Arendt, as for Adorno, the task of criticism is to conceptualize theological concepts after their final disappearance, and this, I argue, means that critique, yet again, is shown to be dependent on theology. Next, I suggest that this type of critique of theology enables us to gain new insights into Arendt's support of a modern *novus ordo seclorum* (which Arendt translates as "a new order of the world"). A new and secular order not only relates to the ongoing erosion of Christian dogma in public life, but also, and somewhat antithetically, to a political return to the Roman religious tradition (as in, for example, the context of modern revolutions). I conclude by illustrating how such an argument—connecting Arendt's understanding of secularization and her reference to theology—may also be extended to explain her famous shift from her early discussion of "radical" (or "demonic") evil to her later preference for the "banality" of evil. The latter represents an understanding of evil in "secular settings" that are born, however, out of her theological considerations.

The book concludes with an epilogue that weaves together the four different critiques of theology. Anchored in Jewish and Christian traditions, worldly and divine law, mysticism, negative theology, and tripartite theology, these thinkers' critical redeployment of theology is specifically designed to engage with "the world in which we live." Extrapolating from these specific cases, I reflect on the predominant image of the secular separation from theology, contesting in this way recent claims regarding the so-called "return" of religion to a formerly "disenchanted" secular society. I also ask whether the desire to dissociate critical investigations from religion may suggest a refusal to acknowledge the fallibility that may exist behind the veneer of scientific rationality, partly because of the political meanings derived from it. I argue throughout the book, however, in favor of transforming the way we think about criticism in general. I go on to suggest that such a transformation is most essential today, given our collective responsibility to democracy in times of political crisis, which includes, one may argue, a dangerous narrowing down of the options that are available to us socially as well as politically. Indeed, in rethinking the relation between critique and theology we may find an opening up of a fruitful dialogue between modern secular thinking and religious traditions, a dialogue that represents, perhaps, our own "demand of the day" in a growingly intolerant and partisan world.

CHAPTER 1

Wit and Law

A Lawgiver

DEEPLY SIGNIFICANT STORIES

In a letter dated June 12, 1897, Freud shared with his then intimate friend, Wilhelm Fliess (1858–1928), a surprising confession. "Let me confess," Freud writes, "that I have recently made a collection of deeply significant Jewish stories" ("tiefsinniger jüdischer Geschichten").[1] The "stories" were Jewish jokes, anecdotes, and witticisms about *schnorrers* (beggars), *shadchanim* (matchmakers), and other comic (in Freud's eyes) figures, taken mostly from Eastern European Jewish experience. Starting such a "significant" collection was, for Freud, closely tied to the death of his father in 1896 (which he termed "the most important event, the most poignant loss, of a man's life") and the beginning of his famous self-analysis in 1897—the two formative events of his personal and professional life.[2] Thus, in recognizing that "the ostensible wit of all unconscious processes is closely connected with the theory of jokes and humor," Freud associated jokes with his first steps into what would later mature as a new science.[3] Freud was, no doubt, aware of the rise of scholarly attention at the turn of the nineteenth century to humor, the comical, and witticisms, but his deep interest in jokes also developed out of the connections he made between his personal experience and the founding of psychoanalysis.[4]

His book, *Jokes and Their Relation to the Unconscious* (*Der Witz und seine Beziehung zum Unbewussten*), was born out of these connections.[5] Published in 1905, eight years after starting the collection mentioned above, Freud's book presented an analysis of jokes (or *Witze*, which Freud presented as being an equivalent to the English term "wit") and of their social and psychological significance. The large number of "deeply significant stories" that Freud included in this work prompted scholars like Ernst Simon, Elliott Oring, and Sander Gilman to regard it as a "Jewish" document of minor significance to the understanding of Freud's psychoanalytic theory or metapsychological work.[6] However, for Freud, the book was much more than just a minor "side issue."[7] It represented a significant contribution to his early body of work that included his magnum opus *The Interpretation of Dreams* (1900), his *Psychopathology of Everyday Life* (1901), and his *Three Essays on the Theory of Sexuality* (1905)—the latter written concurrently with his book on jokes.[8] The study was thus juxtaposed by Freud with his work on sexuality and dreams, and belonged to his formative corpus that, as Ernest Jones pointed out, contains "permanent elements" to which he "adhered all his life."[9]

In this chapter, I suggest that the main enduring element in Freud's study of jokes relates to his critical engagement with the notion of law and lawgiving ascribed by a religious tradition. Indeed, what integrates his personal experience and psychoanalytic investigation in this book is the notion of law. By presenting jokes as a mechanism of social critique, I argue, Freud expresses a critique of law that is informed by theology. In what follows, I set out then to explore the relation between critique and theology in Freud's book and the manner in which it points to Freud's critique of theology.

Before doing so, I would first like to provide a context for this perhaps unorthodox reading of Freud's book. Especially in the years leading up to its composition, Freud expressed a deep interest in the notion of law and its association with religion and theology that related to him personally as well as professionally. His first expedition to Rome from 1901 exemplifies this point rather well and merits a more detailed description. In that year Freud overcame his "phobia of railways" (*Reisefieber*) and, for the first time in his life, took the train from Vienna to Rome, transgressing imaginary borders and breaking new ground.[10] The need to make this journey was brought about by a personal drama: his promotion to the position of Professor Extraordinarius (*ausserordentlicher Professor*) at the University of Vienna kept being delayed because of "denominational considerations," which essentially referred to Freud's Jewish origins. The legal constraints imposed on him left him feeling "inferior and an alien because I was a Jew."[11] They were then accompanied by a series of dreams related to

Catholic Rome, which represented for Freud both the "promised land" and the ultimate enemy, source of all Jewish persecution, compelling him to leave Vienna by heading to Rome.[12]

The point to note is that for Freud, this no doubt painful private affair mainly underlined a problem that related to the notion of law: "Learning the eternal laws of life in the Eternal City," wrote Freud, somewhat waggishly, to Fliess, "would be no bad combination."[13] It took the perspicacious self-analysis of Freud to later add in the same witty spirit: "If I close with 'Next Easter in Rome' I would feel like a pious (*frommgläubiger*) Jew," ironically reflecting on his personal complex (in the playful substitution of Jerusalem with Rome in the well-known Jewish expression).[14]

Freud's attitude toward the law in this context seems then to stand out vividly. First, he brings together "eternal laws" and denominational considerations, in this way associating religious symbolism with the legal drama that formed the backdrop to his expedition. Laws and eternal laws are thus correlated in a way that explicitly expresses Freud's critique of religion and society—a scrutiny of the social circumstances that are for Freud informed by religious considerations. That is to say that in Freud's analysis there is a link between his personal experience in a particular social and political reality, and a long and ongoing Christian hostility toward Jews that is emblematically represented, for him, by two Catholic cities: Vienna and Rome. Second, both the references to the law, eternal or otherwise, and the irony with which these references take shape assume a role in these partly painful, partly playful, richly associative and critical reflections. The use of witticism, no doubt, served Freud's emotional needs under such difficult circumstances. It was, perhaps, a way of expressing, or ventilating, feelings of frustration and discontent. But the jesting also provided Freud with an analytical instrument itself worthy of analysis. In his witticisms, Catholic Rome supplants Vienna, while Jerusalem (another eternal city of religion) is, to some extent, humorously presented as interchangeable with both. In an amusing way, Freud combines Rome and Jerusalem to reflect "eternal," divine law, against the background of his unresolved legal status related to his Jewish identity in a hostile (and Catholic) Vienna. Freud's witty approach, then, is also the prism through which he offers his social critique. It expresses his critique of social circumstances (i.e., the conditions in which he is regarded as "inferior" because he is a "Jew") to the same extent that this critique relates to religious and theological imagination. By means of irony and wordplay, there is a blurring of the boundaries between persecution and deliverance (symbolized by the clever exchange between Rome and Jerusalem) that relates to Freud's actual legal impasse. In all these areas of reflection (law, legality, religion, and theology), Freud seems to play with interchangeability, induced perhaps by the transgression of physical and imaginary borders that his excursion to Rome required. Freud, it seems, was not just going on a vacation. In his eyes, he was on his way to confront an eternal, malicious, redemptive, detested Rome-Jerusalem, a locus of concurrent identification and repulsion.[15] It was not for nothing that Freud called his pilgrimage "the high-point of my life," which could be read as a serious and ironic self-observation.[16]

If the road to Rome provided fertile ground for Freud's composite and witty reflections on law, religion, and theology, his arrival in the "eternal city" kept him going very much in the same direction. In what seems to be a fitting continuation of the chain of associations between social, legal, political, and theological spheres, Freud was struck—after crossing his personal "Rubicon" as Didier Anzieu puts it—by the sight of Michelangelo's *Moses* in the church of San Pietro in Vincoli (Saint Peter in Chains), an imposing marble figure adorning the tomb of Pope Julius II.[17] Freud would return to this statue of the "law-giver of the Jews" six times, on each of his subsequent visits to Rome.[18] He later asserted in an essay entitled "The Moses of Michelangelo": "[for] no piece of statuary has ever made a stronger impression on me than this."[19]

To the extent that Freud's last controversial publication, *Moses and Monotheism*, gave the final word on a long-lasting personal interest (as many scholars argue), his first visit to Rome stood for its naissance.[20] However, the main point to note here relates to Freud's insistence on bringing together critique, law, and theology. What we are dealing with, in particular, is Freud's response to a masterpiece of art through which Michelangelo essentially introduced Jewish law into the Christian framework with the aim of expressing his own critique of Christianity. This critical significance of the sculpture, Freud claimed, passed "suddenly through me" ("plötzlich, duch mich") like a personal revelation.[21] What struck him in this context was a combination of three integrated postures of Moses, which contributed to the "inscrutable" nature of his statue.[22] All three physical positions relate to falsifications and inversions of original meaning, orchestrated by a cunning artist who delivered his critical message in a rather shrewd way.

The first of Michelangelo's clever twists, Freud suggested, was the positioning of the Hebrew "law-giver" not only as a feature of the tomb of Pope Julius II, but rather as the "guardian of the tomb."[23] In Freud's eyes, the placing of the figure of Moses at the heart of a sacred Catholic space represented a double critique of the church. First, it presented the supremacy of divine law over and against the pope: Moses's "role in the general scheme" of Michelangelo is to direct "a reproach against the dead pontiff," serving as a reminder that the eternal law is "superior to his own nature."[24] Freud, undoubtedly, communicates the German intellectual tradition in which Judaism was considered to be the religion of law. Indeed, the figure of Moses unequivocally represents the law. It is in this critical sense that the "law-giver" of the Jews' "immediate counterpart" was to have been "a figure of Paul."[25] If Paul symbolized the Christian rejection of Jewish law, Moses, one could say, stood for Michelangelo's own revolt against the church.

Second, there is the falsification of Moses's status as a Jewish lawgiver, because Moses is now engraved as a Christian icon. This, then, is Freud's second critical observation. It relates to Michelangelo's own reproach to Judaism. For Freud, Moses is made to falsely represent something relating to "the individuality of Julius himself."[26] The imagined split between the figures of Paul and Moses is presented as a witty, somewhat psychological reflection on the pope's persona. But it also points to what such a persona theologically represents for Christianity. The positioning of Moses thus illustrated for Freud an array of dexterous inversions: the representation of a pious pope, which was, at the same time, a reproach against him; a Jewish Moses who is central only in virtue of being a guardian of a Catholic tomb; and a reminder of the supremacy of law, which is nevertheless located as an exclusive part of a Christian theological message.

The third distortion operative in the statue, according to Freud's account, can be observed in the way that Michelangelo's *Moses* is characterized by "a mixture of wrath, pain and contempt."[27] This hints at "a new Moses of the artist's conception," a false Moses, who, ironically, does not shatter the tablets inscribed with divine law, but rather contains his anger when the mob celebrates the false idol of the golden calf.[28] Here, once again, we encounter a fabricated Moses who replaces the lawgiver presented in the scriptures. What is being falsified is mainly Moses's performance. Instead of breaking the tablets, he preserves and rescues divine law. The biblical story becomes distorted and a new Moses replaces the mythical figure.

This last interpretation is the most valuable for Freud's argument regarding the artist's critique of law. It relates to "the very unusual way in which the Tables are held."[29] The Tables, representing the law, are "upside down" (*umgekehrt*).³⁰ Inverted, they stand "on their heads," but this is only because they are "easier to carry" in this way.³¹ The inversion of the law serves to ease the burden it imposes. Michelangelo's representation of the Tables as preserved (i.e., tamed wrath) is accompanied by a sort of overturning of their content. The purpose of this lies partly in the practical function of supporting Moses's physical posture in marble. But the main issue for Freud relates to the symbolic value of this reversal, which not only evokes the overturning of the law but also questions the (re)positioning of the lawgiver within the wider theological scheme. All of this reflects back on the artist's decision to place Moses at the entrance to the pope's tomb as guardian.

There is here a point to note that relates to a threefold falsification (*verfälschen*) that is captured in a theological image of a lawgiver with whom Freud would identify throughout his life.³² First, the law is preserved, but only inversely, a reversal that also supports the structure of the statue and Moses's physical stance, as a matter of practicality. Second, the prospect of wrath is sensed, but tamed and thwarted. Third, Moses maintains his position as an original Hebrew "holy man" and "lawgiver" but only as a Christian and, for Freud, a fabricated one. Here, a fake Moses replaces the original. The artist's display of faith, Freud concludes, "might almost be said to approach an act of blasphemy."³³ The inversions and falsifications that inform such "blasphemy" are not described by Freud as opposite poles but as a playful spectrum of well-devised inversions, transgressions, turns, and overturns.

Echoing his witty wordplays and ironies that related to his expedition to Rome, Freud's reflections on the statue of Moses demonstrate his interest in critical engagement with law and lawgiving ascribed by a religious tradition. A critique of the law and its relation to theology seems to be central in both cases. In his response to a fake Moses of artistic imagination, Freud brings together observations on theology and politics, faith and political action, heresy and deliverance. In Vienna, he examined the connections between the long history of religion and his personal predicaments; his analysis of Moses does this too, while at the same time bringing to the fore the importance of the use of cunning inversions and subversions. Wider critical and theological considerations are brought into play. Indeed, both Freud's critique of Vienna and his interpretation of Michelangelo's critique of the church encompassed playful transpositions, involving Rome and Jerusalem on the one hand, and Christianity and Judaism, Saint Paul and Moses on the other. In both cases, Freud seems to critically reflect on eternal social and political laws, while at the same time (and perhaps more importantly) considering how such laws are transgressed, overturned, held "upside down," circumvented, or subverted.

As mentioned above, the point of this rather long exposé was to set the scene for Freud's early interest in what associates critique, law, and theology with witty transgressions and subversions—the very connections that I wish to trace in his book on jokes. Ernest Jones's observation that this particular book contains "some of [Freud's] most delicate writing" is apt, mainly because the book seems to integrate Freud's dominant personal and professional quests at that time.[34] But Freud himself made the case rather clear when suggesting that the vital importance of his collection of stories stems from the fact that "only the setting (*Beiwerk*) is Jewish, the core (*Kern*) belongs to humanity in general."[35] Such a notion may explain why Freud's autobiographical retrospective presented the book as a particular "contribution to the psychology of religion."[36] Perhaps like a statue of Moses over the tomb of a pope, jokes have grave importance because they are conceived by Freud as guardians of a universal message. One may argue that it is this message, or "core," that he sets out to examine.

In particular, what invites our attention, then, is the development of Freud's thinking on critique of law and on its relation to religion and theology that ornamented, for example, his reflections on Rome as much as his thoughts on the "lawgiver of the Jews." In this sense, the *Moses* of Michelangelo may not only relate to "dream-work" as Asher Biermann suggested, but also to "joke-work."[37] Still, some of Freud's reflections on law and lawgiving from these early years come across as plainly amusing, while others remain somewhat vague or underdeveloped (for example, in his correspondence). Freud recognized that deeper analysis was required. The importance of the book on jokes lies in providing such an analysis, "intimately interweaving"—to paraphrase Freud—critical considerations with religious sources, theology with its secularization, and Judaism with modernity, to the extent of offering fresh insights into Freud's critique of theology, as discussed next.[38]

A MECHANISM OF SOCIAL CRITIQUE

What is then a joke for Freud and how does it relate to the notion of law? To answer we may start with the fact that for Freud a joke is a mechanism of social critique. Two main points support this claim. First, jokes for Freud represent a social device aiming to induce pleasure through and because of an "economy in psychical expenditure."³⁹ Such an "economy" denotes rather simply the saving of mental energy. Second, this energy is saved because of two interrelated factors: jokes are subversive and they are brief.⁴⁰ The brevity of jokes will be discussed in the next section, but the subversive character of jokes is of particular significance here because it underlines jokes as a reaction to imposed social norms, cultural requisites, or rules of behavior. Subversion in this context denotes a release of sorts from social structures, or from cultural and moral demands internalized by adhering individuals. To put it differently, the joke is made to resist these imposed burdens by subverting and, in this particular sense, resisting them.

An elaborative, rather representative, example of the dynamics of combined subversion and resistance is a witticism that Freud adopts from Heinrich Heine. In his *Reisebilder* Heine introduces the comic figure of Hirsch-Hyacinth of Hamburg, who, so the deeply important story goes, had a personal meeting with Baron Rothschild, one of the wealthiest Jews of that time. He then recalled his experience as follows: "And, as true as God shall grant me all good things, Doctor, I sat beside Salomon Rothschild and he treated me quite as his equal—quite famillionairely."⁴¹ Freud, like Heine, seems to be amused by this particular Jewish pun, and uses it as a central example of the technique of jokes that preoccupies him in the first section of his book dedicated to the analysis of jokes. The subversion embedded in the joke, he explains, results from an irregular condensing of two words into one (familiar and millionaire). The unusual melding of these two words, however, enables the criticism of a social structure in which familiarity may go only "so far as a millionaire can," a criticism that, under regular social conditions, would not, perhaps, be made so readily easily.⁴² In this subversive way the joke mainly discloses a resistance to social norms—in this case the relations between the privileged and the underprivileged—and it is this characteristic that makes it a matter of pleasure. Freud's psychological emphasis on the mental "economy of expenditure" reveals a critique of society and that mainly means an argumentation that comments on the social sphere, through a performance of resistance to an existing social order.

The construction of the invented word, "famillionaire," therefore, communicates a cutting criticism of society. It makes us aware, albeit in a condensed way, of a social structure from the point of view of the underprivileged, and sharply underlines its difficulties. In this context, criticism means simultaneously presenting and resisting a social order imposed on individuals. In this particular sense, jokes are critical because they set out to identify and resist what holds sway in society. In short, jokes are equated with the mechanism of social critique.

The concept of critique may be then applied to Freud's examination of jokes in two main ways. First, in his analysis of the origins, application, and extent of jokes, which he articulates psychoanalytically. To study jokes critically, in this sense, is to present the rationale, function, and limits of a psychological phenomenon. In the strict Kantian sense, critique means a form of analysis of the content or object of study, which includes charting its sources (*Quellen*), extent (*Umfang*), and boundaries (*Grenzen*).[43] In taking the faculty of reason as an object of study, for example, critique aims at "removing all those errors" ("Abstellung aller Irrungen") associated with this faculty.[44] For Kant this approach to critique provides a cleansing or purifying (*reiningen*) of a "ground that was completely overgrown."[45] Freud seems to endorse this approach to critique to the letter. This does not necessarily entail that Freud thinks as a philosopher, as Emmanuel Falque recently argued, but rather that his critique of jokes appears as a method of critical investigation, transposed to the field of psychology.[46] It not only represents a way of "removing" errors by charting the scope and limits of jokes but also (and more profoundly) includes, to some extent even promotes, a "cleansing" of former mistakes and misconceptions that blur understanding.

This critical quest is reflected in the book's tripartite structure. The first "analytic" part presents the rationale of jokes by pointing mainly to their underlining psychological logic. The second "synthetic" part explains the function of jokes (which for Freud is mainly social), from which Freud deduces the existence of different types of jokes. The third "theoretical" part underscores the limits of jokes by distinguishing between jokes and parallel psychological mechanisms (like dreams) on the one hand and social mechanisms like comedy and humor on the other hand. The book's structure thus shows how a critical study of jokes for Freud is about presenting their sources (the first part), mapping out their function and content (the second part), and outlining their scope and limits (the third part).

However, critique more importantly attests to the social function of jokes. Here, the concept of critique appears to correspond more closely to social critique because it relates to the normative dimension—a breaking down of (and thus resistance to) the social reality in question, even if by means of subversive suggestions. Heine's wit makes a case for such resistance because it cleverly creates a humorous association that unveils social structures and, one may argue, power relations, by making a joke out of them. Because of its subversive character, the joke enables criticism that would not be acceptable in any other way. This subversive procedure is for Freud a common characteristic of all jokes, making them critical by nature.

Since the value of the joke in Freud's thinking lies in its social critique, his critical interest is directed not only at the analysis of the scope, content, and limits of jokes, but more profoundly at how jokes demonstrate resistance to social structures and imposed demands. In this second sense, critique relates to wider normative considerations. It is about emancipating human beings from domineering social circumstances. Here, what seems to be important is the manner in which jokes relate to the social order in which human beings live, which they internalize, and to which they otherwise adhere constantly.

With this in mind, social critique indicates a critique of law. We return here then to the relation between wits and law. Indeed, according to Michel de Certeau, Freud assumes that there is an "a priori of a coherence to be found" in society and it is this deep-seated supposition that constitutes his recourse to the notion of "*law.*"[47] The main point that de Certeau makes seems to be that Freud understands the law in the most general sense, not as a narrow set of legal rules, but much more broadly as a concept that corresponds to the pressing demands of society. In his seminal essay "Nomos and Narrative" the legal philosopher Robert Cover makes an analogous case for this broad understanding of law.[48] Cover, who to some extent built on Talmudic tradition, suggested that we should regard a worldly order as a "law" to which we constantly relate.[49] Reference to the law needs to be understood, says Cover, not in its more common, narrow, legalistic sense, but rather as a symbolic configuration of an overarching order (social, cultural, political, or religious) with which we continuously engage. For Cover there is a nomos—"a normative universe" that we constantly shape and to which "the conventions of a social order" belong.[50] Once understood in such a way, "law becomes not merely a system of rules to be observed, but a world in which we live."[51]

The world in which we live, therefore, means the law according to which we live. We endow such a world/law with meaning "by using the irony of jurisdiction, the comedy of manners that is *malum prohibitum*, the surreal epistemology of due process."[52] This jesting, however, is not just a technical device used within a narrow legalistic context. It relates, in Cover's eyes, to issues ranging from violence and power, to the difference between "creating" and "maintaining" law, and questions of redemption and of human and religious demands.[53]

There seems to be a range of themes that connects Cover's metajuristic inquiry with Freud's metapsychological analysis of jokes (including the allusion to humor and irony, or religious symbolism). Nonetheless, Cover's definition is most helpful in the way it shows how de Certeau's broader understanding of the concept of law fits in with Freud's case. We have seen how in Freud's engagement with the statue of Moses, or in his personal predicaments in Vienna, he repeatedly employs a concept of the law and associates it with the rules that govern human life. The "learning of eternal laws," or enthusiasm for the "lawgiver" of the Jews are examples of a wider understanding of the law in association with the "normative universe" in which we live. The point to make is that the notion of subversion that Freud attributes to jokes runs along the same lines of argumentation. As a critique of social order (including norms, modes of behavior, imposed cultural rules, and so on) the joke turns against the a priori coherence or logic on which this order is based. Jokes are subversive inasmuch as they undermine a pre-given social structure of imposed requirements, ethical imperatives, and normative demands, all of which are encompassed by the concept of law. To the same extent that jokes represent social critique, they stand for a critique of law.

Particularly in the case of principles of behavior, rules of social conduct, and ethical imperatives, which result from the law that governs us, the joke represents subversion because it aims directly at disclosing inhibited thoughts and suppressed wishes. Thus, the joke according to Freud "must bring forward something that is concealed or hidden."[54] While the joke unveils these hidden thoughts and concealed wishes, it deceives the censorship and judgment of reason, which is an outcome of adhering to the social requirements that suppress our impulses and innermost drives. Freud is referring here to any thought or wish that has been restrained, suppressed, or prohibited by our conscious censors. Arguably, these censors are themselves a product of imposed social and cultural prerequisites, and therefore represent the lawful order of the social world we inhabit. In presenting itself as a joke the hidden thought "bribes our powers of criticism and confuses them" and in this way cheats our censorship.[55]

We may recall Heine's character, Hirsch-Hyacinth, and his joke based on the invention of the word "famillioniare," which combines two words to create a new meaning. Our censors are confused by the irregular use of words and by the manipulation of the normal rules of language to which we are accustomed.[56] Moreover, the social critique of a "rich man's condescension" can be communicated because the joke cheats our normative modes of expression (including a certain twisting of grammatical laws) and in this particular sense "confuses" us.⁵⁷ Confusion here means a technique used to articulate social critique but only inasmuch as it hides behind wordplay. In such a way the joke critically subverts the social norms of correctness.

Another joke in Freud's repertoire offers a somewhat different example of the subversive character of jokes vis-à-vis the laws by which we live. The story goes:

> The doctor, who had been asked to look after the Baroness at her confinement, pronounced that the moment had not come, and suggested to the Baron that in the meantime they should have a game of cards in the next room. After a while a cry of pain from the Baroness struck the ears of the two men: "Ah mon Dieu, que je souffre!" Her husband sprang up, but the doctor signed to him to sit down: "It's nothing. Let's go on with the game." A little later there were again sounds from the pregnant woman: "Mein Gott, mein Gott, was für Schmerzen!"—"Aren't you going in, Professor?" asked the Baron. "No, no, it's not time yet." At last there came from next door an unmistakable cry "Ai waih, waih geschrien!" The doctor threw down his cards and exclaimed: *"Now* it's time."⁵⁸

It is rather questionable whether this joke with its insinuations can be considered funny or socially acceptable today. Nonetheless, the aim of referring to this particular joke is to point to Freud's focus on the subversive, and thus critical, element embedded in the mechanism of jokes. This time, the mechanism that "cheats" and "bribes" our censors lies not in the structure of the joke or in a wordplay, but rather in its playful content. This content relates mainly to the three different cries of pain that can be heard coming from the other room—"mon Dieu," "mein Gott," "Ai waih." First, as Elliott Oring pointed out, these exclamations represent for Freud a universal claim regarding the human condition: the idea that a painful state of emergency enables our inner untamed, primal essence to transgress all cultural façades.⁵⁹ At such a moment there is neither baroness nor cultivated German woman, but simply a human body in pain. When the cultural laws, rules, and norms are suspended—in this case because of the painful urgency—"primitive nature" surfaces.⁶⁰ Social sensibilities are dismissed when hidden nature springs out. In other words, the law is suspended in a state of emergency. To some extent we may be dealing here with a joke about the meaning of jokes: one whose content points to the mechanism of bringing forward some concealed or hidden reality relating to the oppressive social order.

Yet, there is another layer to the joke. Is it not also possible that the three cries represent three different languages: French ("mon Dieu"), German ("mein Gott"), and finally Yiddish ("Ai waih")? The argument, which the English translator discounted, was made by both Christopher Hutton and John Murray Cuddihy.[61] The "unmistakable cry" in the joke relates to a third language, hinting at a more particular, surreptitious truth: namely that the French, well-educated (*gebildet*) baroness is an *Ostjude*—an Eastern European Jew, whose suppressed mother tongue—her *mamme loshen*—is Yiddish. In no other way, apart from via a joke, could such an idea be suggested or accepted. The subversive characteristic of the joke points, then, to a particular Jewish theme, or more precisely to what connects Jewish settings with a more general truth, conveying Freud's view of Jewish jokes as guardians of a universal message.[62] Here, however, the opposite might also be correct: namely that the learning of the "eternal laws" of human nature communicates, somewhat resourcefully, a particular underlying Jewish reality.

This specific joke, then, is another example of critique of law, because it discloses a concealed reality that in any other social conditions could not be exposed. It does so in two ways: first, in the content of the joke, which is about the suspension of rules of behavior and social conduct in a state of emergency; second, in its message, insinuating a true, surreptitious identity beneath all the false layers of culture and social etiquette. By moving through the layers of civility and delving into the primal sources of our social contracts, the joke presents us with an argument about hidden truths and how their expression breaks through our normative expectations. Here, irony and law, universality and particularity, human nature and Jewish identity are condensed into one ingenious example of wit. There is good reason for suspecting that this particular joke amused Freud (who probably identified with all the characters of the joke—the scientific doctor, the civilized respectable baron, and the hidden Eastern European Jew). Perhaps more poetically, in his own eyes he could identify with the newly born child of the joke who came into the world amid a somewhat absurd assembly of three figures: science, culture, and Judaism.

When we tell a joke, which is accepted as such, we may then express meanings that cannot be expressed in any other manner to another person, and perhaps not even to ourselves. The critical element embedded in the telling of such a story relates to the way in which the joke identifies a certain lawful structure, and works against it in an act of defiance and liberation. What allows such a maneuver is the fact that the joke is subversive. By using jokes, we can overcome the codes of moral censorship, cultural norms, or rules of behavior and thereby resist what is imposed on us.

The opposite should also be true for Freud, namely that in a social or cultural context in which we cannot overcome the judgment of morality or the political laws of correctness, the critical mechanism of jokes remains out of reach. If the law cannot be deceived, jokes have no space to perform. Rudolf Herzog shows how the Nazi dictatorship represented a regime that was "deeply humorless," and how, on the other hand, political jokes played out, albeit in hiding, as forms of defiance.[63] In such a way, jokes presented the last resort of human freedom in an otherwise totalitarian reality. One may recall Arendt's shrewd remark that one disarms totalitarian regimes only by using the armament of humor and the weapons of irony. Where there is irony, humor, and witticism, the theory goes, there is at least some form of liberty. An indication of critique, freedom, and defiance, jokes dare to disclose hidden, untamed thoughts while undermining the censorship imposed by the rules, norms, and laws of social and political correctness. Where laws cannot be subverted, jokes are excluded.

The Body and the Soul of Wit

Brevity

Jokes, however, are not only subversive. They are also brief. This is the second main point that Freud makes concerning the critical characteristics of jokes. He does so mainly in his passage from the first "analytic" to the second "synthetic" part of the book. "Brevity," argues Freud, "is the body and the soul of wit, it is its very self."[64] In this passage Freud is quoting Shakespeare's *Hamlet*. "Brevity is the soul of wit" says Polonius, somewhat insouciantly, in reflecting on the essence of being reasonable. In loosely exchanging wit for *Witz* Freud reiterates this passage because for him it relates to a central characteristic of jokes: the quality of being concise and brief, and this implies a particular connection between reason and witticism.

Jokes are brief exactly where we should take a longer and much more complicated route if we wish to follow cultural rules or codes of social engagement. Operating critically, then, also includes brevity. Jokes, however, can be long and wordy. The story of the baroness, for example, is somewhat lengthy, involves information in several languages, repetition, and a scene that is built up slowly. Nevertheless, jokes, and even that particular joke, always convey their critical point in fewer words than normally called for. When the doctor says "*Now* it's time" he means something like, "Now that untamed nature (or true identity) is disclosed by cutting through all the cultural façades, and given what we know of human nature, I can be absolutely sure that labor is on its way." This fuller statement, however, is hardly funny. The point is that making critical comments on the relationships between culture and nature, or between society and identity, is quite a long-drawn-out affair. Joking about it, however, is smart, direct, and pierces the heart of the matter.

Puns that Freud finds amusing exemplify the same argument. For example, Heine's comment that at school he had to put up with "so much Latin, caning and Geography." The addition of "caning" to the list of subjects condenses a potentially long story about the horrors of a harsh education into a concise and funny comment, while at the same time conveying disdain for the violence inflicted on the child.[65] And again Heine, this time on his deathbed: "When a friendly priest reminded him of God's mercy and gave him hope that God would forgive him for his sins, he is said to have replied: 'Bien sur qu'il me pardonnera: c'est son métier' " (Of course he'll forgive me: it's his job).[66] The reference to God's vocation is the essence of the matter. In between the lines, there is a final, somewhat testimonial critique of religion in which "what was supposed to be the created being revealed itself just before its annihilation as the creator."[67] The deeply critical approach, however, is hardly funny when put in these terms. In its brevity, the joke makes the same critical point and amuses the listener.

Through the wide range of examples that Freud gives to illustrate jokes, puns, irony, and wordplay, he aims to show how jokes display their brevity in two main ways: in their techniques, and in their tendencies. These two points deserve some attention. Condensation, displacement, indirect representation (including representation by using opposites), and the use of allusion or absurdity are central techniques of humor that Freud presents in the first "analytic" part of the book. The "famillionaire" joke offers an example of condensation by cleverly soldering two words together. The use of absurdity (God's job) characterizes the witty comment of Heine on his deathbed. Meanwhile, the technique of displacement is achieved by operating a quick shift in the meaning of a sentence, thus playing with the overall message received. This is illustrated, for example, in the following joke: A horse dealer recommends a horse by saying, "If you take this horse and get on it at four in the morning you'll be at Pressburg by half past six." The customer, however, replies, "What should I be doing in Pressburg at half past six in the morning?," thus displacing the dealer's original meaning (crediting the horse with speed) by entering "into the data of the example that has been chosen."[68]

This range of techniques is important because, once more, jokes are displayed as a critical mechanism that is always abridged. Brevity is, in this case, the essence of jokes because it enables their critical operation vis-à-vis the law. This means for Freud that although jokes are similar to dreams (a point that he emphasizes in the third "theoretical" part of the book) they also represent a widely different subject matter. On the one hand, dreamwork (*Traumarbeit*) and joke-work (*Witzarbeit*) are similar because they construct images (dreams) or wordplay (jokes) that condense, mix, play with, relocate, displace, or amalgamate various notions. In this sense, they are always epigrammatic. On the other hand, only jokes function in this way in order to convey social critique.

"Tendentious" jokes are another, perhaps more complicated, case in point. A joke becomes "tendentious," according to Freud, when it serves one of four ends: hostility (for the purpose of aggressiveness or defense), obscenity (aimed at exposure), cynicism, or skepticism.[69] In all these cases we express inhibited thoughts, aggressions, vulgarities, or hidden and to some extent brutal content matter in the form of jokes. When we do so, we are able to touch base with inner wishes (which may be hostile, obscene, or violent) that are usually left unspoken, or better, suppressed. Sexuality, violence, hostility, masochistic or sadistic pleasures, and similar natural (for Freud) and clandestine drives commonly form the substance of such jokes.

Eastern European (and in particular Galician) Jews are the butt of a type of hostile joke that Freud seems to rather enjoy, perhaps even against his best wishes. One example is as follows: "Two Jews met in a railway carriage at a station in Galicia. 'Where are you going?' asked one. 'To Cracow,' was the answer. 'What a liar you are!' broke out the other. 'If you say you're going to Cracow, you want me to believe you're going to Lemberg. But I know that in fact you're going to Cracow. So why are you lying to me?'"[70]

Another example to illustrate the exposure of vicious tendencies starts, once again, with a Galician Jew who is traveling alone by train:

A Galician Jew was traveling in a train. He had made himself really comfortable, and unbuttoned his coat and put his feet up on the seat. Just then, a gentleman in modern dress entered the compartment. The Jew promptly pulled himself together and took up a proper pose. The stranger fingered through the pages of a notebook, made some calculation, reflected for a moment and then suddenly asked the Jew: "Excuse me, when is Yom Kippur?" "Oho" said the Jew, and put his feet up on the seat again before answering.[71]

These are offensive jokes at the expense of Jews originating from Galicia that according to Freud were "created by Jews and directed against Jewish characteristics." Even so, they reiterate Western European racial classification of Eastern European Jewish sociability (or lack of it). Jokes involving sexual obscenity, mainly targeted at women, are of the same character because they involve stories or puns that aim at exposing deeply buried sexual drives. In this particular case, Freud's analysis of jokes resonates well with some aspects of his theory of sexuality, composed at the same time.[72] The main buried desire in this context relates to the touching of sexual organs (even if only in words and imagination). Obscenity, in particular, is a type of violence and hostility that is "difficult or impossible" to enjoy because of the acquired forces of "repression." Obscene tendentious jokes, however, "*will evade restrictions and open sources of pleasure that have become inaccessible.*"[73]

Because of these traits, such tendentious jokes are always deeply suspicious and may not even be considered tolerable. But for Freud, jokes are not originators of hostile, brutal, obscene, or violent impulses, which exist, he presupposes, on our mental maps. The main issue at hand in his view relates to the critical mechanism of jokes designed to release these hidden impulses in an act of defiance of the law. Here, again, tendentious jokes are critical because they are brief. The unflattering portrayal of Galician Jews shares a critical message (that is, resistance) in relatively few words. The short story involving "Yom Kippur," for instance, points in a compact way not only to the alleged questionable behavior of Eastern European Jews but also to the comfortableness of Jews, supposedly at ease only when among their kin. The brief monologue relating to Cracow addresses a range of critical associations—from a racial, highly problematic categorization of the Jews as being tricky by nature, to a critique of the Jewish tradition of pilpul.

These somewhat malicious displays of passing judgment would remain silent if we observed codes of behavior. However, the concise nature of these jokes subverts our censure and overcomes the obstacles presented by these codes. Thus hostility becomes accessible, and perhaps may even go unnoticed, if there is a "bribing" of the laws of civility, or of any relevant ethical consideration. If cultural conditions or acquired sensitivities are not suspended, the joke would pass only for a vulgar statement. Such is the case with obscene jokes. If our inner ethical censors are not bribed, any wordplay would be considered wholly unacceptable. In such a way, jokes can be considered funny not because they enable the disclosure of preexisting hostility (which would have been left unspoken otherwise) but because they do so while repealing our censorship.

It is in this last sense that in order to work, the joke must suspend the law. For Freud, the laws against which the "joke-work" is directed are perceived by the individual as being oppressive. In all the cases observed above, a person is required to suppress a wide range of wishes, needs, and impulses that represent the surreptitious substance of jokes. Suppression in this context means an investment of mental energy. Energy is spent in order to keep certain thoughts or wishes suppressed, to subdue impulses, or to avoid untamed desires. Adhering to the law that governs our lives means an expenditure of mental energy. We invest mental energy according to our internalization of social demands. By working with these "materials," however, jokes help to eschew social demands or "save" energy. Thus, in making the suppressed matter (e.g., thoughts, wishes, impulses, desires) available to us, albeit by means of subversion, the joke overrides the mental investment, presenting an "economy in psychical expenditure": the energy spent adhering to and maintaining the imposed laws is avoided. Imposing these restrictions on ourselves demands an investment; overcoming them in this case results in a discharge. We consequently experience pleasure in jokes because their brevity and subversion enables economy. "All these techniques," Freud writes, "are dominated by a tendency to compression, or rather to saving. It all seems to be a question of economy. In Hamlet's words: Thrift, Horatio, Thrift."[74]

THE PRINCIPLE OF PLEASURE

Pleasure is an important outcome of the critical mechanism of jokes. Eventually, the very aim of resisting the law is the attaining of pleasure. Freud examines this "principle of pleasure" mainly in the second, "synthetic" part of the book, following two principal lines of thought. First, he presents the manner in which jokes induce pleasure because they present us with shorter routes on our mental maps. Second, he connects this condensation with the critique of law.

Pleasure arises because brevity and subversion save mental energy. Freud explicitly argues, especially in relation to tendentious jokes, that "*economy in expenditure on inhibition or suppression* appears to be the secret of the pleasurable effect of tendentious jokes."[75] Pleasure, in this case, is a form of relief. If energy is saved, the individual experiences a liberation of sorts, even if only for a short duration of time. This mechanism may explain why Freud remains somewhat appreciative of jokes, even if and perhaps because they may express socially unacceptable notions. Jokes seem to constitute the liberating of energy that is already there and that needs to be somehow reworked. In such a way Freud seems to connect liberation from the burden of constant mental investment with a notion of pleasure. The experience of pleasure is not directly linked to the aggression or obscenity that may form the content or aim of jokes. Rather, jokes induce pleasure because they bring short-lived relief from the heavy burden we constantly carry on our mental shoulders. This is another way in which jokes differ from dreams. While dreams "serve predominantly for the avoidance of un-pleasure," jokes, conversely, are made "for the attainment of pleasure."[76]

If the cunning and succinct characteristics of jokes enable the enjoyment of relief, they also point to jokes as a critical affair.[77] In other words, the mechanism of condensation is connected with a critique of law. This is, then, the second point to note. Pleasure relates to such critique because in Freud's theory it is available not to the person who tells the joke—the instigator of the joke—but to the person who hears the joke—the joke's addressee.

We do not aim jokes at ourselves. Rather, we seek to stimulate pleasure in a third person (or third party), who is not the subject or originator of the joke, but its audience.[78] This aspect of communication underlines for Freud the social role of jokes. In particular, the subversive message of the joke needs to be expressed in words and in a way that can be readily understood and unpacked by a willing listener if it is to be considered funny. In other words, jokes (again, unlike dreams) need to be communicative to someone else and are thus part of the social sphere, inducing a sort of "being together" with fellow human beings. The joke's addressee may experience pleasure only when he or she understands the underlying critical message. If Heine's social and cultural critique, for example, was not available to the listener, his joke would remain at the very least opaque. This is not about understanding as such. The addressee experiences pleasure only when he or she understands the particular critical attitude directed against the law under which we live. The critique of law, if understood, overcomes or cheats this person's suppressing censors.

With particular regard to the third party, Freud articulates the principle of pleasure as a result of the relation between wit and law. Experiencing a relief is made of a certain recognition of the critique of law that was communicated by a clever and inventive creation of language plays; for example, the points raised by the offensive jokes in relation to an alleged Eastern European Jewish mentality, or to the arrogance of the rich vis-à-vis the poor. Or the painful truth, at least for Freud, who was born in Moravia before migrating to Vienna at the age of four, was that beyond the thin cultural façades would always lie, perhaps, an *Ostjude*.[79] These could be considered funny, if only in a rather excruciating way, when the subversive message is picked up by a willing listener whose imposed censors vis-à-vis rules, norms, and cultural codes are bypassed, bribed, or overcome. Pleasure is then, and only then, available to us. "Let us assume," argues Freud:

> that there is an urge to insult a certain person; but this is strongly opposed by feelings of propriety or of aesthetic culture that the insult cannot take place. If, for instance, it were able to break through as a result of some change of emotional condition or mood, this breakthrough by the insulting purpose would be felt subsequently with unpleasure. Thus the insult does not take place. Let us now suppose, however, that the possibility is presented of deriving a good joke from the material of the words and thoughts used for the insult—the possibility, that is, of releasing pleasure from other sources which are not obstructed by the same suppression. This second development of pleasure could, nevertheless, not occur unless the insult were permitted; but as soon as the latter *is* permitted the new release of pleasure is also joined to it.[80]

The principle of pleasure here stems from a cunning maneuver, connecting the expression of a suppressed impulse with the cheating of the censure of a willing listener and a reduction in the sum of energy spent on the suppression of these impulses. In this way, critique of the law may be pleasurable. As a result of this pleasure—again, pleasure induced by taking a shorter route and saving energy—a third person may laugh. Laughter is, therefore, a result of this particular principle: "We should say that laughter arises if a quota of psychical energy which has earlier been used for the cathexis of particular psychical paths has become unusable, so that it can find free discharge."[81] A "free discharge" (*Abfuhr*) in the form of laughter is the apex of the principle of pleasure. Like Bergson, Freud attributes this expression of enjoyment to the overcoming of our social and ethical censure. For Bergson this censure is mainly responsible for our identification with the object of a scene or story to which we are exposed and that sanctions any pleasure.[82] Once the disapproval is overcome, laughter is possible. In Freud's theory, however, laughter is consequently described in terms of a "short circuit" (*Kurzschluss*). It is thus for Freud "the pleasure in a joke arising from a 'short circuit' like this" that takes the form of a vocal expression of amusement.[83]

Laughter is an outburst resulting from a short circuit in an energy system that has its wires crossed. But the point Freud wants to make seems to be more than just an allusion to electrical metaphors. The reference to the concept of a short circuit underlines the way in which Freud brings together the saving of mental energy and the taking of shorter routes where usually longer ones are the rule, norm, or common law. The pleasure arising from the joke is always greater "the more alien" the circles of ideas brought together are.[84] Freud then concludes: "Our insight into the mechanism of laughter leads us rather to say that, owing to the introduction of the proscribed idea by means of an auditory perception, the cathectic energy used for the inhibition has now suddenly become superfluous and has been lifted, and is therefore now ready to be discharged by laughter."[85] The critical role of jokes culminates in a free discharge of energy through laughter. We may laugh in this sense against our better judgment, and perhaps even unwillingly when "energy used for the inhibition" becomes "superfluous." This end result is connected with the concept of a "short circuit" in which ideas are brought together in a way that shortens, so to speak, their "circles."

One may argue that the discharge of "cathectic" energy and the short circuit are in themselves additional forms of brevity. In the social sphere, in particular, brevity assumes the guise of a burst (laughter). The process in which a critical message is picked up by the audience culminates in such a surge. Here, energy is saved through a discharging effect that abbreviates normal, regulative flows and cuts through their energy current. The description in terms of energy, however, relates to the critical mechanism of jokes and to how such a mechanism affects us. Through its compact character and its critical content, a joke releases the audience's burden in a way that results in laughter. If brevity is the soul of wit, free discharge and short circuit constitute its social guise.

Critique and Theology

Shortcut

Brevity; taking shorter paths than the norm; the saving of mental energy; thrift; abbreviation; a short circuit and the end result in the form of an immediate outburst or discharge of energy. Could we not argue that these central characteristics of jokes, and of the social critique they engender, amount to an overarching concept, that of a shortcut? This single term may encapsulate the range of different ways in which Freud's analysis characterizes the joke as a critical mechanism that cuts through the normative means of expression, modes of conduct, laws of behavior, rules of social engagement, and so on. Jokes are critical because they take shorter routes where longer ones are the norm. They save energy where this is habitually spent. They induce pleasure (in the form of a "short circuit") that remains otherwise out of reach. In such a way, jokes are about charting shorter routes on our mental maps and cutting through all that is ascribed to us by the cultural, social, and political rules, norms, or regulations that govern our lives.

The notion of a shortcut seems to capture Freud's definition of jokes as a form of social critique. It applies in this sense not only to the mechanism of jokes but also to the critique of laws (in the broader sense of the term) embedded in jokes. Resistance to or defiance of the social order is possible because jokes make a long story short, condense language, or compress critical messages. Brevity enables resistance and defies codes and norms. Shortcuts are in this sense transgressive. Transgression here denotes the capacity to break the law, cross boundaries, violate rules, regulations, habits, and norms. It points to the manner in which the joke outwits, and in this sense violates, the social and (by means of internalization) psychic regulatory obstacles that hinder free expression of hidden substance (e.g., wishes, aggressions, drives). In other words, the joke is made to transgress imagined borders set by laws, in playful defiance of these laws.

Freud appears to carry this argument on into some of his later works. His paper on "Humor" presents a case in point. In this essay Freud associates the transgressive potential of jokes with the work of the "id" as it makes its way into our conscious ego.[86] By drawing such parallels between "joke-work" and what could be termed "id-work," Freud seems to suggest that the untamed impulses, drives, and suppressed wishes of the id transgress our conscious censure that is a result of the law under which we live.

In this later development of ideas, Freud suggests that the transgressive work of the id also underlines the main characteristic of jokes.[87] For Freud, we enjoy jokes precisely because of the transgressive potential embedded in their subversion and resistance. We laugh because of the moment of defiance, of boundary crossing, of violation, and of release of mental excess. And vice versa: the fact that jokes circumvent the censorship of reason, or the dictates of acceptable social behavior, does not mean that they perform a reasonable nor prudent diversion following an imagined, careful, and longer route than usual; nor does it entail that jokes are socially expected. On the contrary, it implies a more rebellious act of cutting through the censure, thus enabling the safe discharge of accumulated energy in the same way, perhaps, as a lightning rod enables high-voltage static energy to be redirected and safely discharged to the ground without damaging the struck structure.

A shortcut is then a form of transgression. We may recall Freud's early engagement with the law in anticipation of, during, and following his first visit to Rome, and how he interpreted Michelangelo's false Moses (including his inverted Tables) as an emblem for his critique of Christianity. The mechanism of critique that Freud ascribes to jokes points to the development of overarching thoughts on transgressing laws that always tie together, it seems, personal drama with universal claims. Thus, inversions are an integral part of the transgressive mechanism of jokes that brings relief that would otherwise stay out of reach. Falsifications are, obviously, central to the subversive character of jokes, encompassing all their playful turns and overturns. Taming pain, wrath, or aggression (albeit by means of disclosing its hidden sources) may be seen as another central function of the shortcutting joke because of its content. In a more ironic tone it is possible to say that jokes are a shining example of our ability to make a crack through or, perhaps, out of, imposed lawful limits.

Such an association between shortcut and transgression means bringing closely together wit and law, because in wit, critically resisting the law denotes its violation. The crossing of lawful boundaries is especially important if one considers the experience of its addressee. The addressee is made to laugh—sometimes against his or her best wishes—because of the momentary experience of violating the laws in the shortcut of the joke. But Freud is not only making an analytic observation. Rather, because of his clear interest in the question of the "safe" discharge of inner, suppressed drives (whose existence he presupposes) he seems to display a favorable attitude toward the use of jokes as a certain stance "against the world."[88] Thus, Freud's association between shortcuts and such a defiant stance highlights the positive implications of transgression in the social arena. Transgressions in this sense are endorsed by Freud rather than rejected. Where inner impulses and drives could be dismissed, or ventilated, reticent materials may become socially available without damaging the social structure. Shortcuts as a form of transgression underline, then, a positive area of social critique that Freud wishes to support.

A shortcut as a form of transgression is, however, not a Freudian innovation. It is a central religious theme, touching the very heart of the relationships between individuals and imposed laws. The Jewish religious tradition may serve as a case in point mainly because of Freud's own focus on the links between Judaism, law, and lawgiving. Thus, for example, in Jewish rabbinic literature, taking a shortcut (or *kapandaria*) through the Temple is prohibited because it communicates disregard for (and therefore a violation of) the sacred space of the Temple.[89] The Mishnah unequivocally states that: "A man should not enter the Temple mount with his staff or with his shoes on or with his wallet or with his feet dust-stained; nor should he make it a shortcut [*kapandaria*], and spitting [on it is forbidden] a fortiori."[90] *Kapandaria* is characterized here as a form of disgracing the sacred space of the Temple. The Temple, representing a holy domain, cannot be used for the purpose of taking a shortcut because this would represent an abuse, and in this sense a transgression, of the sacred arena.

The Mishnah develops the same preclusion to include the space of a synagogue. Even after its demolition (echoing, perhaps, the destruction of the Temple, too), a synagogue represents a sacred space through which one is not allowed to take a shortcut.[91] Thus, the Mishnah says: "Rabbi Yehudah further stated: A synagogue that has been destroyed [must be treated with respect and] one may not eulogize in it, nor does one twist ropes or spread nets in it [or any other type of labor] and one may not spread produce to dry on its roof, nor may it be used as a shortcut, as it is written: 'I will desolate your sanctuaries' (Leviticus 26:31), implying that they retain their sanctity even when they are desolate."[92] There is a stark contradiction between the sacred character of the synagogue and the sacrilegious nature of a variety of prohibited actions, which include shortcuts. In the case of shortcuts, the synagogue is endowed with the sort of holiness that is ascribed to the Temple.[93] The reference to the Bible makes the case rather clear, since it relates to the sacredness of "your sanctuaries" (in Hebrew, *mikdashechem*, which literally means "your temples") even when rendered vacant. A shortcut is prohibited because it violates the sacred character attributed to the synagogue.

The transgressive performance embedded in shortcuts is brought up again in a short entry relating to Rabbi Eleazar ben Shammua (a second-century rabbi and one of Rabbi Akiva's disciples). When asked by his pupils about the secret to his long life, he listed three reasons, one of which was: "Never have I made use of a Synagogue as a shortcut."[94] Clearly, the suggestion was that long life depended on renouncing shortcuts through the sacred space. The Talmud expands on this point relating to the synagogue. In a relevant passage in *Berachot* the prohibition on shortcuts through the synagogue ("Ein ossin beit ha'knesset kapandaria") is more closely linked with human intentions. The rabbinic discussants suggest that if one enters a synagogue "not intending to use it as a shortcut" (Rabbi Nahman), or if "there was a path there originally" (Rabbi Abbahu), or "if one entered a synagogue [with an intention] to pray" (Rabbi Helbo), walking across the synagogue is not prohibited.[95] What seems to be the crux of the matter here is whether or not there is the intention to degrade the sacred law. When such a resolve is absent, crossing from one side of the synagogue to the other is devoid of transgressive meaning and rendered acceptable. Shortcuts, on the other hand, are intentional and count as sacrilegious acts, violating what is regarded as the sacredness of the Temple and the synagogue.[96]

The association of intention with the Hebrew prohibition ("Ein ossin beit ha'knesset kapandaria") seems to be central. There is the indication of a compound meaning, because the prohibition to physically take a shortcut through the synagogue is linked with an ethical proscription to relate to the synagogue as a space of profanation—two different possible readings of the Hebrew original statement. The short entry relating to Rabbi Eleazar ben Shammua may serve as an example. The making "use of a Synagogue as a shortcut" ("Meolam lo assiti beit haknesset kapandaria") indicates both a physical movement and a moral judgment. Mere physicality is arguably linked to deeper ethical dimensions of faith.

The connection between physicality and faith seems to be underlined in the discussion. Physically, taking a shortcut by walking from one side of the Temple or synagogue to the other is proscribed. The Mishnah and the Talmud indeed open the discussion by pointing to the distance between the gate of entering the Temple and the "Holy of Holies" that lies on the exact opposite side of the Temple. This observation refers to walking from one side to the exact opposite side of the Temple or, by extension, the synagogue. One can enter and exit the sacred space via different locations such that time and effort are saved, but only if this is not done in a calculated or deliberate way. To put it differently, the sacred space cannot serve economy in physical expenditure when this is done intentionally. But shortcuts are prohibited mainly because they show disrespect toward the sacred space, and the sacred cannot be used as a means to an end. Clearly, *kapandaria* does not mean merely walking from one side of the sacred space to another. It also encompasses wider and arguably more abstract notions relating to transgression of the divine order, or profanation of the sacred.

Shortcuts assume then a transgressive guise in rabbinic literature. They violate the sacred because they represent an act against the lawful and eternal order of things. They point to the boundary crossing that is prohibited and are associated with mortification. While there is economy in physical expenditure, at the same time there is disrespect and an act of rebellion against God. Put differently, a shortcut is prohibited because it is a form of profanation.

Freud was probably ignorant of these rabbinic discussions. But he was not completely uninformed about religious tradition and the theological imaginaries that these discussions represent.[97] The point was made, for example, by Karl Abraham (1877–1925), one of Freud's disciples. Abraham suggested in a letter to his mentor that not only did psychoanalysis in general show Talmudic qualities, but also that elements in Freud's book on jokes, in particular, were "completely Talmudic." "After all," Abraham argued, "the Talmudic way of thinking cannot disappear in us just like that."[98] One can only imagine Freud's reaction to this observation. Nevertheless, the statement might not be entirely out of place. By associating the critique embedded in *Jokes* with different manifestations of shortcut, Freud reengages with the relationships between the law and its forms of violation, central to religious deliberations.

From this point of view, is it not possible to argue that Freud's analysis of jokes further extends a long religious tradition in which law and lawgiving is central and within which the trope of shortcuts as forms of transgression surfaces? This question seems to resonate with what scholars like Eric Santner and Harold Bloom saw as the deep "theological significance" of Freud's psychological theory.[99] This means that "the very religious tradition in which Freud was raised" endowed his thinking in general and specifically his disciplinary vocabulary with a basis.[100] For Santner there is a "spiritual" component in Freud's psychoanalysis that needs to be acknowledged and that calls for a "new awareness of the theological dimensions of Freudian thought."[101] The concept of theology relates in this case especially to Freud's alignment with a Jewish tradition in which the universal divine law exerts "too much pressure" and induces the seeking of a "release or discharge" from the so-called Jewish "tension of election."[102]

Other scholars, notably Yosef Haim Yerushalmi, and recently Ruth Kara Ivanov-Kaniel, have pointed to a similar theological sensitivity.[103] This is not to overlook Freud's unfavorable, if not derisive, discerning of what the psychic mechanisms of the religious illusions (or "obsessional neurosis") were made of. But it is also hard to overlook the range of ways in which Freud himself repeatedly engaged with the deep theological dimensions of his thought. For example, when a patient told Freud his dream that featured "a very compact but stupidly designed church," Freud, who was certain that the dream related to the "church" of psychoanalysis, suggested that it was the way it was because it had been built by "a Jew."[104] For Freud the dream's critique of psychoanalysis involved religious considerations that did not only insinuate anti-Semitic tendencies of his patient but also disclosed his own thoughts on the religious core of the science he founded. A rather similar theological frame of reference seemed to capture the final dramatic scene of Freud's life, on his own deathbed. When the pain of cancer became unbearable, Freud asked his friend and physician, Max Schur, to execute a well-devised mercy death. The gloomy death of the intellectual giant occurred on September 23, 1939, which coincided that year with Yom Kippur, the Jewish Day of Atonement.[105] Freud's body was cremated and the ashes were put in a Greek vase, as Freud had requested, depicting Dionysus and a maenad (one of the crazed and ecstatic female followers of the god). There is here, one could say, an orchestrated turn against Jewish law in the form of a *Selbstmord* (self-imposed death) on Yom Kippur.[106] But at the same time this is arranged as a gift of the gods, showing perhaps how the "tension of election" expresses Freud's last will and testament.

In his analysis of jokes as shortcuts, especially, these issues are central. Indeed, here we find a formative example of how the unfavorable assessments of the religion of an "unrepentant Jew" are contrasted by "the spiritual dimension of the new science he founded."[107] Through an association of shortcuts, transgressions, and subversions of laws, Freud's examination of jokes seems to show an early, to some extent decisive, engagement with the "theological significance" of his work. At the heart of this significance lies an eternal law that Freud takes issue with and a long discursive tradition of laws and transgressions (to which the rabbinic discussions belong) that forms the basis of his discussion. This theological basis is as relevant to his examination of Michelangelo's *Moses* as to his analysis of jokes. In both cases, a critique of law involves an engagement with its role in religion, as much as with a turning against it. Against this background, the social implications of transgression in Freud's account carry the theological significance of law, lawgiving, mortification, and desecration. The connections between wit and law are thus reminiscent of his reference to denomination and theology, and the tension between Judaism and Christianity in his analysis of Rome and Moses. In such a way Freud's endowing the critical mechanism of jokes with a "release or discharge" points to a deep theological significance.

A Critique of Theology

It is possible, then, to argue that Freud's critique of law presents us with a critique of theology. By using such a term, the aim is not to argue for Freud's critical attitude toward religion, but to capture the intersection of critique and theology in his analysis of jokes. Such an intersection points to a concept of social critique that emerges out of a theological tradition. What seems to be noteworthy here is the transgressive capacity that Freud ascribes to jokes. Through such a capacity the critical mechanism of jokes reformulates a certain rebellious logic that relates in the Jewish religious tradition to the violation of eternal laws, and which Freud reapplies to the mainly social laws by which we live. In such a way critique still engages with "learning the eternal laws of life," as Freud rather artfully put it, but does so by applying it to the social arena, demonstrating the relocating of "the eternal within the earthly."[108]

The manner in which such a repositioning of theology also means its secularization will be discussed shortly. The point to note here is that the relation between critique and theology goes beyond just a critical analysis of the psychological content of theology or origins of religion; it also suggests that the critique that Freud attributes to jokes can be traced back to a theological vocabulary and imagination. Freud's modeling of the shortcut as transgression exemplifies these last points rather well because the correlation between shortcuts and transgression resounds with a religious tradition that engages with this very association. As in the rabbinic discussion, Freud perceives a shortcut as an act of resistance, disavowal, and renunciation of a law by which we normally abide. And he does so, it seems, for the same end: describing an emblematic mode of mortification. In bringing these issues to bear on the content, scope, and aim of jokes, Freud makes their critique of the law dependent on a theological discussion that relates to the "too much pressure" of divine law. Jokes for Freud are, no doubt, a social phenomenon that violates socially imposed rules. But we may speak of a critique of theology because their mechanism of critique is informed by religious associations between the notions of shortcut, violation, and transgression. Furthermore, the link forged between jokes and universal law is redolent of rabbinic engagement with eternal law. Within this context, the relation between wit and law continues to convey a theological significance tied up with the ideas of boundary crossing, committing offenses, and profanation. By seeing in jokes a mechanism that cuts through the imposed norms, rules, and imperatives, Freud makes a case for understanding a shortcut as a rebellion against the order of things, showing how a theological argumentation serves as a basis for social critique.

Yet, in Freud's critique of theology the concept of a shortcut also undergoes a notable transformation. There are two points to note. First, Freud endorses rather than rejects such an idea of insurgence. By cutting through the rules and laws enforced—one could say—from above, the critique that jokes put on display represents a positive arena of freedom. The need to ventilate the overwhelming pressure of emotional excess (e.g., wrath, sexual desires, and aggression) arguably justifies the existence of such a mechanism of resistance. More importantly, however, it is Freud's endorsement of standing "against the world" that seems to underline his affirmation of such a "release or discharge." In opposition to the rabbinic view, Freud seems to support rather than reject this type of transgressive shortcut, which shows the extent to which for him violation and suspension of the law, and not identification with it, may bring people together.[109] It is in these moments of defiance that we may enjoy a release from the slings and arrows of outrageous laws.

What Kant sees as freedom from the guidance of an "other" (*Die Leitung eines anderen*) seems to receive here particular interpretation. Especially in *The Conflict of the Faculties*, Kant associates critique with freedom from the guidance of a divine "Other" but also, and perhaps more importantly, from the social control of the state. Thus, in Kant's vision, the philosophical faculty should represent freedom from the two different forms of tutelage. But Freud seems to go even further by associating between the two forms of control (divine and social) because critique denotes a liberation from the "excessiveness" of social oppression that nonetheless builds on a theological representation of divine pressure. To the extent that the joke rebelliously works against the law, it also intertwines its theological and social connotations. Here, unlike the religious outlawing of shortcuts because they work against the eternal rules of God, to which the individual is requested to adhere, Freud endorses them for the same reason by applying them to the social arena.

At the same time, however, the critique that the joke represents actually enables the norms, rules, and codes of social conduct to continue to hold sway over our lives. This is the second, somewhat opposite, point to note. Despite its rebellious content, critique of law also means its validation. In facilitating a discharge of mental energy the joke also liquidates rebellious aggression, suppressed wishes, or untamed impulses. In this second sense, it is meant to spare, perhaps even save, the same rules against which it operates.

We may recall here the image of a law that is held "upside down" introduced in Freud's observations of Michelangelo's *Moses* earlier in this chapter. One of the falsifications of Moses lies in "the very unusual way" in which the Tables, representing the law, "are held": the fact that they stand "on their heads" symbolizes an overturning of the law, which makes it "easier to carry."[110] The lawgiver inverts the law, according to Freud, for the sake of easing its burden: an overturning of the law for the sake of its preservation. In the same vein, Freud's concept of discharge also entails the dropping of energy that was accumulated, a process that ends with the preserving of social norms rather than their dismissal. A hidden desire, once revealed, albeit by "bribing" the censors, is also aired. A concealed thought, once exposed, also disintegrates. The power that surreptitious truths have over our lives is moderated if these painful truths are unveiled. That is to say that in aerating the rebellious wish or drive, the shortcut also disarms it. In such a way, it also enables the persistence of the rules and norms that it set out to oppose.

We can thus observe the double role of critique: it simultaneously rebels against and perpetuates the law. This means that critique permits the continued carrying of the burden of norms and rules that surround and shape the individual. Arguably, then, in Freud's critique of theology a transgressive turn is made against the law that at the same time enables its persistence. The universal law that interested both Freud and the rabbinic discussions is preserved rather than fully dismissed. To put it in Mosaic terms: in their cunning turns and overturns, jokes tame our wrath and make the law easier to carry. Here, it is our disobedient turning against the imposed demands that verifies our support of and obedience to the rule of law.[111] In short, the turning against the law affirms, one may say returns to, the law.

The last point (underlining a turn away from a godly domain that symbolizes, however, a return to it) resonates well with a rather similar argument that was presented by Michel Foucault in his extensive paper *A Preface to Transgression* (*Préface a la Transgression*).[112] The relevant issue, I suggest, relates to how Foucault reflects on the notion of transgression and its theological origins. Theology is central to the paper's account of transgression, because Foucault finds the origins of this offense in the Christian mystical tradition of "fallen bodies" and "sin."[113] This tradition mainly concerns profane sexual acts. It is then in the mystical tradition of sin that sexuality enjoyed its highest free, immediate, and natural "felicity of expression."[114] The sinful, heretical expression of pleasure (i.e., pleasure that is attained through such a free sexual burst or a discharge, so to speak) represents a turn against demands of God; a "felicity" of free expression that is a path to mortification. But it also stands, concurrently, for a return to "the heart of a divine love" ("coeur d'une amour divine").[115] Here, a turn against God aims, rather explicitly, to return to the God-loving domain. In such a way, the rejection of God enables the persistence of God. Sin, therefore, is an act of faith, in a way that is reminiscent of redemption by sin.

This theological convolution resembles for Foucault "a source returning upon itself" ("la source en retour").[116] Such a "returning" means that the rejection of God is made in order to return to God. Sinful acts display therefore a somewhat circular movement between the turn against and the return to their divine source. In this theological imaginary, the core of the godly domain—the so-called "heart of a divine love"—is the origin of this double movement (away from and back to God) and in such a way God also stands as the instigator, locus, and purpose of such a movement. In the heretical tradition, God provides the source for the rebellious impulse, which then seeks a faithful return to the core from which the impulse originated. By means of sin, original divine love turns against itself and returns back to its "core." Thus, in the theological origins of transgression the divine love moves against and back to itself, pointing in such a way to the meaning of transgression as a turning against God (through a profane sexual act) carried out for the sake of complying with God's loving call to return.

For Foucault, however, this heretical tension has been "denatured" in modernity.[117] Modern sexuality stands for human desire alone, with no reference to an original divine domain as in the heretical tradition. Without movement of divine love (away from and back to itself), sexuality in modern theories (such as Freud's) "points to nothing beyond itself."[118] Under its new modern conditions sexuality is not only limited to "the law" of a "universal taboo,"[119] it also epitomizes our own limits, which we cannot transgress in the absence of divinity.

We are dealing then with the modern, godless context, in which transgression changes its meaning. Accordingly: "Profanation in a world which no longer recognizes any positive meaning in the sacred—is this not more or less what we may call transgression?"[120] The emphasis now seems to fall on the modern conditions to which "we" are subjugated. Within such a new framework we redefine transgression as an empty act of defiance, outlined by the absence, rather than the presence, of God.[121]

The new, modern, and arguably secular circumstances that Foucault has in mind relate, rather simply, to the "death of God." But Foucault's understanding of such a "death" is anything but simple: it does not signify the disappearance of God but rather suggests a new way in which the divine may continue to hold sway over our lives. Thus, for Foucault: "The death of God is not merely an 'event' that gave shape to contemporary experience as we now know it: it continues tracing indefinitely its great skeletal outline."[122] Here, God's death denotes only a repositioning of his continuing presence. In tracing the shape of our experience God remains a player in our world, albeit absent from it. In the "death" of God, one may speak, perhaps, of the continuing presence of an absent God: "Not that this death should be understood as the end of his historical reign or as the finally delivered judgment of his nonexistence, but as the now constant space of our experience."[123] What Foucault seems to outline is the theological meaning of transgression in modernity. He does so by suggesting transgression as a transformation of the original heretical impulse into a defiant social action devoid of the original divine object of defiance. The "source" that returns "upon itself" still reflects the same currents of movement in turning against and returning. Under modern conditions, however, its action cannot fall back on a "dead" source that is not available anymore. From such a point of view, transgression in modernity may continue to echo an original heretical disobedience (including an interplay between turning against and returning to God), albeit in a world devoid of a sacred "heart," or perhaps more poetically a world in which the divine loving core is a void. Taking such a transformation into consideration, a modern form of transgression, it could be said, can only appear for Foucault as a secularized form of heresy.

It is interesting to read Freud's critique of theology against the backdrop of this line of argumentation. In particular, because such a critique is made of a reference to a law that persists by transgressing itself. The double role of the joke (the critical turn against the law that enables its continuation) is important here because the act of transgression that the joke embodies is both rejection and affirmation, a mechanism of turning against and returning, as Foucault so elegantly outlined. Specifically, through the shortcutting character of jokes the law enables its own persistence by turning against itself. The joke's transgressive act could be described, to build on Foucault, as a "law returning upon itself" (or "la loi en retour"). The turn (against) and return (to) the law are not only connected but also delimited within its sphere of legitimization.

We may recall again Freud's engagement with the statue of Moses. The notion of a law in its returning to itself seems to encapsulate rather well some of the main issues that Freud accentuated in his analysis of Michelangelo's work. The inverted manner in which the Tables—representing the divine law—are held indeed serves as a case in point. Such an inversion is captured by the physical manner in which the divine message is held "upside down," if only to "support" Moses's (and perhaps also Freud's) position. It is also an attempt to locate the most emblematic figure of Jewish law not only as a broadcaster of the Christian turn against it but also as the core element of a theological adversary and historical persecutor.

Freud's attempt to reinstate Moses as a lawgiver of the Jews points to a similar composition of turns and returns. It does so because it takes some critical distance from the artist's image of the Hebrew lawgiver: on the one hand accepting Michelangelo's positioning of Moses within a Christian scheme, and on the other hand turning against such a compartmentalization of the original lawgiving. Therefore, accepting Michelangelo's theological critique of the pope also involved a critical turn against it. To some extent, then, we encounter a twofold engraving of a new lawgiver according to "the artist's conception." First, there is Michelangelo's *Moses*. Second, there is Freud's Michelangelo. Both conceptions seem to work within one interpretive configuration though Freud blurs the boundaries between them, eventually leaving his reader—perhaps like in a "Purim spiel"—with no fixed notion of "who is who and which is which."

Freud's critique of theology, central to his analysis of jokes, represents a crucial moment in the development of this mechanism. It underlines the way in which any turning against the law remains restricted to the overall structure of the law because transgressive moments of rejection of the imposed norms, regulations, or imperatives do not evoke their full dismissal. On the contrary, the power these laws hold over our lives is facilitated by such a transgression. The joke is then derived from the restrictions to which it remains limited. In such a way we encounter in Freud's discussion of jokes a law that "turns upon itself" as an underlying principle of the joke's defiance of the law, whose origins are the law and whose entire "trajectory" is bound up with that law. A law thus is turned physically (as in the case of Moses's Tables, or the crossing of the sacred space), but also symbolically, for Freud. To turn against a law, and in this sense to transgress it, means merely to suggest an exercise that originates in and is limited by the lawful sphere of legitimation. Thus, transgression is about the crossing of an imagined divine boundary that remains, nonetheless, delimited by what is being crossed.

The last point underlines the relation between transgression and secularization. What was evocative in Foucault's reading of transgression seems relevant to Freud's critique of theology as well. Secularization here means that Freud presents a shift from reverence of "eternal" laws to a clear focus on the universal laws that govern a world devoid of God. Lawgiving in this sense is not about inscribing the divine word on tables (as in the case of the statue of Moses), but rather articulating the "nomos of the earth" as Robert Cover would call it, that is, the laws of social order.

Nevertheless, Freud's approach to secularization is anything but simple because his focus on the social world merely brings a religious logic to bear on social argumentation. Santner's suggestion that in Freud we see an enclosing of "the eternal within the earthly," cited previously in this chapter, seems to be rather apt.[124] The "supremacy of the law," in the religious sense, is still upheld, but this is because it is reapplied to the relation between the individual and society alone. In such a way, secularization denotes not a dismissal of theological symbolism but its transformation. For Freud such "immanentization," as Agata Bielik-Robson calls it, "does not announce the demise of the transcendence, but, to the contrary, inaugurates *nova era* in uncovering the latter's new modes of being."[125]

Within this context, Freud's secular approach endorses the type of transgression that was rejected in the rabbinic discussion, with the aim, however, of verifying the rule of law. It seems that rather than transgressing the religious importance of preserving the law, Freud saves religious argumentation by turning it on its head, so to speak: he inverts its meaning (from a full taboo against transgression to its endorsement) and yet preserves its end (a defense of the law by which we live). Here the main point is that a secular approach does not express a simple opposition to a religious point of view; nor is it a reiteration of religious obedience. Both interpretations fall short of fully describing Freud's mechanism in which the rejection of the law marks its justification.

One of the implications of this type of secularization of religion is that Freud's critique of theology diverges from Foucault's secularization of heresy. In Freud's case, transgression relates to the law rather than to love, and to the position of the religious lawgiver rather than to any numinous unity with the divine. The transgressive affair strongly resists any retreat to mysticism because it remains restricted to the world and to the "terms of being" that are part of such a world. If Foucault falls back on mysticism, Freud has recourse to a rabbinic notion of law as a normative universe that surrounds us.

This difference between Freud and Foucault might also point to Foucault's misunderstanding of Freud's theory of sexuality. In Freud there is not a "denaturing" of an original religious message, as Foucault argued, but a reworking of a religious imaginary that simply diverges from the one evoked by Foucault. What Foucault does not seem to consider is the possibility of a theological resource for modern secular thought other than Christian mysticism. The sharp contrast, then, lies not between a Freudian dismissal of religious symbolism and a Foucauldian reconstruction of it (albeit in a world devoid of God), but between two dissimilar religious sources.

This last point is crucial. Christoph Schmidt, for example, noted that modern forms of secularization of mysticism include a turn away from the law—indeed a flight "beyond the law"—and toward unmediated connections with a divine loving sphere.[126] For Schmidt this means, in particular, a transformation of the theological claim for a numinous unity of the human being with the divine, which includes entering into the "enigma" of "the hidden depths of the self."[127] This might be true of Foucault. But in Freud's case, it is the question of obedience to laws that lies at the center of transgression. To put it differently, there is no division between "enigma" and law. If the most evocative, transgressive and, one may say, antinomian acts are still contained within the law, there seems to be no area of human expression for Freud that lies beyond its normative organization. Here there is no refusal of a "hidden" self—there is always a surreptitious inner truth to consider, as illustrated by the joke involving the baroness—but rather a capturing of it to represent an unresolved tension between the law and its own terms of being, with no reference to an imagined external sphere beyond.

From this perspective, there is no mysterious unity with the divine but a more entangled sphere of a discontent lawfulness, in keeping with the idea that critique of the law is for the purpose of keeping, saving, and affirming it. In these terms, critique does not mean a "denaturing" of transgression, as Foucault would argue, but rather a secularization of it in a way that is still reminiscent of the eternal order of things. "Joke-work," therefore, denotes the transformation of a particular religious tradition that brings the relation between individual and eternal laws to bear on affairs within the social, and in this sense worldly, order. The Freudian notion that "we cannot fall out of this world" may be thus extended to imply an enclosing of human existence within this immanent world that includes, rather than excludes, transcendence.[128]

Does this argumentation also reflect on Freud's famous self-portrayal as a "Godless Jew" (*gottloser Jude*)?[129] By giving himself this label, Freud seemed to communicate the position of a secular modernist who completely rejects the Jewish religious tradition of obedience.[130] Freud's adherence to the modern secular culture translated more concretely into his self-portrayal as "a liberal of the old school," at a time when the "traditional liberal culture" of "reason and law" was in deep crisis.[131] But surely if Freud's engagement with wit and law is taken into consideration, his continuous concern with the relation between his secular outlook and Jewish terms of being may be articulated as a form of interplay, perhaps a continuum, rather than a division. In the image of a "Godless Jew" there is indeed a turn against the law of the father, to put it in Freudian terms. This turn against the law, however, is compartmentalized within the terms of the law, in accordance with the idiom of a law that returns upon itself. Its transgressive mechanism thus marks the opposite possible preserving of what was dismissed—that is, Judaism. In rooting for modern ideals like progress and freedom, Freud therefore seems to suggest a complicated approach to the notion of an "old school" liberal, one that intertwines seemingly opposing elements—on the one hand the secular, critical appeal, and on the other hand its theological sources, supporting the persistence of the tradition of lawfulness that is concurrently rejected.

From the standpoint of subversion and resistance we may endow Freud's self-reflection with a double meaning: a secular, godless turning away from religious Judaism and thereby an expression of the reverse endorsement of a Jewish core in defiance of the modern and secular, exemplifying perhaps what Freud's concept of a "short circuit" could have meant for him. A continuation, not a dichotomy, describes the connection between the two poles that Freud endorsed and frequently rejected between his "birth and death, etc."[132] To put it polemically, Freud's concept of law does not express an "undefined sense of Jewishness" as Peter Gay would have it, but rather a definite sense of purposely undefined Judaism.[133]

The concept of an undefined Judaism may explain why Freud expresses his view of "the very essence" of Judaism by using a wide range of theologically oriented metaphors such as "miraculous," "enigmatic," and "mysterious."[134] As argued above, however, it would be wrong to claim that Freud's critique of theology falls back on mysticism.[135] On the contrary, thinking in terms of enigma seems to encapsulate the mechanism of a law—"our God logos"[136]—in and within itself and not of any numinous unity with an ideal essence or true being that lies beyond it. This mechanism, nonetheless, is now composed as a cunning, perhaps uncanny, enclosing of itself as a riddle.

CHAPTER 2
A Theory of Youth

An Age of Youth

Rebellion and Quest

Freud's analysis of jokes, although unique in its combination of wit and law, was not alone in pointing to the theological sources of critique. Walter Benjamin's extensive engagement with the concept of "youth" (*Jugend*) (encompassing the meaning of being young, the call for "youthfulness," and its success or failure) generated another, albeit contrasting, contemporaneous discussion in which critique was dependent on theology. In contrast to the religious elements found in Freud's analysis of jokes, this chapter shows how Benjamin's conceptualization of youth offers social criticism of mystical lore. I start by illustrating what youth means for Benjamin, how he articulates such a meaning theologically, and in what way theology of this sort relates to mysticism. The final section of this chapter is dedicated to the manner in which the mystical underpinning of youth informs Benjamin's concept of critique and what can be considered Benjamin's critique of theology.

Youth was no doubt central to Benjamin's early, mostly posthumously published writings from the period 1910–17. These writings include a variety of short philosophical works and fragmented texts, such as "The Life of the Students" ("Das Leben der Studenten"), "The Metaphysics of Youth" ("Die Metaphysik der Jugend"), "The Youth Is Still" ("Die Jugend Schwieg"), "Experience" ("Erfahrung"), "Socrates" ("Sokrates"), "Two Poems by Hölderlin: The Poet's Courage (*Dichtermut*) and Timidity (*Blödigkeit*)," and "Dostoyevsky's *The Idiot*."[1] They cover a wide range of themes and issues, like the sources of language, the question of freedom, the origins of tragedy and its relation with play, and aesthetics. But it was mainly the trope of youth and its intersection with these different issues with which Benjamin grappled in most of his early writings before and during the First World War.

To some extent, Benjamin's extensive engagement with the idea of youth is not surprising. Youth, youthfulness, and being young were all widespread metaphors in the German cultural and intellectual sphere at the turn of the nineteenth century. As historians such as Walter Rüeggs, Frank Trommler, and Robert-Jan Adriaansen have pointed out, a concept of youth was employed as an emblem for an abstract breaking away from modern cultural, social, and political reality.[2] The reinvention of youth as a symbol for a social and cultural rupture occurred against the backdrop of growing distrust in positivism, materialism, and the rationalist "demystification" of the world that was also regarded as the signature of a modern secular culture. Endemic to a range of cultural, intellectual, artistic, and scholarly trends in the late nineteenth and early twentieth centuries, such a breaking away from modernity was visible in various neoromantic, post-Nietzschean, and spiritual impulses that were highly attentive to the idea of a true human essence, or original term of being, that transcends articulation and understanding—the "hidden depths of the self" with which the human being may have an unmediated relation.[3]

Within this cultural and intellectual context, the concept of youth often stood simultaneously for an iconoclastic revolt against oppressive modern conditions and an iconographic quest for an alternative return to nature, to community, and to a spiritual reverence for life.[4] Against the Wilhelmine social and political order it represented a cultural revolt—a counterculture, as it were—offering a remedy to feelings of alienation and to existential crisis. To the extent that modernity signified alienation, youth represented a return to an authentic, true human essence, or original term of being, that had allegedly been lost in the process of modernization, although what exactly such originality actually meant remained heavily disputed. Where modern life oppressed, youth redeemed.[5]

Youth, then, encapsulated rebellion and quest. This particular interpretation of youth received attention in a wide range of cultural, artistic, literary, and intellectual spheres. Intellectuals such as Erich Gutkind and Oswald Spengler, for example, related, each in his own way, to a concept of youth as a symbol of prehistorical originality that stands over against modernity.[6] In a rather similar abstract vein, Carl Jung used the archetype of *Puer Aeternus*—"forever young"—to describe a psychological mechanism that not only refuses boundaries and limits but also "represents our totality, which transcends consciousness."[7] From a social perspective, Karl Mannheim placed the quandary of youth and of its reaching maturity at the center of his discussion of "generationality" (*Generationalität*), a dilemma that, to some extent, constituted the main theme in Frank Wedekind's play *Spring Awakening*.[8] Similarly, Fidus's popular drawings depicted the free and naked aesthetic figure of the young body, and the overall new style of art nouveau was endowed, at least in its German variant, with the meaning of a "youth art" (*Jugendstil*).[9]

The emergence and rapid growth of the German Youth Movement was perhaps the most salient example of the social and political impact of the new concept of youth.[10] From the *Wandervogel*'s modest beginnings in 1896 in the Steglitz Quarters of Berlin, the German Youth Movement (and its later variant the *Freideutsche Jugend*) quickly became a significant cultural phenomenon, spreading far beyond the borders of the German Reich over the next decades. For members of the German Youth Movement, activities such as hiking, camping, singing, or experiencing nature were a way of demonstrating rebellion against the modern way of life and were seen as being crucial to the quest for independence and self-assertion. Thus, in 1913, during the first all-German meeting of the youth movements at the Hoher Meissner mountain near Kassel, being young was defined as a search for an autonomous and free life, devoid of external interference; this entailed assuming the responsibility of following one's untainted inner convictions, whatever they may be. This "Meissner formula" demonstrated the extent to which youth culture (*Jugendkultur*) offered an antidote to feelings of crisis and alienation induced by the modern way of life. It represented what historian Hartmut Böhme has called "the utopian potential of youth" in the eyes of many contemporary young German scholars, writers, intellectuals, and political activists, mostly young men, who belonged to the well-established educated bourgeoisie.[11]

Benjamin was one of these young men. Making sense of what youth means marked for him both a personal quest and a sign of the times, bound up with notions of crisis and youth, rebellion and quest, alienation and redemption.[12] "We are living in an age of Socialism, of the women's movement, of traffic, of individualism" wrote the enthusiastic eighteen-year-old Benjamin. "Are we not headed toward an age of youth?"[13] The social as well as metaphysical meanings of such an "age of youth"—"youth's two bodies," to play on Kantorowitzc's famous concept—truly captured his intellectual imagination.

Around 1910 Benjamin was already deeply engaged with thinking about "an age of youth" and its relation to the social and political reality of Wilhelmian Germany.¹⁴ Between the summer of 1912, when he was twenty years old and a student at the University of Freiburg, and the outbreak of World War I, he became involved with what was then known as the "radical faction" of the German Youth Movement, which took its inspiration from Gustav Wyneken (1875-1964).¹⁵ Being "radical" denoted a commitment to an ideal of youth rather than to a particular practice or political alignment. For the members of this faction, it was important that the concept should remain politically unaligned and not reduced to the common practices and rituals of other contemporary youth movements. Upon returning to Berlin in the winter semester of 1912-13, Benjamin, still a committed Wynekenian, devised the *Sprechsaal* (talking room)—a free association of friends who joined together in the spirit of "radical" youth. He attended the 1913 youth rally at the Hoher Meissner and in the summer of 1914 finally succeeded in being elected as chair of the Berlin Independent Students' Association, where he immediately arranged lectures from Martin Buber on his new book *Daniel* and from Ludwig Klages on his "life philosophy" (*Lebensphilosophie*).¹⁶ From 1912 he was also involved in Zionist student circles (his famed friendship with Gershom Scholem to follow) and combined his thoughts on youth with questions of Jewish identity and politics. Following the outbreak of World War I and the dramatic suicide of his close friend, the poet Christoph Friedrich (Fritz) Heinle, Benjamin turned away from his early enthusiasm for Wyneken's formula of youth and emphasized the failure of youth culture.¹⁷ Heinle's tragic suicide was a particularly decisive factor in Benjamin's eventual withdrawal from a positive approach to youth.¹⁸ With this in mind, he composed his 1917 piece on "Dostoyevsky's *The Idiot*," which represents his last explicit engagement with the concept.¹⁹

TRANSCENDENCE, DIVINITY, AND ETERNITY

What, then, is the "age of youth" for Benjamin? When Benjamin speaks of an "age" he is not simply talking about a distinct historical era (or "spirit" of the times, as evoked in German philosophical discussions since Hegel). More profoundly, he takes the notion of "age" to represent a human spiritual core that transcends social and historical circumstances. This means that the notion of spirit (*Geist*) does not signify a particular culture or historical stage; it refers instead to an innate and not-of-this-world characteristic of human beings. There is for Benjamin a human "individual time" that is not equivalent to a particular biological phase (for example, adolescence), but rather to an inner spiritual core of the human being that is free from any temporal (i.e., social and historical) conditioning.[20]

An age of youth stands for such an inner spiritual core. This is what an "intellectual autonomy of the creative spirit" signifies for Benjamin.[21] Not just an inner human resistance to particular social and cultural circumstances (for example, a bourgeois upbringing, one's educational background, or moral codes), but more radically a spiritual independence of all forms of external social, cultural, or political influences.[22] Thus, for Benjamin, the "meaning of the word 'youth'" lies in the fact "that from youth alone radiates new spirit, *the* spirit."[23] In the same vein, and in contrast to a "philistine" experience "devoid of meaning and spirit," Benjamin presents an image of youth as "the voice of the spirit": a site of human independence and freedom from any conditioning by history and society.[24] Representing for Benjamin an inner human spiritual core—"the pure word for life in its immortality"—youth could be termed a site of "beyondness" because of its alleged existence beyond all possible social and historical binding circumstances.[25]

It is this inner human element that lies beyond society and history that Benjamin articulates theologically, on the basis of three characteristics: transcendence, eternity, and divinity. This is, then, another important issue to note because it points to a clear theological underpinning of the concept. Youth is transcendent because Benjamin conceptualizes it as an unmalleable inner human essence, separated from all worldly demands. To "faithfully serve the true spirit" is to remain above all transitory historical or social settings.[26] Youth, one may say, transcends worldliness.[27]

Benjamin's short essay "The Life of the Students" illustrates this last point.[28] The text opens with a clear differentiation between two historical approaches: first, a "view of history" that is concerned with the ways in which "people and epochs advance along the path of progress," and second, Benjamin's analysis of history that aims at grasping a "metaphysical structure, as with the messianic domain or the idea of the French Revolution."[29] Though embedded within history, such a "metaphysical structure" lies beyond its historical appearances and different manifestations. It is also separated from any historical notion of "progress" and advancement. In referring to a redemptive "domain" (that of messianism) or to an "idea" of a historical event (rather than to the event itself), it contains for Benjamin a certain "spiritual" essence that points to a double meaning—the logic of history, but also and more importantly, a differentiated inner core that transcends the social and historical.

This separation between history and the "spiritual" essence that transcends it informs Benjamin's distinction between true and false education, central to his "The Life of the Students." Benjamin clearly distinguishes between academic "vocational training" and an autonomous student "spirit."[30] True education, for Benjamin, is about "living and working *sub specie aeternitatis*," a reference to Spinoza that he reiterates in a range of texts from this time.[31] Echoing neoromantic notions in particular, Benjamin represents true education as an "erotic" and "creative" core that "cannot be captured in terms of the pragmatic description of details (the history of institutions, customs, and so on)" but rather eludes them.[32] The true "spirit" of education here relates to an imagined human essence that escapes social conditioning. Its fulfillment is not aligned with the requirements of society, and though it could be distilled from a certain social context (for example, that of the students in Wilhelmian Germany) it marks an essence that lies beyond social circumstances. What Benjamin then calls the "perversion" of universities lies in their attempt to transform "the creative spirit into the vocational spirit."[33] Conversely, Benjamin pleads for "a hazardous self-dedication to learning and youth."[34] "All these institutions," argues Benjamin, "are nothing but a marketplace for the preliminary and provisional, . . . they are simply there to fill the empty waiting time, diversions from the voice that summons them to build their lives with a unified spirit of creative action, Eros, and youth."[35] There is therefore a conflict between social institutions and the inner calling of Eros and youth. As Benjamin explains in a letter to Carla Seligson, Eros for him combines Platonic heavenly desire with Christ's "Kingdom of God."[36] It connects a passionate desire for self-formation (according to the concept of *Bildung*) with self-elevation to the divine realm of truth, beauty, and totality.[37] This entwining of youth with Platonic and Christian symbolism was a central theme in his fragment "Socrates."[38] Figuratively, self-formation of the individual appears as a reenactment of the Socratic winged chariot in its trajectory of returning to the dominion of the divine, albeit in the Christian redemptive sense. Youth resonates in such a way with a *theia mania* (divine madness), and human life is thus reenchanted.

Pedagogically, such a reenchantment of human existence is not about learning a specific curriculum that prepares the young person for a productive and meaningful life in modern German society and culture; it is instead about transcending this curriculum. As the next chapter of this book discusses, half a century later, Adorno returns to these notions in his own take on education from the 1960s. In Benjamin's early vocabulary, an educational mission offers "the Eros of creativity" over against "bourgeois security."[39] For Benjamin, this radical approach takes the Humboldtian kind of "freedom," with which he was familiar, to its logical end—a *Freiheit zum Grunde*, which is a conclusive form of freedom from all types of limiting actions.[40]

If transcendence signifies Eros and self-fulfillment, it also aims at the "Kingdom of God." Benjamin's reference to the divine points to a second theological aspect of his concept of youth. His notion of youth and the sacred realm are interwoven, and transcendence seeks the divine. The combination of human existence and divine presence was central to Benjamin's theory of language of that time.[41] His much discussed 1916 fragment "On Language as Such and on the Language of Man" ("Über Sprache überhaupt und über die Sprache des Menschen"), for example, underlines the "communion" of human language "with the *creative* word of God."[42] This is a rich text that encompasses a wide range of issues and themes that lie, however, beyond the scope of the discussion offered here. The relevant point to note is that especially in the text's explicit reflections on the Bible, the communion between language and the divine "word" (also: logos) is seen as a form of "immanent magic" that represents a mythical moment of creation and revelation, providing language with its logic.[43] The creative word of God enables human language to operate but also remains an "un*mediated*" element that elevates the "*gift* of language" above nature.[44] The aim of using written language, writes Benjamin to Buber, is therefore: "to lead the reader toward that which escapes the world; only when this non-verbal realm is opened up in its pure, inexpressible power, can the magic spark fly between word and motivating deed to the point of unity between these two equal realities."[45] What "escapes the world" is the divine word that represents a "nonverbal realm" and opens up to the human being who may then share "the same language in which God is the creator."[46]

Such a prelapsarian connection between humans and God is encapsulated in the human ability to "name" things. In pointing to this human competence, Benjamin relates to the biblical myth in which Adam "gave names" to all living creatures (Gen. 2:19). Hannah Arendt's later remark that it was "not Plato but Adam, who named things" seems to relate to

Benjamin's theory of language since for him "God rested when he had left his creative power to itself in man. This creativity, relieved of its divine actuality, became knowledge."[47] In human naming, then, there is a transformation—but also a "fall"—of the divine "word" into human knowledge, which means "the translation of the nameless into name."[48] Translation denotes at this point a migration of divine elements into the profane realm of this worldliness. The translation into human language, however, does not entail the classification, grouping, or identification of objects that may serve as a common ground for human communication. "Naming," in this sense, is not "a means to an end"; nor is it to be understood as a "way for people to converse."[49] Rather, "naming" for Benjamin is about a form of creation, a way for humans to touch upon a divine pure essence, which they share. Language is thus "Name" ("Sprache ist Namen") in the Hebrew sense of relating to God (Hashem, which literally means "the name"). Scholem's famous 1926 "confession" (sent to the moribund Franz Rosenzweig) resonates with this point rather well. Language, writes Scholem, "is Name" and in the name "the power of the sacred speaks out."[50]

Benjamin's theory of youth runs along similar lines. Youth represents the presence of the divine within a transcendent human (spiritual) essence. In youth, as in the "name," the sacred speaks out. In this sense, youth points to a certain human divine essence. We are dealing, then, with "youth by the grace of God."[51] The human being has a divine "spiritual"—or youthful—core; an element that the human being incorporates and may experience, but that, in its referring to God, escapes classification. Like language, youth represents a creative, divine, transcendent element that the human being incorporates, may experience, but cannot grasp.

Following divinity, eternity is the last main aspect in Benjamin's theological conceptualization of youth. Denoted by *kairos*, youth-time is the "now" (*Jetztzeit*), or, better, represents the eternal-now moment.[52] Benjamin reiterates a distinction between two concepts of time: the flow of time that characterizes this worldliness, and the other, removed, transcendent-eternal time of youth. Thus, for example, in "The Life of the Students," understanding such "life" means for Benjamin thinking in terms of its everlasting, eternal nature.[53] Here, the distinction between two concepts of time appears in the form of a separation between the time of history and that of youthful eternity.

In temporal terms, youth may denote, then, what contemporary sociologists had termed "moratorium"—a time in which all social laws, regulations, and duties are suspended by the young person.[54] The point is worth mentioning, because it may provide a sociological explanation for Benjamin's theory of youth. Yet Benjamin does not seem to be thinking here in sociological terms. Nor is he focusing on a psychology of youth as merely a break from infancy in anticipation of adulthood—as "a period of preparation" or a "period of waiting for marriage and a profession."⁵⁵ Rather, Benjamin aims at articulating the relation between eternity and temporality, informed by a theological association between divinity and eternity. The suspension of world-time points to such a theological aspect of Benjamin's theory of youth exactly because it denotes for him the true divine time that lies beyond historical linearity; it echoes a religious dualism between transcendence and immanence; and it is meant to play on the gnostic themes of redemption and fall.⁵⁶

Mystical Allegories

YOUNG MAN, I TELL YOU, STAND UP!

Transcendence, divinity, and eternity point to the theological imagination invested in Benjamin's theory of youth. This imagination should be regarded, more particularly, as mystical. In order to make sense of the type of mystical thought that informed Benjamin's symbolism, it would be helpful to consider Meister Eckhart's (1260–1328) writings, not just because of their strong mystical import, but also because of what could be viewed as Eckhart's own theory of youth.

Eckhart was a Dominican priest who served as the first provincial of Saxony and as vicar general of Bohemia in the late thirteenth and early fourteenth centuries. He was condemned, posthumously, for heresy by Pope John XXII (who himself was later accused of holding unorthodox views).⁵⁷ The accusations brought against Eckhart stemmed from the connections drawn between his mystical views and heresy. His accusers traced their suspicion back to his main work, *The Book of Divine Comfort* (1308), along with a range of "German sermons" composed in *Mittelhochdeutsch*, which were considered his most explicit mystical writings. These various texts were singled out as "spreading dangerous doctrines among the common people."⁵⁸

The importance of these mystical writings for the discussion of Benjamin's theory of youth lies in their modern reception. As Ingeborg Degenhardt's pivotal study has shown, Eckhart's mystical writings received particular attention among intellectuals at the turn of the nineteenth century, when mysticism was once again "in the air."[59] In the nineteenth century especially, Eckhart was credited with being not only "the father of German mysticism" but also "the father of German idealism."[60] In 1857 Franz Pfeiffer published the first modern edition of Eckhart's sermons, treatises, and lectures, which prompted a growing interest in Eckhart, culminating in 1903 with the appearance of two new German editions of the mystic-theologian's writings—Gustav Landauer's *Meister Eckharts Mystische Schriften* and Hermann Büttner's *Meister Eckeharts Schriften und Predigten*, the latter being the more comprehensive and influential of the two.[61] Eckhart's impact was then visible in a wide range of literary, poetic, intellectual, and scholarly outputs, as well as in the formation of *völkisch* aspirations and in the rhetoric of German nationalism.[62]

Eckhart's mystical scripts presented modern enthusiastic readers no less than Middle Ages excommunicators with a theologically explosive substance. His allegorical interpretations of biblical texts were central and presented the birth of Christ not as a historical affair, but as an allegory for the manner in which God can potentially "awaken" his "son" in every human soul. The "son" becomes an emblem for a transcendent ground or the essence of the soul that can be "awakened" from slumber by the "father." Jesus thus provides an allegory for the divine "son" within us all. Here, Eckhart adopted the formula of the "son" in the "soul" (underlined in the condemnatory bull of John XXII) to express the relationship between God and the human being, interpreted not historically but mystically.[63] This relation is the fruit of a fusion between the rejection of worldliness and the move toward inner human experience, which, through being "united" with God, transcends this world.[64]

In Eckhart's thinking, the image of an awakened "son" was symbolized by youth. Youth, therefore, marked an important aspect of the idea of divine presence embedded within human experience. He accentuated this last point in numerous sermons that became accessible through Pfeiffer's collection and partly through Büttner's translation.[65] In three of these sermons, Eckhart focuses in particular on an episode from the gospels in which Jesus comes across a "widow" whose only son has died. As the coffin is carried forth, Jesus touches it and cries: "Young man, I tell you, stand up!" ("Adolescens, tibi dico: surge!," Luke 7:14).

Eckhart reads this passage as an allegory in which Jesus is seen to underline the divine, transcendent, and eternal characteristics of being young. Here, there are three points to note. First, the text is charged with symbolic meaning. According to Eckhart, the widow represents the human soul devoid of God.[66] The young man stands for the "son" or the (divine) essence of the soul—"the highest intellect"—that "can receive the divine light" and thus be awakened by God.[67] Youth is where the soul is "Godlike: *there* she is an image of God."[68] And Eckhart comments: "Why did he say 'young man'? . . . 'Young man': All the powers that belong to the soul do not age. . . . Therefore, 'Young man.' The masters call 'young' that which is close to its beginning. In the intellect man is ever young. . . . Now he says, 'Young man, arise.' What does it mean 'arise'? 'Arise' from the work, and let the soul 'arise' in herself!"[69] If "youth" represents the divine within the soul, it also transcends this worldliness. It connects the "now," the divine spoken word ("he says"), a command ("arise"), and youth—all are but elements of an inner development (an awakening, as it were) within the human "soul."

A second point to note is that Eckhart's symbolism involves images of femininity and masculinity. Elliot Wolfson, for example, pointed aptly to the significance of such images in Christian and Jewish mysticism.[70] In Eckhart's variation, the soul is presented as a "widow" while the young core within is seen as a virile "son." Eckhart, then, does not only see youth as transcendent and divine, but also imagine it as masculine. Yet, while for Eckhart the figure of youth is masculine, he presents also an exchange between such a masculine characteristic of the soul and its feminine aspect. This exchange stands for the "intellect" or the "citadel" of the soul that enables its evolution.[71] Thus, for him the soul is "virginal" (*Jungfrau*—also suggestive of a young woman) when it is free from "alien images."[72] It elevates itself to the position of "bearing fruit" and evolves into a "wife" only on being suffused with the "young man."[73]

Finally, youth is eternal. In Eckhart's account, youth is the faculty of the human being that "touches neither time nor flesh," otherwise defined as the "eternal now."[74] In her dissertation, Hannah Arendt argued that this "eternal now" was also Saint Augustine's conception of divine time, as distinct from the future–past linearity of this-worldliness.[75] This is true also of Eckhart. For him, in particular, the "eternal now" denoted being young, corresponding to the notion of the "eternal life" of the soul.[76] It is where the soul is "free from time," which means that it remains transcendent and separated from the world.[77] There is here, it seems, a dualism between the eternal-divine and the temporal-worldly. This central theological trope, however, is reframed by Eckhart's introduction of an eternal presence within the human experience. The godly-eternal is located within the young core of the human being, which remains therefore "free" and in this sense withdrawn from worldly affairs. Arguably, the location of the divine within the human ensures the possibility of salvation by means of a human regression into the innermost sublime, eternal-young, alien core. This also means that the retreat to the self rather than a connection to the world characterizes the redemptive feature of Eckhart's mystical theory of youth.

Read through the prism of Eckhart's allegories, in the mystical Christian tradition the essence of the human being is viewed as eternally young, and as such resides in a unity with the divine. In this way, youth guarantees salvation. It could be argued that such a theory of youth also points to the manner in which human time and worldly time are disconnected, because the first entails a divine presence, while the second is discussed in the wake of its absence. Whereas the divine remains forever young, the worldly is transitory, temporary, and decadent. This also helps to explain why youth represents an inner core that cannot be grasped or articulated by the human being in any given way. To put it differently, for Eckhart youth represents a nothing, or a *nihil*. One of the celebrated aspects of Eckhart's mysticism is that nothingness is not specifically identified with the notion of complete emptiness. Rather, it underlines an ideal demesne that is categorically foreign to us because it lies beyond our capacities to understand, know, or imagine, and even eludes any notion of nothingness that we may have. In this sense, nothingness indicates a completely transcendent, alien, not-of-this-world, free, youthful form of being.

THE METAPHYSICS OF YOUTH

It is useful to address the manner in which Benjamin's theory of youth incorporated a reworking of such mystical allegories. Benjamin probably became familiar with Eckhart's writings long before he enriched his personal library with a copy of Eckhart's sermons.[78] In using the pseudonym "Eckhart. phil" for his 1912 essay "School Reform: A Cultural Movement" he made clear, at the very least, his awareness of Eckhart. The main issue, however, is not whether Benjamin was directly influenced by Eckhart's theory of youth, but rather in what manner he was precociously attuned to the type of mysticism that Eckhart's writings exemplified. As presented above, Benjamin's concept of youth reiterated notions of transcendence within a human spiritual core, the eternal-present, and the numinous unity with the divine realm that are central to the mystical imagination.

In the same vein, his understanding of youth as an emblem of free experience, or better, the fundamental experience of being free, radiated mysticism because it reflected the same metaphors—like "awakening," the "alien" soul, and the "divine" essence of "youth." This does not mean that Benjamin's articulation of youth did not bring together a wide range of other influences, including the contributions not only of romantics like Hölderlin, Novalis, and Schelling but also of early modern philosophers such as Spinoza and contemporaneous thinkers like Bergson. However, the mystical symbolism relating to the numinous unity with the divine, or to the "awakening" of the soul, became a central characteristic for Benjamin through his allusion to this range of influences (mainly German romanticism), or, more accurately, through his presentation of these textual and historical traditions with their theological common denominator.[79]

Perhaps the most striking text into which Benjamin engraved his reworking of mystical allegories was "The Metaphysics of Youth." The essay was written between 1913 and 1914, and according to Gershom Scholem it was left unfinished.[80] As Steizinger points out, the text aimed at explicating the concept of "youth" in a way that integrated the prevalent themes from various other texts that Benjamin had written prior to that point.[81] It did so, however, by employing a highly enigmatic style, which resists systematic scrutiny.[82] Consequently, its value to an understanding of Benjamin's philosophy, rather than poetics, remains heavily debated.

The style and content, nonetheless, seem to be useful for a more detailed analysis of Benjamin's mystical orientation. At its core, the text describes a range of ordinary experiences from everyday life—dancing, conversing with friends, writing a diary, plus addressing sexual desire in venues that were then fairly common to members of the young bourgeoisie. Benjamin, however, does not wish to relate to this range of everyday experiences plainly. Rather, he opens with a call to his readers—most probably the circle of friends among whom the text was circulated—to decrypt the "uncomprehended symbolism" that "enslaves us" in our everyday life.[83] This opening statement, together with Hölderlin's poem, which Benjamin selected as a motto for his text, resonates well with Benjamin's quest to understand the student's life "as a metaphor, as an image of the highest metaphysical state of history."[84]

The reading of everyday life "as a metaphor" presents the issue at stake here. Can we not argue that it reflects a tension between the description of mundane experiences characteristic of youth (dancing, writing a diary, conversing with friends) and the elevation of these activities to an allegorical, and for Benjamin profound, order? Benjamin, arguably, reads life allegorically. As Talal Asad observed, for Benjamin allegory became "the appropriate mode for apprehending this world."[85] Such an "apprehending" of the world means that mundane experiences are seen as symbolic reflections of more abstract, metaphysical themes, raising these everyday experiences "onto a higher plane."[86]

It is this allegorical mechanism that is highly relevant to Benjamin's metaphysics of youth. Indeed, taking on Benjamin's call to engage with the text's symbolism seems to be particularly fruitful in gaining insights into its interplay with mysticism. The text has three sections, labeled "Conversation," "Diary," and "Ball." Read allegorically, the first (conversation) explores youth mainly in terms of language and gender; the second (diary) conceptualizes youth in reference to time and temporality; the third (ball) may be seen as focusing on space and transcendence.

Benjamin's "conversation" relates to language and gender because it is composed of an interaction between a "speaker" (appearing rather bluntly as "he") and a "listener" (referred to as "she") who also stand for masculinity and femininity, respectively.[87] Here, Benjamin expands on a variety of rather challenging concepts, like "genius" and its counterpart "prostitute" (*Dirne*), manhood (*Mannheit*) and its feminine (*weiblich*) equal. These, however, could be seen as symbols of an inner human experience—partly carried over from German romanticism—and not as references to individuals or social categories.[88] They point to what Paul North called "a silent conversation in the soul."[89] As such, speaker and listener, masculinity and femininity, are aspects of the human soul, engaged in the elusive instigation of truth and meaning.

Thus, the speaker "receives meaning" from the "silent" listener, who is "the unappropriated source of meaning."[90] In this case the "source of meaning"—eventually what youth should stand for—is located in an experience (which Benjamin calls "silence") that cannot be appropriated or grasped by the language of conversation. "Silence" in this particular way seems to be reminiscent of "the name" that Benjamin evokes in his theory of language. Such a connection is possible since Benjamin terms silence as "the internal frontier of conversation," which he relates to the eternal and to the true, spiritual, and divine essence.[91] Like "the name," silence points to a conversation that cannot appropriate its divine source, which it nonetheless shares. It is through silence, perhaps, that the divine speaks out. It then becomes a paean to the fall of language in echoing "the name" that has been "lost" through its modes of operation.[92] Here, and somewhat preceding his thoughts on language, Benjamin's allegory presents the lost divine origin as the "source of meaning," which also corresponds to the innate feminine essence of the masculine (*Sein Weiblich-Gewesenes*).⁹³ It is possible, therefore, to see the variety of propositions relating to the woman, who according to Benjamin "protects meaning from understanding" or who is referred to as "the guardian of conversation," as allegories for the unappropriated source of meaning, which is innate in the human soul.

These are not random images. For Eckhart, being mute (*ohne Laut*), for example, characterizes the "original experience" (*ursprüngliche Erfahrung*) beyond understanding.⁹⁴ In Benjamin's adaptation of the idea, the focus on experiencing a moment beyond understanding is decisive. The enigmatic character of the text that Benjamin composes, for example, could be seen as intended to break with understanding. As in Eckhart's mysticism, the source of meaning is internal, located within the human unmediated experience and points to an embedded transcendence of sorts.

The reading of Benjamin's essay against the background of its mystical sources, could be relevant also of his application of masculine and feminine symbols, although these have a more elusive, abstruse appearance in the text. The feminine aspect that Benjamin plays with relates to two of the missions apparent in Eckhart's writings. For example, the dialogue between the two figures Benjamin calls a "prostitute" and a "genius" may be taken as symbolizing the human soul devoid of the divine presence of "greatness," and youth.⁹⁵ Because of this lacuna "greatness has no claim upon her, for greatness comes to an end when confronted by her."⁹⁶ In playing with mystical symbolism, Benjamin's "prostitute" echoes, arguably, human existence devoid of God (Eckhardt calls this the "widow"), in opposition to the so-called "virginity" of the spiritual soul.⁹⁷ However, the feminine (*weiblich*) aspect of the soul marks, concurrently, the opportunity—the conditions, as it were—for human beings to touch upon their inner youthful and divine essence. Woman, therefore, is where the human "receives the silence."⁹⁸ The soul is, to begin with, feminine, in alignment with a long mystical tradition that, as mentioned above, has both Christian and Jewish variants. It appears, however, as part of the masculine, and as in Eckhart's mysticism "the female is comprised in the male."⁹⁹ In being "the female of man"—in the words of Elliot Wolfson—woman is "the guardian of conversation," the structural conditions, as it were, for the rise of "the youth of mysterious conversation."¹⁰⁰

The second section of Benjamin's text, the "Diary" ("Tagebuch"), explicitly engages with the question "In what time do men live?"¹⁰¹ In his answer, Benjamin articulates two forms of time in which the human being lives. The first stands for the past–future linearity of this worldliness, whose human characteristics are "mortality," "emptiness," "hopelessness," and loss of meaning.[102] Like in Heidegger's *Being and Time*, and preceding it, existence is articulated by Benjamin as a living toward death.[103] Indicating finitude, however, death also stands for being empty, hopeless, and devoid of meaning.

Over against this "emptiness of time," there is the second "eternal," "youthful," "true," and "immortal" time: "That time, our essence, is the immortality in which others die."[104] Eternity, here, marks a characteristic of youth and its "immortality" stands against the finitude that is associated with the temporality of this-worldliness. Benjamin thus contrasts world-time (mortal, empty, moving toward death) and eternal-time (youthful, true, immortal).

As a "book of time" the diary points to the possible "act of liberation" from this-worldly temporality (characterized by the "living toward death") and the entering of the eternal-time. As "pure time," it suspends worldly temporality by the very experience of "timelessness" and "the birth of immortal time."[105] Against the "calendar time, clock time, and stock-exchange time," where "no ray of immortality casts its light over the self," the diary embodies the potential for the emergence of its opposite when "an 'I' that we know only from our diaries stands on the brink of an immortality into which it plunges."[106] Here, the "immortal" time stands on the other side of world-time. It penetrates world-time in the form of an "interval" (*Abstand*—to be read as "distance" too). Such an "interval" also represents "the diary's silence," showing how the source of meaning is put in temporal terms.[107] A diary becomes a symbol for the eternal-present youth, a point that also demonstrates the extent to which Benjamin's accentuation of the interval as "pure time" relates to his overall theory of youth.

The stark distinction between the eternal and timeless on the one hand and the linear and worldly on the other hand should command our attention. Because of this distinction between what Hans Blumenberg called life-time (*Lebenszeit*) and world-time (*Weltzeit*), a dualism of the kind expressed by Eckhart remains here a sound basis for Benjamin's thoughts. As a "ray of immortality" the eternal may pierce into this-worldliness and in this sense it is of a different constitution; as a suspending "interval" it cannot act through this-worldliness or, better, cannot act by its means. The image that Benjamin seems to evoke relates to a certain act of penetration: eternity may erupt, disturb, suspend the other temporality, but cannot be reconciled or combined with it. Rather, it remains alien to it.

Benjamin seems to propose what Harry Jansen called "incarnated" time, which rejects rather than accepts a Hegelian conceptualization of the cunning of history, in which the advent of the divine-eternal is fulfilled by the workings of the worldly-temporal.[108] To put it more polemically, Benjamin advocates not the advent of transcendent reason through history but rather its implosive irruption in history and against it. There is, then, the constant potential for salvation, for divine time may always, and at any given moment, implode in history. Though always present, and possible, this potential remains, however, out of human control and beyond historical reach.

It should also be noted how, at this point, the mystical theme of "awakening" (*erwachen*) becomes meaningful to Benjamin.[109] Ansgar Hillach rightly suggested that for Benjamin a concept of "awakening" is informed by a "utopian movement of the spirit."[110] Within the context of the diary, this utopian movement maintains the meaning of "resurrection" when "time rises up at the end of time."[111] The trope of "awakening youth" seems, therefore, to be not just about obtaining self-consciousness. Indeed, Benjamin explicitly connects his concept of time with the "awakening" of the human being, in the same way that Eckhart talks of the redemptive awakening of the "son" embedded within each of us.[112] The utopian movement relates in such a way to a mystical imagination. More profoundly, it represents for Benjamin the mission of the "new religion" in which "the spirit of youth will awaken in *all*." In other words, it is the mystical opening up of "a spiritual reality."[113] "Awakening," writes Benjamin under the pseudonym Eckhart.phil, ". . . is a consciousness of the unconditional value, the gaiety and seriousness of this new youth."[114]

Shifting the focus from time to space, the last section of the text, entitled "Ball," could be seen as the succinct culmination of these discussions. Benjamin takes the example of a prom night to symbolize "a space for Elysium, the paradise that joins the isolated into a round dance."[115] In the allegory, this heavenly space of interaction between man and woman is where "we are truly in a house without windows, and a ballroom without world."[116]

We are dealing here, it seems, with a free space (i.e., free from external reality). One may argue that in an inner experience "without world" there is an image of immanent freedom on display that denotes the joining together of the different forces of our mental lives, which are part of the inner conversation of the soul. Youth is associated in this way with complete freedom and implies—one could say—a room of one's own. It stands for a singularity in which "time is captured," located not in the outer universe but rather within our inner experience—on the other side of the "outside world."[117]

Described from a mystical perspective, this singularity depicts the numinous unity of opposites. In alignment with mystical symbolism, the mysterious unity of opposites is embodied in Benjamin's poetics by the joining together of the virile and the feminine aspects of the human inner experience that was explored in the first part of his text.[118] The "ball" culminates in such a unifying "dance" and thus dovetails with the potential of salvation—existing, but beyond reach; celebrated, but out of sight.

There is, then, a reiteration of mystical allegories that can be observed in the three sections of "The Metaphysics of Youth." Jean-Luc Nancy pointed out—in quoting Meister Eckhart—that this type of mysticism brings the "nothing" into the center of "the world." We are returning, then, to the notion of "nothing," as presented in Eckhart's mystical allegories. Such a notion represents that which eludes all possible articulations, presentations, or imagination of divinity. For Nancy it is about praying to God to make us "free of God" (in keeping with Eckhart's famous appeal).[119] The act of awakening, according to Nancy, affirms an inner freedom, a pure spiritual singularity, beyond the possible, and as an imagined limitless limit that only nothing—*nihil*—can represent.[120] Such an affirmation of nothing looks "where time and place have never entered" that is "beyond time, in eternity."[121]

Similarly, an affirmation of the nothing that remains is what Benjamin seems to be driving at. Youth, in this sense, depicts a pure, uncontaminated, not-of-this-world, original, creating being. This being is truly transcendent to the extent that it contains no substance that could be captured by any form or articulation; it is truly divine if it is fundamentally detached from the world while remaining its creative force; eternal only in being nontemporal; existing in its nonexistence; realized by not being realized.

Benjamin's notion of nothingness did not go unnoticed. Gershom Scholem, for example, saw in it the most profound element in Benjamin's work, placing him at the heart of Jewish mystical and messianic thought.[122] The "nothingness of revelation"—as Scholem later termed it—is an integral part of the Jewish mystical and Kabbalistic interpretations of redemption.[123] It points to "the potential for redemption" that is embedded in every present moment; a fulfillment of time that is redemptive and therefore signifies the end of time. "This idea of fulfilled time," wrote Benjamin, "appears in the Bible as its dominant historical idea: the messianic time."[124] To emphasize this, Benjamin at one point played with the Jewish concept of the Shechinah, which he articulated as the symbol of divine potency embedded in the world.[125]

But especially within the theory of youth, Benjamin's approach to messianism is not exclusively based on one single source.[126] The messianic undertones of Benjamin's theory of youth present, perhaps, more of an admixture of Christian and Jewish mystical sources, or, to follow Elliot Wolfson, a deep-rooted area of thought in which both sources concur—"Christian ethics (or Jewish ethics, if you will)" as Benjamin rather cunningly put it (the proposition "or" signifying affinity, not differentiation).[127] Thus, for example, the "messianic time" is redolent of the type of allegories that Eckhart expressed in particular because it is not about divine involvement in and through history, but rather the breaking of, indeed the suspension of, its engagement with historical time. In messianic terms, the youthful "time of the now" represents a nothingness that can occur only as an "extra-historical" event within history.[128] It can be fulfilled in history, one may suggest, only by not being historically fulfilled. In his "Theological-Political Fragment" from 1921, Benjamin shows the extent to which this point remains for him decisive. "Nothing that is historical," writes Benjamin, "can relate itself, from its own ground, to anything Messianic."[129] The messianic moment is openly separated from historical temporality. As in the Jewish tradition, fulfillment of time is not concerned with the transformation of eschatological time into historical progress, but rather separates the two. In this way, however, messianism involves what could be termed the tension of constant expectation: in symbolizing a break from temporality it includes the unwavering, ever-imminent possibility of a rupture within history.[130]

True Criticism

A Critique of Theology

Youth, however, is not only a theological concept. It is also a critical category. The point to note is that Benjamin's "metaphysics of youth" does not only depict the most intimate stances of the mystical mystery: the fortress of the soul, unity with the beyond, femininity and eternity, nothingness and the fulfillment of time; all are indeed part of the young Benjamin's enthusiastic—perhaps too enthusiastic—imaginaries. It also brings the mystical allegories to bear on his social criticism.

Critique is already a central concept in Benjamin's early writings. The point is made, for example, by Richard Wolin who argues that for the young Benjamin, taking a "critical" approach means exercising understanding and in so doing gaining knowledge in accordance with the tradition of the Enlightenment.[131] From such a point of view, Benjamin's critical thinking (like Freud's) mainly includes charting the sources (*Quellen*), scope (*Umfang*), and boundaries (*Grenzen*) of its object, while at the same time "removing" all possible "errors" "independently of all experience" ("unabhängig von aller Erfahrung").[132] But especially in his theory of youth Benjamin articulates such independency of "all experience" in a unique way: a liberation of a certain potential from all social and historical manifestations. "The sole aim of criticism" is then "by means of knowledge, to liberate the future from its deformation in the present."[133] Bernd Witte rightly pointed out that this particular passage presents for the first time Benjamin's emphasis on critical thinking and its meaning.[134] "True criticism," Benjamin adds, means an "exposing" of a pure and hidden "inner nature" from its entrapment in historical and social circumstances.[135]

Liberation from errors and independency of all experiences denotes such an act of liberation. Arguably, then, the object of critique (the "essence" that needs to be released) appears in the form of a "future" potency because it resists an already existing social and historical reality. What Benjamin seems to point to is an act of liberation (and in this sense exposure of a hidden potential) that resonates with a distancing from any of its manifestations that are expressed in society and over history. "Independency" from experience in this sense means a departure from social and historical conditioning. This is not about emancipating concepts from particular historical, material, or social circumstances, but from worldly circumstances as such.

This last point may explain why Benjamin articulates critique in temporal terms. He simply perceives experience as historical experience, misuse as past articulation, and a "purified" concept as a "pure" potency that endures the transience of temporality. This, however, does not imply an advancement of reason in history because the potency that Benjamin evokes transcends all historical appearances, even if embedded in history. As a way of freeing its object from any preexisting conditioning, critique, for Benjamin, stands for the liberation of the pure essence of a certain concept or idea from all present settings. One may then argue that the "tutelage" of the "other," which Kant had in mind when encapsulating his idea of freedom, denotes here worldliness. In the same vein, a "cleaning up" of the "completely overgrown" ground may mean the liberation of a "pure" concept from its former worldly appearances—also to be understood as a liberation from all possible circumstances, whereby some imagined pure essence is freed, not from a particular misuse, but from any of its former binding articulations. "True criticism" is therefore about liberation from all worldly conditions.

Youth stands for such an act of critique. If anything, being young represents for Benjamin freedom in this exact sense. A spiritual core of the human being, beyond understanding and articulation, youth indicated an arena of pure deliverance from all social and historical conditions. Youth is thus a critical category, releasing a potency of the human being that transcends existing distortions. This is not just to say that youth is an object of study for Benjamin's analysis, but that it epitomizes for him the notion of liberation from present "deformations" and corresponds to a release or a discharge of a pure inner human "nature" from social and historical entrapment.

This act of liberation, however, exposes an inner surreptitious truth that Benjamin understands theologically. This point is crucial because the pure, youthful, fundament of the human being that escapes the world is transcendent, eternal, and divine. What is liberated from the different material or worldly appearances, by means of critique, is the godly constituent of human existence. Especially here, critique seems to be much more than an analysis that brings about understanding, as Wolin would argue. It also comprises a release of a "pure," divine, young core from the tutelage endowed by all its former, one may say enslaving, circumstances. It could be then said that Benjamin expands on the notion of liberation (from "errors" and from "all experience") that formed part of Kant's definition of critique. This liberation, however, now includes a theological argumentation about a release of an eternal and transcendent "spirit" from the immanent worldly reality.

Can we not argue, then, that "true criticism" is starkly informed by the mystical notion of liberation, central to the concept of youth? What enables such a conjecture about critique and mysticism is that Benjamin's critique presents a mechanism of liberation of a hidden, "pure" element from its materiality, and such an idea can be traced back to its theological, and in Benjamin's case mystical, sources. To put it differently, critique is about "awakening": informed by mystical categories of transcendence, eternity, and divinity, it aims at a deliverance of an imagined spiritual core from all possible worldly conditions. As in the mystical allegories of youth, there is a pure essence to be salvaged from its enslavement, and critique presents the manner in which this act of deliverance can be addressed. Articulating "true criticism" as a form of "exposing" the "inner nature" of a certain object means that there is always some eternal essence to be liberated from its range of worldly, and in this sense deformed, appearances.

The association between critique, release from worldliness, and deliverance seems to characterize many of Benjamin's references to critique in his early writings. His speaking of critique in terms of the "decomposing" of a particular substance may present one salient example. This is no doubt a somewhat opaque chemical metaphor. But it refers to the release of a matter's imagined essence from its own materiality. Indeed, what could be more suggestive of Benjamin's theological articulation of critique than the metaphor of the extraction of the genuine, original essence of a matter from its concrete, worldly, and in this sense nongenuine material appearance?

Benjamin's somewhat associative allusion to humor and laughter may offer another example. The trope of humor is quite different from that of decomposing matter, but Benjamin's argument seems to be comparable. The point to note is that the "distinguishing between the genuine and the non-genuine"—which is the task of criticism—constitutes the concern of humor. Thus: "Only in humor can language be critical. The particular critical magic then appears, so that the counterfeit substance comes into contact with the light; it disintegrates. The genuine remains: it is ash. We laugh about it."[136] Not very far removed from Freud's theory of jokes (though without arguing that Benjamin was necessarily aware of it), criticism acts as a form of revelation. As in the case of the metaphor of decomposing, what is revealed is some "genuine" essence in the form of a residue or "ash." Laughter simply erupts when a surreptitious truth is revealed, as Freud argued. And for Benjamin as well, all this relates to "the metaphysical origin of a Talmudic witticism [that] comes to mind here."[137] Nonetheless, the difference between Benjamin and Freud is also noticeable. Unlike the turning of the law against itself for the purpose of supporting its composition, so central to Freud, Benjamin's critique suggests a full retreat from any such conformation. For him, the essence at stake lies beyond any possible articulation of the law by which we live, and it enters the magical arena of the "nothingness" of mysticism. Informed by

A Theory of Youth | 77

mysticism, critique endeavors to defend, perhaps even save, the eternal and divine spirit from all that is transient and worldly.

Benjamin's critique is then of mystical lore. Here, we are presented with another form of critique of theology, in which a social critique emerges out of a theological tradition. Like in the case of Freud, the concept refers not to a critical attitude toward religion, but rather to the intersection of critique and theology, central to Benjamin's conceptual commitments. In particular, we are dealing with an immanent critique that redeploys mystical imagination. No doubt, critique could be accentuated as containing a normative dimension: the acting against and overcoming of the circumstances that limit freedom. Max Horkheimer, one of the instigators of critical theory, made a similar argument by suggesting that a critical approach aims at "human emancipation"—the liberating of human beings "from the circumstances that enslave them."[138] For Horkheimer as well such a critical approach is mainly concerned with revealing the "secret" of a given social and historical reality. Such an act of revealing differentiates, for example, critical theory from a "traditional" one.[139] In Benjamin's case, however, it would be wrong to make sense of this "task of criticism" without fully taking into account its mystical underpinning. Critique is mystically informed because its aim is to rescue the pure experience of a transcendent truth, indeed to rescue the ability to defend such an experience, which is inaccessible to any classification within this world. It entails, therefore, a theological redemptive (one may argue messianic) mission to go beyond limits and into the limitless that only nothingness can represent.[140] The same goes for the concept of liberation, which is not only liberation from the shackles of this world, but also the liberation of a religious experience of nihility, or better, the rescuing of the liberating potential of such an experience.

It is for this reason that "Kant's system of critique," as Benjamin called it, "must be conscious of eternity" and "must account for religious experience in the modern age."[141] Such consciousness includes a revisiting of the theological sources of any philosophical critique, making the "handmaid of theology" redolent of mysticism. In this particular sense "the new philosophy is thus synonymous with theology."[142] There is here, it seems, a modern appeal for a "new religion" that aims at connecting "the religious significance of our times" with "the religious significance of knowledge."[143]

One of the possible implications of such a critique of theology, however, is that transcendence is restricted within an exclusively human, critical endeavor. I believe this last point deserves attention because it presents Benjamin's redeploying of mystical sources in a complicated light. On the one hand, the presence of the divine in Benjamin's theory of youth still reverberates with the same mystical logic as expressed in Eckhart's writings. On the other hand, as a form of critique, youth reframes transcendence within an independent human experience in the world and in such a way stands for a distancing from the original mystical orientation toward the divine. Is it not possible, then, to argue that Benjamin's critique of theology evokes mystical notions and turns against them at the same time? What is emphasized, in this sense, is Benjamin's mystical turn against mysticism.[144] To follow this idea through, Benjamin's modern reworking of mysticism takes mysticism to its radical, heretical conclusion: it signifies a break with the mystical tradition, which is nonetheless a performance that is consistent with this tradition's original message (that of a break with a tradition).

Such a compound structure of thought is not exclusive to Benjamin. Adolf von Harnack's *Marcion*, for example, makes an analogous case.[145] Published in 1924, ten years after Benjamin composed his "Metaphysics of Youth," von Harnack's book suggests that Marcion of Sinope was the true disciple of Paul because he introduced a type of radical, and for von Harnack gnostic, dualism that breaks with the Pauline tradition. Here, however, a specific break with a theological tradition represents a pure theological formulation of that tradition. Marcion is thus an inventor of a "new religion" precisely because he follows Paul's theological message to the letter. Bernhard Grainer and Christoph Schmidt pointed out that such an exercise maintains the religious principle (i.e., rebellion, transgression, the turning against) while rejecting its former historical religious manifestation.[146] They regard this exercise as a "dialectic" form of liberating a theological principle from its bondage to previous historical expressions. The turn against a theological tradition constitutes, in this sense, its pure fulfillment. To put it differently, a theological tradition is fulfilled by not being fulfilled.

Benjamin's critique of theology seems to present a similar argument. The critical compartmentalization of transcendence within human experience, the human self-awakening, or the relocation of the divine constitute a turn against mysticism that nonetheless does not lose sight of the original mystical message. These compositions signify, perhaps, being religious to a fault (to put it ironically), or pushing the limits of a religious message, such that an original doctrine is taken so seriously that it is broken altogether. Mysticism, one could argue, is here fulfilled by means of its critical rejection, or perhaps by not being fulfilled. In such a way Benjamin presents a turn against mysticism that nevertheless aims at its confirmation. A reference to theology, then, means taking critique to its radical end and it is the mystical modes of standing against the world that power critique's distancing from mysticism. As in Benjamin's suggestion of a critique that is "conscious of eternity," we are dealing here with a mystical idiom in which an awareness of the eternal and transcendent God marks a precondition for freedom from God.

This last statement may indicate how in Benjamin's critical-theological interchange each form of thinking (critical or theological) is conditioned by the other. On the one hand, for Benjamin operating critically means acting in a way that always involves the eternal, transcendent, and divine. On the other hand, theology perceives being critical in its most radical, and for Benjamin pure, sense. Theology is therefore not demarcated as a language of faith but as pure criticism, while operating critically is defined, circularly, as a theological endeavor. The gaining of knowledge through critique is endowed with religious significance, and theology is secularized because it is reduced to a systematic, conceptual examination (rather than exercising devotion, or proving the existence of God), even if such examination originates in an object that lies beyond any possible examination.

Arguably, the interdependency between critique and theology denotes the obscuring of the boundaries between the two forms of thinking. Such obfuscating of the two concepts disintegrates any ability to clarify each of them independently. Indeed, Kirk Wetters illuminates rather brilliantly how Benjamin associated such a structure with an idea of "ambiguity" or, more accurately, "demonic ambiguity" (which goes back to its mythical origins through Goethe's "Demon").[147] For Wetters, such ambiguity—combining the idea of medium with that of a mythical force, the very concept seeming to be evidence of its content—aims at fusing together laws and their transgression, philosophical concepts and their theological orientations. Laws in general, and modern norms in particular, "remain ambiguous in essentially the same way as transgressions against the demons were for primitive man."[148] The concept of ambiguity itself, relevant to Benjamin's later work (for example, his "Critique of Violence"), is thus ripe with theological significance.[149] In the case of the relation of critique to theology, ambiguity seems to work in a way that supports the pairing of reason and revelation, the divine "word" and human "knowledge." Thus,

80 | Critiques of Theology

only as a theological endeavor, critique can present human beings with the type of knowledge that it was designed to facilitate.

SECULARIZATION AND POLITICAL IMAGINATION

Critique of theology is also its secularization (*Verweltlichung*) in the sense that it reframes transcendence within independent human experience in the world. Arguably, what interests Benjamin is this experience in the world in which humans live. Buck-Morss, for example, pointed out how Benjamin's literary critique represents "a form of secular revelation," a kind of secular thinking that does not lose sight of its theological origins.[150] In still referring to its theological sources, secularization seems then to denote two interrelated issues. On the one hand, it implies a holding to mystical language and symbolism. Benjamin's critique of theology is thus mystical in its retreat to the numinous unity with the divine, which Benjamin describes as an eternal-present messianic moment of awakening and salvation. On the other hand, secularization also points to a certain transformation of such notions because the human being encounters an alleged human inner true self—i.e., youthfulness—without, however, leaning on simple faith in a unity with God. When Benjamin, for instance, discusses the "awakening" of the inner transcendent capacity, he focuses on an exclusive human experience. In Benjamin's allegory what "awakens" the humanity of the human being is the human being; a self-referring self, one might say, that stands for the former mystical "divine self-revelation."[151] As Kohlenbach argues, such a "self-reference" serves as an image "of the absolute, or of a God who is no longer found in traditional religion."[152] The traits that were associated with a divine sphere are reset to define an autonomous, critical, and self-referring human being.

As in the case of the "Metaphysics of Youth," the notion of God is relocated (rather than disappearing—God is not "dead" in the strict sense) because transcendence is compartmentalized within human experience with no excess beyond it.[153] Put differently, a mystical interaction between the human and the divine is restructured as an exclusively human affair. Transcendence is maintained by pointing to an innate human faculty, rather than the presence of an almighty God; a spiritual trait that may be fulfilled in any mundane human action or simple communication (such as dancing, conversing, or composing a diary), yet that is not conditioned directly by divine providence. Secularization thus implies a transformation of mysticism that is marked, however, by the tracing back of modern critique to religious symbolism.

Arguably, then, the mechanism that powers Benjamin's secular thinking is not secular but rather mystical and it is theology that informs critique's secular focus on this world. Moreover, those are the mystical ideas that power the secular distancing from mysticism. In this sense Benjamin offers a form of immanent critique that redeploys rather than dismisses theology, and it is this structure of a critique that is born out of theology that guarantees the coherence of the secular. The notion of an "eternal within the worldly" that was relevant to Freud may be of the essence here, even if this means in Benjamin's case a play on mysticism rather than a reference to the law. Here as well we find an "immanentization" that "does not announce the demise of transcendence" but rather underlines its "new modes of being."[154] Applied to Benjamin's concept of the secular, such an "immanentization" captures a compartmentalization of the eternal, transcendent, and divine within a stark interest in the human experiences in this world.

Because of this particular interest in worldly affairs, Benjamin's critique of theology may provide some insights into his early engagement with politics. If, for example, youth stands for a "higher, mystical principle of authority," it points not to a rejection of a particular political authority, but of all forms of political control.[155] Arendt's observation that Benjamin's theology was aimed at refusing all available forms of (mainly political) tradition could be seen as relating to this last point.[156] It underlines a comprehensive refusal that segues from a commitment to a pure, not-of-this-world, spiritual principle that is represented by youth and that leads to a clear distancing from all the political options that were then available. We are dealing, perhaps, with a critique of politics that denotes a radical resistance to all political ideologies. If the possibility of redemption lies beyond history (even if this does not mean that it is external to it) it also resides, ceteris paribus, beyond any concrete political realization. Taking Talal Asad's argument that "the political" is a sphere "necessarily (not just contingently) articulated by power" as a point of reference, Benjamin's critique makes a case for a complete resignation.[157]

This last point seems to remain central in Benjamin's much discussed paper "Critique of Violence" ("Zur Kritik der Gewalt") from 1922.[158] Here Benjamin examines the use of violence, contextualized by the social unrest and political instability that characterized the Weimar Republic. This is particularly demonstrated through a range of textual references to a political reality comprising labor strikes, economic struggle, parliamentary weakness, military presence, and police brutality. For Benjamin, violence is a means to a political end, and the main question in this context seems to be: When and in what way could the use of violence be justified?[159] Since political "ends" are always connected to the rule of law, violence can be seen either as a mechanism for "preserving" existing rules and directives (legislated, for example, by state institutions) or as an element of "lawmaking" in that it creates new dictates by its action (e.g., by filling lacunas that are not covered by existing laws, or more radically by revolting against the power of the state).[160] But the main differentiation that Benjamin makes is not between "lawmaking" and "law-preserving" violence. Rather, it is between the political (or "legal") violence that these two forms represent and "pure" violence. The latter is manifested in divine action that originates beyond the political sphere. Here, in particular, Benjamin rearticulates the stark divide between the realm of law and politics (which he also identifies with "mythic violence") and that of God. Permeating the political sphere from outside, divine violence is, however, nonviolent in essence because it presents a category of power that escapes any political terminology (including that of violence).[161]

This point is emphasized, for example, in Georgio Agamben's essay "On the Limits of Violence."[162] Writing with Arendt's *On Violence* in mind (a point to which I shall return in chapter 4 of this book), the young Georgio Agamben points out that the main problem for Benjamin lies "in identifying a just violence," which means "a violence oriented towards something radically new, a violence that can legitimately call itself revolutionary."[163] This type of violence, however, is understood in terms of a "pure and immediate violence, which seeks to impose no law, not even in the form of *ius condendum*."[164] What transcends the political, or else the law, is "sacred violence."[165] Thus, it is in this sense that divine "pure power" stands "outside the law, as a pure immediate violence."[166] The type of revolutionary thinking that Benjamin attributes to Georges Sorel is dependent on this strong distinction between the "pure divine" and the political. This means that "revolutionary violence is not a violence of means, aimed at the just end of negating the existing system." Rather, it escapes all ties to worldly, political affairs—a messianic moment that Agamben associates with "self-negation and self-sacrifice."[167] But such violence is nonviolent in principle because it cancels out the political. Thus, only on this theological basis may one speak of revolutionary "non-violence" that "nullifies all the ideological consequences of every possible social policy"; and it is "anarchic" for it destroys "state power."[168]

Here, anarchism means that which eschews the arena of politics. Because of its theological underpinning, this radical rejection of politics may indeed represent what scholars have termed "theocratic anarchism," bringing Benjamin closer to the so-called anarchic *Antipolitik* of Gustav Landauer.[169] Nonetheless, anarchism in Benjamin's case induces a stark refusal of all known forms of politics, Landauer's socialism included. What is being separated, then, is the messianic potency from the actual political sphere. One may argue that the possibility of an actual political theology—though not the concept itself—is rejected and that the flow of history continues to be differentiated from its embedded messianic potential. This conclusion may extend to the political notion of authority. Indeed, Benjamin points out that divine violence may be called "sovereign" violence.[170] We are dealing, however, with a "higher principle of authority" beyond any possible articulation of authority that we may put to the political test. To the extent that such "higher" authority relates to the nothing of mysticism, it may be upheld only by being nullified. Freedom may therefore point to a full retreat from the sphere of power that authority represents.

Are we not dealing here also with a radical interpretation of the notion of exile? This particular term, central to Jewish political imagination, does not appear in Benjamin's early writings on youth. But it does, nonetheless, seem to encapsulate rather well his approach to politics. Exile may represent the complete refusal of any worldly form of authority, control, and power. What makes this notion radical is its universalization. It does not signify the loss of Jewish sovereignty in particular, but rather a withdrawal from the realm of politics in the most general sense. This argument may be extended to include the political character of youth. Here, to the extent that youth lies beyond this-worldliness, its endorsement includes being exiled from all political affairs. Youth thus demonstrates the definitive, redemptive, not-of-this-world nothingness that Benjamin contemplated, perhaps as a prelude to becoming "a peripatetic exile."[171]

Thinking of exile in such a way brings Benjamin's social criticism closer to his engagement with particular Jewish political themes.[172] "The problem of the Jewish spirit," writes Benjamin to Buber in 1916, "is one of the most important and persistent objects of my thinking."[173] Arendt, in rare agreement with Scholem, took this statement seriously enough to argue that the young Benjamin's coming to terms with Judaism became an "eminent personal question."[174] The Jewish "question"—to follow Arendt—corresponded to Benjamin's notion of a true and transcendent, not-of-this-world, spiritual being. Judaism thus represented for Benjamin "the most distinguished bearer and representative of the spiritual."[175] The "spirit of Judaism" is in this way elevated to match the "abstractness of pure spirit" that is called youth, as Witte, for example, pointed out.[176] Judaism is, to put it bluntly, a spirit of exile.

This last point seems to be important. Unlike the "essence of Judaism" as articulated, for example, in the context of the *Wissenschaft des Judentums* and some of its later variants, Benjamin's spiritual "essence" is designed to escape any historical, social, or political framing. It cannot be rationally grasped, studied, or articulated in historical terms. At the same time, it is not about adherence to divine laws. One may think of Leo Baeck's 1905 famous book *The Essence of Judaism*, which presented—in answering von Harnack's *What Is Christianity?* (*Das Wesen des Christentums*)—a "character of Judaism" that rests on an ongoing response to the divine law.[177] Conversely, Freud's early engagement with the trope of jokes presented a secularization, and to some extent a universalization, of such adherence to laws, which entails a turning against the law in order to enable its continuous sway over human life. Even if in widely dissimilar ways, both Leo Baeck and Freud related to laws and commands.

The Jewish "spirit" for Benjamin, however, seems to deviate from this range of possibilities. In accordance with his modern approach to mysticism, Benjamin does not endorse the law, but rather underline what always remains beyond our conceptual and normative reach—the so-called "ash"—a potent metaphor for that which remains. The ongoing suspense of the potential of redemption, at any given moment, is not brought about by the thick normative walls of adherence to the law. It is, somewhat differently, realized by the constant nonrealization of the messianic moment. One may suggest that Judaism itself may be thus fulfilled by not being fulfilled, pointing to the extent to which Benjamin's "Jewish spirit" is aligned with his critique of theology.

One of the implications of this approach is that Benjamin expresses a stark critique of the so-called "assimilation" of Jews.[178] Such a critique of the Jewish "bourgeois milieu" was rather dominant among many of his friends at that time.[179] His allusion to a Jewish spiritual core, however, makes a unique case because it underlines his rejection of the very possibility of assimilation of a Jewish "spirit" in existing social and political circumstances. In virtue of there being such a fully transcendent core, a complete assimilation is not made undesirable but rendered impossible. Thus, a retreat to an original spiritual sphere—the so-called "Jewish spirit"—invited a call for migrating away from assimilation, although what could be entailed in such a call, in practice, remains rather vague.

Yet, this is also true of Benjamin's critique of Zionism. In these early years, Benjamin was already exposed to Jewish nationalism through his encounters with Zionist student circles in Freiburg and Berlin and his subsequent close friendship with Gershom Scholem.[180] "Here," wrote Benjamin, "for the first time I have been confronted with Zionism and Zionist activity as a possibility and hence perhaps as a duty."[181] His reproach of these circles was nonetheless evident. For him "their personality was inwardly by no means defined by Jewishness; they preach Palestine but drink like Germans."[182] Though articulated rather polemically, Benjamin's reproach echoes a more fundamental issue. For Benjamin, Zionism, with all its baggage of sovereignty, authority, and control, could not dovetail with his arguments for a true, Jewish, not-of-this-world, spiritual singularity.

I would like to suggest that there is a Benjamin–Scholem controversy on the topic of youth along these lines. Like Benjamin (and given the beginnings of their friendship at that time), young Scholem also wrote extensively in these early years and during the upheaval of the First World War about the meaning of youth and being young for the "awakening" Jew.[183] This was particularly evident in his blatant attacks on the Jewish youth movements. Over against what he characterized as the loss or absence of the element of "movement" (*Bewegunglosigkeit*), he advocated a youth movement that was marked by a return to "wholeness, spirit and greatness" ("Ganzheit, Geist und Größe").[184] While the first (loss of movement) represented for him a spiritual vacuum, the second (return to wholeness, spirit, and greatness) stood for the renewal of a youthful, spiritual core. For the young Scholem, Zionism represented this reemergence of youth, or what he would later term a "religio."[185] Indeed, years later, Scholem would still maintain retrospectively that "it should never be forgotten that Zionism was essentially a youth movement," reiterating to some extent his early attention to the symbol of youth and its political implications.[186]

Scholem's Zionism is, of course, the object of continuous fascination and long-standing scholarly interest. The point to make here, however, is much more modest. It relates particularly to what could be seen as Scholem's theory of youth. For the young Scholem, youth is a spiritual venture that is interwoven with the call for Jewish sovereignty. Youth, in this sense, is an emblem for a concrete political theology. To take part in a metaphysical quest for youth is therefore "to move totally and in totality to Zion."[187] Through the interaction between notions of youth and politics, the Zionist mission becomes a call for a political articulation of Jewish life and a reminder of a messianic articulation of politics.[188]

Totality or wholeness, however, leads Benjamin to the exact opposite conclusion. In accordance with the complete resignation of his mysticism, a true, youthful, spiritual, Jewish core refuses the type of Zionist aspirations that Scholem advocated. Making an "example" of domination, Benjamin replies to the fervent Scholem, should be replaced by the devotion of a total spirituality that Benjamin takes to be the sign of "tradition."[189] Such a tradition constitutes the refusal of all forms of its realization in terms of worldly authority and political control.

Benjamin's critique of theology therefore invites a shift from Scholem's political theology. As in Scholem's case, it presents a return to messianism, even if in its secular guise. But it also stands for the exorcism of the demons of sovereignty that are entailed in this return. One may conclude that Benjamin's critique of theology is not about the final judgment of messianism, but rather about maintaining its enduring suspension. However, this approach goes hand in hand with the intention to hold onto messianism. In such a convoluted messianic approach one holds onto an unholdable object of redemption—perhaps a conscious withdrawal from the full burning implications of messianism, if put to the political test.

Especially in the light of this controversy over youth, Benjamin's approach could be captured by his own slogan "myth and modernity" ("Mythos und Moderne"), which means, in this context, a critical take on mysticism, which is aimed at, perhaps even constructed for, drafting answers to modern Jewish social and political conditions.[190] Here, modern critique and mystical symbolism come together to bear on Benjamin's overly far-reaching thoughts that extend from secular modernity to "envision a place for Jews in the polity."[191] Like Freud, he seems to suggest something of a program for an imagined "discharge" of the "tension of election" embedded in Jewish political life, even if differently thought out and rather inversely concluded. Yet, is it really possible to create a tangible political program on the basis of constant distance, and continuous metaphysical refusal? Is it not probable that a liberating critical mechanism may very well end up becoming an oppressive myth if it intrinsically relates to a not-of-this-world object and remains a guiding beacon beyond reach? Nothingness may present a rather shaky basis for a valid political agenda, and a mystical "higher" principle of authority could collapse in the wake of an emergent need for the protection that only an actual political constitution, state, or social institution can provide. Benjamin's critique of theology could be seen, then, as more than simply evidence of his rich and vibrant intellectual world, standing "at the crossroad of the modern intellectual landscape."[192] It is also a reminder of a vulnerability that perhaps accompanied its author to the last crossroad of his life.

CHAPTER 3

Education Ex Machina

A Translation of Theological Conceptions

AFTER AUSCHWITZ

Critique and its relation to theology constitutes a central, albeit understudied, element in Adorno's postwar reflections on education spanning the decade 1959–69. In this chapter I wish to focus on these reflections and to show how the vicissitudes of critique in its relation to theology, from antiquity to modernity, provided them with a leitmotif. In particular, I demonstrate that for Adorno critique both depends on and saves theology, and I discuss the manner in which modernity represents for him a distortion of this relation. Finally, I present how Adorno responds to this difficulty by calling for an education for "critical self-reflection," designed to reengage with the mission of saving theology.

Adorno regarded education, rather broadly, as the arena of human cultivation, and he developed his educational thinking in a wide range of texts as well as public and classroom lectures. His engagement with themes related to education and cultivation led to a series of annual public lectures and talks, broadcast by the Public Radio services of Hessen (Hessischer Rundfunk). The most representative of his published works from that time that took issue with the concept of *Bildung* is an extensive paper "Theory of Pseudo-Culture" ("Theorie der Halbbildung"), while his popular university survey courses paved the way for his *Negative Dialectics*.[1]

Positioning himself, one could argue, as a public intellectual in a nascent Federal Germany, Adorno focused his attention on a central mission: "no more Auschwitz." Thus, for Adorno, the "premier demand upon all education is that Auschwitz not happen again."[2] Auschwitz represented for Adorno an evocative symbol for the extermination of human beings and he was clearly suggestive here of a new categorical imperative, aimed at precluding the potential for another such catastrophe. However, largely because of this overarching mission, Adorno's lectures, talks, and written compositions devoted to education "after Auschwitz" were not limited to a narrow focus on issues of teaching and learning alone, even if he certainly addressed these, for example, in his radio talks (particularly with reference to the education of young children).[3] It would also be wrong to claim that Adorno's thinking was confined within the framework of education as an academic discipline, or as a profession; nor did he wish to develop a new comprehensive theory of pedagogical practice, didactics, or teaching methods, although his talks on education certainly related to such concerns. Rather, in his postwar thinking Adorno was especially interested in the cultivation of critical thinking as an antidote to the "conditions" that made Auschwitz possible.[4]

It is here that the relation of critical thinking to theology receives a central position. The centrality of this topic is conveyed rather explicitly in the content of the previously mentioned survey courses that Adorno offered. From its Greek origins, critique, Adorno openly argues, is the essence of metaphysical inquiry dedicated to "the teaching of the good life" ("die Lehre vom richtigen Leben").[5] In his view, this should be the main priority of education. Adorno presents his students with two clear lines of argumentation that highlight the link between critique devoted to such "teaching" and its theological sources. The first main point that Adorno makes relates to the definition of metaphysics. He defines metaphysics as a "critical practice," denoting "the form of philosophy which takes concepts as its objects."[6] Critique then becomes an instrument of reason that may clarify concepts, including their scope of validity, while testing their content and limits. It is in this sense that Kant, for example, spoke of a quest for metaphysics that "cleans" a territory from former errors. But Adorno connects such an understanding of critique with the original quest of Greek philosophy for "the first principles and causes" that Kant dismissed.[7] Therefore, for Adorno, metaphysics represents not just a critical examination of concepts, but an analysis that assigns them "to a higher order of being."[8] This critical quest for transcendence is, in Adorno's interpretation, the hub of metaphysics. Thus, in metaphysics "nothing can be even experienced as living if it does not contain a promise of something transcending life."[9]

Theology provides this metaphysical (i.e., critical) inquiry with a foundation. This is the second point that Adorno accentuates. Theology, he argues, is a "mythical" way of thinking about the beginning of being (as a first cause of all things) in terms of mythology—the gods who transcend life and offer a "higher order of being." The search for the "first principles and causes" that can be applied in conducting a "good life" and assigned to a "higher" order was originally a central feature of thinking about God, or else theology. In its critical dedication to the same issues, however, metaphysics took over such theological thinking. It substituted theological explanations with a critical investigation provided by human reason alone. Yet, the point to note is that for Adorno, this means that critique relates to its theological precursor in a unique way that he terms "secularization": "It is undeniable that metaphysics itself is a phenomenon of the secularization of mythical and magical thinking, so that it is not so absolutely detached from superstitious ideas as it understands itself to be, and as it has presented itself in the history of philosophy."[10] The notion of a type of "secularization" that is not "absolutely detached" from its theological sources is paramount here.[11] It denotes the intricacy dominating the relation between critical and "mythical" thinking. On the one hand, secularization is about scrutinizing being by means of reason, rather than through belief in the myth of divine creation—a disenchantment of the world, as it were. On the other hand, in being "not so absolutely detached" from mythical explanation, it still resonates with its theological forerunner and, as far as explaining the meaning of being is concerned, its adversary. Secularization, Adorno adds, is also a "translation" of theology rather than its full rejection: "It could be therefore said that metaphysics is a translation of theological conceptions into categories of reason, that it is a conceptualization of those conceptions."[12] Critique therefore means a "translation," or else a reconceptualization of theological conceptions.[13] Translation in this case entails a transmutation of the theological substance. As in Benjamin's early writings, there is a certain original meaning—which Benjamin articulated in terms of a "pure" substance, an "ash," or residue—that the translation releases from its former appearance. This reflects on what Benjamin would later term "the task of the translator." For Adorno, this task attests to the fact that theological "conceptions" are not dismissed by metaphysics but are rather reframed through their reconceptualization.

Critique in this specific sense can be traced back to its theological origins even if in a compound manner. But Adorno goes even further and argues that critique is not only a reformulation of theology. It is specifically designed to rescue theology: "Metaphysics in the precise sense I have set out here is both a critique and a reprise, a resumption, of theology. It is a peculiarity of metaphysical thinking, . . . that the conceptual operations it performs, which aim initially at something like a critique of mythological beings, repeatedly end in reinstating these mythical beings, or the divinity; but it no longer does so in a belief in the direct experience of the sensible perceptibility or the substantial existence of the divinities or divinity, but *on the basis of conceptual thought*."[14] Furthermore: "What I said earlier about the rescuing intention which accompanies the critical aim of all metaphysics now takes on its precise meaning, which is quite simply that metaphysics attempts to rescue through concepts what it simultaneously calls into question through its critique."[15] From this perspective, critique is not only about replacing theological thinking with categories of reason. It is also about "rescuing" theological concepts that are replaced by critical terminology. Metaphysics as a form of critique carries out a double mission of working against and, in so doing, holding onto the same object—that is, theology. This double mission is represented by "the unity of a critical and a rescuing intention."[16] Such a unity is maintained because the "conceptualization" of theological "conceptions" must still uphold their original meanings.

The reference to critique as a conception of theological concepts seems to be the decisive point in Adorno's teachings. It denotes an arena of thinking in which theology is not refuted but rather rethought. To rethink an object of reference, by means of critique, indicates for Adorno that the object of this rethinking endures. The crux of the matter is the idea that any reconsideration of theological conceptions works only by means of disbelief in these concepts. Put differently, critique preserves theology by working against it.[17] This is a rather clear dialectical articulation of the relation between critique and theology, in which critique represents both the end and the recovery of theology. In critique, theological conceptions are held by means of their dismissal.

Even if the argument that Adorno makes refers to the Greek origins of critique, it is clear, at least in the context of his own teaching, that what is at stake for him are the modern political implications. Arguably, Adorno's lectures were engaged with one burning question: whether and in what way it could be possible to save the teaching of metaphysics in the face of "Auschwitz." The Holocaust changed the concept of metaphysics "to its innermost core" and made "the presence of a positive meaning or purpose in being" clearly "impossible."[18] This exact mission was later reflected in his *Negative Dialectics*. "The intention of saving metaphysics," wrote Adorno to Scholem, "is in fact the central point of 'Negative Dialectics.'"[19] What clearly interested Adorno was to bring his discussion of critique to bear on contemporary social and political questions. Adorno, it seems, was drawn to the theological origins of metaphysics in the light of the educational implications of its possible end. The "civilizational break," to cite Dan Diner, represented by "Auschwitz" conditioned Adorno's quest for the theological roots of critique.[20] In this sense, he wanted to reconstruct a history of metaphysics from antiquity to modernity (motivated, inversely, by looking from modernity back to antiquity) in order to show his students what a "demand for a new beginning" meant at that time in Germany.[21]

Adorno's call for a "democratic pedagogy" further illustrates this last point. The importance of this call is that it constituted a central element in his public lectures on "critique."[22] Here, Adorno makes connections between the decline of critique (that is, a "secular" resuming of theology) and the collapse of Greek democracy. But the waning of critique that Adorno speaks of also explicitly and even more strongly relates to the collapse of modern democracy because it enabled the "delusional mania of nationalism" that "possessed the nation."[23] Clearly, in referring to such "mania" Adorno has in mind the modern political experience of his country. Athens was an allusion to Weimar. Adorno's pedagogical call for "democratic" education is thus mainly designed to bring about an awareness of and resistance to the modern social and political conditions that he associates with a retreat from critique. Critique and resistance to the modern political setting are thus inextricably linked and it is because of the recent delusion of "nationalism" that critique is, for Adorno, "essential to all democracy."[24] Not surprisingly, then, Adorno teaches his students that metaphysics is "something fundamentally *modern*."[25] From such a perspective, the idea of "working through the past" ("Aufarbeitung der Vergangenheit"), a central educational theme for Adorno, receives particular attention. It refers not only to an urgent call for pedagogy to engage with recent historical events, but also and perhaps more profoundly to the need to understand the strong ties between critique, as an instrument of "rescuing" theology, and democracy.[26]

The concept of critique acquires an additional meaning here. Critique does not only mean an ordering of concepts, nor is it limited to the resumption of theology. It also mediates theology and what Adorno calls, in passing, "the world in which we exist."[27] As in the case of Freud's analysis of jokes, and Benjamin's concept of youth, such a focus on "the world" refers to the social and political context to which we are subjugated and to which critique relates.

The manner in which critique corresponds to the liberation of human beings from the "enslaving" social mechanism of domination and control will be examined in the next section of this chapter. Here, however, I wish to underline the fact that our critical concepts that relate to the political sphere are based on former theological ones. The idea that our political categories are "secularized theological concepts" constitutes the hub of Carl Schmitt's notion of "political theology."[28] The claim also seems to be relevant to Adorno's teachings, which associate critique as a "secularization" of theology with politics. In view of Adorno's critical focus on "the world," we are dealing, then, with a political theology of sorts. Yet the dissimilarity between Schmitt and Adorno is noticeable. Adorno, for example, dismisses Schmitt's strong emphasis on the power of the sovereign. Mitigated through critique, Adorno's political theology promotes resistance to political conditions, including resistance to any form of authority and control. This point seems to me to have been decisive in Adorno's repudiation of Schmitt's legal theory. The "political theological predicament" (a concept that concerns the diagnosis of the relation between politics and theology as much as its reconstruction) is clearly central to Adorno, too, but acquires, it seems, a new guise.[29] In Schmitt's theory what defines the sovereign is the capacity to declare a "state of exception" (*Ausnahmezustand*) and this capacity to "decide" remains analogous to the domain of divine authority. In Adorno's concept of critique, however, there is an opposite, perhaps intentionally opposing political theological image of resistance to the overwhelming power of the sovereign. As in Schmitt's political theology, political categories were formerly theological, but they do not indicate the "decisionism" of the potentate, but rather its negation. Christoph Schmidt, for example, pointed out that the emphasis on such a theological conceptualization of resistance to political circumstances uncovers its reliance on biblical images of exodus and deliverance from "slavery."[30] It is, to follow Schmidt, not the power of the sovereign, but rather the freedom from such power that indicates what a "state of exception" may have meant for Adorno.

A Critique of Theology

Is it not possible to argue that a critique of theology is being put forward here? As in Benjamin's modern mysticism, and Freud's recourse to the "law," composed in the first decades of the twentieth century, a critique of theology denotes in this case a concept of critique that is starkly dependent on theology. Adorno did not teach critical thinking as something that is exterior to theology, but as a reconceptualization of theological concepts. Arguably, then, with the "secular" emphasis of critique, theology loses neither its sway nor its centrality. As a form of analysis that saves theology, and a political category, critique emerges from former theological concepts and can be traced back to them. Critique of theology is also, in this sense, a form of immanent critique because it points to a redeployment (rather than a dismissal) of theological constellations.

Critique of theology thus indicates a dialectical relationship between theology and its critical adversary and successor, in which the latter holds up the former by overriding it. This point seems to be important because it is in this particular sense that one may speak of the ways in which religious modes of critique power critique's secular distancing from religion. The critical endeavor is designed to replace theology as a precondition of its maintenance, and theology is thus sustained only in terms of its critical surrogate that relates concurrently to conceptual thinking and to society and politics (i.e., the "world in which we exist"). And vice versa: critique addresses these issues by secularizing, and therefore translating, theological concepts. The mission of rescuing theology, which Adorno ascribes to metaphysics, is a critical-theological undertaking of this kind. And the question he poses as to the extent to which one may still hold onto metaphysics in the postwar era attests to his endeavor to salvage theology by means of a return to the teaching of critique. If anything, the postwar, social, and political context to which Adorno relates only emphasizes the need to reengage with what could be referred to as a critical theological predicament—regarding not only the analysis of the relation between critique and theology but also its reconstruction.

History provides Adorno with the central arena for such analysis and reconstruction.[31] We have seen, for example, how in his classroom lectures the relation of critique to theology is revealed in the course of history from antiquity to modernity. Adorno was particularly concerned with the description of a historical process, from "Aristotle's theology" to Christian cosmology, and Hegel's philosophy.[32] The centrality of Hegel's philosophy to such an overarching, and for Adorno "universal" (even if clearly Eurocentric), process will be discussed next. Here, I wish to point to the manner in which not only theology in general but also gnostic theology in particular marks a central aspect of Adorno's classroom presentation of the historical unfolding of critical thinking.

Gnosis is the main theological issue because Adorno starts his historical overview with theological dualism. Dualism for Adorno originates in Aristotle's clearly theological concept of "unmoved mover," which marks a glaring opposition between being and beings (i.e., the so-called ontological difference). This points to being as a "pure concept" of thought and as an "absolutely perfect entity" that is separate from all beings (or else it would not have been an "unmoved" and "perfect" origin of things). Such an idea was redolent of theology because it was not only about a "radical dualism of matter and form, the divine and the earthly, body and soul," but also represented "the ancient precursor of the ontological proof of God."[33]

Indeed, Christianity inherited from Aristotle's metaphysics this theological dualism in which being "resists identity" with beings. "Resistance" means an innate nonidentity between form and matter, God and the world.[34] Thus: "What you have here is, fundamentally, the later problem of Christian theology: why the world created by God is not a divine world, why it is not already perfect. This, too, is answered in accordance with the same dualistic principle, which states that creation opposes, or in some way resists, pure identity with the creator."[35] By means of its emphasis on dualism, Aristotle's secularization of theology (i.e., his critical thinking) informs, perhaps ironically, Christian theology. But the point that Adorno makes here is that Christianity is consumed by the unequivocal opposition between a benevolent god and its counterpart, an evil world. Christianity, it seems, does not fully dismiss its secular, critical forerunner, in much the same way as Aristotle's metaphysics did not fully dismiss its own theological precursor. It thus continues to engage with a theological problem that is dominant in the construction of critical thinking.

Yet why associate such dualism with gnosticism? The reference to gnosis, I suggest, is pertinent not only because it was relevant, for example, to Benjamin (as described in chapter 2), but also and especially in the light of the increasing interest in gnostic theology in intellectual discussions in Germany in the 1950s and 1960s.[36] In these discussions gnostic theology stood for a radical distinction (i.e., dualism) between a completely transcendent (other, alien, true) God and the world.[37] This is a perspective that encloses the hidden character of the true, absolutely other God, who is conceptualized as removed from a world governed by other forces. Gnosis, to put it bluntly, is the theology of dualism.

This dualistic theology was addressed in the writings of scholars like Hans Blumenberg, Eric Voegelin, Jacob Taubes, Ernst Bloch, Hans Jonas, and Gershom Scholem in the decades that followed the Second World War (the last two already began taking an interest in gnosis in the 1920s and 1930s). In a variety of ways, at times contradicting, these scholars integrated gnosis into their different historical descriptions and, not less importantly, social and political imaginaries. This array of references was directed less at questions relating to the existence of a dualistic or Manichean faith in antiquity (e.g., What constituted such faith? Who were its agents? When and where did it proliferate?). The focus was rather on the symbolic significance of gnosis for an analysis of modern society and politics.

Voegelin's "revolt against modernity," for example, was based on his move to identify gnostic heresy with all modern social and political ideologies.[38] For Voegelin, the common denominator of all modern political phenomena—without differentiating, for example, between liberalism and communism—is that they are gnostic. His critique of modernity relied on this supposition, which pointed not only to a connection between gnostic theology and modernity but also, more profoundly, to an identity between them. At the same time, Jonas critically reconsidered his own early enthusiasm for gnosis (beginning in the 1920s) and connected it with Heidegger's philosophy.[39] In a rather convoluted way, Jonas wished to highlight the gnostic characteristic of his former mentor's existentialism, which made it even more susceptible to "the absolute pit" of nihilism than its theological portent.[40] Unlike gnosticism, which classifies the world as evil, Heidegger's existentialism goes even further and empties the world of all meaning (whether good or evil). To overcome gnosticism, Jonas argued, meant to combat such nihilistic existential theology and to do so by rethinking the relation between God and the world.[41] In the 1960s, Hans Blumenberg's *Legitimacy of the Modern Age* picked up these different engagements with gnosis. Underlining, however, modernity as a successful attempt to "overcome" gnosis, Blumenberg presented an explicit retort to Voegelin's association between modernity and gnostic theology.[42] For Blumenberg, gnostic theology appears and reappears in the course of history as an upshot of failed attempts to explain the endurance of evil. One falls back on dualism when all other possible theological explanations for the coexistence of evil and good are rendered invalid. However, modernity breaks loose from this theological inheritance by introducing "the immanent self-assertion of reason through the mastery and alteration of reality."[43] In the light of human "self-assertion" any imagined dichotomy between the world and God is meaningless. By overcoming gnostic dualism, modernity is in such a way "defended" and to some extent celebrated because it presents a final, perhaps redemptive, liberation from all former theologies of redemption.

Similar overarching reflections on gnosticism, the course of history, and the meaning of modernity are visible in Ernst Bloch's utopian imagination (which he associated with "revolutionary gnosis"), Jacob Taubes's critique of modern political theology, and Gershom Scholem's writings on Jewish modernity from the 1960s.[44] Scholem's scholarship is a particular case in point because the concept of gnosis was central to his ongoing studies of Jewish messianism and in particular Sabbatianism. For instance, as early as 1937, in his celebrated "Redemption through Sin" he underlined the strong association between the Sabbatian heresy and gnostic theology.[45] This association was then central to Scholem's ongoing studies of Jewish mysticism, which always incorporated a reference to a dualist theological speculation that necessarily accompanies the mystical notion of an "alien" God.

Adorno was, no doubt, familiar with this wide scholarly context, elaborated in brief above. In one of his early letters to Scholem, he confessed his interest in what ties together gnosis, Jewish mysticism, and the modern works of Kierkegaard, Benjamin, and Kafka.[46] His critique of theology, especially in its anchorage in the history of dualism, may thus be suggested as his own way into the discussion. In Adorno's critique of theology, the historical process is described in terms of the separation between God and the world, proceeding from its Greek theological and metaphysical origins to Christian theology, and continuing into modernity. Such a dualistic worldview represents in particular the "problem" that was transmuted from Christianity into modern forms of critical investigation. Put differently, the history of critique, grounded as it is in theology, is marked mainly by the relation between critique and gnosis. Modernity, especially, inherited ontological dualism from Christianity and, not a far cry from Blumenberg's thesis, is characterized, according to Adorno, by endeavors to overcome this gnostic inheritance.

These endeavors culminate in Hegel's idea of progress (*Fortschritt*). We are returning here to the centrality of Hegel's philosophy in Adorno's lectures. For Adorno, Hegel's idea of progress marks an attempt to overcome gnostic dualism because it points to a historical process that ends in "oneness," identity, or unity (*Einheit*) of the divine spirit with the world. This unity between God and the world (or Being and beings) denies a stark separation between the two and is achieved by the progressive process of systematic negations and the negations of these negations, whose summative result is the identification of all negations with a positive, final, one may say all too final, redemptive confirmation.[47]

To some extent, what Adorno presents here is a philosophical reconceptualization of the Christian theological struggle against Judaism, central to Hegel's *The Spirit of Christianity and Its Fate*.[48] Hegel's "progress" is in such a way considered an upshot of his understanding of Christian eschatology.[49] Here Adorno seems to simply reiterate Karl Loewith's thesis that all modern categories—and specifically Hegel's philosophy—are reformulations, and thus secularization, of Christian eschatological notions, although Adorno is not sedulous in disclosing this source.[50] Modernity for Adorno "is still linked to redemption by Christ, as the historically successful redemption." The theological concept of redemption, however, is translated into "an immanent teleology and the conception of humanity as the subject of all progress." Hegel's progress, then, means that the advent of the divine spirit is achieved in the world through a worldly process and it culminates in a final identification, or else redemptive oneness, of this spirit with the world.[51] Because of the unity between God and the world, metaphysics slips "into material existence," which means that it offers a critique in which the essence of Being is not separated from beings, but rather absorbed into their worldly existence.[52]

In Hegel's dialectics, one may argue, the problem of gnostic dualism is resolved because unity (or identity) elevates gnostic conflicts (i.e., nonidentity between God/world, matter/form, object/thought) to a higher "positive" unity of all conflicts within this worldliness. But the final unity of matter and spirit, world and God, history and eternity, cosmology and soteriology, not only presents a modern solution to old theological problems. It also stands for a new and, for Adorno, far more precarious predicament: if transcendence is transformed to indicate an immanent, historical process, this process "receives the aura of redemption even though redemption failed to occur and evil persisted unabated."[53] The new problem that Adorno identifies stems from the fact that in modern Hegelian critique "Christian soteriology—in other words, the science of salvation, the doctrine of salvation" is "completely absorbed into the *civitas terrena*, its Augustinian counterpart."[54]

In *Minima Moralia* Adorno clearly points out that such an association between soteriology and cosmology means no more than to "justify the diabolical positive, naked interest."[55] What makes such a process "diabolical" is that dualism is replaced with the oneness of transcendence and immanence, thus clinging to a "religious authoritarian pathos without the least religious content."[56] The theme reappears, therefore, as educational content. Much like Aristotle's metaphysics, Hegel's dialectics is endowed with a secular shift from the divine to the worldly in a way that also preserves the original theological connotations. In both cases, a theological argument is refuted, and held onto concurrently by critique—a structure that attests to the continuing presence of theology at the heart of all critical endeavors. Adorno then concludes that dialectics takes over metaphysics: "One of the mystical impulses secularized in [Hegel's] dialectics was the doctrine that the intermundane and historic is relevant to what traditional metaphysics distinguished as transcendence—or at least, less gnostically and radically put, that it is relevant to the position taken by human consciousness on the questions which the canon of philosophy assigned to metaphysics."[57] What the canon of philosophy "assigned to metaphysics" was the original theological argumentation concerning a transcendent being, absorbed, in Hegel's secular scheme, into the "universal" historical process. This process of secularization, however, has the effect of diluting transcendence. As a result, there is a difference between modern and ancient critique. Only the modern critical approach identifies Being with beings, history with salvation, and critique with an adaptation to existing conditions. Critique, arguably, becomes enslaved to the existing social and historical circumstances. Furthermore, modern critical thinking does not fulfill its calling to "rescue" theology, but instead attenuates it by representing a worldly and immanent process as if it were divine and transcendent.

In this way Hegel's dialectic ends not with the "freedom" of subjectivity but rather with its absolute enslavement to a new form of total domination and control.[58] Under such new circumstances, historical events "work themselves out at the expense of human beings, human beings are their victims, history stretches its hand out over all human beings."[59] Adorno then goes on to describe the total "entrapment" of the human being.[60] A complete "adaptation" to reality with no possibility of escape, entrapment is the result of a mechanism of total domination and control, which Hegel's theology of "unity" stands for.[61] This conclusion brings Hegel closer, perhaps, to Spinoza's pantheistic identification of God with natural necessity and the consequent exclusion of transcendence. But the point that Adorno seems to make is that "entrapment" still culminates in "oneness," "identity," and "unity"—the focus of all eschatological anticipation. It does so because it is merely a material process (i.e., social and historical) with no reference to any divine or transcendent sphere. In the same vein, history still maintains the ideal of unity of thought and matter, subjectivity and external conditions, freedom and law that characterizes the continuing relation between critique and theology. This, however, becomes devoid of any notion of the eternal, transcendent, and divine, at least in the sense that the historical operation encloses its inner rationale within itself and for itself. It becomes a *modus ponens* of sorts—a process that affirms itself by the very operation of its own mechanism. One may argue, then, that Adorno's critique of theology portrays here an image of an all-consuming mechanism in which deliverance is re-formed as the bare technical reason of a worldly apparatus.

Entrapment and Education

From *Bildung* to *Halbbildung*

The "entrapment" of critique, following the disappearance of theology, is especially visible in the context of modern education.[62] The fact that the cultivation of human beings provides a central arena for thinking about the theological roots of critique and their modern implications is particularly underlined in Adorno's extensive essay, *Theorie der Halbbildung*, which (given the rich meaning of the term *Bildung*) may be translated as a Theory of Pseudo-Culture and as a Theory of Pseudo-Education.[63] The paper's reference to education is obvious since *Bildung* represents for Adorno the educational ideal of the Enlightenment, denoting the "self-formation" of an individual who practices universal rationality and makes autonomous decisions.[64] In the tradition of the Enlightenment, the development of such a critical individual is accomplished by means of self-formation (*Bildung*) whereby the individual's inner capacities advance toward a "complete and consistent whole."[65] Especially in the light of Humboldt's dominant view, self-formation indicates the inner progression of free individuals toward a better understanding of themselves, fulfillment, and self-growth, which, as Bauer rightly argued, was considered to be a characteristic of human beings that may eschew any direct social control.[66] Critical thinking is thus entwined with freedom from social circumstances because the cultivation of the "self" is not supposed to yield to external guidance but is rather directed "by each individual of himself and his own free will, according to the measures of his wants and instincts, and restricted only by the limits of his powers and his rights."[67]

This rather traditional view of *Bildung* was a generational truism. Steven Aschheim, for example, has pointed out that among twentieth-century German intellectuals finding fault with *Bildung* signified the "abandoning" of the rational, universalist ideals inherited from the Enlightenment.[68] This is also true of Adorno. For him, *Bildung* denoted what Fritz Ringer called the "ideological position" of the German "*Bildungsbürgertum*"—endowing their emerging liberal ethics and idea of "progress" with a foundation.[69] In such a way, *Bildung* referred to education, to culture, and to an ideology at the center of which lay an idea of progress, absorbed into the development of each individual. As an educational ideal it also represented the cornerstone of class identity "of the educated middle classes under the circumstances of political impotence," thus connecting the ideals of the Enlightenment, i.e., liberal ethics, with concrete social and political aims.[70]

The main point to note is that Adorno sought to develop the particular theological aspects that Benjamin ascribed to *Bildung*. Theology is central here because for Adorno self-formation secularizes the concept of the godlikeness of man (*imago Dei*) found in Christian theology.[71] This notion of secularization is decisive. It underlines the manner in which education epitomizes the history of critique discussed above. Arguably, we are presented with a stage on which theological ideas are translated into rational categories of critique—replacing, but in so doing rescuing, these ideas. Aimed at the refinement of a rational, autonomous individual, *Bildung* comes to represent the overall idea of progress by means of self-fulfillment, designating self-perfection.[72] This overall mission of progress toward the "good life" carries with it a secularized version of human creation according to the image of God, with all its redemptive overtones. These overtones are connected to what Gotthold Ephraim Lessing labeled "revelation coming to the individual man," which Adorno understood as a process in which theological notions are central because they are invested in the formation of an ideal type of rational, autonomous, critical human being.[73] From this perspective, the secularization of revelation contained within the concept of *Bildung* offers a reconceptualization of theological concepts.

Yet, while the cultivation of humanity provides Adorno with the forum for discussing the relation of critique to theology, it also becomes the locus of its entrapment, when *Bildung* is transformed into "a socialized pseudo-education (*Halbbildung*), the ubiquity of the alienated spirit."[74] For Adorno this transformation of an educational ideal means "regression" (*Rückbildung*), a term that indicates a shift from self-formation that critically resists social dominance to self-formation that is absorbed by such a controlling influence. What enables regression is the "spiritualization" (*Vegeistlichung*) of self-formation.[75] As in *Dialectic of Enlightenment*, the spiritualization that Adorno evokes does not refer to the making of a concrete substance more abstract or removed from the world, but rather to the loss of the original theological horizon of critique.[76] Following such a process, social and political reality absorbs the theological hopes for redemption invested in human self-formation. In this way, "the dream of associating critique with freedom from the dictate of means (*Mittel*), from obdurate and sterile utility, is falsified into an apology for the world guided by the same dictate."[77] An entrapping education, somewhat cunningly, replaces an original theological mission by means of its falsification.

This last point seems to be crucial. An unctuous pseudo-education represents for Adorno an emblem for the "entrapment" that was central to his discussion of the relation between critique and theology in his lectures. What was imagined as a site of "freedom" and "autonomy," because it was still saturated with theology (even if by working against it), is distorted in such a way that it comes to represent an educational call for adaptation to social structures and heteronomy.[78]

The prefix "pseudo" points to such a distortion and corresponds to an educational surrender to what Horkheimer categorized as "enslaving circumstances."[79] The image that was relevant to Benjamin's social critique reappears in Adorno's reflections on education. This means that pseudo-education does not just refer to the reduction of education to mere practical, narrow knowledge, although this is certainly a characteristic. More importantly, it signifies that education is replaced by a devious doppelgänger (i.e., pseudo-education), which does not imply that people are uneducated but that they "hypostatize limited knowledge as truth" and equate limited schooling with personal growth.[80] Deceitful education does not leave people uncultivated, but rather entraps them in a mendacious reality.

In the spirit of today one may call this, perhaps, fake education. A fake educational ideal stands for a type of cultivation that reduces humans to controllable things. Bearing this particular argument in mind, Adorno's assertion that "pseudo-education made the secret kingdom into an everything" means more than just making hidden truths "available to all."[81] It implies (with Benjamin's "Kingdom of God" in mind) that a theological imagination referring to the divine, clandestine "kingdom" is absorbed by its opposite—a reified, worldly, fully material, and for Adorno technological, polity. Material reality substitutes the divine, and practical knowledge presents itself as if it were critical reflection. The crux of the matter lies not in replacing one ideal of critical education with a different one. More accurately, it is about the corruption of a critical theological educational mission that is turned into its opposite because of mechanisms that were already embedded within this mission.

In the light of this, we may understand some of Adorno's prevalent concepts such as "reified consciousness" and "coldness." Discussed especially in his lectures on education, reified consciousness—a concept that Adorno adopts from Lukács—characterizes a person who is fully absorbed into existing conditions.[82] As Brian O'Connor has noted, "by reification Adorno means the perception of what is qualitative as quantitative."[83] It is where the human being is reduced to an entity "with certain socially useful capacities." This is also where there is no "sphere of life" that is independent of "the requirements of society."[84] "Coldness," in the same spirit, encompasses an aspect of reification because a person who is absorbed by "what happens to be the case" is also indifferent to others, or else "cold."[85] In both cases, however, the argument that Adorno wishes to make is not restricted to human submission but more profoundly extends to the effects of fake education. We are dealing, then, with the different outcomes of the transformation of a theological imagination into its opposite. An important consequence is that the original mission of critique (a mission anchored in theology) is rendered hollow.

Adorno's reference to a "short circuit in permanence" ("Kurzschluß in Permanenz") offers another example of total submission to worldly conditions.[86] In chapter 1, we saw how Freud used the concept of "short circuit" to indicate a complicated relation between the law (broadly understood) and its forms of transgression in which a law that turns against itself simultaneously enables its own persistence. Falsifications, in particular, were for Freud a mechanism that supported such an operation. Adorno seems to work along similar lines of argumentation because he takes the concept of a "short circuit" to signify the manner in which in pseudo-education the divine is transformed and thus turned against itself. However, a clear difference between the two approaches can be observed. In Freud's theory of jokes, short circuits stand for antinomies that enable, nonetheless, the persistence of "the law by which we live" and that Freud therefore endorses. For Adorno, conversely, such a law seems to lose its immediate positive connotation. It represents a complete subordination to the world, which denotes a clear, and one may say, final distortion of the law's theological origins. Adorno does not address this end result in terms of the success of untamed impulses, nonrational desires, or suppressed wishes, as Freud's theory of jokes indicates, but rather in terms of the opposite triumph of rationality over such impulses. One could say that the law at stake is now rethought and redefined as an industrial, arguably technological, logic, with no possibility of transgression. Such a conclusion may demonstrate not that antinomian moments of defiance and relief win the day, but rather, conversely, that they are fully lost.

Moloch

I would like to zoom in at this point, albeit briefly, on the entanglement of entrapment, reification, and technology that Adorno's discussion of education brings to the fore. It is clear that Adorno's critique of theology brings together these notions, and it is valuable to unpack some of their central implications for education. Even if this rich symbolism was addressed in Adorno's lectures and written compositions in the 1960s, I find the Weimarian image of a "Moloch"—depicted melodramatically, for example, in Thea von Harbou's and Fritz Lang's *Metropolis*—a fruitful way to encapsulate rather elegantly the association of this array of different notions and of their theological connotations.[87] The "strength of an image," to evoke Adorno's own conceptualization, can capture the philosopher's pedagogical constellations.[88]

The term Moloch refers to the biblical Canaanite god, associated with human, especially child, sacrifice. In the German intellectual milieu of the late nineteenth and early twentieth centuries, the terms *Moloch* and *molochitisch* were typically used as allegories of destruction and annihilation. For instance, for members of the George Circle they signified the main characteristics of a repressive modern culture that represented the "sworn enemy" of life. Ludwig Klages's blatant anti-Semitism was a case in point, because he associated this metaphysical foe of life with the Jewish God of creation.[89]

For the viewers of *Metropolis*, however, Moloch was developed to represent a modern, all-embracing machine-god that demands human sacrifice; a human-made principle of reality that consumes the human being within the very framework of modern society and its cruel demands.

In one of the film's decisive moments, the protagonist of the film, Freder Fredersen, cries out "Moloch" when envisioning, for a brief, elusive moment, the machine-god as the essence of an industrial society whose fruits he was born to rather insouciantly enjoy at the brutal expense of others. Moloch, to put it bluntly, controls and consumes all aspects of life. There is, therefore, a clear association between technology and theology, at the center of which lies a human-made enemy of the humane: an idol of self-sacrifice.

This image seems to resonate rather well with the interweaving of entrapment, reification, and technology that Adorno's critique of theology highlights. This is not to argue that Adorno had seen *Metropolis* or that he had been influenced by it. But at the heart of Adorno's symbolism lies, it seems, an analogous dramatic association between theology and technology, encapsulated by the image of Moloch: an association between a divine and an all-embracing worldly mechanism that operates with its own sacrificial logic and rationale, where human beings are but victims. This is, arguably, what Adorno means when he points to the transformation of transcendence into an immanent, universal and mechanical, consuming reality with no possibility of escaping its domination and control, even if Adorno predominantly has in mind the secularization of Christian theology rather than the notion of a pagan deity.

The association between a theological argument and mechanical imagery is one of the main points to note here. What specifically entraps critique is a mechanism of worldly domination that enslaves humanity with its sacrificial logic. Freud's civilizational "discontents" in which "civilization itself produces anti-civilization and increasingly reinforces it" may come to mind.[90] But for Adorno this "discontent" mainly means a sadistic "pleasure machine" and, thus, a form of "torture" in which any resistance to the "adaptation of people to collectives" is futile.[91] Gershom Scholem's critical remark that Adorno's concept of history acts as a "deus ex machina" seems to present the case rather fittingly. In Adorno's postwar thought, Scholem finds a Hegelian notion of an organizing "totality" that binds everything to its logic, although such a mechanism does not resolve the tragic plot but rather embodies it.[92]

Is it possible to argue that Adorno is reacting to Kant's statement that the human being is "more than a machine" ("mehr als eine Machine")?[93] Kant's somewhat hopeful avowal closes his famous "An Answer to the Question: What Is Enlightenment?," central to which was the notion of a human "release" (*Ausgang*) from self-imposed tutelage. In this closing passage, Kant seems to think that both human freedom and human "dignity" depend on the separation between human and machine. Critique is a central element of this imagery because it represents the main capacity of the human being to act as a rational, autonomous, and self-dependent free agent. From this point of view, the problem that Adorno identifies for education may be related to the fact that such a separation was lost. Especially because of its entrapment in the totality of history, the humanity of humans becomes enslaved by a working mechanism. The human being, therefore, is not "more than a machine" but is rather adapted to its modes of operation.

Adorno often seemed to accentuate and apply this particular imagery. The celebrated "Culture Industry" that he and Horkheimer composed is one of the more widely discussed cases. The notion of an industry is visibly the main topic here. This notion relates to the "standardization" of objects themselves and to the "rationalization of distribution techniques."[94] These two categories (standardization and rationalization) affect individuals to their innermost core. They do so even to the extent that "imagination is replaced by a mechanically relentless control mechanism which determines whether the latest imago to be distributed really represents an exact, accurate and reliable reflection of the relevant item of reality."[95] And thus: "The massive concentration of economic powers, and consequently of political and administrative ones as well, to a large extent reduces every individual into a mere functionary of the machinery."[96] Humans become "an appendage of the machinery" representing merely "an object of calculation."[97] Here, mechanization represents a central image for both thinkers, one that encapsulates the modern human condition. Such mechanization is not just about mass production of factories, though this seems to be part of their social imagination. More profoundly, in referring to notions such as sameness and reproduction, mechanization represents an emblem for dehumanization. As in the Weimarian image of Moloch, the "technological rationality . . . makes souls into things," and it is exactly this theologically imbued notion that Adorno in particular develops further in his concept of mechanized, technological totality.[98] One could say that, perhaps in stark opposition to Heidegger, there are no traces of "techne" (craftsmanship, skill, art) in Adorno's concept of technology.[99] On the contrary, modern technology is devoid of such qualities. It is thus not about a "revelation" of Being, as Heidegger would argue; instead, it is a matter of exposing the "demonic" termination of the human being.

Adorno clearly has Auschwitz in mind. We are returning here to the overriding concern of education, the call for "no more Auschwitz." An emblem for annihilation, Auschwitz is a product of a critique that distorts theology. Secularization and annihilation are in such a way connected through an evocative image of "barbarism," which Adorno evokes (in parallel and in contrast to Hannah Arendt, who will be discussed in the next chapter) in many of his lectures and oral presentations on education. With his reference to "barbarism" Adorno aimed at presenting his audience with the absolute bottomless pit of extermination. As Terence Holden rightly pointed out, however, Adorno takes such a notion to represent more profoundly the absolute evil of theology.[100] As a form of evil, barbarism reflects the full extent of the absorption of transcendence within immanence, making the first (transcendence) void and the second (immanence) malicious. Barbarism, then, is not characterized by its impulsive or irrational aspects, or by a refusal to comply with the norms of correct or acceptable behavior. It is, rather, described as being consumed by an all-embracing "machine," or else as a full capitulation to the mechanism of social rule, cultural habits, and political coercion. It is where human beings are "one with domination"—with special emphasis, though, on the theological connotation of "oneness" and "dominion"—a catastrophic play on the imaginary end result of the Christian promise of redemption through sameness, oneness, and identification with Christ.[101]

These theological associations not only relate to the horrifying systematic murdering of Jews, although this was certainly of central concern to Adorno, whose Jewish origins might have condemned him to such a fate had he not escaped Germany.[102] More universally, they represent a full withdrawal of society and culture from humane considerations, culminating in the *Endlösung*—which Adorno sees as the complete loss of humanity.[103] Here, a control mechanism denotes the extinction of humanity by reducing the human being to represent nothing more than a part of a machine—an image that persisted later in a wide range of philosophical and popular ideas, from the speculations of nomadic theory to the science fiction of *Star Trek* that brought us the ominous collective "Borg."

Critical Self-Reflection

Sabotage

Against the critical theological image of entrapment in a sadistic "pleasure machine," Adorno endeavors to throw "wrenches into the machinery."[104] One could fairly say: an act of sabotage. In the field of education, the notion of sabotage seems to be important because it points to the acute need to rethink cultivation in a way that saves human beings from the machine. While the consumption of a human being by a mechanism of total control is an image that represents the end result of a critique that dilutes its theological sources, sabotage may denote the opposite in saving the human being from such a fate. To put it more metaphorically, it is about an education ex machina. By using this metaphor, the aim is not to appeal to the supernatural dramatic appearance of God by means of the machine (a deus ex machina as Scholem, for example, suggested) but to the no less theatrical allure of rescuing human beings from the Ananke of entrapment. Thus, to the extent that education represents for Adorno an arena for demonstrating how human beings are part of the machinery (as in the case of *Halbbildung*) it also serves as the showground for sabotaging the instruments of control, with all its critical and theological overtones.

"Critical self-reflection" is the main educational concept reflecting this aim. I suggest this point because in many of his lectures Adorno pitted an education centered on "critical self-reflection" and one based on "reified consciousness"—the latter characterizing, as noted above, people who are "an appendage of the machinery"—against each other.[105] Critique, however, indicates sabotage in a distinctive way: it reflects the recovery of the critical endeavor to "save" theology (even if by turning away from it), against the background of the impossibility of recreating the educational tradition of self-formation, devoted to this mission. In the notion of "critical self-reflection," arguably, Adorno presents a reconceptualization of the educational concept of critique that has been rendered invalid.

The point to note relates to Adorno's double reference to the original mission of critique. On the one hand, "critical self-reflection" still resonates with the hope that the human being is "more than a machine" and in such a way echoes the "Kantian idea of the humanity in our person."[106] On the other hand, it takes into consideration the conversion of *Bildung* into *Halbbildung*, which renders this original ideal inaccessible. The question that Adorno seems to underline with regard to an education ex machina is whether and in what way it is possible to reengage with the mission of critique, in the face of the impossibility to do so.

One may consider Adorno's celebrated notion of negativity in this educational light. Paul Mendes-Flohr pointed out how negativity, perhaps *the* concept that is most associated with Adorno's postwar thought, is a theological concept that appeals to "an entire other," and as such it means resistance to identity (the type of unity between God and the world that Adorno ascribes to the source of fake education); "nonidentity" is presented in its stead.[107] In the educational arena, such a notion may suggest something further still. In signifying the retreat of critique from any belief in a final positive unity, goal, or end for human self-formation, negativity also presents the only viable way to still hold onto these ideals. Put differently, it is about reengaging with the mission of critique, against the background of its disappearance. This is, then, what negativity stands for: the only possible way of holding onto an unholdable object.

This last point is crucial. Peter Gordon recently suggested that in Adorno's postwar "dialectic of secularization" we see a clear "migration into the profane" ("Einwanderung ins Profane") from which "all metaphysical authority" evacuates.[108] In his reflections on education, however, we see, perhaps, a more nuanced approach to such a migration in which there is a turn against metaphysical authority in order not to lose sight of it. Since the ideal of *Bildung* is transformed into its fake-educational doppelgänger, one must scour any naive faith in the redemptive hopes that are invested in the enlightened perfect "personality" (*Persönlichkeit*) in which self-formation is supposed to culminate. In particular, "the concept of personality," Adorno argues, "cannot be saved."[109] Nonetheless, in evoking the need for critical self-reflection these ideals are not forsaken. On the contrary, Adorno strove to reengage with their critical calling. This reengagement, however, is possible only at the expense of dismissing the actual (but not the potential) realization of the original theological mission of critique.[110] To put it differently, critique's theological promise can be realized only by not being realized.

This point is developed, for example, in Adorno's reflections on the educational role of philosophy. Constituting a central element in many of his oral lectures (e.g., "Philosophy and Teachers," "Why Still Philosophy?," and "Notes on Philosophical Thinking"), philosophy attests to the grasping of the theological mission of critique that cannot be held onto anymore. Thus, on the one hand, the role of philosophy is to resist the machinery's consumption of human beings by continuing to hold onto critical thinking.[111] Offering such a form of resistance generates "a force that opposes the narrow-minded acquisition of factual knowledge, even in the so-called philosophical specialties."[112] For "specialists" (Heidegger's existentialism and logical positivism represented clear examples for Adorno) thinking is contracted to disclosing "pre-given data." In still avowing the original role of critique, however, philosophy works "against the justification of what happens to be the case."[113]

On the other hand, however, "philosophy is no longer applicable to the technique of mastering one's life."[114] Here especially, philosophy withdraws from the original mission of the critical quest of metaphysics, which it can no longer guarantee. Philosophy can thus appear in the field of pedagogy only "as critique, as resistance to the expanding heteronomy" and as a "powerless attempt" not to offer truth but to expose "untruth."[115] In such a way, philosophical education holds onto a tradition—in this case that of critical inquiry—only by rejecting its positive aims. Adorno put this duality in the following terms: "The only responsible philosophy is one that no longer imagines it had the Absolute at its command; indeed, philosophy must forbid the thought of it in order not to betray that thought, and at the same time it must not bargain away anything of the emphatic concept of truth. This contradiction is philosophy's element. It defines philosophy as negative."[116] Forbidding the mission of philosophy in order "not to betray" it seems to be the main issue here. Defining philosophy as negative means a dialectical move away from a theological conviction (i.e., the belief of having the "Absolute" at our command) in order to save it. The association of such a notion of negativity with so-called negative theology and "*Bilderverbot*" (the biblical prohibition of making images) will be presented in the last section of this chapter. Here, the point to note relates to the manner in which Adorno underlines the effort to hold onto an unholdable theology—not "betraying" the theological endeavor that must be considered lost at the same time. Critique's theological promise can thus be realized only by not being realized, precisely because philosophy does not "bargain away" its conceptual commitments by dismissing them.

Many of Adorno's concepts of education point in the same direction. For example, Adorno's "return to the subject," or else "a turn toward the subject" accentuates a belief in the success of the project of humanism while dismissing its underlying positive aspirations (i.e., those that relate to its material realization) altogether.[117] This is also true of the "individual element" that education needs to nurture. It still attests to the "enduring persistence of particularity" without, however, pointing to its realization through the perfection of the human being.[118] The same can be said with reference to "universal history." For Adorno, this is something that "must be construed and denied."[119] There is a critical act at stake in which the only way to "construe" a lost object is to deny any positive ability to do so.

What is denied in Adorno's appeal to foster "critical self-reflection" in education is not the theological horizon of critique but rather the belief in a progressive advancement toward the realization of its redemptive mission. Again, we should bear in mind the sort of critique that entails a reconceptualization of theological concepts, indicating a critical adversary and successor to theology that ensures its continuation by overriding it. A critical retreat from redemption to reflection demonstrates this method. The redemptive mission is about perfection; the new negative mission of education is about a retreat to the "refuge" of reflection.[120] Reflection rather than perfection means self-formation that does not correspond to a process of advancing or progressing toward a final redemptive end in any positive sense. Neither is it about losing sight of that theological aspect; it is a question of holding onto that which always remains the source of critique and its ability to offer resistance to "enslavement."

The idiom of holding onto an unholdable object seems, then, to capture such a "negative" approach to critical self-reflection rather well. It encapsulates the extent to which Adorno distances himself from the "final" unity of God and the world, in order not to lose sight of its theological underpinning. "Destroying immediacy" thus signifies the sabotaging of the modern (and, for Adorno, mainly Hegelian) attempt to establish a link between the advancing of history and the advent of redemption.[121] Indeed, it is not a matter of resisting the theological image of a perfect, redeemed "utopia." Instead, it is a type of resistance that "sabotages its realization."[122]

Can we speak, in this context, of an orchestrated return to gnosis? We have seen above how the unity that Adorno seems to have worked against represented for him a failed attempt to overcome gnosis. The focus on nonidentity may thus be regarded as a reengagement with the traditional differentiation between God and the world, which falls back on theological dualism.

If we concede that to dismiss unity, sameness, and identification is to save them, however, we must also acknowledge an implicit resistance to stark dualism. On the one hand, the notion of a totally alien "other" (as Mendes-Flohr, for example, put it) is indeed redeployed by Adorno in order to eschew its unity with the world. On the other hand, and concomitantly, such a dual approach is not meant to dismiss the relation of God to the world and reseparate them. Rather, it is intended to point to the only way that remains available in order to hold onto such a relation, and this can only happen in a negative sense. The patent separation between the "Absolute" and the world is resisted by holding onto it, and perhaps this represents what a reconceptualization of gnostic conceptions might have meant for Adorno.

A Love Supreme

Love represents another important, perhaps surprising, feature of critical self-reflection that holds onto an unholdable theological mission. A close examination of love seems to be fitting because Adorno repeatedly, albeit far from systematically, associates love with critique in his lectures on education.[123] In his university course on metaphysics, for example, he talks of the type of love that needs to be directed "towards evil" and rebukes the "unqualified love" that is an "uncritical" attitude "in the face of what is."[124] Earlier, in his radio address "Philosophy and Teachers" Adorno made connections, though somewhat loosely, between love and "the ability to engage with intellectual matters" and between the lack of love and the mere learning of bare facts.[125]

In "Education after Auschwitz" Adorno expands on these connections. People with "reified consciousness" are discussed in terms of their deficit in love: "With this type who tends to fetishize technology, we are concerned, baldly put, with people who cannot love."[126] A person who cannot love resembles for Adorno a "societal monad" whose "coldness" and "indifference to the fate of others" displays "the pathogenic character" of the tendencies that led to Auschwitz.[127] Thus: "Those people are thoroughly cold; deep within themselves they must deny the possibility of love, must withdraw their love from other people initially, before it can even unfold."[128] In the same vein, the "power of reflection" is also considered in terms of love, because to be able to reflect critically means to be able to belong "to *all* people without exception as they exist today."[129] The universal character of love is then amplified, Adorno reasons, by the fact that love is indifferent in that it does not differentiate between worthy and unworthy objects, "for the people whom one should love are themselves such that they cannot love, and therefore in turn are not at all that lovable."[130] Specifically, through these considerations, Adorno articulates the concept of critique in association with love. The absence of the one entails especially for education the nonexistence of the other.

It might seem bizarre that one of the instigators of critical theory should bring together two seemingly unrelated concepts (critique and love) in this way—perhaps simply the romantic glitch of a philosopher. But love and its relation to critique did not represent a new theme for

Adorno at that point, and certainly not one that he considered a matter of rhetoric or trifle. As early as 1939 Adorno published an extensive essay "On Kierkegaard's Doctrine of Love."[131] Published the same year that Adorno and Horkheimer began their collaboration on their "Dialectic of the Enlightenment," the essay on Kierkegaard extended Adorno's early interest in the so-called Young Hegelian tradition, which was already evident in his professorial thesis, published in 1933.[132] While the latter focused on Kierkegaard's religious thinking as an aesthetic construction, his stand-alone paper scrutinized more specifically Kierkegaard's Christian doctrine of love, presented mainly in *Leben und Walten der Liebe* (*Works of Love*), as a critical endeavor. Adorno's key points in this paper expand on the relation between critique and theology in Kierkegaard's "collection of so-called edifying discourses," and it is this connection, Adorno argues, that should command our attention.[133]

There are three points to note. First, according to Adorno, Kierkegaard converts the Christian notion of love (agape) into social categories.[134] This means that for Kierkegaard loving people is equivalent to resisting the modern conditions that enslave them. The Christian motif of *A Love Supreme*—to use the title of John Coltrane's 1965 jazz album—operates as a type of critique of the reification of human beings.[135] Adorno's main thesis is that Kierkegaard's doctrine of love enables him "like few other writers, to perceive decisive character features of the typical individual of modern society," which means that "Kierkegaard regards the criticism of progress and civilization: as the criticism of the reification of man."[136]

For Adorno "it is this awareness which invests Kierkegaard's critical motives with their genuine earnestness and dignity."[137] It is not only that Kierkegaard's doctrine of love has "critical potential."[138] More particularly, love is a critical category. This means that love liberates human beings from entrapment in enslaving circumstances because it turns into hostility "toward the dominating mechanisms of a society that turns human beings into a mass."[139] To love implies in this sense to be critical of entrapment, and thereby resist its sway over human lives.

Kierkegaard's love is thus a form of critical theology. This is the second point to note. Critical theology means that the Christian supremacy of love is reformulated as a critique of modernity. Critique denotes a resistance to the "machinery" of the modern world that make people into things.[140] The concept of critique is of relevance here precisely because Adorno ascribes to Kierkegaard's doctrine of love what he applied to the definition of a critical theory. To some extent, such an argument enables

Adorno to distance Kierkegaard's existentialism from Heidegger's "jargon of authenticity."[141] It also endows Kierkegaard with an almost prophetic critique of modern "mass society." Indeed, "in speaking of the mass meetings of the 1848 period," writes Adorno, Kierkegaard "seems to have heard those loudspeakers which filled the Berlin Sportpalast one hundred years later."[142] However, what is crucial here is the fact that, for Adorno, Kierkegaard does not simply bring the theological notion of agape to bear on philosophical scrutiny. More profoundly, he points to the clear dependency of critique on theology. Such dependency is reflected, for example, by the relation between critique and the divine object to which love refers. Critique may attain knowledge of the divine "absolute" only by "sacrificing itself."[143] Self-sacrifice is, arguably, a devout measure adopted by critique. As a religious measure it indicates "not so much the expropriation of philosophy by theology as the transplantation of theology into the philosophical realm."[144]

What concerns Adorno most is the fact that Kierkegaard's critical theological attempt to deny the "reification" of human beings ends in failure. This is the third and last point: Kierkegaard's critical theology, according to Adorno, fails.[145] This failure means that Kierkegaard's approach "acknowledges the very same reification of man against which Kierkegaard's doctrine of love is directed."[146] Love in such a way ends up supporting reification rather than dismissing it.

The reason for such a failure lies in the fact that love, for Kierkegaard, remains "a matter of pure inwardness"—a retreat to an "interior" realm of the subject over against the external world that includes other people. Consequently, Kierkegaard's love is directed by the individual to his or her own subjectivity alone.[147] The love of God becomes a love that "is determined only by the subjective qualities of the loving one, such as disinterestedness, unlimited confidence, unobtrusiveness, mercifulness, even if one is helpless oneself, self-denial and fidelity."[148] In this way love denies not only reciprocity but also the separate existence of another beloved subject. To love God, or better to love the love of God, is consumed by the loving subject alone. Thus, love can only be an appropriation of self-love.

The appropriation of love also means that love is a positive form of critique because in resisting the world it is directed at affirming the inner qualities of the individual that it wishes to constitute or to possess. Thus: "What is introduced here as an exegesis of Christian Love, is revealed, through a more intimate knowledge of Kierkegaard's philosophy, as supplementing his negative theology with a positive one, his criticism with something edifying in the literal sense, his dialectics with simplicity."[149] For Adorno, the main problem with such a "positive" appropriation of love lies not in its "simplicity" per se, nor in its cultivating character, but rather in the way it renders other human beings superfluous. In other words, the subject retreats to an "interior" realm, as opposed to the external social world.

Peter Gordon rightly pointed out that such a "philosophy of the interior" means that Kierkegaard's love is "object-less" because the individual directs love to his or her own subjectivity. Indeed in his paper, Adorno accentuates the consequential fact that Kierkegaard's love is "universal" in being a love of no one. "Perhaps one may most accurately summarize Kierkegaard's doctrine of love," Adorno argues, "by saying that he demands that love behave towards all men as if they were dead."[150] Love can then "easily turn into its opposite, a universal hatred of human beings." It "threatens, at any given moment, to become transformed into the darkest hatred of man."[151] Love, Adorno concludes, becomes "demonic love"—a retreat to pure inwardness to the extent of exhibiting animosity toward an imagined hostile exteriority that, again, includes all human beings.

As a type of theology, "demonic" love is arguably gnostic because it points to a stark dualism between the loving individual who encompasses the love of God, and the devious external world. Earlier in this chapter, Adorno's critique of theology was associated with his contribution to the debates on gnosticism in the 1950s and 1960s, and one may see in "demonic love" an earlier example of this association. Here, in particular, Adorno seems to flesh out the type of radical, perhaps narcissistic "inwardness" that is a central characteristic of the gnostic "knowledge" of the divine core that lies within the depths of the human soul. Adorno makes the case rather clearly, since for him "Kierkegaard is unaware of the demonic consequence that his insistence on inwardness actually leaves the world to the devil."[152] The demonic characteristic of love therefore emphasizes that Kierkegaard's Christian love ends up reinstating the problem of gnostic dualism between the benevolent God and the evil world (or in this case a demiurgic power). The particular failure that Adorno attributes to Kierkegaard also implies the modern failure to overcome gnosis in general.

One of the main outcomes of this failure is an inconsistency between the inward character of love and the critique of social domination that love is supposed to have represented. The demand to love other human beings is impossible to fulfill when, for example, "the love of the neighbor" is no more than "the reduplication of one's own ego," or when love means viewing all other people as if they were dead.¹⁵³ With the emphasis on others, Kierkegaard's orientation toward this-worldliness is at stake for Adorno. Certainly, what makes other human beings lovable is their inherent feature of being made in God's image. But if for Kierkegaard humans are loved because they are nothing but a replica of God, are they not marked by the instrumental "sameness" that he condemned? Arguably, loving the image of God in the "other" (and especially as a reproduction of self-love) means that all other human beings represent nothing more than an instrument for the love of God rather than an end in themselves. By converting human beings into instruments of love, they become things. Adorno seems to clearly distinguish here between loving the God-given feature of humanity and loving concrete human beings; between caring for particular others in all their diversity, uniqueness, and actual individuality and the love of the humane that renders such a notion of others redundant. Kierkegaard's critical theology fails, then, because it reemploys the type of instrumental relationship that characterizes the demonic feature of reification, against which he set out his critique of social domination. This critique ends, therefore, with a demonic hatred of humans and Adorno concludes that "the presuppositions of this doctrine of the neighbor and, at the same time, of love itself, are untenable."¹⁵⁴ Love cannot fulfill its critical calling.

Adorno's own "edifying" discourse seem to drive at overcoming this failure of critique. The following lines from "Education after Auschwitz" may hence be read as though they had been composed with Kierkegaard in mind: "One of the greatest impulses of Christianity, not immediately identical with its dogma, was to eradicate the coldness that permeates everything. But this attempt failed; surely because it did not reach into the societal order that produces and reproduces that coldness."¹⁵⁵ To "reach into the societal order," however, does not mean for Adorno an abandonment of Kierkegaard's love but rather a more compound holding onto it by resisting its "demonic" potential—ensuring a theology of love by critically overriding it. We are engaged here with another mode of reconceptualization of theological concepts that saves a theological charge by its dismissal. Under such a composition, love is still "something immediate and in essence contradicts mediated relationship" as Kierkegaard argued.¹⁵⁶ It is still redolent of its universal (belonging to "all people"), indifferent (not differentiating between potential worthy and unworthy objects of love), and spontaneous ("something immediate" and contradicting mediated relationships) characteristics that Anders Nygern, for example, strongly associated with the Christian "agape motif."[157] In the same vein, love remains a critical category exactly because of these characteristics, which is perhaps the central feature that Adorno ascribes to Kierkegaard's doctrine.

Nonetheless, Adorno assumes these theological orientations in order to turn away from Kierkegaard's solitude of "inwardness." He interlocks the "power of reflection" with interpersonal love (the "belonging to *all* people as they exist today"), and this is key. In showing some similarity to Levinas's ontological quest from that time, Adorno seems to present education with a shift from "solitude" to "relation."[158] Redeploying theology by means of critique points in this case to an intention to relate to the "world in which we exist" rather than to retreat into the solitude of the self. This new understanding of a "love supreme" is critical because it offers resistance "to the expanding heteronomy."[159] Still imbued with this theological image, critique therefore aims at fulfilling its original calling when the world of human beings, and not the solitude of the loving individual, stands as the arena of noninstrumental love.

The last point may perhaps show some similarity between Adorno's critical self-reflection and the Jewish concept of mitzvah (an obligation that is performed in the world and mostly as a duty to others). However, one may certainly question the extent to which Adorno was aware of this connection between interpersonal love, with which he expressed his distancing from Christianity, and relational duties, which brought him closer to Jewish religious vocabulary. No less interesting is the fact that the concept of "a love of the world" may be seen as embedded in a turn away from inwardness to a relation to others, even though such a concept is more commonly associated with Hannah Arendt than with Adorno.[160] In Adorno's loving (and in this sense critical) commitment to the world, one may speak of a de-demonization of love because it shifts from a "demonic" hatred of humans to an interpersonal relation that informs a critical resistance to social domination. It is also possible to invoke in this case Adorno's concept of "inverse theology" by suggesting that in the context of education the inversion relates to a turn away from Kierkegaard's movement inward to an emphasis on ensuring that "suffering be remedied and society redeemed."[161]

Kierkegaard's love is therefore not refuted, but rather upheld by being disavowed in accordance with an immanent critique that redeploys theological concepts. A lost theological mission is saved by a subversive turning against it, thus respecting the most intimate core relation between critique and theology. Subversion, resistance, and possibly irony are parts of the critical promise of theology. Perhaps reminiscent of Freud's analysis of the Mosaic tablets, love is turned upside down—from self-love to the love of others, from inwardness to the redeeming of society, from the inner qualities of the loving subject to the obligation (of education) to one's fellow human beings.

Messianic Passion

I wish to conclude the discussion of Adorno's critique of theology, featured in his reflections on education, by pointing to its relation to messianism. There is, it seems, a connection between Adorno's call for an education centered on critical self-reflection and his articulation of messianic expectations. Adorno's approach to messianism is captured rather well by Elliot Wolfson. For Wolfson, Adorno's "decisively secular" thought is nonetheless "rooted in what has been called the 'Jewish passion for the impossible,' a fidelity to the idea of redemption that assumes the form of its refusal—in the traditional idiom, the Messiah can be present only in the absence of being present."[162] This extract points to Adorno's messianic "passion" because the quest for "uttering the unutterable" gives a "valid redemptive response" that "involves turning away from redemption."[163] Thus, in what has been termed in this chapter holding onto an unholdable object, "the possibility of redemption" is inescapably bound to the "impossibility of its actualization."[164] In such a compound way one may endow Adorno with a "non-eschatological eschatology" that is, to emphasize again, a turn away from redemption that is made, however, for the sake of retaining the theological hope that it represents.[165]

With this messianic passion in mind, one may reflect on some of Adorno's main arguments discussed above. For example, we have seen that Adorno simultaneously clings to and dismisses Hegel's secularization of eschatological expectations. Here Adorno turns away from Hegel's positive hopes for redemption while, nonetheless, holding onto the idea of redemption—a point that Adorno already stresses in the closing statement of *Minima Moralia*.[166] One maintains the messianic idea only by revoking it. The same may be said in relation to the notion of critical self-reflection, central to Adorno's discussion of education. In calling for critical self-reflection in education Adorno holds onto an object that can be realized only by not being realized and thus takes distance from any redemptive hopes concerning "the Absolute" in order "not to betray" such redemptive hopes.

Love represents, arguably, the clearest example of these interconnections since the act of advocating interpersonal love points to a double resistance. On the one hand, there is a resistance to the social and political conditions that enslave us. In accordance with Kierkegaard's love (as Adorno interprets it), resistance represents a thrust against "coldness" and the "lack" of love that enable the subordination of human beings to the "machine," sharply exemplified by the transformation of *Bildung* into *Halbbildung*. Here, the gift of love denotes the critical capacity of human beings to transgress such social domination by subversively working against it. On the other hand, Adorno also presents a resistance to Kierkegaard's arguably narcissistic self-love, which imagines it has the absolute under its command; and in this turn away from Kierkegaard's theology Adorno holds onto what Wolfson underlined as a redemptive approach that is bound to the "impossibility" of its actualization. One may see here not only a philosophical commitment to theology, but also, one could argue, a rather clever appeal to one theological tradition (Jewish messianism) in order to amend another (Christian faith).

Arendt's rather shrewd comment that Adorno was Walter Benjamin's only student seems to be rather fitting here. Adorno explicitly identifies with Benjamin's messianism. For him it is Benjamin's type of "messianism" that attempts "to formulate a materialist conception of history, albeit one that is shot through with theological ideas that are presented in terms of a highly negative dialectic."[167] As presented in chapter 2, Benjamin's nihilism suggests a messianic time that is nevertheless embedded within history (in every "present moment") but not revealed by the course of history. In this last sense Benjamin holds to a messianic potential that is innate in historical time (and the immanent world) while lying beyond its worldly flux. This type of complete resignation, associated with a notion of exile, and supported by a separation between history and redemption—cosmology and soteriology—represents, for Adorno, Benjamin's concept of a "messianic arrest of happening": the potential for a messianic irruption that may penetrate history but that is not actualized within its course.[168]

Adorno's explicit critique of messianic traditions may be read against such a backdrop. The theme was discussed, for example, in his last classroom lecture on metaphysics. Here Adorno stressed his opposition to the mystical traditions that claim to have access to "primal religious experiences."[169] But what Adorno seems to rebuke is "affirmative or positive" forms of messianism. Such is, for example, the case of Schelling's "positive philosophy" that adopted a speculative theological model that was introduced by the Zohar.[170] Messianism, then, in Adorno's view, may still correspond to valuable "religious experiences." These are, however, positive interpretations of redemption that "simply become blasphemies" because they form a perspective that "effectively demonizes the absolute" in a way that "turns God into an abyss."[171]

The "blasphemy" inherent in such a messianic "turn" relates to "vulgar materialism," which means that a positive redemptive meaning is enclosed within history. In a more concrete tone, messianism cannot be about the affirmation of faith, the attainment of redemption through acts of sovereignty, the justification of nationalism, the fighting of "just wars," or the oppression of others. Neither can it support political theological national arguments about historical rights or God's promise. Especially in the context of the 1960s, this approach may imply a specific distancing from the ideas of fulfillment and sovereignty that characterized Jewish nationalism. But one may think also of Adorno's mistrust in the social and political activism of the German student movement in the 1960s, expressed, for example, in his famous correspondence with Marcuse.[172] In pointing to the students' "streak of coldness," Adorno seems to be concerned less with their lack of critical awareness and more with their transformation of critique into an ideological zeal.[173] This was, arguably, a moment in which critique itself became what Isaiah Berlin called a "positive doctrine of liberation by reason" by offering an actualization of critique's redemptive promise.[174] In a play on Adorno's own argumentation, we may speak of a critique that is not realized by being realized because it is fulfilled by suggesting itself as worthy of compliance and in this sense by working against itself. In such a case, unrefined materialism simply means a bowdlerizing of transcendence by transforming the content that was associated with it to represent nothing more than another mechanism of violence.

To some extent, Adorno connects the messianic materialism that he identifies in contemporary political agendas with "the intricate interrelationship between gnosticism, Neoplatonism, the Cabbala, and later Christian mysticism" and in particular the adaptation of the "Sohar" in German Idealism.[175] It might be hard to defend this bringing together of a rather broad array of redemptive and messianic traditions in one stroke. Still, Adorno's educational aim is to point to the vulgarization of messianism, based on the intertwining of transcendence and immanence, cosmology and soteriology, divine time and historical time, even if at the expense of scholarly precision. He therefore turns not against a messianic interest in this world, but rather against a particular expression of such an interest.

Wolfson's reference to the Jewish messianic idiom—"the Messiah can be present only in the absence of being present"—seems indeed to illuminate Adorno's view of these messianic traditions, and of their political implications, on the one hand, and his own quest for a critical messianism (so to speak) that is based on "uttering the unutterable" on the other hand. The "messianic idea" (as Benjamin put it) is only that which always remains constantly absent. One may talk of a "heretical" turn against all former messianic heresies that rejects their various historical appearances for the sake of holding onto their core theological rationale nonetheless.

Such an approach to messianism exemplifies what has been presented in research as Adorno's negative theology.[176] There is, however, a particular standpoint to consider. Signifying the limits of our capacity to represent and in this sense have knowledge of the limitless, the eternal, the transcendent, and the divine, negative theology is about the exclusive articulation of nondivinity (or, to put it simply, an articulation of what is not God). I tend to agree that such an apophatic approach is part of Adorno's argument. Nevertheless, one must not overlook his particular understanding of negativity in this context. Rather than an inability to represent the divine, negativity points to the possibility of representation by means of nonrepresentation. Adorno openly and uniquely associates the *Bilderverbot* (the biblical prohibition on the making of idols and images) with this negative theological imagination.[177] There is indeed a prohibition of making an image of God. But this prohibition is imposed not because it is impossible to have any knowledge of the divine but rather because it is the only viable way to still hold onto the possibility of such knowledge in a material reality that is now pregnant with a theological, indeed messianic, passion. Thus, for Adorno: "It is only in the absence of images that the full object could be conceived. Such absence concurs with the theological ban on images. Materialism brought that ban into secular form by not permitting Utopia to be positively pictured; this is the substance of its negativity. At its most materialistic, materialism comes to agree with theology. Its great desire would be the resurrection of the flesh, a desire utterly foreign to idealism, the realm of the absolute spirit."[178]

In absence, then, we may conceive what is inconceivable. Our attention could be drawn at this point to Adorno's reflection on "fruitless waiting"—a Weberian image that refers particularly to Jewish messianic expectations—that concluded his classroom lectures on metaphysics.[179] Contrary to Weber, however, Adorno upholds such waiting to be "no doubt the form in which metaphysical experience manifests itself most strongly to us."[180] Is it not this very "waiting" that embodies the "absence" (of a messiah) as the only possible way of conceiving deliverance within the boundaries of the "world in which we live"? In its association with "fruitless waiting," metaphysics, and thus critical thinking, demonstrates a subtle rejection of messianism, which is the only way to retain a hold on its passion. This is also true, ceteris paribus, of education. Perhaps as a type of "melancholic" engagement with the cultivation of humans, education should not aim at mourning a lost object, but rather at being attentive to the ever-present possibility of its resurrection.[181] Its critical mission navigates itself in such a way through the troubled waters whirling between an imagined Scylla and Charybdis: "rescuing" the messianic and at the same time suspending its worldly realization.

CHAPTER 4

Tradition

All Roads Lead to Rome

TRADITION, TRADITION, TRADITION

"Tradition" is the title of the opening song of the celebrated Broadway show (later made into a movie) called *Fiddler on the Roof*, which tells the agonizing story of a struggling Jewish family in Eastern Europe. Tradition (in Hebrew *massoret*), says Tevye, the main protagonist, is the reason "we keep our balance for many, many years," for it plays an essential role in the organization of family, community, and Jewish life. "Because of our traditions," he adds, we show "our constant devotion to God." Though having no clue as to "how this tradition started," it forms for him both the pillar of his identity and the foundation of everyday life in his community, which lives "in simple peace and harmony." And if tradition is where the story begins, its slow evaporation marks a central element of the personal drama that ends with deportation. A crisis of modernity, at least from an Eastern European Jewish perspective, is inextricably linked with the loss of tradition.

Hannah Arendt is certainly no Tevye, and the notions of devotion to God, or simple peace and harmony, are hardly part of her vocabulary. But some of the main aspects of Arendt's postwar writings on tradition (especially her works from the 1960s) seem to dovetail with the milkman's standpoint rather well. The grounds for community and identity; the relationship between past and present; the reference to mythic unknown origins; and the modern calamity resulting from the disappearance of tradition—all are essential parts of Arendt's argumentation. Not without a grain of irony, perhaps, one could say that Arendt's analysis of the crisis of modernity in the wake of two world wars, and the rise of totalitarianism and extermination, starts where Sholem Aleichem's drama left off, that is, with the loss of tradition, although without the same stagy pathos or moral intentions in mind.

In what follows, I would like to show what tradition means for Arendt and the ways in which it represents a theological category. This will invite an examination of how tradition informs her conceptualization of critique and in particular her critique of modernity, making it dependent on theology. As this chapter shows, it is in the postwar context of renewed interest in tradition that Arendt adopts a subtle, certainly distinctive approach to the relation of critique to theology, disclosing her unique critique of theology.

In her political writings from the 1960s in particular—texts that demonstrate, according to Dana Villa, Arendt's shift of focus "from totalitarianism to tradition"—Arendt presents two main arguments concerning the meaning of tradition.[1] First, tradition means the intergenerational transference of a sacred testament. Second, tradition is a Roman concept. In one of the more evocative passages of a chapter entitled "What Is Authority?" she writes: "Tradition preserved the past by handing down from one generation to the next the testimony of the ancestors, who first had witnessed and created the sacred founding and then augmented it by their authority throughout the centuries."[2] This somewhat dense statement (encompassing a range of notions such as foundation, augmentation, and authority) encapsulates Arendt's overall understanding of political tradition.[3] Stemming from the Latin (and for Arendt, this means Roman) *traditio*, the concept refers to both the act of "handing down" from one generation to the next as well as the particular "sacred" content that is being handed down.[4] The first aspect of tradition (as an act of passing on a certain message, which corresponds to the German term *Überlieferung*) denotes the linkage between each generation and the one that preceded it.[5] The second aspect of tradition (as a certain content) refers to a unique and "sacred" set of core principles, originating in a mythic past. Here, tradition has a theological connotation because of the particular sacred parcel—a "testimony of the ancestors"—and the moment of revelation to which it relates and that is being transmitted from one generation to another. In this way, tradition relates to religion, and religion is understood in terms of its ties to a sacred, revealed experience in the past.

The theological dimension of tradition is important. For Arendt the intergenerational transference of a sacred testament suggests an element of revelation. Such an element relates to a formative moment of creation that involves divine presence and is augmented by each passing generation. Augmentation (deriving from a Roman word, *augere*) means that this mythic past serves as the foundation of what continues to bind people together. In this way, the notion of temporality (the past that we share) is permeated by a layering of theology. Put otherwise, the sacred origin of tradition appears, to cite Mircea Eliade, as "a sort of eternal mythical present."[6]

It is this capacity that makes tradition an adhesive religious substance that underpins the shared existence of human beings, binding them to their common ground. Arguably, a mythic and "sacred" past—involving divine presence—is here evoked as an object of reference to which all generations relate because they see themselves—or must see themselves—reflected in it, as if they too were present in the formative experience. This experience serves as a religious condition of communality that is accessible by means of the transmission of the sacred testimonial moment that tradition stands for.

While tradition may be defined as the intergenerational transference of a sacred testament, its origins are to be found in the Roman "spirit." This is the second point that Arendt makes: tradition is a Roman religious concept. Arendt particularly builds on the Roman experience and in such a way takes part in what Dirk Moses called "Das römische Gespräch" (the Roman debate or discussion), which he defined as the "long-term recuperation of the distant European past for present purposes" that "had been underway in the West since the eighteenth century."[7] "A rich tradition," Moses further suggests, "Roman republicanism offered her a variety of positions on questions of war, conquest, and reason of state (raison d'état), and she drew on them both explicitly and implicitly."[8] Notwithstanding the undisputed importance of Greek philosophy for Arendt, it is—as Dean Hammer convincingly argued—the Roman experience that mainly provides her with her arsenal of concepts, themes, and models for thinking about "how we might discover the past for ourselves" including reflection on the earlier Greek example.[9]

A similar religious image of tradition is also central in the Jewish heritage: the sacred core principles that were revealed in a mythic moment on Mount Sinai were taken to represent divine law and handed down from generation to generation until the present day. In chapter 1 we saw how

Freud was rather explicit in suggesting that Michelangelo's *Moses* attests to the "tamed wrath" of the prophet in the aftermath of the revelation of God's testament. Freud associated this theological imagery with the artist's reproach of a "Catholic Rome," which he himself shared. But Arendt may have presented overlapping (rather than antagonistic) theological similes. Samuel Moyn's suggestion that Arendt "connects between the Jewish and Roman sources of her thought" is particularly pertinent here because Arendt presents a definition of Roman tradition that was considered central to the Jewish experience as well.[10] The idea that it was a Jewish polity that was established at Sinai, an idea that has been debated by Jewish intellectuals since Spinoza, seems to bring the two sources of Arendt's thought together.[11] Indeed, in the Roman tradition there is, according to Arendt, a testimonial, sacred substance that was revealed in a mythic moment of the past and from that moment on conveyed from one generation to the other, providing all generations with a shared political foundation.

I will return to the combination of Roman and Jewish elements in Arendt's thought below. Here, I wish to highlight the centrality of Saint Augustine to her discussion of tradition. Arendt was by no means a highly systematic thinker, perhaps even an eclectic one, who drew on a highly diverse range of sources.[12] But in her discussion of tradition, her "debt" to Augustine is unequivocal.[13] Starting with her 1929 dissertation, and throughout her meticulous editing of its various English translations in the 1960s (a project she never completed), Arendt takes Augustine to represent not only the most notable Christian thinker but also the most representative Roman one.[14] An understanding of the "Christian Augustine" can be fully grasped, Arendt argues, only "if we take into account the ambiguity of his existence as both a Roman and a Christian."[15] As the "greatest theorist of Christian politics," Augustine was "still firmly rooted in the Roman tradition."[16] When Arendt points out that none of the influences that Augustine absorbed throughout his life were ever "radically excised from his thinking," she is referring less to his Manichean past and much more to the Roman origins of his thought.[17] Moreover, because of Augustine, Christianity became for Arendt a "religion" only by the merits of its consolidation with the Roman religious imagination. Thus: "Thanks to the fact that the foundation of the city of Rome was repeated in the foundation of the Catholic Church, though, of course, with a radically different content, the Roman trinity of religion, authority, and tradition, could be taken over by the Christian era."[18] A Roman trinity was absorbed into a Christian one. The church consequently "adapted itself so thoroughly to Roman thinking" because it saw the Apostles as "the founding fathers" and claimed for itself the old authority of the Senate, which embodied divinely sanctioned authority, leaving worldly power to the secular rulers—illustrating the separation of the two earthly and divine "bodies" central to Ernst Kantorowicz's thesis.[19] In this sense, it was Augustine, rather than Paul (or Adolf von Harnack's Marcion for that matter), who could be seen as the inventor of a new religion.[20]

Augustine's concept of love particularly exemplifies for Arendt the intersection of Roman and Christian theologies.[21] The main point to note is that Augustine speaks of love—perhaps the most significant of all concepts of Christian theology—as a Roman. As a Roman thinker Augustine displays in his notion of Christian love an "uncritical use not only of Stoic but also of Neoplatonic categories."[22] It is the intertwining of these categories with Pauline theology that "could not help but lead him into inconsistencies, if not into outright contradictions."[23] "So strong is Augustine's dependence upon these non-Christian currents of thought," Arendt adds, "that he even uses them occasionally for a description of God."[24] In such a way, "the strong influence of Stoic and Neoplatonic terminology on Augustine's early thought takes its revenge here."[25] The "revenge" relates to the failure of Augustine to exorcise from his theological imagination a Roman religious take on earlier Greek origins. The Roman religious sources of Augustine's thought "remain active in each set of Christian problems, peculiarly transforming them (even concealing them) from a purely Christian point of view."[26] The Roman religious tradition thus continues to haunt Augustine's thought, even if "against his own wishes."[27]

Yet, what was the Roman religious tradition that Augustine absorbed so unwillingly into his conceptualization of love? In her dissertation, Arendt's answer to this question seems to point to Augustine's "tripartite hierarchy" of love.[28] This "hierarchy" simply reiterates the Roman translation of the Greek concepts of love—storge, eros, and agape. These concepts correspond to the Roman *amor*, *dilectio*, and *caritas*, which Augustine uses, according to Arendt, rather "loosely."[29] Augustine then takes: "*amor* to designate desire and craving (that is, for love in its largest, least specific sense); *dilectio* to designate the love of self and neighbor; and *caritas* to designate the love of God and the 'highest good.'"[30] In line with his Roman sources, Augustine presents here an order of love. This order, or "hierarchy," relates to "what is above us (*supra nos*), what is beside us (*inxta nos*), and finally what is beneath us (*infra nos*)."[31] The first indicates God, the second points to our neighbor, and the third relates to the (physical) body.

Augustine's adoption of a Roman "hierarchy of love" leads to inconsistencies that Arendt attributes to the result of a fusion between two elements. The first element relates to a separation between two forms of love: worldly and divine, with divine love representing the "highest good." The second, contradicting element, however, relates to the classification of three spheres of love—physical, social, and divine—all three indicating forms of presence of divine love in the world.

In the first element, Augustine still holds to a dichotomy between the divine (the "highest good") and the worldly, in a way that demonstrates the sway of Platonic dualism over his thought, also explaining why he saw Plato as being "closest to the Christian faith."[32] Here, Augustine makes a case for two forms of love that are separate: desire, which Augustine terms *cupiditas*, and which represents "the root of all evil," and *caritas*, which "seeks eternity and the absolute future" and stands for "right love."[33] But in the second element, divine love is described not in terms of dualism (divine versus worldly) but rather as constantly present within all physical and social experiences in and of the world, too. The theological view that can be observed here relates to the belief that there is divine presence in the world in three different modalities (physical, social, and mythic).

Arendt (who thereby dissociates Augustine from a stern Manichean dualism) concludes that the tripartite scale of love (physical, social, and mythic), relating to three types of divine presence in the world, overrides the Platonic dichotomy between God and the world for two main reasons. First, because a tripartite order of love means that, for Augustine, love of God informs all modes of love in this world, desire included. Thus, "every particular act of love receives its meaning, its raison d'être, in this act of referring back to the original beginning," which means "a return to God."[34] There are, arguably, no traces of dualism here because desire, in its "return to God," also includes, rather than excludes, divine love. For Arendt, this means that a return to the heart of a divine love—a main feature of Christianity—is not only already present in the entire spectrum of craving, but also endows it with a positive connotation: "strictly speaking," writes Arendt, "he who does not love and desire at all is a nobody."[35]

Second, and perhaps more importantly, the dichotomy between the two terms of love (worldly and divine) does not fully apply to Augustine's theological speculations because he articulates love of God itself as a type of "desire." One desires the "highest good" and in this particular sense loves divine love. As Anders Nygren rightly pointed out, this amalgamation of love of God (agape) and desire (eros) is hardly justified from the point of view of a strict Pauline dichotomy.[36] It diverges, therefore, from an original Christian message. Arendt, it seems, offers a corresponding argument in relation to Augustine: "Insofar as Augustine defines love as a kind of desire, he hardly speaks as a Christian."[37] The dichotomous relations between God and the world, love and desire, agape and eros, go through some transformation, according to Arendt, making Augustine's concept of love different from that of Paul.[38]

Such a view of "the Roman" Augustine reflects mainly on the type of love for one's "neighbor" that interests Arendt the most. This love also relates to God and in such a way "depends on something outside the human condition as we know and experience it."[39] Here, it is important to note that "the love of my neighbor, or generally love between human beings, derives from a source altogether different from appetites and desires" and that it stems from the same divine source that also informs these two dispositions (appetite and desire).[40] For Augustine, this implies the human capacity to share the world with others because such an aptitude harks back to the mythic moment of the past, which is the main principle of tradition.

Roman tradition, one may argue, conditions love. Human communality consequently becomes "a social organism" that is based on love because it originates in a mythic, divine moment, and it is characterized from that moment on by the "passing away and succeeding" of generations, as the Romans understood it.[41] So unequivocal is Arendt's argument concerning the relationships between love, tradition, and community that she accentuates the Roman origins of Augustine's formulation (later to become a leitmotif in her writings): "That there be a beginning, man was created."[42] Though trying to reconcile this Roman conception with the biblical story of Adam, Augustine nonetheless merely points to a "source of being itself" that is "altogether different" from the Christian one: "When Augustine asks about the origin of the human race, the answer, as distinct from the self-sameness of God, is that the origin lies in the common ancestor of us all. . . . In this second sense, man is seen as belonging to mankind and to this world by generation."[43] Conditioned by tradition, the origin of humanity points to the sacred testament of the mythic past that brings people together generation after generation. It is then interesting to note how Augustine's neighborly love is deeply informed by such a notion of tradition. Such a love still represents for Augustine "an occasion to love

God" and not a love of our fellow human beings for their own sake.[44] In chapter 3 we saw that in his reading of Kierkegaard's *Works of Love* Adorno concluded that this love of God leads to "pure inwardness," eventually leaving the world to the "devil." Arendt, however, concludes the opposite. Since we are dealing here with a divine dwelling in the human world in the Roman traditional sense, love of God is always entwined with its presence in the human political and social sphere. The world is consequently not left to the "devil" because it is redolent of divinity. In the development of Arendt's idea, love of God is not presented only as diametrically opposed to the world—as "wordless"—but also as entangled with the world—as "worldly."[45] Gershom Scholem, not without a controversial amount of hostility, pointed to Arendt's lack of "love of Israel" ("Ahabat Israel" [sic]) and this may resonate rather well with this last point.[46] While Scholem's accusation is usually considered to be a reproach against Arendt's alleged lack of loyalty to the Jewish people, it could also be construed as a rather crafty comment on the Roman-Augustinian sources of her concept of love.

Arendt wishes, then, to present an area of thought that goes beyond Augustine's explicit arguments in order to explore what "Augustine himself has merely implied."[47] What is implied are the Roman origins of his conceptualization of Christian love. Given the central importance of such a concept for Christian faith, Arendt's argument may be seen as rather radical in this implication: Christianity was never exclusively Christian. Arendt may seem to echo a long, somewhat controversial, modern German scholarly penchant for separating Christian theology from its Jewish origins (F. C. Baur in the nineteenth century and Adolf von Harnack in the twentieth century are distinct examples). Nonetheless, one may also argue that in Arendt's case such a separation calls into question Christian theology, rather than the Jewish religion, because its pagan sources are underlined. These origins are, to emphasize again, anchored in the Roman concept of tradition, fleshing out in particular the theological substance of this tradition. This theological matter relates to the three main loci of divine presence in the world (physical, social, and mythic) that Augustine absorbed from the Roman religious heritage. Regarding tradition, therefore, Arendt is not arguing for a type of theology that starts with a transcendent, out-of-this-world godhead, but rather, perhaps conversely, a religious imagination that involves an immanent, in this world, divine presence; a divine attendance that conditions reality is also imagined as dwelling within the political, natural, and mythical human experiences of this world.

Theologia Tripartita

The three loci of divine assurance bring us to the crucial point. Can we not say that Arendt more than "merely implies" that tradition is made of a tripartite theology (*theologia tripartita*)—a division between physical, social, and mythical modes of divine presence in the world? Though a "Christian Augustine" may have unequivocally rejected this theology, the Roman Augustine, to follow Arendt, could not avoid incorporating it into his own "hierarchy" of love.

Augustine's explicit engagement with this particular Roman heritage may support such a claim. For Augustine, the "tripartite theology" was articulated mainly by Varro and it represented a central characteristic of Roman civil life, which he precluded. This is made clear specifically, though not exclusively, in Books 6 and 7 of *The City of God*. Varro's distinction between mythical, social (or political), and physical theologies represents the main object of scrutiny for Augustine. Granting Varro the extraordinary status of "a man universally informed," Augustine nevertheless castigates him for being "most hostile to the truth of religion."[48] Thus, he adds: "What ought we to think but that a most acute and learned man—not, however made free by the Holy Spirit—was overpowered by the custom and laws of his state, and, not being able to be silent about those things by which he was influenced, spoke of them under pretence [sic] of commending religion?"[49] "The custom and laws of his state" are made of the "three kinds of theology" in which "one is called mythical, the other physical, and the third civil."[50] The first, mythical or "fabulous" (derived from the Greek μῦθος which Augustine translates as "a fable"), is acted out by poets and "stage-players" who sing or act "such things as are derogatory to the dignity and the nature of the immortals."[51] The second (physical), which Augustine also calls "natural," relates to a philosophical examination of the nature of being. It is theological to the extent that it discusses gods in natural (i.e., philosophical) terms. The third kind is a political theology "which citizens in cities, and especially the priests, ought to know and to administer."[52] It is here, as far as we know, that the term "political theology" first emerges.[53] Augustine thus concludes that according to Varro, "the first theology . . . is especially adapted to the theater, the second to the world, the third to the city."[54]

Augustine unequivocally rejects all three theologies as "fables."[55] His rejection, however, remains for Arendt incomplete. Augustine's reference to Varro's idiom "God is the soul of the world" is a key point.[56] For Varro "the soul of the world and its parts are the true gods," interoperating in such a way with Plato's "three grades of the soul in universal nature."[57] The first is defined as the most general in that it "pervades all the living parts of the body, and has not sensation, but only the power of life." The second is articulated as being positioned somewhat higher in the hierarchy and relates to a certain level of understanding of the world that is provided by the senses.[58] The third in the hierarchy "is the highest, and is called mind, where intelligence has its throne. This grade of soul no mortal creatures except man are possessed of. Now this part of the soul of the world, Varro says, is called God, and in us is called Genius."[59] Augustine explicitly rejected Varro. But, at the same time, his hierarchy of love seems to be rather close to this "tripartite" order of souls. In particular, Augustine's theological distinction between what is above us (*supra nos*), what is beside us (*inxta nos*), and finally what is beneath us (*infra nos*), much like his association of these modalities with nature, society, and myth, dovetails with Varro's God as "the soul" of the world.[60] Varro's souls seem to be rearranged in Augustine's thought as elements of a theological speculation about the three types of divine presence in love. Souls, one could argue, are simply transformed into loves.

Arendt, then, strongly points to an area of thought in which Augustine's explicit rejection of Varro may be seen as accompanied, tacitly, by an adaptation of his structural differentiation between three modes of divine presence. Even though one may argue that the Roman mythical form of worship, which Varro ascribes to the poets, withdraws from Augustine's tripartite division, it is nonetheless reformulated as a type of knowledge of divine truth. There appears to be a reconceptualization of a mythical theology that stands higher up, rather than lower down, in the hierarchy, exemplifying what Arendt means when she argues that Augustine thinks rather "loosely" as a Roman.

Augustine, however, did not integrate the Roman tripartite theology willingly, openly, or even knowingly. He does not wish to endorse the Roman religious legacy. On the contrary, he argues against it. There is, for Arendt, an unresolved tension between the tacit Roman tripartite theology that Augustine unwillingly absorbed and the explicit Christian language and terminology that he overtly promotes. Moreover, in her view, Augustine remains mostly unaware of the Roman inheritance that informs his theology. Roman theology remains a hidden, to some extent suppressed, perhaps unconscious, element throughout the history of Christianity.

The notion of a "hidden tradition" may therefore apply to Arendt's examination of Roman theology. This issue seems to deserve attention as it reflects back on what was considered above as the interweaving of Roman and Jewish sources in Arendt's thought. On the one hand, Arendt coined the notion of "hidden tradition" in her early writings before and during the Second World War, when referring specifically to Jewish history. The "hidden" tradition of which she spoke related to the endurance of a Jewish political "spirit" within an overall apolitical (and, for Arendt, "worldless") existence imposed on, and self-imposed by, the Jewish people following the fall of their sovereign state in the first century AD. Thus, for example, the messianic political mission of seventeenth-century Sabbatianism represented for Arendt a last, failed attempt to restore the political "hidden" capacity of Jews that had become buried hundreds of years earlier.[61] In modernity, in particular, the hidden political tradition was maintained, according to Arendt, but also transformed into a plea for worldliness rather than a messianic fight for sovereignty (an argument that seems to be consistent with her growing distance from Zionism in those years). It became the main characteristic of the "conscious pariah"—a term that plays on Weber's "social outcast"—which Arendt ascribed, in a variety of writings, to a somewhat lively assembly of figures including Heinrich Heine, Rahel Varnhagen, Franz Kafka, Charlie Chaplin, and Walter Benjamin.[62] As Richard Bernstein suggested, Arendt endowed these figures with the status of rebel and pariah, a position that she, one may argue, not only acclaimed but also reclaimed for herself.[63] Against the Jewish imposed, and self-imposed, worldlessness—representing for Arendt "a form of barbarism" and "apolitical" stance—the conscious pariah acts as a "rebel" who continues to fight for a modern Jewish place in the polity, working against (external and inner) forces that prevent Jews from entering the modern political sphere.[64] Thus: "As soon as the pariah enters the arena of politics, and translates his status into political terms, he becomes perforce a rebel."[65]

On the other hand, Arendt also applies a similar argument to the Roman religious tradition. As a "hidden" source of Christianity, the Roman religious "spirit" endured from antiquity and throughout the development of Christianity and on into modernity. Arguably, it is the translation of the Roman religious heritage into modern political terms—especially in order to "rebel" against these—that Arendt wishes to evoke in her discussion of tradition. The "hidden" Roman tradition thus serves as a constant historical factor, applied wherever the "Roman-Western" (for Arendt this also means "Western-Christian") civilization is to be found. And it penetrated "wherever the *pax Romana* created Western civilization on Roman foundations."[66]

With this approach in mind, the plot that related to Jewish history is endowed with a universal meaning, shifting the discussion from the specific Jewish context to the general political theater, relevant to the understanding of Western history and Western modernity as a whole. Ron Feldman's remark that Arendt's "view of the modern Jewish condition serves as an introduction to her political theory" may be correct in relation to Arendt's notion of "hidden" tradition.[67] But, at the same time, the opposite could also be said, namely that her early engagement with the "Roman" Augustine in the 1920s served as an introduction to the evolution of her thought on Jewish modern politics. In both the Jewish and Roman cases, the concept of a "hidden" tradition represents a core, albeit concealed, religious element that endures throughout history and speaks to modernity.

Hidden tradition, then, implies that Arendt is not shy of suggesting a Roman-Augustinian relevance to the thinking of modernity. In particular, by applying such a notion to the Roman tradition, Arendt shows the extent to which she is interested mainly in the "crisis" of modernity, rather than the history of antiquity. Especially as a Roman thinker, Augustine resonates as a "fundamental chord which sounds in its endless modulations through the whole history of Western thought."[68] He is also the one who "speaks across centuries to Luther, and also to the emerging movement of German phenomenology in the void created by the crises of modernity."[69] The connection that Arendt would repeatedly make over the years is rather plain. Augustine, her "old friend and benefactor" as she calls him, is: "The great thinker who lived in a period which in some respects resembled our own more than any other in recorded history and who in any case wrote under the full impact of a catastrophic end, which perhaps resembles the end to which we have come."[70] Arendt associates not only two different eons, but more particularly two "catastrophic" ends—the fall of Rome in late antiquity, and the recent destruction, unprecedented death, and extermination.[71] From within this array of somewhat loose, arguably questionable, connotations Augustine's relevance to an analysis of modernity is brought to the fore. Indeed, in the next section I wish to show that it is the background against which Arendt composes her critique of a modern world in crisis that includes a reliance on a "hidden" Roman religious tradition and its embedded tripartite theology.

A Tripartite Critique of Modernity

A Critique of Theology

In Arendt's *Between Past and Future*, the relation between critique and tradition is made explicit. Here, critique stands for "a critical interpretation of the past" whose main aim is "to discover the real origins of traditional concepts in order to distill from them anew their original spirit which has so sadly evaporated from the very key words of political language—such as freedom, and justice, authority and reason, responsibility and virtue, power and glory—leaving behind empty shells with which to settle almost all accounts, regardless of their underlying phenomenal reality."[72] Defined as an analysis of "traditional concepts" that have "evaporated" in modernity, Arendt's critique aims at uncovering the "real origins" of mainly political concepts, liberating in such a way their "original spirit" from all later, "empty" manifestations.[73] As in Freud, Benjamin, and Adorno, we find a concept of critique that refers not only to an analysis of concepts (including their scope, content, and limits), but also to a "release" of their underlying truth or original meaning. Arguably, we are dealing here, once again, with the same notion of critique: the act of rediscovering a certain surreptitious truth, which has got lost, buried, or suppressed, or has faded away in the existing social and political conditions. Arendt uses a rich range of metaphors to express such an endeavor—from "pearl diving" (which she ascribes to Benjamin) and "treasure" seeking, to the excavating of a deeply submerged reality that lies beyond all of its mere historical appearances. In all these cases, the mission of critique seems to be about recovering, or else saving a tradition that has disappeared with the arrival of modernity.

The lost tradition is the Roman religious one. Arendt's critique is focused, therefore, on one particular theological legacy, and this is not only because the concept of tradition is Roman. There is also the idea that the lost treasures evoked (e.g., freedom, authority, virtue, or power) are those that relate to the bringing together of truth and revelation in philosophy, politics, and myth, originating in a Roman religious experience.

In Arendt's political writings, ideas that have come to lose their constitutive meaning originally endowed by the Roman tripartite theological tradition to which they belong are emancipated, making it possible to rescue them by reengaging these original meanings critically.

Critique and theology are thus intimately interwoven, to the extent that another, rather unique, critique of theology emerges—one that takes the Roman religion into consideration. There are two points to note. First, theology is clearly a type of content that forms the object of critique because the latter focuses on the disappearance of the Roman theological heritage from the modern theater. What Arendt's critique conveys is a rather simple argument: modernity represents the loss of the Roman tripartite tradition that tacitly informed Augustine's theology and reverberated, albeit as a hidden constituent, throughout the history of Christian civilization. Especially with regard to this religious tradition, all that was solid—to paraphrase Marx—melted into air. This focus on the "evaporation" of tradition in modernity was no doubt induced by Arendt's mentors, Karl Jaspers and Martin Heidegger, even if their emphasis was different and to some extent opposing.[74] In Arendt's variation, however, what becomes lost is a sacred moment of foundation and revelation, which was responsible for producing a divine testament that bound people together in the Roman religious sense.[75] In relating to these "traditional concepts," critique means a scrutiny of theology.

The adopted maxim "Our heritage is left to us by no testament," with which Arendt opens her book *Between Past and Future*, exemplifies this point since it refers to a type of modern existence that has severed all ties with any mythic testament from the past. Such a void denotes a crisis of modernity not only because "the whole dimension of the past" is endangered, but more profoundly since the sacred testament that binds people together in the Roman sense has no relevance anymore.[76] What is lost, therefore, is the particular tradition anchored in the myth of a sacred testament.

Yet, critique not only takes Roman theology as an object of study, but also emerges out of this theological tradition. This is the second, albeit more elusive, point to note. Arendt's conceptualization of critique can be traced back to theology because she endows this concept with the task of tradition: the harking back to and thus the revealing of a shared "origin" for society and politics. For her, this marks also Kant's understanding of critique because he evoked it as a source of community.[77] The point to note is that critical undertaking itself is articulated in a way that reformulates the definition of tradition as a return to a shared foundation that brings people together. The task of criticism, which is to distill "anew," and in this sense to save the original "spirit" of a lost Roman theological tradition, also implies that critique puts this tradition into practice (i.e., returns to the "original" formative experience of the past). To wit: while in the Roman tradition divine revelation binds human beings together, in critique it is the revealing of this "lost," theological tradition that presents us with the original shared core. Like tradition, and arguably, by replacing it, critique offers the only viable way to preserve the past under the conditions of its final disappearance. Critique, one may argue, applies the logic of tradition to tradition, perhaps showing what it means for Arendt "to live with creative confusion."[78]

In chapter 3 we saw how Adorno's critique of theology operates a reconceptualization of theological concepts, in which critique rescues theology by overriding it. In Arendt's critique of theology, we encounter a rather analogous argument in which critique replaces tradition in order, however, to liberate, and thus to rescue, its central elements. Critique, to follow this analogy, presents a reconceptualization of traditional concepts in the context of their ultimate evaporation. This is not to say that Arendt was directly influenced by Adorno (or vice versa), but she shows in her postwar writings a parallel susceptibility to the dependency of critique on theology, even if differently articulated and differently thought out. Here, again, the mechanism of critique has theological origins. What critique then presents through its scrutiny (designed to rediscover a lost truth) is the traditional concept of revelation. It does so, however, by replacing the theological image of a revealed divine presence in the world with a focus on revealing a tradition in which such a presence is central. The next section will show how such a reconceptualization of theology illuminates Arendt's particular understanding of secularization. Here I simply wish to highlight the manner in which a theological tradition is not only an object of critique but also provides the basis for its argumentation. By redeploying traditional concepts, Arendt's critique of theology exposes the ways in which critique is immanently dependent on the Roman religious tradition it discusses, disclosing it, to paraphrase Arendt, as "the ground on which we stand and the sky that stretches above us."[79]

Such an interpretation of critique is relevant, for example, to an understanding of Arendt's celebrated concept of "gap." Central to her book *Between Past and Future*, the "gap between past and future" serves as a leitmotif of the crisis of modernity. The temporal fissure denotes a crisis because human beings find themselves in a certain "here" (*Da*) in which time is "broken in the middle."[80] As a consequence, modernity is mainly characterized by an inability to offer a valuable connection to our common heritage and, consequently, to solidify a shared desired future. The point to note, however, is that this evocative image of a "break" marks a clear reformulation of a theological concept advocated by Augustine. Arendt makes reference to Augustine most notably in her additional notes to the English translation of her dissertation, composed in the 1960s.[81] Augustine (who follows Plotinus), according to Arendt, articulates a gap as a "now," representing "what measures time backwards and forwards, because the Now, strictly speaking, is not time but outside time."[82] In being "outside time" the Augustinian gap stands for a rupture in time; a certain space, as it were, in between the two temporalities (past and future). What stands "outside time" is the transcendent, divine, eternal-present temporality. Thus, in Augustine's terms, a gap signifies not only a rupture in time but also, concurrently, the "present" divine revealed truth that complements and thus guarantees the temporal flow.[83] Arendt concludes that, for Augustine, "there are three times; a present time about things past, a present time about things present, a present time about things future."[84] Standing "outside" time is the divine presence underlying the fabric of temporality.

In symbolizing the crisis of modernity, the theological concept of a "gap" still represents a rupture in time for Arendt. There is also a certain "now" that denotes a space of temporal arrest of happening (in the words of Walter Benjamin). Arendt leans, then, on the image of a gap as standing "outside" time, and she is concerned with tracing the religious heritage that originally provided this image with meaning and yet disappeared. Since this gap demonstrates, in her view, the crisis that characterizes modernity, her critique of modernity is openly dependent here on previous theological argumentation. But such a dependency also means that Arendt rearticulates rather than merely restates Augustine's theology. For Augustine, a gap means both a rupture in time and, coevally, the divine guarantee of its resolution. For Arendt, however, a gap means a breach, with no divine guarantee to fall back on. Especially because of the evaporation of the Roman-Augustinian tradition, the Augustinian trust in the eternal present that guarantees temporal coherence is lost. Confined to these modern circumstances, critique depends on human action alone in which "his [the human] standpoint is not the present as we usually understand it but rather a gap in time which 'his' constant fighting, 'his' making stand against past and future, keeps in existence."[85]

There is, no doubt, a new basis in human action, rather than in divine assurance, but Arendt's turn away from God toward the human being does not mean the exorcising of a theological imagination, but rather its rearticulating. It is evident that Arendt's critique of theology distances itself from Augustine's trust in a divine presence, guaranteeing the temporal continuum. Such a distancing from theology, however, rearticulates and in this sense maintains the theological vocabulary in which a divine guarantee is central and on which her critique is based. The shift from the divine domain to the human condition marks a reconceptualization of traditional concepts and those are the theological mechanisms that empower critique's distancing from theology. In such a convoluted way, the critique of a modern world in crisis puts theology into practice by replacing it, and offering, arguably, a rearticulation of a religious heritage in the aftermath of its disappearance.

Arendt's examination of Walter Benjamin's philosophy brings to mind another consideration. Like Theodor Adorno and Gershom Scholem, Arendt presents, particularly in her *Men in Dark Times*, a version of Benjamin's early enthusiasm for theology that she distinctively associates with his "traditionalism."[86] Here especially Arendt wishes to uncover the "theological background" of Benjamin's early critique of modernity and in particular the manner in which his social criticism saves a theological tradition by replacing it.[87] In this context, "traditionalism" means that for Benjamin, critique aims at analyzing "the break in tradition which took place at the beginning of this century" with the aim, however, to rescue the theological tradition under the conditions of its final withdrawal.[88]

This was especially evident in Benjamin's work with quotation, representing for Arendt his main method of critical investigation. Signifying "a new way of dealing with the past," quotations bring traditional theological concepts to the fore in two main ways. First, they reiterate theological vocabulary by citing it. Second, and more importantly, they reveal the deep theological significance of texts that was rendered unavailable to us once the tradition that carried this significance had dissolved.[89] Thus, in quotations we encounter not "an unveiling which destroys the secret, but the revelation which does it justice."[90] The "secret" revealed is an eternal primal-phenomenon (*Urphänomene*) that Benjamin articulates theologically and associates with the eternal and transcendent God.[91] For this reason, Arendt concludes that, for Benjamin, "to quote is to name." Therefore: "Naming through quoting became for him the only possible and appropriate way of dealing with the past without the aid of tradition."[92]

Since, for Benjamin, "to name" means to take part in the "word of God" (as he articulated it in his early theory of language), quotations recover a "sign of origin," the "name," or God.[93] "As to their weight in Benjamin's writing," Arendt then argues, "quotations are comparable only to the very dissimilar biblical citations which so often replace the immanent consistency of argumentation in medieval treatises."[94]

As the traditional transmission of the sacred substance is not available anymore, quotations remain for Benjamin the only possible way to reach out to the original divine content. Critique, to stay with Arendt's argument, replaces tradition because the "modern function of quotation" simply replaces "the transmissibility of the past" (and this mainly includes the communication of the divine "secret") by "its citability."[95] In "citability" we therefore find a critique that adopts the role of theology (and thus saves it) by replacing it.

Arguably, the type of critique of theology that Arendt ascribes to Benjamin seems to resonate rather well with the intimate connection of critique to theology in Arendt's political writings. In both cases, we are dealing with a critique that replaces tradition. In substituting tradition, nonetheless, critique does not aim at refuting it. On the contrary, its objective is to reveal the lost original (mythic) truth that tradition can no longer transmit, because of its disappearance. Critique, then, evokes the religious tradition that it dismisses, a point that is as relevant to Arendt's theory as it is relevant to her discussion of Benjamin.

As in Adorno's postwar writings, and in parallel to them, Arendt's political writings propound a critique of theology that relates to a theological tradition against the impossibility of doing so. In both cases, the mechanism that powers critique's distancing from theology is of theological origin. If anything, the postwar context left both scholars with an acute need to reengage, even if differently, with the so-called "critical theological predicament," involving the analysis as much as the reconstruction of the relation of critique to theology—even if they present a "fidelity" to different, and to some extent contesting, theological traditions.

Philosophy, Myth, and Politics

I would like, at this point, to look more closely, however briefly, at how Arendt's critique of theology presents three main loci of modern "crisis"—philosophy, myth, and politics. This is of particular importance to a further understanding of her reconceptualization of traditional concepts.

Roman tripartite theology was based on these three concepts of divine presence in the world, and Arendt seems to bring this type of thinking to bear on what could be seen as her own tripartite critique of modernity.

Especially for the Romans, philosophy stood for a natural theology. The quest to understand the essence of nature, or else the truth of being, was the objective of philosophical inquiry, which assumed "that truth is what reveals itself, that truth *is* revelation."[96] Revelation requires a phenomenological trust "that things appear as they really are."[97] For the Romans, philosophy associates this fundament of nature with an idea of God, and the revelation of truth with the disclosure of the divine. For Arendt "the meanings of this revelation" are not the same in philosophy and in Christian theology. There is, for example, a difference between the Greek concept of truth, *Aletheia* (ἀλήθεια), which the Romans adopted, and the eschatological expectations that characterize divine revelation in Christianity. The former (philosophy, or natural theology) relates to a discovery of the essence of the world as the essence of the gods, and the latter (Christianity) to a disclosure of the divine ruler of the world. Nonetheless, both types of truth concern a divine (immanent or transcendent) domain and are in this sense theological. As such, they converge in the Roman-Augustinian tradition and continued to underlie all philosophical endeavors for centuries.[98]

In modernity, however, this type of theology came to lose its sway. According to Arendt, Marx in particular "buried" the "revealed truth" that was central to the philosophical tradition.[99] His dictum that "labor and not God created man" implied that Plato's ideas had "lost their autonomous power to illuminate the world and the universe."[100] When Marx declared that human existence, which he called "society," conditions truth through the emergence of "socialized men" he broke ties with this philosophical legacy, which led to the evaporation of natural theology.[101]

A crisis of modernity includes, then, this retreat from theology. Arendt's critique, on the other hand, aims at revealing the philosophical-theological tradition that was lost in the modern age. One may speak here of an attempt to redeploy theological concepts. However, for Arendt, this reengaging with tradition does not mean restoring the same trust in a revealed truth that forms the content of that tradition. Rather, it presents a critique that evokes a philosophical tradition in which this theological concept of revelation is central.

Arendt makes a rather similar argument in relation to a mythic theology, which represents a second theological aspect of the lost Roman tradition. Framed by Augustine as a theology of things divine, a Roman mythic theology stood higher up (i.e., "what is above us"), rather than lower down, in his hierarchy of love, informing the idea of transcendent love. We have seen above how divine love, perhaps the most central aspect of the Christian faith, stems from mythic Roman origins. This is also true for Arendt of the Christian "fear of hell," relating to an avenging God. Here, Christianity can be seen to have adopted a Roman theological take on Plato's myth of the immortality of the soul, albeit by introducing an element of violence that "diluted" the original Roman mythological theology.[102] Thus, while the Romans viewed immortality as "the standard according to which cities may be founded and rules of behavior laid down for the multitude," Christianity used it to convey the image of eternal punishment, inflicted on the unbeliever by an avenging, transcendent God, and this became a new standard "for rules of behavior" in society.[103]

Modernity broke all ties with such a myth, including a retreat from its Roman sources.[104] This constitutes, therefore, the second aspect of the crisis of modernity. In particular, the myth of "future states," central to the Christian take on Roman theological myths, disintegrates as a central adhesive force of society. With no heritage concerning "rules of behavior," social "standards," and God-given sanctions to lean on, a theology of things divine disappeared from the modern theater altogether. Arendt's critique, on the other hand, aims at reengaging with this lost tradition. This is not to argue that a critique of modernity expresses a hope to return to such myths. Rather, it aims at rediscovering the type of theology to which these myths were indebted, as a source for bringing people together—a critique that saves lost theological concepts by conceptualizing them anew. As in the case of her examination of natural theology, Arendt is not suggesting a return to the theological content of tradition, but rather offers a critical examination that redeploys its logic.

Notwithstanding the importance of these two aspects of modern "crisis," the withdrawal of Roman political theology (the third locus of a lost tradition) represents a key point of discussion. She strongly identifies the world in which human beings live with the "political world," while conversely linking "wordlessness" with being "apolitical."[105] The concept of the "political" indicates somewhat loosely a "togetherness of men in speech and in action" as she repeatedly put it.[106] In this particular sense, the political world that we share is equivalent to the world in which we live. All our thoughts, behaviors, actions, and interactions are conditioned by political "togetherness" and for Arendt this also includes human thinking—perhaps the most personal, intimate, and individualistic feature of the Western tradition ("inherent in the philosophical experience" from Athens to modernity)—which she compartmentalizes within the arena of human politics.[107]

The importance of theology to this conception of politics is fundamental. Here again we may speak of a reconceptualization of theological concepts because Arendt's definition of the political sphere of action simply harks back to Roman political theology in which the "immediate revealed presence of the gods" is central.[108] These are the Romans whom Arendt already defines in *The Human Condition* as the "most political" people, for whom living signified being among human beings (*inter homines esse*).[109] Furthermore, it was the Roman religious (and for Arendt republican) experience of divine revelation that made "the world" in which we live and the "political world" that joins people together interchangeable.

In such a way, the concept of the political is redolent of theology, an argument that may also be extended to include Arendt's reflection on Heidegger's notion of *Miteinandersein*. As Emmanuel Levinas noted, the preposition "*mit*" (with) describes the social relation of being "side by side, around something, around a common term and more precisely, for Heidegger, around truth."[110] When Arendt points out that the notion of "with" reverberates with its original Roman-Augustinian sources, however, she seems to suggest that this terminology has Roman origins. Particularly in the case of Augustine's theology, the Roman association between truth and revelation entails the capacity to secure human communality with the gods' willing approval.

We saw at the beginning of this chapter how the political concepts of foundation and authority are integrated into Arendt's definition of tradition, relating explicitly to a "sacred founding" moment in the past, and to its augmentation by virtue of the "authority" of the ancestors who have witnessed it. Thus, as a Roman political theological concept, foundation denotes "the initial getting together" of humans and implies "an authentic and undisputable experience common to all" in the Roman religious sense.[111] Arendt somewhat echoes Jaspers's concept of an "origin" as a unique beginning of things when she points to a "unique event" that cannot be repeated in history; one that goes back to a mythic past (i.e., the foundation of the city) as the source of "its own" legitimacy, conditioning all later historical events.[112] The "absolute new beginning" of foundation thus has divine origins.[113] "The binding power of the foundation itself," argues Arendt, "was religious, for the city also offered the gods of the people a permanent home."¹¹⁴ These were the gods who "gave Romulus the authority to found the city," and so: "All authority derives from this foundation, binding every act back to the sacred beginning of Roman history, adding, as it were, to every single moment the whole weight of the past."¹¹⁵ Stemming from foundation, authority denotes a divine approval "of decisions made by human beings" and represents in such a way "the source of its nature" ("die Herkunft seines Wesens"), as Heidegger put it. For Arendt, this source refers to "a god who, as long as he dwells among men, as long as he inspires their deeds, saves everything."¹¹⁶ Like foundation, then, authority is a Roman political concept since "neither the Greek language nor the varied political experiences of Greek history shows any knowledge of authority and the kind of rule it implies."¹¹⁷ This political concept (denoting a hierarchical "pyramid" of power, running "top to bottom" and making it "the least egalitarian of all forms") is dependent on theology because of the particular Roman take on the earlier Greek experience, and thus: "That the source of their authority, which legitimates the exercise of power, must be beyond the sphere of power and, like the law of nature or the commands of God, must not be man-made goes back to this applicability of the ideas in Plato's political philosophy."¹¹⁸ When Arendt speaks of "the source of authority" that is "always a force external and superior to its own power," she means an "external force which transcends the political realm" and from which "the authorities derive their 'authority.'"¹¹⁹ Transcendence, however, implies the godly sphere in the Roman sense; a type of transcendence that dwells in the world, among people, rather than one that is external to it.¹²⁰ Authority therefore represents divine approval as interpreted through the Romans' immanent theology: "The binding force of this authority is closely connected with the religiously binding force of the *auspices*, which, unlike the Greek oracle, does not hint at the objective course of future events but reveals merely divine approval or disapproval of decisions made by men."¹²¹ Foundation and authority do not fall back on the notion of an unknown god. They are based, nonetheless, on divine revelation as a sign of patronage and guidance from a familiar divinity, making truth, revelation, and authority interchangeable.¹²²

The disappearance of authority, in particular, underlies the modern condition in which "practically as well as theoretically, we are no longer in a position to know what authority really *is*."¹²³ Here Arendt arguably takes her thesis of modern crisis to its extreme: Roman political theological concepts cannot be substituted, or replaced, by later political categories, nor can they be reduced to earlier Greek ones. Representing the theological origins of politics, these concepts have "vanished" completely from the modern world.[124]

Foundation and authority, therefore, represent key elements of the lost tradition. At the same time, however, they also stand for vital features of Arendt's political theory. Reworking these theological categories for modern needs, in Arendt's view, means not only highlighting their disappearance from the modern theater but also pointing to their possible areas of recovery. In this sense, Arendt's critique (i.e., the distilling of traditional concepts) does not merely underline the political sphere lost to modernity; it also indicates its possible retrieval. Consider, for example, her reliance on the Roman concept of foundation. Concluding her *The Burden of Our Time* (later to become *The Origins of Totalitarianism*) with the somewhat dramatic call to create "a new foundation for human community," Arendt seems to make the association between the concept of foundation and a modern recovery of "the political" rather clear.[125] In particular, she discusses freedom—"the most important principle of all political life"—in terms of the capacity to "embark" on something altogether new in the Roman sense.[126] Being free does not relate to freedom of choice, or to the absence of external restrictions. For Arendt, it means an "absolute new beginning" in the sense of a new foundation, and this is especially relevant for her when reflecting on the postwar political context.[127]

This is also true of "natality" (or birth), one of the more celebrated concepts that Arendt introduced to political thought.[128] With "natality" Arendt, no doubt, turns against the Heideggerian idea that it is "death" that "works with us in the world" and "humanizes" us.[129] She does so, however, by leaning on the Roman idea of foundation, since for Arendt "natality," like freedom, signifies the political capability to start something altogether new. In such a way, Arendt links Roman theology to the religious maxim "A child is born," underlining that the human capacity to deliver to the world something completely new "always appears in the guise of a miracle."[130] In all these cases (foundation, freedom, and natality) there is a reworking of political theological vocabulary since Arendt bases her modern political theory on traditional Roman concepts, demonstrating the extent to which criticism reformulates a tradition, declared lost, with regard to contemporary needs.

While the association of foundation, freedom, and natality demonstrates the dependency of Arendt's political theory on Roman theology, her critique of violence points to one of its vital implications. Arendt presents violence (mainly, though not exclusively, in her book *On Violence*) as an instrumental coercion, the use of an external force as a means to an end. Distinguishable from the use of power, violence, she says, should be excluded from the modern political sphere.[131] Yet to make her case, Arendt builds her analysis on Roman political categories. These categories present an area of power and authority that is dissociated from the deployment of violent force. Indeed in Arendt's analysis violence and authority are at odds and authority "precludes the use of external means of coercion; where force is used, authority itself has failed."[132] The power of authority, originally embodied by the Senate in the Roman experience, also differs from an open process of argumentation and persuasion.[133] More importantly, however, it renders violence unnecessary. In the modern context it resembles, one may argue, a constitutional principle that is bound by the law and that needs "neither the form of command nor external coercion to make itself heard."[134] What is more, it is grounded in divine, loving approval that is translated into advice or recommendations that simply cannot be ignored.

In chapter 2, we saw how Benjamin's "Critique of Violence" strongly separates divine potency from the political arena. For him, the only type of violence that can be considered justified, and thus rendered nonviolent, is one that eschews the political and relates to the divine. In her own critique of violence, Arendt seems to outline a contesting theological schema. Like Benjamin, she argues against political violence, but she does so, nonetheless, by offering a political category of authority (as the Romans understood it) that is inherently free of violence. We are dealing with a divine nonviolence that dwells within the political sphere—not separated from it. Agamben's "On the Limits of Violence" may be helpful here, too, because it points to the theological aspect of Arendt's political categories. Because of its nonviolent character, the authority at stake, according to Agamben, relates to divine and "sacred" power (which he associates with the demand for the human being's self-negation). This power therefore represents the "messianic halt" that is "capable of opening a new chronology (a *novus ordo saeclorum*) and a new experience of temporality—a new History."[135] The area of nonviolence that Arendt evokes for modern needs harks back to the reliance on a divine presence in the world, endowing the political with its own authority.

To exclude violence from the modern political sphere is, therefore, to respect Roman theological argumentation. However, as in the case of foundation, natality, and freedom, this does not mean that critique aims to reinstate a dependency on divine presence, which is no longer available. Rather, in the modern context, criticism reveals a Roman religious tradition in which divine authorization is central, thus reconceptualizing the concept of revelation within the framework of its final disappearance.

CRITICAL AND POLITICAL THEOLOGY

There seems to be wide agreement among scholars that Arendt formulates her political theory in opposition to Carl Schmitt's political theology.[136] Anna Jurkevics's study, for example, shows how Arendt's braiding of the political sphere with the "intimate connection or relationship" between human beings (the so-called "togetherness of men") starkly contrasted not only with Schmitt's early grounding of politics in the friend–foe dichotomy but also with his later notion of an earthbound nomos (central to his *Theory of the Partisan*).[137] This opposition seems to be made clear through Arendt's emphasis on a political arena that is not defined by the "decision" of the sovereign but rather by the agreement—"in speech and in action"—of the people.

The departure from Schmitt, however, does not mean that the political arena as a shared (republican) public interest is not informed by theology. This point seems to be significant in the light of contemporary scholarly efforts to dismiss the importance of "the political theological predicament" for Arendt's political theory.[138] For Arendt, whose political theory, as we have seen, can be traced back to its Roman sources, political categories are based on previous theological ones. Nonetheless, it is true that Arendt suggests a different type of theological underpinning for politics than Schmitt. For Schmitt, the divine source of authority is external to the political arena and endows the unwavering "decision" of the sovereign with its legitimacy. For Arendt, it dwells within such an arena, and is revealed only by the "togetherness" of human beings in discussion.[139] In tradition, divine approval is revealed as advice rather than as a dictate from above. Even the concept of authority, which requires a "transcendent source" for its legitimation, points to divine revelation in a Roman sense. If Schmitt's concept of the political is dependent on a transcendent, commanding God, Arendt's comparable concept is built on an alternative theological imaginary centered on the intimacy of divine visitation in the world.

One may argue, then, that Arendt's retort to Schmitt does not dismiss but rather revises political theology. One of the points that were made in the previous chapter in relation to Adorno was that his clear response to

Schmitt's theory did not lose sight of the theological origins of our political categories. Arendt, it appears, makes a similar effort. In Arendt's critique of politics there is still a promise relating to a moment of creation and salvation. The moment at stake, however, harks back to the Roman religious imagination. This is not to deny that Arendt displays opposition to the theology of "absolute truth" and divine "transcendence" (at least in its Schmittian variation), as Peter Gordon, for example, argues.[140] Such opposition, nonetheless, does not imply that she distances herself from political theology. On the contrary, it demonstrates her unique contribution to it.

To exemplify this point, we may consider how modern revolutions are intertwined with the state of emergency in Arendt's thinking. Central to Schmitt's theory, the ability to declare a state of emergency defines the sovereign. The "exception," which is reserved for emergencies, "is analogous to the miracle in theology" and it is the capacity to perform such a miracle that classifies sovereignty.[141] Arendt then integrates this close association between theology and political emergency into her discussion of modern revolutions. Thus, in focusing mainly on the French and (for her) American revolutions, Arendt argues that revolutions embody "the only salvation which this Roman-Western tradition has provided for emergencies."[142]

With their grounding in Roman political theology, revolutions are modern phenomena that epitomize not a "break with tradition" but rather traditionalism in disguise.[143] They are "events in which the actions of men are still inspired by and derive their greatest strength from the origins of this tradition."[144] The American Constitution, for example, stands for "a sacred document" and a "constant remembrance of one sacred act, and that is the act of foundation."[145] It echoes the search for a God-given authority, which means "to be tied back, obligated to the enormous, almost superhuman and hence always legendary effort to lay the foundations, to build the cornerstone, to found for eternity."[146] This reliance on Roman political theology, where founding a community "for eternity" is central, is also true of Machiavelli, whom Arendt (like Leo Strauss) regards as "the spiritual father of revolution," and "the sworn enemy" of religious considerations in political affairs.[147] In wishing to "repeat the Roman experience through the foundation of a unified Italy," the nemesis of religion nevertheless made a "passionate effort to revive the spirit and the institutions of Roman antiquity."[148] On this basis, Machiavelli articulates authority in terms of "a God-given authority."[149]

This means, however, that unlike the terms of Schmitt's definition, the "miracle" of revolutions does not relate to the absolute power to proclaim the exception, but rather to the freedom from such absolute power, inherent in the new beginning and reserved for the political sphere that brings people together. It is, then, for this reason that "the greatest event in every revolution is the act of foundation."[150] Such opposition to Schmitt, one may then conclude, does not dismiss the theological sources of political phenomena; the opposition is to his particular version of such a connection.

Thus, it is true, as Margaret Canovan has argued, that Arendt's notion of revolution depicted a "classical republican tradition" with which she could identify.[151] Arendt, however, is especially attentive to the theological roots of this tradition and consequently to the presence of theology in the recovery of a modern political experience. In the same vein, Samuel Moyn's suggestion that Arendt saw in the American Revolution an experiment aimed at discovering a "secular proxy for religion" may also be correct, to the extent that the Roman theological grounds for such a "secular" experiment are taken into consideration (the next section of this chapter discusses Arendt's concept of the secular more closely).[152]

To think of Arendt's political theology, it seems, is also to acknowledge the particular characteristics of her own "traditionalism." Modern revolutions serve as an example of Arendt's debt to tradition because she presents them as conservative and restorative, rather than progressive phenomena. The word "revolution," argues Arendt, originally meant "restoration," and in this sense, the "new spirit" of a revolution is intended to imply the recovery of "old rights and liberties." From its naissance, then, a revolution aspires to recreate a mythic past and hold onto what Gershom Scholem called "hope that mainly turns backwards," embodying "freedom by God's blessing restored."[153]

Nonetheless, it is also important to point out that the term "radical conservative," which is associated with Arendt, may be somewhat misleading in this context.[154] Arendt sees all modern revolutions as restorative because they are traditional (republican, egalitarian, or denoting a free "togetherness" of human beings) and not because they support conservative values (in particular those referring to social stability, political order, control, or any belief in an organic society). Arguably, what is illuminated here is a difference between conservatism and Arendt's traditionalism. The first stresses a loyalty to a specific set of values, and social and political

Novus ordo seclorum

THE DIALECTICS OF SECULARIZATION

Arendt's critique of theology both reconceptualizes and secularizes theology. Secularization appears in Arendt's interpretation, it seems, in two main ways. First, it refers to the decline of a Christianity that characterizes modernity. "The decline of Christian civilization," Arendt writes to Eric Voegelin, "is, as it were, the framework within which the whole of modern history is played out, and that means for me, speaking as one who is not a Christian, both good and evil."[155] The weakness of religion also includes the disappearance of the "hidden" Roman tradition that Christianity absorbed. But secularization also refers, somewhat antithetically, to the critical distilling, and in this particular sense the rescuing, of the "hidden" Roman tradition that disappeared from the modern theater. We have seen above the diverse ways in which such a mechanism is central to Arendt's conceptualization of her critique of modernity. Alongside the "decline" of theology, secularization also means, conversely, a redeploying of traditional theological concepts.

The point that seems to me worth noting is that the combination of these two rather opposing elements—the decline of Christianity and a reengagement with Roman theology—constitutes for Arendt the characteristics of a *novus ordo seclorum*, which she translates as "a new order of the world" ("Die neu Ordnung der Welt").[156] This new order is secular because it is confined to the human world. The focus on "this world," however, is still redolent of theology (a point that Agamben, for example, illustrated rather well) because it is dependent on a particular theological tradition central to which is the presence of God within the world. Because of such a reliance on theology, one may argue, secularization, to paraphrase Bruno Latour, has never been fully secular.[157] It does not exorcise the shadows of theology but outlines them in a new way.

The concomitant withdrawal and resumption of theology may be termed "dialectic of secularization."[158] Evoked, for example, by Christoph Schmidt, such a "dialectic" points to the admixture of rejection and avowal of theology, in which the former is conditioned by the latter. The idea seems to be fitting here, to the extent that for Arendt, as well, even though "traditional religious beliefs" cannot be simply accepted anymore, they are, for this very reason, never fully excluded.[159]

Modern revolutions, discussed above, exemplify rather well the centrality of this "dialectic" in Arendt's critique. We are returning here to the meaning of revolutions as a "secular proxy for religion." Above I argued that this definition of revolution should take into consideration the Roman theological sources of the "revolutionary energy of the new."[160] On the one hand, revolutions present a secular turn away from divine salvation toward human action, and on the other hand they anchor this movement in a Roman religious basis. This means that the notion of a "new" and secular beginning that distances itself from theology is at the same time grounded in a theological imagination. A "secular" political phenomenon dismisses one type of theology while being rooted, nonetheless, in another.

It is in this spirit that Arendt discusses the failure of revolutions to recover a lost theological heritage.[161] She locates the problem not in the revolutionary tendency to connect politics and theology, but rather in the erroneous correlation between a "new" secular beginning (in the Roman religious sense) and the approval of an "immortal legislator" (issued from Christianity) who can validate "man-made law."[162] Arendt's argument seems to focus on the intertwining of two different theological orientations rather than on the dismissal of theological impulses for revolution. Machiavelli's authority, for example, "had to be designed in such a way that it would fit and step into the shoes of the old absolute that derived from a God-given authority, thus superseding an earthly order whose ultimate sanction had been the commands of an omnipotent God and whose final source of legitimacy had been the notion of an incarnation of God on earth."[163] The father of modern revolutions mistakenly associated the Roman religious grounds of authority with the Christian theological imagination (relating to an "omnipotent God") he set out to dismiss. The same difficulty is visible in the French and American revolutions, which had "to plead for some religious sanction" coming from the divine absolute.[164]

What Arendt accentuates is a rather false association between two theological traditions. Her approach to secularization, then, does not communicate a critique of its reliance on theological argumentation. Arendt points out instead the ways in which secularization translates original theological categories, and what she opposes in this context is simply the mixing of theological Roman sources with their later Christian distortions.

154 | Critiques of Theology

Parallels with Adorno's concept of the secular can be observed here because for him, as well, the "secularization" of theology that critique represents requires a translation of former theological concepts. What I termed "holding onto an unholdable object" characterized his secular endeavor because the problem that Adorno wishes to address in the postwar context is the possibility of recovering metaphysical inquiry under the conditions of its final disappearance. Can we not argue that such a line of argumentation may be applied to Arendt's engagement with tradition, as well? In Arendt's case, "secularization" also encompasses the recapturing of a theological tradition that cannot be revived. In this sense, her critique demonstrates the same problem of holding onto the unholdable object of tradition.

This last point, however, may also demonstrate the main contrast between Arendt's theological considerations and the type of mysticism that dominated Benjamin's and Adorno's thinking. Central to both thinkers is a radical, out-of-this-world, transcendent Being that cannot be grasped. For example, in Benjamin's secularization of mystical allegories we find a radical transcendent God that could only be represented by a *nihil*. Benjamin's concept of "awakening" (*erwachen*) redeploys a mystical notion of "birth," denoting a radical or absolute transcendence (described in terms of a "naked truth" or "heart of God") that is located beyond any possible image or articulation.[165] A somewhat similar theological rationale could be identified in Adorno's association between education, critique, and negativity in which the only feasible way to hold onto an "absolute" divine object is to not hold onto it—forbidding that thought "in order not to betray that thought" as Adorno puts it.

In Arendt's critique of theology, we find the somewhat opposite notion of divine presence in this world. Here, the mystical "birth" is replaced by the concept of "natality" anchored in a "holy" beginning in the Roman sense.[166] This is not to argue that Arendt dismisses the mystical moment of revelation, central to Benjamin's and Adorno's understanding of society and politics. She secures such a moment, however, in the contingent presence of divine assurance in the world and not in its absolute nonappearance.

This secular reworking of Roman theology may explain why Arendt, in a reference to Kafka's story "He" ("Er"), accentuates the incapability of human beings to elevate themselves to the degree of an observer or a judge outside of, and beyond, the worldly reality in which they exist.[167] While showing a strong similarity to Freud's engagement with the law (though not with the same intentions in mind), Arendt makes no reference to any pure or radical transcendent arena, which means that there is no "outside" of the world that endows the world with a meaning. In the same vein, Arendt portrays philosophical luminaries like Kant and Lessing as committed to the human reality of this world, and to the constant "self-formation" (*Bildung*) of the human being by the human's own hands.[168] For them, "illuminating" the world meant a "commitment" to a "real relationship to the world."[169]

But if Arendt's critique demonstrates such a secular, dialectic reliance on Roman theology, what could be said about her view of the prevailing thesis in the 1950s and 1960s that "the modern historical consciousness has a Christian religious origin and came into being through a secularization of originally theological categories"?[170] As presented in the previous chapter, this thesis was advocated most notably by Karl Loewith, and it related to modernity as a "secularization of the Christian eschaton." This argument dominated Loewith's book *Meaning in History*, published in 1949.[171] Presenting a genealogical description (starting with modern categories and tracing back their origins to earlier theological ideas), the book mainly accentuates the roots of modernity in the "theory of the three ages" of the twelfth-century Italian monk Joachim of Fiora, and its adaptation of earlier Christian and biblical conceptions of time and deliverance. All our modern categories of history, politics, and progress (presented, for example, in Hegel's idea of the advent of reason) represent, accordingly, later expansions of Christian notions of God's kingdom, redemption, and the end of time. We are dealing here, then, with what could be termed "acute Christianization" of modernity—an argument in which a modern secular world corresponds to a secularized Christian civilization. Christianity in this view provides the standard model for understanding modern culture, society, and politics.

Arendt, like Adorno, hardly refutes Loewith's argument regarding secularization as translation of theological categories. Nonetheless, Roman theology, and not Christianity, is central to her understanding of these categories, showing the extent to which she could be labeled a "post-Christian" thinker.[172] As in the case of her revising (rather than dismissing) political theology, she presents a unique, perhaps consciously rebellious, way into a prevalent intellectual approach. Secularization still signifies, for her, a transformation of Christian symbolism, but only, and more importantly, as a vehicle for carrying a Roman religious experience into modernity. In moving away from the "Christianization" of modernity that Loewith suggested, Arendt's critique of modernity points to the dialectic of loss and revival of those aspects of the Roman tradition that provided the Christian concepts of redemption, divinity, and love with a basis.

The Problem of Evil

I wish to conclude this discussion of Arendt's critique of theology with a note on her concept of evil, and specifically its relation to her secularization of theology. Evil is important to the discussion because it is central to Arendt's postwar thought. In 1945, profoundly shaken, no doubt, by the horrors of Nazism, Arendt declared that "the problem of evil will be the fundamental question of postwar intellectual life in Europe."[173] As such a vital issue, this "problem" underlay much of Arendt's investigation over the next decades—from her examination of totalitarianism, Nazism, and anti-Semitism in the 1950s to her political writings in the 1960s. Yet over the course of these two decades, Arendt's treatment of evil was also dominated by a clear shift from a definition of evil as "radical" or "absolute" (exemplified most notably in her book on totalitarianism) to her later claim that evil is "banal" (culminating in her *Eichmann in Jerusalem: A Report on the Banality of Evil*).[174] Indeed, "banality of evil" is probably the most well-known expression associated with Arendt, representing for many "a kind of icon in the discourse surrounding Auschwitz and related crimes."[175] The point that seems to me to deserve attention, however, is that this shift also represented for Arendt a clear answer to the question "How can we approach the problem of evil in an entirely secular setting?"[176] A banalization of evil marks, it seems, not only a response to secularization but also a secular approach to "the problem of evil," and it is this secular approach that I wish to associate with her critique of theology.

We may start by noting how Arendt's early definition of evil involves theological considerations, mainly developed from Kant's terminology of "radical evil." Kant presents a type of evil that serves as a ground, and in this sense a transcendental condition, for any deviation (*Abweichung*) from the moral law.[177] For Kant, "radical" evil denotes such a condition because it cannot be reduced to or explained by the transgressive acts or moral deviations that are dependent on it. In her *The Burden of Our Time* Arendt rather loosely expands on such an understanding of evil, a point that Seyla Benhabib articulated rather well.[178] She speaks of such "grounds" in terms of an "unpunishable, unforgivable, absolute evil which could no longer be understood and explained by the evil motives of self-interest, greed, covetousness, resentment, lust for power, and cowardice."[179] Embodying an absolute malevolence that lies beyond punishment, which is unforgiven, and which cannot be grasped by human reason, "absolute evil" is also "radical" in that it transcends not only human "evil motives" but also human explanation, or else the possibility to explain such evil from a human standpoint. Absolute evil "transcends the realm of human affairs and the potentialities of human power," both of which it destroys whenever it appears.[180] Absolute evil, to follow Arendt, resembles potency—an active power—that transcends this-worldliness.

Kant's transcendental condition is in such a way transformed by Arendt into a transcendent force in action. In so doing, Arendt seems to propound a theodicy. Coined by Leibniz, theodicy refers to any type of analysis of and response to the problem of evil (including not only a response to the query "Why does evil exist?" but also an answer to the question "What is evil?").[181] It involves for Leibniz theological considerations because it means resolving the embedded tension between the coinciding existence of evil and that of a benevolent God. These considerations constitute an important aspect of religious thought, which needs to reconcile the problem of evil in view of the coexistence of two contradicting elements (evil and God). The question "If God is good, how can evil exist?" is therefore central to any theodicy.

Arendt's theodicy responds to the problem of evil by pitting against each other a fully out-of-this-world transcendent evil and a concrete worldliness. There is, therefore, a stark dualism at work between an absolute evil force and the world in which humans live, not only because the two are completely separate but also since the former transcends the latter. In this manner, the sway of the evil force becomes in Arendt's analysis immeasurable in a way that resembles the power of a demiurge, the traditional gnostic counterpart of the loving benevolent God.

The reference to gnosis seems to be fitting because of its role in the intellectual, historical, and political imagination of many of Arendt's colleagues in the postwar era, briefly presented in the previous chapter. In engaging with unexplainable evil power (beyond anything human) Arendt, it seems, makes a unique contribution to the debates around gnosis and its modern implications. Modernity is not an era of "overcoming" gnosticism, as Blumenberg, for example, argued. At the same time, unlike Voegelin, Arendt does not argue that all modern political phenomena are gnostic. In fact, in totalitarianism she considers political categories to be based on a radical, "demonic" evil, explaining in such a way their vicious practices.[182]

Understanding evil in "secular" terms, undoubtedly, marks a turn against such a dualistic theodicy. For this purpose, and as noted above, especially in her writings from the 1960s, Arendt underlines what was formerly radical and describes it as "banal." Culminating in the famed passage from her *Eichmann in Jerusalem*, banality was thus clearly associated with a turn against the "diabolical or demonic" characteristics of Eichmann's criminality: "He [Eichmann] was not stupid. It was sheer thoughtlessness—something by no means identical with stupidity—that predisposed him to become one of the greatest criminals of that period. And if this is 'banal' and even funny, if with the best will in the world one cannot extract any diabolical or demonic profundity from Eichmann, that is still far from calling it commonplace."[183] Thinking of evil as a type of simple "thoughtlessness" explicitly indicates a retreat from "diabolical or demonic" dimensions. Evil is a human, all too human, deficiency. In being "banal," evil is secular because it does not involve any "radical" or "absolute" characteristic that could be traced back to gnostic dualism.

This notion of secular banality, however, is not Arendt's creation. Indeed, if her radical, transcendent, evil power expands on Kant, her thinking of evil as banal can be traced back to Jaspers. In a letter to Arendt dated August 17, 1946, Jaspers took "a banality of evil" to stand at odds with any "satanic greatness" that could be, for him erroneously, attributed to Nazi perpetrators.[184] "It seems to me," writes Jaspers, that "we have to see these things in their total banality, in their prosaic triviality, because that's what truly characterizes them."[185] Arendt then takes this clearly theologically imbued idea to represent her secular retreat from former references to an absolute "satanic" dimension. Evil is secularized because it relates to human "thoughtlessness" and does not stem from a "radical" transcendent power in action. "The very phrase: 'banality of evil,'" Arendt writes to Mary McCarthy, "stands in contrast to the phrase I used in the totalitarianism book, 'radical evil.'"[186] And in her last interview she makes it evidently clear that "there's nothing deep about it [evil]—nothing demonic!"[187] As always, Jaspers's shrewd articulation makes the theological case rather clear: "Now you have delivered the crucial word against 'radical evil,' and the gnosis!"[188]

Jaspers's theological note refers specifically to Arendt's controversy with Gershom Scholem surrounding the publication of her *Eichmann in Jerusalem*. Arguably, the turn against "the gnosis" that he attributes to Arendt's secularization of evil relates mainly to the centrality of the gnostic apostasy in Scholem's study of Jewish messianism. Scholem himself made a similar observation by underlining the difference between Arendt's analysis and his engagement (lasting "more than forty years") with the "near demonic" aspects of Jewish history.[189] Jaspers seems to locate the root of the controversy in this particular theological disagreement. If evil is banal, so the argument goes, the concept of the "demonic" that Jaspers holds to be important, in particular to Scholem's understanding of Judaism, becomes obsolete. Under such a new "secular setting," a dualism of the gnostic kind is refuted; the interplay between the themes of redemption and fall, hidden divinity and heresy, central not only to Scholem's analysis of Jewish history but also to his engagement with modern Jewish politics, disintegrates.

Nonetheless, Arendt's secularization of evil is still dependent on theology, especially because of her emphasis on this, rather than an "other," world. This point seems to be crucial to understanding Arendt's particular secularization of theodicy. On the one hand, the "secular setting" clearly contests the metaphysical dualism that is inherent in Arendt's retreat from a notion of radical transcendence. On the other hand, it leans on Arendt's critical reengagement with a theological tradition in which a focus on this world is central. It could be argued here that her particular reconceptualization of traditional concepts informs her critique of evil. The "distilling" of such concepts "anew" (i.e., the meaning of criticism) offers the basis for an understanding of evil as banal. The point to note, then, is that Arendt's secular emphasis on a banal evil negates only one particular theological tradition (that of a "radical" or "absolute" transcendent force), while building on another. Given the religious sources of her critique of modernity, Arendt's critique of evil delineates theological considerations; it does not exclude them, as usually argued. In its emphasis on this world, a banal evil, one may argue, is a concept that is no less theological than "radical" or "absolute" evil; it simply relates to a different theological imagination, offering a critique that is theologically informed.

From such a perspective, one may explain why Eichmann's crimes are clearly not lessened by Arendt, as Michal Ben-Naftali noted.[190] It would be wrong to claim that the reference to the banality of Eichmann's crimes is intended to make them more conventional, or acceptable. The actions of "one of the greatest criminals of that period" remain unforgivable in Arendt's view. Situated especially against the backdrop of her discussion of tradition, however, his unprecedented criminality is perceived as an intolerable injury to the sacred fabric that joins people together, and it is on this theological basis that his crimes are indefensible.

The focus on evil, then, may present a unique example for a new secular order in which theology powers the mechanism of turning against theology. In particular, the denial of a transcendent, "demonic" force is informed by immanent religious considerations, showing how the critical distilling of lost "traditional concepts" denotes their modern reconceptualization. Arguably, then, in Arendt's postwar writings we may find another version of "immanentization" whereby "new modes of being" are attributed to transcendence, in a way that was relevant, in various forms, to Freud, Benjamin, and Adorno.[191] Indeed, throughout the twentieth century, a critical attitude—relating to the psychological mechanisms of jokes, the social significance of youth, education, or tradition—was characterized by the concomitant termination and recovery of theology, demonstrating, perhaps, the range of loci in which modern secular thinkers have passionately endorsed the impossible.

Epilogue

The World in Which We Live

The claim that religion has returned to the center stage of society, culture, and politics has dominated academic discussions over the past two decades. Jürgen Habermas, for instance, was one of the first to suggest that such a return of religion heralds a "post-secular" society, which must "adjust itself to the continued existence of religious communities."[1] Charles Taylor concludes his book *A Secular Age* with the claim (and perhaps, for him, the hope) that we are at the beginning of "a new age of religious seeking."[2] In a similar vein, the sociologist Brian Turner points out that instead of a version of Weber's increasingly disenchanted secular world, we are witnessing a "religious turn," which means that "public space has been resecralized insofar that public religions play a major role in political life."[3] Likewise, philosopher Slavoj Žižek argues that we are experiencing the return, "with a vengeance," of theology, a view largely shared by Hent de Vries, who brought to the fore what he conceptualized as the "reenchantment, if not outright remythologization," of the secular modern world.[4]

These scholars and many others who debate the return of religion remain, to a large extent, divided as to the nature of the "new era," its major characteristics, the variety of phenomena associated with it, or its (more or less) dark materials.[5] Is the issue the return of orthodox and institutionalized religions or the emergence of new spiritual paradigms? Is the phenomenon limited to what Habermas calls "affluent societies of Europe or countries such as Canada, Australia and New Zealand," that is, a Western version of secularized Christianity, or is it relevant, even if in different ways, to additional societies, cultures, and religions? To what extent can we speak about the blurring of boundaries between "the secular" and "the religious," or the redrawing of these boundaries? How do theological arguments reshape the political contours of conflicts around the world? These are issues that did not lose their importance during the recent coronavirus pandemic and the Russian invasion of Ukraine.

However, despite their many differences, it appears that these scholars share at least one common image. They all postulate both the narrative of the waning, or perhaps even disappearance, of religion in the framework of secular modern life, and its apparent reemergence in recent decades. To speak about the "return" of religion, to argue that it constitutes a "reenchantment" of a formerly secular and disenchanted world, or to distinguish between secular and "postsecular society"—where the latter ostensibly replaces and succeeds the former—means to assume that there is a contradiction between the secular world and its religious "other." There is the overarching idea that religion somehow lost its place from the modern intellectual, social, and political domains, only to somewhat magically reappear.

The presence of theology in the writings of such major and influential modern thinkers as Freud, Benjamin, Adorno, and Arendt challenges precisely this arc of assumptions and distinctions. These modern thinkers are indubitably secular, perhaps the most secular of their time. Nonetheless, their writings reveal four different composites of the secular modern position containing a vibrant inventory of theological terms. In presenting these combinations, I have not attempted to put forward a normative argument that gives preference to one approach over another or to demonstrate which is better established. I believe that my examination of these thinkers might also contain a certain partiality for the array of complexities, inner tensions, incompatibilities, contradictions, and refractions that characterize their approach with regard to religious traditions—an approach that echoes, perhaps, the implied defiance in the words found in Ecclesiastes: "It is good that thou holdest fast to the one and withdrawest not thine hand from the other" (7:18).

Thus, in these cases, the relation between the "secular" and the "religious" does not point to a contradiction, as one may assume, but rather to what can be called a secular–religious continuum. It is within the framework of such a range that the critical concept relevant to each thinker is expressed. On the one hand, for these thinkers, criticism constitutes the essence of secular heroism. On the other hand, their works, which were explored in this book, point to the broad spectrum of ways in which the analysis of the content, validity, and boundaries of concepts, as well as critical narratives of modernity, touch upon Jewish and Christian traditions, divine law, mysticism, and negative or tripartite theology. To speak of a secular–religious continuum implies a critique that concurrently emerges from theological sources and can in many ways be traced back to them. Moreover, and however paradoxical it may sound, it is the reliance of critique on theology that guarantees the coherence of the secular. Accordingly, these thinkers not only explore religious concepts using the disciplinary tools available to them, but they also visit the world of religious thought in an intimate fashion. For them, critique of theology is therefore a visitation of criticism in theological domains, even if occasionally—to paraphrase Arendt—this happens against their better judgment.[6] Indeed, each one of these thinkers articulates a different conception of critique, relates to a different religious tradition, and expresses the ways in which they intersect differently. Still, in all of these cases, critique does not allow its theological "other" "simply to be reduced, falsified, naturalized, or secularized, once and for all."[7]

One may then cast doubt on the distinction between the aforementioned secular and "postsecular" worlds as much as challenge the division between critique and "postcritique," which has also attained a central status in recent years.[8] There is essentially a reversal of thought here: arguments concerning the disappearance and subsequent return of religion and theology to the secular arena can only be understood within a framework of secular critique where theology occupies a central position. The current focus in research on the place of religion in today's world can be perceived, therefore, not as a reaction to its reappearance, but as proof that theology is inscribed in the very structure of criticism. This is also the case with regard to the crystallization of the "postcritique" approach, which strives, for example, to "blend analysis and attachment, criticism, and love."[9] This endeavor may be indeed anchored in the way in which the "hermeneutics of suspicion," associated with modern criticism, is already entwined with the enabling or rescuing of "non-suspicion."[10]

Even though the scope of the discussion in this book is limited—in terms of the thinkers, historical periods, and texts upon which it focuses—its purpose is somewhat ambitious given that it attempts to reinterpret the compound relationships between the secular modern world and religion. Thus, its aim is to demonstrate that despite these scholars' repeated secular emphasis on critique—in psychoanalysis, social theory, education, and political theory—religious thinking loses neither its place nor its influence. What appears to be particularly prominent is that the modern thinkers' critiques are focused on the world in which we live.

Certainly, this attention is given to what Horkheimer called the realm of immanence, and this emphasizes the secular dimension of their thinking.[11] Still, in all of these cases, secularization does not point, in any simplistic way, to liberation from religious thinking, but rather to the translation or transformation of theological concepts that are constitutive of such thinking, often for the stated purpose of saving them.

For Freud, for instance, the critical role of jokes expresses what Eric Santner described as the "eternal within the earthly," given that Freud secularizes the religious dilemma concerning violation of the law while immersing it in his discussion of the rules, codes, and social norms that shape the psychology of the individual.[12] A similar "theology of worldliness" characterizes critical-theory thinkers.[13] Benjamin's early theory of youth, for example, highlights the "mysticism of this world," that is, the reformulation of theological concepts within the framework of social criticism. In this context, the "nothingness" of a purely transcendent God informs the liberation of mankind from all social and political enslaving circumstances. However, in the final account, Benjamin's interest lies in the way in which mysticism anchors the very prospect of a critique of society. In my opinion, it is important to understand Adorno's perception of education because it continues Benjamin's line of thought into the second half of the twentieth century. Focused on the liberation from enslaving social conditions, the critical self-reflection that Adorno attributes to education constitutes a model for the reconceptualization of theological concepts that he distinguished, for example, from Kierkegaard's withdrawal into pure inwardness. Adorno's "migration into the profane" ("Einwanderung ins Profane") does not offer to relinquish the divine domain ("the nothingness of revelation" as Gershom Scholem called it), but to protect it under the circumstances of its disappearance. This complexity—in the process of relinquishing the substance of theology in order to rescue it—defines the critical dimension of education. With regard to focusing on this world, the critique of theology that emanates from Arendt's political writings is perhaps the most unique because she bases both the concept of criticism and of a new order of the world on the Roman theological tradition. What Arendt objects to is a theological inheritance (centered on a transcendental God and absolute truth) for the purpose, however, of revealing, or returning to, another "hidden" theological tradition. This does not mean Arendt has a special interest in pantheism, and it would be a mistake to assume that she proposes a modern return to paganism. Arendt, I suggest, offers a distinctive version of a theology of this world, in which the "reconceptualization of theological concepts" marks the only way to protect tradition under the circumstances of its complete disappearance.

Arendt's political writings are, perhaps, somewhat atypical. However, it seems to me that something in the traditionalism reflected in her position, despite or perhaps because of its unique texture, projects upon the thinking of Freud, Benjamin, and Adorno to a great extent. Debates on the concept of tradition, on the possibility of distinguishing it from the concept of conservatism, as well as questions about its relevance today perhaps call for a separate task, which exceeds the limits of the present book.[14] Yet, the point here is that the criticism of these thinkers seems to be directed at what Hans-George Gadamer called the "event of tradition" (*Überlieferungsgeschehen*), that is, "a prior condition of understanding" that mediates between the known of knowledge and the unknown that powers it, in which neither remains unaffected.[15] This "event" nurtures these thinkers in their obligation to repair the world as opposed to any detachment from it or its seclusion.

Is the Jewish identity of these thinkers also expressed in their obligation to the world? David Biale has argued that the Jewish tradition centers on the notion that the purpose of theology concerns assuming responsibility for the world.[16] It seems that this kind of argument may also be relevant to the focus these modern thinkers place on social and political issues. It would be accurate to say that for them, Judaism or Jewishness (a term Arendt preferred) "had become hard to parse."[17] Judith Butler's question, "What is finally Jewish about Arendt's thought?," is thus relevant, in different ways, to the other thinkers whose openly expressed attitudes toward Jewish religious practices range from apathy to hostility.[18] Even so, it appears that the difficulty that Butler and others have raised relates to the way in which these thinkers had limited access to the content and practices of traditional Judaism, which was not a major part of their education or way of life and did not shape the formal knowledge they acquired (Freud, in this sense, is perhaps an exception). On the other hand, for them, their Jewish identity, which none of them denied, was not so much linked to formal religious content. It was expressed in their critical perspective on the issues they dealt with, including the possibility to "envision a place for Jews in the polity."[19] This seems significant to me because it can shed light on the importance of critique, particularly for these thinkers. For instance, what Paul Franks referred to as "Kant's appeal to Jewish philosophers" (which, according to Franks, digressed beyond the domain of the neo-Kantian school) can perhaps be understood, with minor modification, as the importance of criticism for these intellectuals.[20] It is in this sense, as Habermas suggested, that Jewish thought "has remained critique."[21] I do not mean to say, however, that the concept of critique was relevant only for Jewish thinkers at that time, or for all modern Jewish thinkers. Yet it is possible that for many of them, precisely because in their eyes Judaism is "something created, not given," being tethered to this tradition constitutes a driving force of critical observation in the world in which they have always felt, as Paul Mendes-Flohr so accurately put it, "cognitive insiders" but "axionormative outsiders."[22] Calling attention to such a possible connection between Jewish identity and criticism may perhaps explain why Horkheimer claimed that critical theory was for him and his peers "Judaism undercover," and why this recognition can be projected upon a wide range of Jewish thinkers of the period.[23]

I have argued throughout this work in favor of a radical change in the way in which we think about criticism. I return to this point because it gives rise to such questions as: Why is there any need to separate critical thinking from religion or theology? The answer, in part, is possibly embedded in a refusal to recognize the fallibility that may hide behind the veneer of scientific rationality, and in part, it is related to the political meanings derived from it. It seems to me, however, that now is the time for such a transformation, given our collective responsibility to democracy in times of crisis. At the time and place of writing, the crisis is particularly acute. Against this background, I wish, however, to propose a position that differs from the contemporary political fault line, situated ostensibly between those who "adhere to the principle of secular reason and those who are ready to embrace the temptations of theocracy."[24]

This clear division was recently expressed by Peter Gordon, who in his latest book distinguishes between religious logic seemingly based on dominance and control and secular critical logic devoted to rejecting such "fantasies." One cannot diminish the importance of Gordon's attempt to oppose the "pathologies" from which we suffer today, manifested in the constant, disturbing, and certainly dangerous departures from the values identified with liberal democracy. In this regard, one can assume that social reality in the postcoronavirus era will only continue to intensify these processes around the world. At the same time, it appears to me that this way of thinking, which in dichotomic terms distinguishes between a worthy secular approach and dangerous religious logic, may invite a "secularist" bias—in Habermas's terms—that continues to justify the former's hegemony over the latter in the public space; within such a framework only "translated," i.e., secular contributions may pass as relevant.[25] Not only does this preference remain deeply suspicious of all things related to the religion external to it, but it also insists that theological concepts have meaning only when they are fully dissolved within their secular "translation." It is unclear, therefore, how it is possible to evade the way in which such an approach holds onto the "fantasy" of the dominance and control of one tradition over another, and sketches once again, even if against its will, the conflictual lines between them.

The problem with such a bias, from my viewpoint, is not merely grounded in the fact that the joining of the "adherents of a religion" to the public sphere cannot, in any case, leave the "preexisting" secular discursive structure intact, as Talal Asad has suggested.[26] Neither does the problem lie in the claim that it is only a Western secularist point of view that transforms religion into a "closed set of ideals and values" and that therefore perceives it as "antithetical to democracy."[27] Instead, it relates to the fact that the binary division between the "secular" and the "religious" upon which it leans does not correlate with the richness, complexity, and perhaps even fluidity of the secular spectrum that always includes an ongoing dialogue with its inherent religious origins.

There is, it seems, a more fruitful distinction to be made than that between secular reason and religious zeal—a distinction between those who continue to dogmatically hold onto this dichotomy (regardless of which side of the fence they are on) and those who reject these types of rigid divisions and point to the existence of a wide secular–religious spectrum as part of secular self-perception.[28] This, I think, is the conclusion that can be derived from critical theory. Especially with Adorno, one can see how secularization, which is the denial of the possibility to maintain the absolute of religion, is important because it constitutes the only way to rescue it. Here there is certainly decisive opposition to any form of messianic realization in the world, but the objective is not to end messianism, but rather to resuscitate it. To wit: there is no doubt that Adorno's critique negates any positive theological meaning, but at the same time, this negation is important simply because it is the only way to continue to hold onto this meaning. We are dealing here, therefore, with an act of amalgamation that does not set criticism against the theological traditions that nurture it, but generates between them a sort of covenant "in time of need."[29]

Is it possible, then—instead of, on the one hand, the darkness descending upon us from forms of religious fundamentalism or, on the other, an increasingly critical rejection of any religious matter—to choose an alternative that acknowledges the tense relation between critique and theology? I am not particularly optimistic regarding the appeal of this alternative view today. However, I daresay that to acknowledge the existence of this type of relation, or continuum, is to invite a fruitful discussion (as opposed to opposition, mutual hostility, hegemony, or violent struggle) between traditions of thought and worldviews, which, to echo Kant's handmaid's tale, may carry the torch for one another, or hold onto the train of the other's dress, and in any case, will not demand exclusivity for themselves in the world of human beings.

Notes

Introduction

1. Michel Foucault, "What Is Critique?," in *What Is Enlightenment? Eighteenth-Century Answers and Twentieth-Century Questions*, ed. James Schmidt (Berkeley: University of California Press, 1996), 382.

2. See, e.g., Foucault, "What Is Critique?," 384–86; Reinhart Koselleck, *Critique and Crisis: Enlightenment and the Pathogenesis of Modern Society* (Hamburg: Berg, 1988), 23–40; Talal Asad et al., *Is Critique Secular? Blasphemy, Injury and Free Speech* (Berkeley: University of California Press, 2009), 1–5.

3. Foucault, "What Is Critique?," 385–86. See also Asad et al., *Is Critique Secular?*, 2.

4. Asad et al., *Is Critique Secular?*, 5.

5. Ibid., vii–viii.

6. Ibid., 55.

7. See, e.g., Steven E. Aschheim and Vivian Liska, eds., *The German-Jewish Experience Revisited* (Berlin: De Gruyter, 2015); Steven E. Aschheim, *Beyond the Borders: The German-Jewish Legacy Abroad* (Princeton, NJ: Princeton University Press, 2008); Leslie Morris, *The Translated Jews: German Jewish Culture outside the Margins* (Evanston, IL: Northwestern University Press, 2018); Kerry Wallach, *Passing Illusion: Jewish Visibility in Weimar Germany* (Ann Arbor: University of Michigan Press, 2017); Scott Spector, *German Modernism without Jews? German-Jewish Subjects and Histories* (Bloomington: Indiana University Press, 2017); Miriam Rürup and Simone Lässig, eds., *German-Jewish Space and Spatiality in Modern History* (New York: Berghahn Books, 2017).

8. A. Dirk Moses, "Genocide and Modernity," in *The Historiography of Genocide*, ed. Dan Stone (Houndmills, UK: Palgrave Macmillan, 2008), 184.

9. Paul North, *The Yield: Kafka's Atheological Reformation* (Stanford, CA: Stanford University Press, 2015), 4.

10. Hans Blumenberg, *The Legitimacy of the Modern Age* (Cambridge, MA: MIT Press, 1966).

11. For the extensive research on the "Judeo-Christian" legacy, relevant also to these thinkers, see, e.g.: David Marshall, *The Weimar Origins of Rhetorical Inquiry* (Chicago: University of Chicago Press, 2020); Benjamin Lazier, *God Interrupted: Heresy and the European Imagination between the World Wars* (Princeton, NJ: Princeton University Press, 2008); Peter Gordon, *Rosenzweig and Heidegger: Between Judaism and German Philosophy* (Berkeley: University of California Press 2003); Ari Joskowicz and Ethan B. Katz, eds., *Secularism in Question: Jews and Judaism in Modern Times* (Philadelphia: University of Pennsylvania Press, 2016).

12. Asad et al., *Is Critique Secular?*, marks a notable exception, although the focus is placed mainly on the relation between a secularized Christian world and Islam.

13. See, e.g., Peter E. Gordon, *Migrants into the Profane: Critical Theory and the Question of Secularization* (New Haven, CT: Yale University Press, 2020); Orr Scharf, *Thinking in Translation: Scriptures and Redemption in the Thought of Franz Rosenzweig* (Berlin: De Gruyter, 2019); Sebastian Musch, *Jewish Encounters with Buddhism in German Culture: Between Moses and Buddha, 1890–1940* (Cham, Switzerland: Palgrave Macmillan, 2019); Paul Mendes-Flohr, *Martin Buber: A Life of Faith and Dissent* (New Haven, CT: Yale University Press, 2019); Vivian Liska, *German-Jewish Thought and Its Afterlife: A Tenuous Legacy* (Bloomington: Indiana University Press, 2017); Joan Braune, *Erich Fromm's Revolutionary Hope: A Prophetic Messianism as a Critical Theory of the Future* (Leiden: Brill, 2014); David Biale, *Not in Heaven: The Tradition of Jewish Secular Thought* (Princeton, NJ: Princeton University Press, 2011); Hent de Vries, *Minimal Theologies: Critiques of Secular Reason in Adorno and Levinas* (Baltimore: Johns Hopkins University Press, 2005).

14. Asad et al., *Is Critique Secular?*, 2.

15. Elisabeth Schüssler Fiorenza, "Feminist Theology as a Critical Theology of Liberation," *Theological Studies* 36, no. 4 (1975): 605–26; Stephen R. Palmquist, *Kant's Critical Religion* (Burlington, VT: Ashgate, 2000); Marc P. Lalonde, ed., *The Promise of Critical Theology: Essays in Honor of Charles Davis* (Waterloo, ON: Wilfrid Laurier University Press, 1995); Marc P. Lalonde, *From Critical Theology to a Critical Theory of Religion: Essays in Contemporary Religious Thought* (London: Peter Lang, 2010); Carl A. Raschke, *Critical Theology: Introducing an Agenda for an Age of Global Crisis* (Downers Grove, IL: Intervarsity Press, 2016); Itzhak Benyamini, *A Critical Theology of Genesis: The Non-Absolute God* (New York: Palgrave Macmillan, 2016).

16. See, e.g., Schüssler Fiorenza, "Feminist Theology"; Palmquist, *Kant's Critical Religion*; Raschke, *Critical Theology*.

17. See also Itzhak Benyamini and Yotam Hotam, "An Outline for Critical Theology from an Israeli Jewish Perspective," *Journal of Modern Jewish Studies* 14, no. 2 (2015): 333–39. De Vries, *Minimal Theologies*, is a rather brilliant recent example because it underlines a search for a new theology, distinguished from the dogmas of "classical theology" on the one hand and from the conceptual analysis that characterizes the modern disciplinary study of religion on the other hand.

18. Foucault, "What Is Critique?," 386.

19. Seyla Benhabib, *Critique, Norm, and Utopia* (New York: Columbia University Press, 1987), 5; Paul Mendes-Flohr, *Divided Passions: Jewish Intellectuals and the Experience of Modernity* (Detroit: Wayne State University Press, 1991), 28; Gordon, *Migrants,* 17; Paul Franks, "Jewish Philosophy after Kant: The Legacy of Salomon Maimon," in *The Cambridge Companion to Modern Jewish Philosophy,* ed. Michael L. Morgan and Peter Eli Gordon, 53–79 (Cambridge: Cambridge University Press, 2007), at 53; Foucault, "What Is Critique?," 387–88.

20. Immanuel Kant, *Critique of Pure Reason,* trans. Paul Guyer and Allan Wood (Cambridge: Cambridge University Press, 1998), 101; Immanuel Kant, *Kritik der Reinen Vernunft* (Hamburg: Felix Meiner Verlag, 1998), 8.

21. Kant, *Critique,* 101. See also Asad et al., *Is Critique Secular?*, 3.

22. Kant, *Critique,* 105.

23. Heinrich Heine, "Nachwort zum Romanzero," in Heinrich Heine, *Romanzero* (Hamburg: Hoffmann und Campe, 1852), 302. See the translation in Hal Draper, *The Complete Poems of Henrich Heine: A Modern English Version* (Oxford: Oxford University Press, 1982), 693–98.

24. Leo Strauss, "Reason and Revelation," in Heinrich Meier, *Leo Strauss and the Theological Political Problem* (Cambridge: Cambridge University Press, 2016), 149.

25. Franks, "Jewish Philosophy after Kant," 55.

26. Ibid., 58.

27. Kant, *Critique,* 14.

28. Ibid.

29. Ibid., 684.

30. Immanuel Kant, "What Real Progress Has Metaphysics Made in Germany since the Time of Leibniz and Wolff?," in Immanuel Kant, *Theoretical Philosophy after 1781,* ed. Henry Allison and Peter Heath (Cambridge: Cambridge University Press, 2002), 394.

31. See also Palmquist, *Kant's Critical Religion,* 7; Stephen R. Palmquist, "Kant's 'Appropriation' of Lampe's God," *Harvard Theological Review* 85, no. 1 (1992): 85–108.

32. Immanuel Kant, *Religion within the Limits of Reason Alone,* trans. Werner S. Pluhar (Indianapolis, IN: Hackett, 2009), 7.

33. James Hering, "Judaism and the Contingency of Religious Law in Kant's 'Religion within the Boundaries of Mere Reason,'" *Journal of Religious Ethics* 48, no. 1 (2020): 74–100.

34. Hans Jonas, "The Concept of God after Auschwitz: A Jewish Voice," *Journal of Religion* 67, no. 1 (1987): 1. For the increasing prominence of theology in Kant's later writings, see Franks, "Jewish Philosophy after Kant," 59.

35. Immanuel Kant, *The Conflict of the Faculties,* trans. Mary J. Gregor (Lincoln: University of Nebraska Press, 1979), 45.

36. Ibid., 84–85.

37. David Sorkin, *The Religious Enlightenment: Protestants, Jews, and Catholics from London to Vienna* (Princeton, NJ: Princeton University Press, 2008), 3. See also Paul Franks, "From World-Soul to Universal Organism: Maimon's Hypothesis and Schelling's Physicalization of a Platonic-Kabbalistic Concept," in *Schelling's Philosophy: Freedom, Nature, and Systematicity*, ed. Anthony G. Bruno (Oxford: Oxford University Press, 2020), 71–92; Paul Franks, "Divided by Common Sense: Mendelssohn and Jacobi on Reason and Inferential Justification," in *Moses Mendelssohn's Metaphysics and Aesthetics*, Studies in German Idealism 13, ed. Reinier Munk (New York: Springer, 2011), 203–15.

38. Benhabib, *Critique*, 5–6. See also Rita Felski, *The Limits of Critique* (Chicago: University of Chicago Press, 2015), 1–5.

39. Willem Styfhals and Stephane Symons, eds., *Genealogies of the Secular: The Making of Modern German Thought* (Albany: State University of New York Press, 2019), 1–2.

40. Peter Gay, *Freud: A Life of Our Time* (New York: W. W. Norton, 1988).

41. Yosef Haim Yerushalmi, *Freud's Moses: Judaism Terminable and Interminable* (New Haven, CT: Yale University Press, 1993); Eric L. Santner, *On the Psychotheology of Everyday Life: Reflections on Freud and Rosenzweig* (Chicago: University of Chicago Press, 2001).

42. Peter E. Gordon, "The Concept of the Apolitical: German Jewish Thought and Weimar Political Theology," *Social Research* 74, no. 3 (2007): 871.

43. Micha Brumlik, "Verborgene Tradition und messianisches Licht: Arendt, Adorno und ihr Judentum," in *Arendt und Adorno*, ed. Dirk Auer, Lars Rensmann, and Julia Schulye Wessel (Frankfurt: Suhrkamp, 2003), 74–75.

44. For example: Margaret Canovan, *Hannah Arendt: A Reinterpretation of Her Political Thought* (Cambridge: Cambridge University Press, 1992); Richard J. Bernstein, *Hannah Arendt and the Jewish Question* (Cambridge, UK: Polity, 1996); Samuel Moyn, "Hannah Arendt on the Secular," *New German Critique* 35, no. 3 (2008): 71–96; Seyla Benhabib, ed., *Politics in Dark Times: Encounters with Hannah Arendt* (Cambridge: Cambridge University Press, 2010); Rebecca Dew, *Hannah Arendt: Between Ideologies* (Cham, Switzerland: Palgrave Macmillan, 2020).

45. See, e.g., Gordon, *Migrants*; Peter E. Gordon, *Adorno and Existence* (Cambridge, MA: Harvard University Press, 2016); Christopher Craig Brittain, *Adorno and Theology* (London: T&T Clark, 2010); Dustin J. Byrd, ed., *The Critique of Religion and Religion's Critique: On Dialectical Religiology* (Leiden: Brill, 2020); Christoph Schmidt, "The Israel of the Spirit: The German Student Movement of the 1960s and Its Attitude to the Holocaust," *Dapim: The Journal of Holocaust Research* 24, no. 1 (2010): 269–318 [Hebrew]; de Vries, *Minimal Theologies*.

46. See, e.g., Colby Dickinson and Stephane Symons, eds., *Walter Benjamin and Theology: Perspectives in Continental Philosophy* (New York: Fordham University Press, 2016).

47. For Arendt's remark, see Detlev Schöttker and Edmunt Wizisla, *Arendt und Benjamin: Texte, Briefe, Dokumente* (Frankfurt: Suhrkamp, 2006), 55. For the controversy, see, e.g., Michael W. Jennings, *Dialectical Images: Walter Benjamin's Theory of Literary Criticism* (Ithaca, NY: Cornell University Press, 1987), 5; Reiner Dieckhoff, *Mythos und Moderne: Über die Verborgene Mystik in den Schrifter Walter Benjamins* (Cologne: Janus, 1987), 13; Richard Wolin, *Walter Benjamin: An Aesthetic of Redemption* (New York: Columbia University Press, 1982); Benjamin Andrew and Peter Osborne, eds., *Walter Benjamin's Philosophy: Destruction and Experience* (London: Routledge, 1994); Eli Freidlander, *Walter Benjamin: A Philosophical Portrait* (Cambridge, MA: Harvard University Press, 2012).

48. Jennings, *Dialectical*, 5; Dieckhoff, *Mythos und Moderne*, 13.

49. Asaf Angermann, ed., *Theodor W. Adorno, Gershom Scholem Briefwechsel 1939–1969* (Frankfurt: Suhrkamp, 2015), 74–75, 78–79.

50. Peter E. Gordon, "The Odd Couple," *The Nation*, June 9, 2016. https://www.thenation.com/article/the-odd-couple

51. "Fingerabdruck des lebendigen Geistes," Theodor Adorno, *Erziehung zur Mündigkeit: Vorträge und Gespräeche mit Hellmut Becker 1959–1969* (Frankfurt: Suhrkamp, 1970), 8.

52. See, e.g., Elliott Oring, "Jokes and Their Relation to Sigmund Freud," *Western Folklore* 43, no. 1 (1984): 37–48; Elliott Oring, *The Jokes of Sigmund Freud: A Study in Humor and Jewish Identity* (Philadelphia: University of Pennsylvania Press, 1984); Ruth R. Wisse, *No Joke: Making Jewish Humor* (Princeton, NJ: Princeton University Press, 2013), 29–58.

53. See, e.g., Jennings, *Dialectical*, 6. Johannes Steizinger's studies are among the few to offer an in-depth examination of Benjamin's theory of youth. See Johannes Steizinger, "Zwischen emanzipatorischem Appell und melancholischem Verstummen Walter Benjamins Jugendschriften," in *Benjamin-Studien*, ed. D. Weidner and S. Weigel (Munich: Wilhem Fink Verlag, 2011), 225–38; Johannes Steizinger, *Revolte Eros und Sprache* (Berlin: Kulturverlag Kadmos, 2013).

54. See, e.g., Dana Villa, *Cambridge Companion to Hannah Arendt* (Cambridge: Cambridge University Press, 2000); Patricia Owens, *Between War and Politics: International Relations and the Thought of Hannah Arendt* (Oxford: Oxford University Press, 2007); Benhabib, *Politics in Dark Times*. For the dispute over the importance of Arendt's political writings to the understanding of her "life of the mind," see Elisabeth Young-Bruehl, *Hannah Arendt: For Love of the World* (Binghamton, NY: Vail-Ballou, 1982), 280; David Arndt, *Arendt on the Political* (Cambridge: Cambridge University Press, 2019), 1–8.

55. Sigmund Freud, *An Autobiographical Study*, trans. James Strachey (Toronto: Oxford University Press, 1948), 118–21.

56. Steizinger, "Zwischen emanzipatorischem Appell," 225–38.

57. See, e.g., Daniel K. Cho, "Adorno on Education or, Can Critical Self-Reflection Prevent the Next Auschwitz?," *Historical Materialism* 17 (2009): 75; Helmut Schreier and Matthias Heyl, eds., *Never Again! The Holocaust's Challenge for Educators* (Hamburg: Krämer, 1997), 3–5.

58. Villa, *Cambridge Companion*, 5. For a similar point, see Gerhard Richter, *Thinking with Adorno: The Uncoercive Gaze* (New York: Fordham University Press, 1919), 40–41; Young-Bruehl, *Hannah Arendt*, 280–85, who emphasizes Arendt's turn away from her more "historical" works composed in the 1930s to the 1950s (most notably, the biography of Rahel Varnhagen written in the 1930s and *The Origins of Totalitarianism* written in the 1940s). See also Evelyn Temme, *Von der Bildung des Politischen zur politischen Bildung: Politikdidaktische Theorien mit Hannah Arendt Weitergedacht* (Frankfurt: Peter Lang, 2014), 10.

59. Michel de Certeau, *The Writings of History*, trans. Tom Conley (New York: Columbia University Press, 1988), xxvi, 287–307.

60. Santner, *Psychotheology*, 23.

61. See also Richter, *Adorno*, 39.

62. Wolfson, *Poetic*, 192–93. See also Christoph Schmidt, "Es gibt Vernichtung: Anmerkungen zu Jakob Taubes' *Die Politische Theologie des Paulus*," in Christoph Schmidt, *Die theopolitische Stunde: Zwölf Perspektiven auf das eschatologische Problem der Moderne* (Paderborn, Germany: Wilhelm Fink Verlag, 2009), 269–302.

63. Gerd Kadelbach's introduction in Adorno, *Erziehung zur Mündigkeit*, 7–9. See also Volker Heins, "Saying Things That Hurt: Adorno as Educator," *Thesis Eleven* 11, no. 1 (2012): 73–74. Following his return to Germany in 1949, Adorno gave more than two hundred radio talks on a variety of outlets such as the Westdeutscher Rundfunk, the Süddeutscher Rundfunk, and Sender Freies Berlin. Between 1959 and 1969 Adorno's visits to the Hessischer Rundfunk included a series of yearly lectures and additional discussions with Hellmut Becker and Gerd Kadelbach. These Public Radio appearances started with the lecture "What Does Coming to Terms with the Past Mean?" ("Was bedeutet: Aufarbeitung der Vergangenheit?") in 1959 and ended with "Education for Maturity" ("Erziehung zur Mündigkeit")—the last speech he gave before his death a couple of weeks later in July 1969. The recordings were revised by Adorno before publication. For the English version of these lectures, see Theodor Adorno, *Critical Models: Interventions and Catchwords*, trans. Henry W. Pickford (New York: Columbia University Press, 2005).

64. Max Horkheimer and Theodor Adorno, *The Dialectics of Enlightenment* (New York: Continuum, 1993), 20. Adorno's scholarly interest in this medium of mass culture was already evident when he participated in the "Princeton Radio Project," which took issue with the listening habits of Americans in the early 1930s. See also Brian O'Connor, ed., *The Adorno Reader* (Malden, MA: Blackwell, 2000), 8. On the relative marginality of his radio speeches in research, see, e.g., Adorno, *Erziehung zur Mündigkeit*, 7–9.

65. Theodor W. Adorno, "Theorie der Halbbildung" (1959), in Theodor W. Adorno, *Gesammelte Schriften*, vol. 8, edited by Rolf Tiedemann (Darmstadt, Germany: Wissenschaftliche Buchgesellschaft, 1998), 93–121. Translated as Theodor W. Adorno, "Theory of Pseudo-Culture," *Telos* 20 (1993):15–38.

66. See in particular his two university lectures from 1964–65: Theodor Adorno, *Metaphysics: Concept and Problems*, trans. Edmund Jephcott (Malden, MA: Polity, 2000); Theodor Adorno, *History and Freedom*, trans. Rodney Livingstone (Malden, MA: Polity, 2006).

67. In the 1960s, Arendt repeatedly insists on being a political theorist rather than a philosopher. See, e.g., Sigwart Hans-Jörg, *The Wandering Thought of Hannah Arendt* (London: Macmillan, 2016), 12.

68. Hannah Arendt, *On Revolution* (New York: Viking, 1963); Hannah Arendt, *Eichmann in Jerusalem: A Report on the Banality of Evil* (New York: Viking, 1963); Hannah Arendt, *Men in Dark Times* (New York: Harcourt, Brace & World, 1968); Hannah Arendt, *Between Past and Future* (New York: Viking, 1961/1968); Hannah Arendt, *On Violence* (New York: Harcourt, 1969); Hannah Arendt, *Crises of the Republic* (New York: Harcourt, 1969).

69. See Young-Bruehl, *Hannah Arendt*, 324–27, 472; Stephan Kampowski, *Arendt, Augustine, and the New Beginning: The Action Theory and Moral Thought of Hannah Arendt in the Light of Her Dissertation on St. Augustine* (Grand Rapids, MI: William B. Eerdmans, 2008), 10; Villa, *Cambridge Companion*, 7; Dana R. Villa, ed., *Politics, Philosophy, Terror: Essays on the Thought of Hannah Arendt* (Princeton, NJ: Princeton University Press, 1999), 192; Canovan, *Hannah Arendt*, 64.

70. Hannah Arendt, *Der Liebesbegriff bei Augustin* (Berlin: J. Springer, 1929). For Augustine's importance, see, e.g., the editor's notes in Arendt, *Love*, 118–19; Roy T. Tsao, "Arendt's Augustine," in *Politics in Dark Times: Encounters with Hannah Arendt*, ed. Seyla Benhabib (Cambridge: Cambridge University Press, 2010), 41; Kampowski, *Arendt*, 13–16.

71. Arendt, *Between*, 18. See also her unpublished letter to Erwin Loewenson dated October 27, 1927, cited in Tatjana Noemy Tömmel, "Vita Passiva: Love in Arendt's Denktagebuch," in *Artifacts of Thinking: Reading Hannah Arendt's Denktagebuch*, ed. Roger Berkowitz and Ilan Storey (New York: Fordham University Press, 2017), 106.

Chapter 1

1. Sigmund Freud, *The Origins of Psycho-Analysis: Letters to Wilhelm Fliess, Drafts and Notes, 1887–1902*, ed. Marie Bonaparte, Anna Freud, and Ernst Kris (New York: Basic Books, 1954), 211; Sigmund Freud, *Aus den Anfängen der Psychoanalyse: Briefe an Wilhelm Fliess, Abhandlugen und Notizen aus den Jahren 1887–1902* (London: Imago, 1950), 224.

2. See, e.g., Max Schur, *Freud: Living and Dying* (New York: International Universities Press, 1972), 108.

3. Freud, *Origins*, 297.

4. For the rise of scholarly interest, see, e.g., Theodor Lipps, *Komik und Humor: Eine psychologisch-ästhetische Untersuchung* (Hamburg: Verlag von Leopold Voss, 1898); Kuno Fischer, *Über den Witz* (Heidelberg: Carl Winters Universitätsbuchhandlung, 1889); Henri Bergson, *Le Rire: Essai sur la signification du comique* (Paris: Quadrige, 1900). See also Ernest Jones, *The Life and Work of Sigmund Freud*, vol. 2 (New York: Basic Books, 1953), 375, emphasizing Theodor Lipps's influence on Freud.

5. Sigmund Freud, *Der Witz und seine Beziehung zum Unbewussten* (Leipzig: Franz Deuticke, 1905); Sigmund Freud, *Jokes and Their Relation to the Unconscious* (New York: W. W. Norton, 1960). The first translation into English was published as Sigmund Freud, *Wit and Its Relation to the Unconscious* (New York: Macmillan, 1916). For the purposes of this chapter, I will use the terms "joke" and "wit" interchangeably.

6. Ernst Simon, "Sigmund Freud, the Jew," *Leo Baeck Institute Year Book* 2 (1957): 270–305; Elliott Oring, *The Jokes of Sigmund Freud: A Study in Humor and Jewish Identity* (Philadelphia: University of Pennsylvania Press, 1984); Elliott Oring, "Jokes and Their Relation to Sigmund Freud," *Western Folklore* 43, no. 1 (1984): 37–48; Sander L. Gilman, "Jewish Jokes: Sigmund Freud and the Hidden Language of the Jews," *Psychoanalysis and Contemporary Thought* 7, no. 4 (1984): 591–614. See also the point made by Robert S. Wistrich, "The Jewish Identity of Sigmund Freud," *Jewish Quarterly* 34, no. 3 (1987): 47–55; Victor Diller, *Freud's Jewish Identity: A Case Study in the Impact of Ethnicity* (London: Associated University Presses, 1991), 109; Moshe Gresser, *Dual Allegiance: Freud as a Modern Jew* (Albany: State University of New York Press, 1994), 13; Ruth R. Wisse, *No Joke: Making Jewish Humor* (Princeton, NJ: Princeton University Press, 2013), 29–58.

7. Sigmund Freud, *An Autobiographical Study* (London: Hogarth, 1948), 120.

8. Sigmund Freud, *The Interpretation of Dreams* (New York: Basic Books, 1955); Sigmund Freud, *The Psychopathology of Everyday Life* (New York: W. W. Norton, 1960); Sigmund Freud, *Three Essays on the Theory of Sexuality* (London: Imago, 1949).

9. Jones, *Life and Work*, vol. 1, 365.

10. Didier Anzieu, *Freud's Self-Analysis* (London: Hogarth, 1986), 171. See also Jones, *Life and Work*, vol. 1, 305.

11. Gresser, *Dual Allegiance*, 13; Earl A. Grollman, *Judaism in Sigmund Freud's World* (New York: Bloch, 1965), 91; Jones, *Life and Work*, vol. 1., 339; Freud, *Autobiographical Study*, 14.

12. For more about Rome as the "promised land," see Schur, *Freud*, 103; Helen Puner Walker, *Freud: His Life and His Mind* (New York: Howell, Soskin, 1947), 24; Jones, *Life and Work*, vol. 2, 18; Ronald W. Clark, *Freud: The Man*

and the Cause (New York: Random House, 1980), 201; Peter Gay, *A Godless Jew: Freud, Atheism, and the Making of Psychoanalysis* (New Haven, CT: Yale University Press, 1987), 15.

13. Freud's letter to Fliess dated August 27, 1899. See Freud, *Origins*, 294. Cited also in Rene Major and Chantal Talagrand, *Freud: The Unconscious and World Affairs* (New York: Routledge, 2018), 120; Clark, *Freud*, 201.

14. Freud's letter to Fliess dated April 16, 1900. Freud, *Origins*, 295. Cited also in Gresser, *Dual Allegiance*, 121; Paul C. Vitz, *Sigmund Freud's Christian Unconscious* (New York: Guilford, 1988), 73.

15. Gresser, *Dual Allegiance*, 112–16; Grollman, *Judaism*, 86; Helmuth F. Braun, *Sigmund Freud: "Ein Gottloser Jude"—Entdecker des Unbewussten* (Berlin: Hentrich & Hentrich, 2006), 34–35; Anzieu, *Freud's Self-Analysis*, 182–83.

16. Freud, *Origins*, 350. Cited also in Jones, *Life and Work*, vol. 2, 16.

17. Anzieu, *Freud's Self-Analysis*, 562; Jones, *Life and Work*, vol. 2, 20. On modern Jewish fascination with the *Moses* of Michelangelo, see Asher D. Biemann, *Dreaming of Michelangelo: Jewish Variations on a Modern Theme* (Stanford, CA: Stanford University Press, 2012), xv.

18. Sigmund Freud, "The Moses of Michelangelo," in Sigmund Freud, *The Standard Edition of the Complete Psychological Works of Sigmund Freud*, vol. 13, ed. James Strachey et al. (London: Hogarth, 1955), 213. Freud's paper was first published anonymously as "***" in *Imago* 3, no. 1: 15–36 (1914); the author's identity was revealed only ten years later. See also Jones, *Life and Work*, vol. 2, 364–65; Braun, *Freud*, 35; Puner, *Freud*, 245.

19. Freud, "Moses," 213.

20. Sigmund Freud, *Der Mann Moses und die Monotheistische Religion: Drei Abhandlungen* (Amsterdam: Verlad Allert de Lange, 1938). For Freud's personal, to some extent compulsive, lifelong identification with the image of Moses, see, e.g., Biemann, *Dreaming*, 38; Gilad Sharvit and Karen S. Feldman, eds., *Freud and Monotheism: Moses and the Violent Origins of Religion* (New York: Fordham University Press, 2018); Yosef Haim Yerushalmi, *Freud's Moses: Judaism Terminable and Interminable* (New Haven, CT: Yale University Press, 1991); Jan Assmann, *Moses the Egyptian: The Memory of Egypt in Western Monotheism* (Cambridge, MA: Harvard University Press, 1997); Emanuel Rice, *Freud and Moses: The Long Journey Home* (Albany: State University of New York Press, 1990); Vincent Brome, *Freud and His Disciples* (London: Caliban, 1984).

21. See also Biemann, *Dreaming*, 51.

22. See also Jones, *Life and Work*, vol. 2, 365.

23. Freud, "Moses," 230.

24. Ibid., 234.

25. Ibid., 220.

26. Ibid., 221.

27. Ibid., 214.

28. Ibid., 230; see also Yerushalmi, *Freud's Moses*, 22.
29. Freud, "Moses," 219.
30. Ibid., 227; see also Jones, *Life and Work*, vol. 2, 364.
31. Freud, "Moses," 227.
32. See also the point made in Biemann, *Dreaming*, 60–61.
33. Freud, "Moses," 230.
34. Jones, *Life and Work*, vol. 2, 12.
35. Freud, *Jokes*, 49; Freud, *Der Witz*, 39.
36. Freud, *Autobiographical Study*, 118–21.
37. Biemann, *Dreaming*, xvi.
38. Freud's reflection relates to the interweaving of his study of jokes and psychoanalysis. See Freud, *Autobiographical Study*, 131; Oring, *Jokes of Sigmund Freud*, 38.
39. Freud, *Jokes*, 119; see also Sigmund Freud, "Humor," *International Journal of Psychoanalysis* 9, no. 1 (1927): 161.
40. See also Abraham Arden Brill, "Freud's Theory of Wit," *Journal of Abnormal Psychology* 6, no. 4 (1911): 279–316.
41. Freud, *Jokes*, 16.
42. Ibid., 17.
43. Immanuel Kant, *Critique of Pure Reason* (Cambridge: Cambridge University Press, 1998), 101; Immanuel Kant, *Kritik der Reinen Vernunft* (Hamburg: Felix Meiner Verlag, 1998), 8.
44. Ibid.
45. Ibid., 105.
46. Emmanuel Falque, *Nothing to It: Reading Freud as a Philosopher* (Leuven, Belgium: Leuven University Press, 2020).
47. Michel de Certeau, *The Writing of History* (New York: Columbia University Press, 1988), 302–3. Emphasis in the original. De Certeau refers specifically to "a law of history" that Freud presupposes, in relation to which human actions, norms, or rules are mere "traces."
48. Robert M. Cover, "The Supreme Court 1982 Term—Forward: Nomos and Narrative," *Harvard Law Review* 97, no. 4 (1983–84): 1–68. See also Robert M. Cover, "Nomos and Narrative," in *Narrative, Violence, and the Law: The Essays of Robert Cover*, ed. Martha Minow, Michael Ryan, and Austin Sarat (Ann Arbor: University of Michigan Press, 1993), 95–172.
49. Cover, "Nomos and Narrative," 4.
50. Ibid., 4.
51. Ibid., 5.
52. Ibid., 8–9.
53. Ibid., 12–18. For Cover's reliance on the Jewish rabbinic tradition, see Suzanne Last Stone, "In Pursuit of the Counter-Text: The Turn to the Jewish Legal Model in Contemporary American Legal Theory," *Harvard Law Review* 106, no. 4 (1993): 813–89.

54. Freud, *Jokes*, 13.
55. Ibid., 132.
56. Ibid., 17.
57. Ibid.
58. Ibid., 81. The English translation of the third and last cry of the baroness ("aa-ee, aa-ee, aa-ee") is here amended to more accurately reflect the cry as presented in the German original ("Ai waih, waih geschrien").
59. Freud, *Jokes*, 81; Oring, *Jokes of Sigmund Freud*, 16.
60. Freud, *Jokes*, 81.
61. See John Murray Cuddihy, *The Ordeal of Civility: Freud, Marx, Levi-Strauss, and the Jewish Struggle with Modernity* (New York: Dell, 1974), 24; Christopher Hutton, "Freud and the Family Drama of Yiddish," in *Studies in Yiddish Linguistics*, ed. Paul Wexler (Tübingen, Germany: Max Niemeyer, 1990), 15. See also Edmund Edel, *Der Witz der Juden* (Berlin: L. Lamm, 1909).
62. Freud, *Jokes*, 49. Hutton points to the pun "Yid-id" that encapsulates, albeit ironically, such connections. See Hutton, "Freud," 20.
63. Rudolf Herzog, *Heil Hitler, Das Schwein ist Tot: Lachen unter Hitler—Komik und Humor im Dritten Reich* (Frankfurt: Eichborn, 2006).
64. Freud, *Jokes*, 4. See also Freud, *Der Witz*, 5, "*Kürze ist der Körper und die Seele des Witzes, ja er selbst.*"
65. Freud, *Jokes*, 69.
66. Ibid., 114.
67. Ibid., 115.
68. Ibid., 54.
69. Ibid., 97, 115.
70. Ibid., 115.
71. Ibid., 80–81.
72. See also Freud's own reference to his theory of sexuality in ibid., 98.
73. Ibid., 103. Emphasis in the original.
74. Ibid., 42.
75. Ibid., 119. Emphasis in the original.
76. Ibid., 180.
77. See also Brill, "Freud's Theory," 309; Jeffrey Mehlman, "How to Read Freud on Jokes: The Critic as *Schadchen*," *New Literary History* 6, no. 2 (1975): 439–61.
78. Freud, *Jokes*, 98–100.
79. Freud's mother spoke Galician Yiddish all her life, and this was also how his parents communicated with each other. See, e.g., Marianna Krüll, *Freud and His Father* (New York: W. W. Norton, 1986), 116; Erika Freeman, *Insights: Conversations with Theodor Reik* (Englewood Cliffs, NJ: Prentice-Hall, 1971), 80; Hutton, "Freud," 10–11.
80. Freud, *Jokes*, 136.
81. Ibid., 147, paraphrasing here Spencer's essay on "The Physiology of Laughter" from 1860.

82. Bergson, *Le Rire*.
83. Freud, *Jokes*, 147.
84. Ibid., 120.
85. Ibid., 149.
86. See Freud, "Humor," 161–66.
87. Ibid.
88. Eric L. Santner, *On the Psychotheology of Everyday Life: Reflections on Freud and Rosenzweig* (Chicago: University of Chicago Press, 2001), 43.
89. "What is the meaning of kapandaria? Raba said: A shortcut, as its name implies." See Babylonian Talmud, *Berachot*, 9, 62b. See also Jerusalem Talmud, *Berachot*, 9, 43 (p. 12, col. 4). For a detailed discussion, see Binyamin Katzoff, "The Relationship between Tosefta and Yerushalmi of *Berachot*" (PhD diss., Bar-Ilan University, 1994), 138 [Hebrew], which points to the Latin *compendiāria* as the possible origins of *kapandaria*.
90. Mishnah, *Berachot*, 9; Babylonian Talmud, *Berachot*, 9, 54a.
91. See the entry "Synagogue" in the *Talmudic Encyclopedia*, vol. 3 (Jerusalem: Talmudic Encyclopedia, 1951), 194–95.
92. The Mishnah, "Megillah," 3c. https://www.emishnah.com/index1.html
93. See the point made in the *Talmudic Encyclopedia*, vol. 3, 194.
94. Talmud, *Sotah*, 39a (in Hebrew: "Meolam lo assiti beit haknesset kapandaria"). See also a slightly different version in the Babylonian Talmud, *Megillah*, 27b: "Never in my life have I made a shortcut through a synagogue" (in Hebrew: "Meolam lo assiti kapandaria lebeit knesset," which can also be literally understood as referring to the road taken to the synagogue).
95. Talmud, *Berachot*, 9, 62b.
96. Ibid.
97. See, e.g., Yerushalmi, *Freud's Moses*; Rice, *Freud and Moses*; Ruth Kara Ivanov-Kaniel, *Birth in Kabbalah and Psychoanalysis* (Berlin: De Gruyter, 2022).
98. See Hilda C. Abraham and Ernst L. Freud, eds., *A Psycho-Analytic Dialogue: The Letters of Sigmund Freud and Karl Abraham, 1907–1926* (London: Hogarth, 1965), 40; Gay, *Godless Jew*, 130.
99. Santner, *Psychotheology*; Harold Bloom, *Ruin the Sacred Truths: Poetry and Belief from the Bible to the Present* (Cambridge, MA: Harvard University Press, 1987).
100. Santner, *Psychotheology*, 8–9.
101. Ibid., 23.
102. Ibid., 8–9.
103. Yerushalmi, *Freud's Moses*; Kara Ivanov-Kaniel, *Birth*.
104. Freud's full answer was: "It is really a Jew that has built the house and is showing you about." Smiley Blanton, *Diary of My Analysis with Freud* (New York: Hawthorn Books, 1971), 45–46. Both patient and doctor agreed that the dream under discussion related to the patient's critique of psychoanalysis that

involved religious tensions. See Anat Tzur Mahalel, *Reading Freud's Patients: Memoir, Narrative and the Analysand* (New York: Routledge, 2020), 87–88.

105. Schur, *Freud*, 529. See also Oring, *Jokes of Sigmund Freud*, 123; Diller, *Freud*, 208.

106. For Freud's self-display as a gift of the gods, see Grollman, *Judaism*, xx. For the so-called Jewish "tension of election," see Santner, *Psychotheology*, 8–9.

107. Santner, *Psychotheology*, 9. See also a similar point made in Joel Whitebook, *Freud: An Intellectual Biography* (Cambridge: Cambridge University Press, 2017), 377, who argues that religion belongs to the core of Freud's psychological theory.

108. Santner, *Psychotheology*, 146.

109. Salvoj Žižek, *Metastases of Enjoyment: Six Essays on Woman and Causality* (London: Verso, 1994), 55. See also the point made in Santner, *Psychotheology*, 96.

110. Freud, "Moses," 227.

111. Santner, *Psychotheology*, 106.

112. Michel Foucault, "Preface to Transgression," in Michel Foucault, *Language, Counter-Memory, Practice: Selected Essays and Interviews*, ed. Donald F. Bouchar (Ithaca, NY: Cornell University Press, 1977), 29–52. See also Michel Foucault, "Préface a la Transgression," *Critique*, no. 195–96 (1963): 751–69. Foucault published the text in 1963 as a eulogy to George Bataille, who had passed away the year before.

113. Foucault, "Preface," 29.

114. Ibid.

115. Ibid.

116. Ibid., 29.

117. Ibid.

118. Ibid.

119. Ibid.

120. Ibid., 30.

121. Ibid., 31.

122. Ibid., 31–32.

123. Ibid., 31–32.

124. Santner, *Psychotheology*, 146.

125. Agata Bielik-Robson, " 'The God of Myth Is Not Dead': Modernity and Its Cryptotheologies: A Jewish Perspective," in *Genealogies of the Secular: The Making of Modern German Thought*, ed. Willem Styfhals and Stephane Symons (Albany: State University of New York Press, 2020), 52.

126. Christoph Schmidt, "Kairos and Culture: Some Remarks on the Formation of the Cultural Sciences in Germany and the Emergence of a Jewish Political-Theology," in *Arche Noah: Die Idee der "Kultur" im deutsch-jüdischen Diskurs*, ed. Bernhard Greiner and Christoph Schmidt (Freiburg, Germany:

Rombach, 2002), 321–46. See also Christoph Schmidt, *Der Häretische Imperative: Überlegungen zur theologischen Dialektik der Kulturwissenschaft in Deutschland* (Tübingen, Germany: Max Niemeyer, 2000); Christoph Schmidt, *Die Apokalypse des Subjekts: Ästhetische Subjektivität und politische Theologie bei Hugo Ball* (Bielefeld, Germany: Aisthesis, 2003).

127. Schmidt, "Kairos," 324.

128. Sigmund Freud, *Civilization and Its Discontents* (New York: W. W. Norton, 1961), 12.

129. Braun, *Freud*, 8; Gay, *Godless Jew*, 5; Yerushalmi, *Freud's Moses*, 8.

130. Carl E. Schorske, *Fin-de-Siecle Vienna: Politics and Culture* (New York: Knopf, 1980), 6.

131. Ibid., 4–7, 185; Schmidt, "Kairos," 321–46; Mladen Dolar, "Freud and the Political," *Unbound* 15, no. 4 (2008): 15–29.

132. See Freud's letter to Mrs. Fliess, July 4, 1901. Cited in Schur, *Freud*, 215. Freud makes an allusion to Goethe's *Faust*.

133. Gay, *Godless Jew*, 133.

134. Ibid., 131–32. See also Freud's introduction to the Hebrew edition of *Totem and Taboo* (Jerusalem: Dvir, 1939), xv.

135. See the claim made by David Bakan, *Sigmund Freud and the Jewish Mystical Tradition* (New York: Schocken), 1965; William Parson, *Freud and Augustine in Dialogue: Psychoanalysis, Mysticism, and the Culture of Modern Spirituality* (Charlottesville: University of Virginia Press, 2013); Joseph H. Berke, *The Hidden Freud: His Hassidic Roots* (New York: Karnac Books, 2015).

136. Sigmund Freud, "Die Zukunf einer Illusion," in Sigmund Freud, *Gesammelte Werke* (Frankfurt: Fischer, 1946), vol. 14, 378.

Chapter 2

1. Some of these texts were published by Benjamin in a variety of journals, and especially in Barbizon and Bernfeld's *Der Anfang*, which was considered the "journal of youth." Most of them, however, remained unpublished in Benjamin's lifetime. See Bernd Witte, *Walter Benjamin: An Intellectual Biography* (Detroit: Wayne State University Press, 1991), 24. The texts were collected in Walter Benjamin, *Gesammelte Schriften*, vol. 2 (1–3), ed. Rolf Tiedemann and Hermann Schweppenhäuser (Frankfurt: Suhrkamp, 1991). An English version of these texts is presented in Walter Benjamin, *Selected Writings*, vol. 1: 1913–1926 (Cambridge, MA: Belknap Press of Harvard University Press, 1996) and Walter Benjamin, *Early Writings (1910–1917)* (Cambridge, MA: Belknap Press of Harvard University Press, 2011).

2. Walter Rüegg, "Jugend und Gesellschaft um 1900," in *Kulturkritik und Jugendkultur*, ed. Walter Rüegg (Frankfurt: Suhrkamp, 1974), 47–59; Frank

Trommler, "Mission ohne Ziel: Über den Kult der Jugend im modernen Deutschland," in *"Mit uns zieht die neue Zeit": Der Mythos Jugend*, ed. Thomas Koebner, Rolf-Peter Janz, and Frank Trommler (Frankfurt: Suhrkamp, 1985), 14–49; Robbert-Jan Adriaansen, *The Rhythm of Eternity: The German Youth Movement and the Experience of the Past, 1900–1933* (New York: Berghahn Books, 2015).

3. See, e.g., Anson Rabinbach, *In the Shadow of Catastrophe: German Intellectuals between Apocalypse and Enlightenment* (Princeton, NJ: Princeton University Press, 1997); William Borrow, *The Crisis of Reason: European Thought 1848–1914* (New Haven, CT: Yale University Press, 2000); Christoph Schmidt, *Der Häretische Imperative: Überlegungen zur theologischen Dialektik der Kulturwissenschaft in Deutschland* (Tübingen, Germany: Max Niemeyer, 2000); Steven E. Aschheim, *Beyond the Border: The German Jewish Legacy Abroad* (Princeton, NJ: Princeton University Press, 2007); Yotam Hotam, *Modern Gnosis and Zionism: The Crisis of Culture, Life Philosophy and National Jewish Thought* (London: Routledge, 2013).

4. See, e.g., Heiko Stoff, *Ewige Jugend: Konzepte der Verjüngung vom späten 19. Jahrhundert bis ins Dritten Reich* (Cologne: Böhlau Verlag, 2004); Yotam Hotam, ed., *Deutsch-Jüdische Jugendliche im Zeitalter der Jugend* (Göttingen, Germany: V&R Unipress, 2009.)

5. Hotam, *Deutsch-Jüdische*, 6; Adriaansen, *Rhythm*, 180.

6. Erich Gutkind, *Siderische Geburt: Seraphische Wanderung vom Tode der Welt zur Taufe der Tat* (Berlin: Schuster & Loeffler, 1914); Oswald Spengler, *Der Untergang des Abendlandes: Umrisse einer Morphologie der Weltgeschichte* (Munich: Beck, 1922).

7. Carl Jung, *Answer to Job* (Princeton, NJ: Princeton University Press, 1969), 73.

8. Karl Mannheim, "The Problem of Generations," 1923, reprinted in Karl Mannheim, *Essays on the Sociology of Knowledge* (New York: Oxford University Press, 1952), 276–322; Frank Wedekind, *Frühlings Erwachen* (Stuttgart: Reclam, 1991).

9. Fidus was the pseudonym of the illustrator Hugo Reinhold Karl Johann Höppener (1886–1948). See also Peter Janz, "Die Faszination der Jugend durch rituale und sakrale Symbole: Mit Anmerkungen zu Fidus, Hess, Hoffmannsthal und George," in Koebner, Janz, and Trommler, "*Mit uns*," 62–82.

10. Walter Laqueur, *Young Germany: A History of the German Youth Movement* (London: Routledge, 1962); George L. Mosse, *The Culture of Western Europe: The Nineteenth and Twentieth Centuries* (Boulder, CO: Westview, 1988); Peter D. Stachura, *The German Youth Movement 1900–1945* (New York: Macmillan, 1981); Hotam, *Deutsch-Jüdische*; Adriaansen, *Rhythm*.

11. Helmut Böhme, "Das Verewigen und das Veralten der Jugend," in *Jugend: Psychologie-Literatur-Geschichte. Festschrift für Carl Pietzcker*, ed. K. M. Bogdal, G. Ortrud, and J. Pfeiffer (Würzburg, Germany: Königshausen & Neumann, 2001), 25–39. Hans Blüher, the first scholar to present a study of the German Youth

Movement, underlined it as a homoerotic phenomenon because of the type of *Männerbund* that the movement represented. See Hans Blüher, *Wandervogel: Geschichte einer Jugendbewegung* (Berlin: Bernhard Weise Buchhandlung, 1912). See also George L. Mosse, *Nationalism and Sexuality* (New York: H. Fertig, 1985); Ofer Nur, *Eros and Tragedy: Jewish Male Fantasies and the Masculine Revolution of Zionism* (Brighton, UK: Academic Press, 2014).

12. Richard Wolin, *Walter Benjamin: An Aesthetic of Redemption* (New York: Columbia University Press, 1982), 5; Momme Brodersen, *Walter Benjamin: A Biography* (London: Verso, 1990), 56–57.

13. Benjamin, *Early Writings*, 26.

14. Walter Benjamin, *Berliner Chronik* (Stuttgart: Suhrkamp, 1970), 33–40; Terry Eagleton, *Walter Benjamin: Or, Towards a Revolutionary Criticism* (London: Verso, 1981), 12.

15. Witte, *Walter Benjamin*, 22–23; Howard Eiland and Michael W. Jennings, *Walter Benjamin: A Critical Life* (Cambridge, MA: Belknap Press of Harvard University Press, 2014), 39–40; Brodersen, *Walter Benjamin*, 50–51.

16. Benjamin, *Berliner Chronik*, 39–40; Walter Benjamin, *The Correspondence of Walter Benjamin* (Chicago: University of Chicago Press, 1994), 69; Brodersen, *Walter Benjamin*, 57; Witte, *Walter Benjamin*, 23; Eiland and Jennings, *Walter Benjamin*, 63.

17. Benjamin, *Early Writings*, 13; Brodersen, *Walter Benjamin*, 90–91; Witte, *Walter Benjamin*, 34–38.

18. See Rolf Goebel, "Einschreibungen der Trauer: Schrift, Bild und Musik in Walter Benjamins Sonetten auf Christoph Friedrich Heinle," *Weimarer Beiträge: Zeitschrift für Literaturwissenschaft, Ästhetik und Kulturwissenschaften* 59, no. 1 (2013): 65–78; Reinhold Görling, "Die Sonette an Heinle," in *Benjamin Handbuch: Leben, Werk, Wirkung*, ed. B. Lindner (Stuttgart: J. B. Metzler, 2011), 55–59; Erdmut Wizisla, "Fritz Heinle war Dichter: Walter Benjamin und sein Jugendfreund," in *Was nie geschrieben wurde, lesen: Frankfurt Benjamin-Vorträge (1988-1991)*, ed. L. Jäger (Bielefeld, Germany: Aisthesis, 1992), 115–31. See also Erdmut Wizisla, "'Krise und Kritik' (1930/31): Walter Benjamin und das Zeitschriftenprojekt," in *Aber ein Sturm weht vom Paradiese her: Texte zu Walter Benjamin*, ed. Michael Opitz and Wizisla Erdmut (Leipzig: Reclam, 1992), 270–302.

19. Johannes Steizinger, *Revolte, Eros und Sprache* (Berlin: Kulturverlag Kadmos, 2013), 222. See also Michael W. Jennings, "Walter Benjamin, Siegfried Kracauer, and Weimar Criticism," in *Weimar Thought: A Constant Legacy*, ed. Peter E. Gordon and John P. McCormick (Princeton, NJ: Princeton University Press, 2013), 127.

20. Benjamin, *Early Writings*, 242.

21. Ibid.,136.

22. Ibid.

23. Ibid.

24. Ibid., 118.
25. Ibid., 278.
26. Ibid., 133.
27. Wolin, *Walter Benjamin*, 16; Steizinger, *Revolte*, 60.
28. This text was based on a speech that Benjamin gave at the Berlin Free Student Group. See Witte, *Walter Benjamin*, 29.
29. Benjamin, *Selected Writings*, 37.
30. Ibid., 37–38.
31. See, e.g., Benjamin, *Early Writings*, 58, 70, 90; Eiland and Jennings, *Walter Benjamin*, 34; Witte, *Walter Benjamin*, 24.
32. Benjamin, *Selected Writings*, 37.
33. Ibid., 41.
34. Ibid., 42.
35. Ibid., 46.
36. Benjamin, *Correspondence*, 92.
37. Wolin, *Walter Benjamin*, 6.
38. Benjamin, *Selected Writings*, 52.
39. Ibid., 42.
40. Wilhelm von Humboldt, *The Limits of State Action* (Cambridge: Cambridge University Press, 1969). On Benjamin's familiarity with Humboldt's writings, see Witte, *Walter Benjamin*, 35.
41. See, e.g., Winfried Menninghaus, *Walter Benjamin: Theorie der Sprachmagie* (Frankfurt: Suhrkamp, 1980).
42. Benjamin, *Selected Writings*, 66–67.
43. Ibid.
44. Benjamin, *Selected Writings*, 68.
45. Benjamin, *Correspondence*, 127.
46. Benjamin, *Selected Writings*, 69.
47. Ibid., 68. For Arendt's remark, see Detlev Schöttker and Edmunt Wizisla, *Arendt und Benjamin: Texte, Briefe, Dokumente* (Frankfurt: Suhrkamp, 2006), 95.
48. Benjamin, *Selected Writings*, 70.
49. Ibid., 67.
50. Gershom Scholem, "Confession on the Subject of Our Language," in *Acts of Religion*, ed. Jacques Derrida (New York: Routledge, 1926), 226–27. See also Galili Shahar, "The Sacred and the Unfamiliar: Gershom Scholem and the Anxieties of the New Hebrew," *Germanic Review* 83, no. 4 (2008): 299–320.
51. Benjamin, *Early Writings*, 101–2.
52. Michael G. Levine, *A Weak Messianic Power: Figures of a Time to Come in Benjamin, Derrida, and Celan* (New York: Fordham University Press, 2014), 27.
53. Benjamin, *Selected Writings*, 37.
54. See, e.g., Reuven Kahane, *The Origins of Postmodern Youth: Informal Youth Movements in a Comparative Perspective* (Berlin: De Gruyter, 1997).

55. Benjamin, *Early Writings*, 41, 207.
56. Steizinger, *Revolte*, 30. See also Agata Bielik-Robson, *Jewish Cryptotheologies of Late Modernity: Philosophical Marranos* (London: Routledge, 2014), 83–122.
57. Meister Eckhart, *The Complete Mystical Works of Meister Eckhart*, trans. Maurice O'C Walshe (New York: Herder & Herder, 2009); Joachim Kopper, *Die Metaphysik Meister Eckharts* (Saarbrücken, Germany: West-Ost, 1955); Niklaus Largier, *Bibliographie zu Meister Eckhart* (Fribourg, Switzerland: Universitätsverlag, 1989).
58. Eckhart, *Complete Mystical Works*, 8.
59. Ingeborg Degenhardt, *Studien zum Wandel des Eckhartbildes* (Leiden: Brill, 1967), 226.
60. Elliot R. Wolfson, "Theolatry and the Making-Present of the Nonrepresentable," *Journal of Jewish Thought and Philosophy* 25, no. 1 (2017): 6.
61. Franz Pfeiffer, *Deutsche Mystiker des vierzehnten Jahrunderts: Meister Eckhart* (Leipzig: G. J. Göschensche Verlagshandlung, 1857); Gustav Landauer, *Meister Eckharts mystische Schriften* (Berlin: Karl Sehnabel, 1903); Hermann Büttner, *Meister Eckeharts Schriften und Predigten* (Leipzig: E. Diedrichs, 1903); Ingeborg, *Studien*, 237.
62. Ingeborg, *Studien*, 239–66; Wolfson, "Theolatry," 8–10.
63. Eckhart, *Complete Mystical Works*, 27.
64. Kopper, *Die Metaphysik*, 33.
65. Eckhart, *Complete Mystical Works*, in particular Sermons 8, 21, 37, 79, and 80. See also Büttner, *Meister Eckeharts*, vol. 2, 149–56.
66. Eckhart, *Complete Mystical Works*, 576.
67. Ibid., 214.
68. Ibid., 396.
69. Ibid., 396.
70. Elliot R. Wolfson, "Patriarchy and the Motherhood of God in Zoharic Kabbalah and Meister Eckhart," in *Envisioning Judaism: Studies in Honor of Peter Schäfer on the Occasion of His Seventieth Birthday*, vol. 2, ed. Ra'anan S. Bourstan et al. (Tubingen, Germany: Mohr Siebeck, 2013), 1049–88. Wolfson points here in particular to the similarity between Eckhart's symbolism and Kabbalah.
71. Eckhart, *Complete Mystical Works*, 77–78.
72. Ibid., 78.
73. Ibid., 214.
74. Ibid., 79.
75. Hannah Arendt, *Love and Saint Augustine*, ed. Joanna Vecchiarelli Scott and Judith Chelius Stark (Chicago: University of Chicago Press, 1996).
76. Eckhart, *Complete Mystical Works*, 148.
77. Ibid., 394. See also Kopper, *Die Metaphysik*, 50–52.
78. Benjamin, *Correspondence*, 178.
79. Reiner Dieckhoff, *Mythos und Moderne: Über die verborgene Mystik in den Schrifter Walter Benjamins* (Cologne: Janus, 1987), 22; Michael Löwy, *Redemp-*

tion and Utopia: Jewish Libertarian Thought in Central Europe: A Study in Elective Affinity (London: Athlone, 1992), 99; Steizinger, *Revolte*, 55.

80. Asaf Angermann, ed., *Theodor W. Adorno, Gershom Scholem Briefwechsel, 1939–1969* (Frankfurt: Suhrkamp, 2015), 46.

81. Steizinger, *Revolte*, 48.

82. See also Eiland and Jennings, *Walter Benjamin*, 56.

83. Benjamin, *Selected Writings*, 7.

84. Ibid., 37.

85. Talal Asad, *Formations of the Secular: Christianity, Islam, Modernity* (Stanford, CA: Stanford University Press, 2003), 64.

86. Ibid., 65. See a similar point made by Bainard Cowan, "Walter Benjamin's Theory of Allegory," *New German Critique* 22 (1985): 109–22.

87. Benjamin, *Selected Writings*, 8.

88. See the point also made by Eiland and Jennings, *Walter Benjamin*, 56, who highlight the close relation to Hebert Belmore's parallel toying with the symbolic significance of the prostitute. On the centrality of the romantic image of the "genius," see also Kirk Wetters, *Demonic History: From Goethe to the Present* (Evanston, IL: Northwestern University Press, 2014), 124; Eli Friedlander, *Walter Benjamin: A Philosophical Portrait* (Cambridge, MA: Harvard University Press, 2012), 75.

89. Paul North, *The Yield: Kafka's Atheological Reformation* (Stanford, CA: Stanford University Press, 2015), 12.

90. Benjamin, *Selected Writings*, 6.

91. Ibid., 6–7.

92. Ibid.

93. Ibid., 8–9.

94. Büttner, *Meister Eckeharts Schriften*, 188.

95. Benjamin, *Selected Writings*, 53. See also Benjamin, *Correspondence*, 35–36.

96. Benjamin, *Selected Writings*, 8.

97. Ibid., 35–36, 53.

98. Ibid., 9.

99. Wolfson, "Patriarchy," 1056.

100. Benjamin, *Selected Writings*, 9–10. For Wolfson, see his "Patriarchy," 1056.

101. Benjamin, *Selected Writings*, 10.

102. Ibid., 11.

103. See also Steizinger, *Revolte*, 66–74; James McFarland, *Constellation: Friedrich Nietzsche and Walter Benjamin in the Now-Time of History* (New York: Fordham University Press, 2013), 241–48.

104. Benjamin, *Selected Writings*, 11–12.

105. Ibid., 15.

106. Ibid., 12.

107. Ibid.

108. Harry Jansen, "In Search of New Times: Temporality in the Enlightenment and Counter-Enlightenment," *History and Theory* 55, vol. 1 (2016): 66–90.

109. See also Johannes Steizinger, "Zwischen emanzipatorischem Appell und melancholischem Verstummen: Walter Benjamins Jugendschriften," in *Benjamin-Studien*, ed. D. Weidner and S. Weigel (Munich: Wilhelm Fink Verlag, 2011), 225–38.

110. Ansgar Hillach, "Ein neu entdecktes Lebensgesetz der Jugend: Wynekens Führergeist im Denken des jungen Benjamin," in *Global Benjamin: Internationaler Benjamin-Kongress 1992*, vol. 2., ed. K. Garber and L. Rehm (Munich: Wilhelm Fink Verlag, 1999), 890.

111. Benjamin, *Selected Writings*, 16.

112. Ibid., 12.

113. Ibid., 133.

114. Benjamin, *Early Writings*, 60.

115. Benjamin, *Selected Writings*, 16.

116. Ibid., 16–17.

117. Ibid., 17.

118. Ibid.

119. Jean-Luc Nancy, *Dis-Enclosure: The Deconstruction of Christianity* (New York: Fordham University Press, 2008), 36; North, *Yield*, 26; Wolfson, "Patriarchy," 1061; Wolfson, "Theolatry," 18.

120. Ashok Collins, "Towards a Saturated Faith: Jean-Luc Marion and Jean-Luc Nancy on the Possibility of Belief after Deconstruction," *Sophia* 54 (2015): 332; North, *Yield*, 26.

121. See Wolfson, "Patriarchy," 1063, who points to Eckhart's concept of "unbirth" that represents the locus of such eternal nothingness, beyond time, located within the human soul and as an essence of God.

122. Gershom Scholem, *Walter Benjamin: Die Geschichte einer Freundschaft* (Frankfurt: Suhrkamp, 1981), 18; Benjamin, *Correspondence*, 82.

123. Gershom Scholem, ed., *Walter Benjamin/Gershom Scholem: Briefwechsel* (Frankfurt: Suhrkamp, 1980), 157. See also the discussions in Moshe Idel, "Transfer of Categories: The German-Jewish Experience and Beyond," in *The German-Jewish Experience Revisited*, ed. Steven E. Aschheim and Vivian Liska (Berlin: De Gruyter, 2015), 25–26; David Biale, *Gershom Scholem: Kabbalah and Counter-History* (Cambridge, MA: Harvard University Press, 1982), 129–30; Robert Alter, *Necessary Angels: Tradition and Modernity in Kafka, Benjamin, and Scholem* (Cambridge, MA: Harvard University Press, 1991), 108–10.

124. Benjamin, *Selected Writings*, 85.

125. See his letter to Scholem: Benjamin, *Correspondence*, 82.

126. On Benjamin's messianism, see, e.g., Stéphane Symons, *Walter Benjamin: Presence of Mind, Failure to Comprehend* (Leiden: Brill, 2013); Peter Fenves,

The Messianic Reduction: Walter Benjamin and the Shape of Time (Stanford, CA: Stanford University Press, 2011); Sami R. Khatib, *'Theleologie ohne Endzweck': Walter Benjamins Ent-stellung des Messianischen* (Marburg, Germany: Tectum Verlag, 2013); Eric Jacobson, *Metaphysics of the Profane* (New York: Columbia University Press, 2003).

127. Benjamin, *Correspondence*, 20. See also the points made by Scholem and Adorno in their correspondence: Angermann, *Briefwechsel*, 462, 467. For Wolfson, see Wolfson, "Patriarchy," 1051–52.

128. Margarete Kohlenbach, *Walter Benjamin: Self-Reference and Religiosity* (New York: Palgrave Macmillan, 2002), 34.

129. Walter Benjamin, *Selected Writings*, vol. 3 (Cambridge, MA: Harvard University Press, 2006), 305–6. The year of composition is not certain.

130. Khatib, *Theleologie*, 217; Jacobson, *Metaphysics*, 28; David Frisby, *Fragments of Modernity: Theories of Modernity in the Work of Simmel, Kracauer, and Benjamin* (Cambridge, MA: Polity, 1985), 220.

131. Wolin, *Walter Benjamin*, 9. See also Michael Trabitzsch, *Walter Benjamin: Moderne, Messianismus, Politik: Über die Liebe zum Gegenstand* (Berlin: Verlag der Beeken,1985), 61–62.

132. Immanuel Kant, *Critique of Pure Reason* (Cambridge: Cambridge University Press, 1998), 101; Immanuel Kant, *Kritik der Reinen Vernunft* (Hamburg: Felix Meiner Verlag, 1998), 8.

133. Benjamin, *Early Writings*, 198.

134. Witte, *Walter Benjamin*, 30.

135. Benjamin, *Correspondence*, 84.

136. Ibid., 94.

137. Ibid. In his letter to Scholem, Benjamin suggests that witticism presents the essence of the whole Talmudic teaching. See in particular Scholem, *Tagebücher*, vol. 2 (Frankfurt: Suhrkamp Verlag, 1999), 206. Irvin Wohlfarth further suggests that Benjamin makes connections between the mythical origin of the law and his idea of "play" or between "*Trauerspiel* and the Jewish joke." See Irvin Wohlfarth, "On Some Jewish Motifs in Benjamin," in *The Problems of Modernity: Adorno and Benjamin*, ed. Andrew Benjamin (London: Routledge, 1989), 191.

138. Max Horkheimer, *Critical Theory* (New York: Seabury, 1982), 244.

139. Max Horkheimer, "Traditional and Critical Theory," in Max Horkheimer, *Critical Theory: Selected Essays* (New York: Continuum, 1972), 188–243.

140. Wolin, *Walter Benjamin*, 29.

141. Benjamin, *Early Writings*, 168.

142. Jennings, *Walter Benjamin*, 88.

143. Benjamin, *Early Writings*, 168.

144. Ibid., 77.

145. Adolf von Harnack, *Marcion: Das Evangelium vom Fremden Gottes* (Leipzig: J. C. Hinrisch'sche Buchhandlung, 1924).

146. Bernhard Grainer and Christoph Schmidt, eds., *Arche Noah: Die Idee der "Kultur" im deutsch-jüdischen Diskurs* (Freiburg, Germany: Rombach Verlag, 2001).
147. Wetters, *Demonic History*, 114.
148. Ibid., 114.
149. Benjamin, *Selected Writings*, vol. 1, 236–52. For the relevance of ambiguity to the understanding of Benjamin's later work, see, e.g., Jennings, *Walter Benjamin*, 165; Kohlenbach, *Walter Benjamin*, 34; Frisby, *Fragments*, 214; Gabriele Guerra, *Judentum zwischen Anarchie und Theokratie: Eine religionspolitische Diskussion am Beispiel der Begegnung zwischen Walter Benjamin und Gershom Scholem* (Bielefeld, Germany: Aisthesis Verlag, 2007), 213.
150. Susan Buck-Morss, *The Origin of Negative Dialectics: Theodor W. Adorno, Walter Benjamin, and the Frankfurt Institute* (New York: Free Press, 1977), xiii.
151. Kohlenbach, *Walter Benjamin*, 50.
152. Ibid., xii.
153. Fenves, *Messianic Reduction*, 34.
154. Agata Bielik-Robson, "'The God of Myth Is Not Dead': Modernity and Its Cryptotheologies: A Jewish Perspective," in *The Making of Modern German Thought*, ed. Willem Styfhals and Stephane Symons (Albany: State University of New York Press, 2019), 52.
155. Guerra, *Judentum*, 126.
156. See Schöttker and Wizisla, *Arendt und Benjamin*, 83.
157. Asad, *Formations*, 185.
158. Benjamin, *Selected Writings*, vol. 1, 236–52.
159. Ibid., 236.
160. Ibid., 240–41.
161. Ibid., 249–50.
162. Giorgio Agamben, "On the Limits of Violence," *Diacritics* 39, no. 4 (2009): 103–11. The Italian original ("Sui limiti della violenza") was published in *Nuovi Argomenti* 17 (1970): 159–73.
163. Agamben, "On the Limits," 105.
164. Ibid., 107.
165. Ibid.
166. Benjamin, *Selected Writings*, 252.
167. Agamben, "On the Limits," 108–9.
168. Benjamin, *Selected Writings*, 246.
169. On Benjamin's "anarchism," see, e.g., Guerra, *Judentum*, 126–35; Jacobson, *Metaphysics*, 28–29. On Landauer and especially on his mysticism, see Yossef Schwartz, "Gustav Landauer and Gerhard Scholem: Anarchy and Utopia," in *Gustav Landauer: Anarchist and Jew*, ed. Paul Mendes-Flohr and Anya Mali (Berlin: De Gruyter, 2015), 172–90; Yossef Schwartz, "Martin Buber and Gustav Landauer: The Politicization of the Mystical," in *Martin Buber: Neue Perspektiven/New Perspectives*, ed. Michael Zank (Tübingen, Germany: Mohr Siebeck, 2006), 205–19.

170. Benjamin, *Selected Writings*, 252.
171. Jennings, *Walter Benjamin*, 3; Witte, *Walter Benjamin*, 28–29.
172. See also a similar point made in Bielik-Robson, *Jewish Cryptotheologies*.
173. Benjamin, *Correspondence*, 79. See also Benjamin's letters to Balmore and Seligson: Benjamin, *Correspondence*, 18, 20.
174. See Schöttker und Wizisla, *Arendt und Benjamin*, 76. See also Eiland and Jennings, *Walter Benjamin*, 4.
175. See Benjamin, *Gesammelte Schriften*, vol. 2, 839.
176. Witte, *Walter Benjamin*, 27.
177. Leo Baeck, *The Essence of Judaism* (London: Macmillan, 1936); Adolf von Harnack, *What Is Christianity?* (New York/London: G. P. Putnam's Sons/ Williams & Norgate, 1902).
178. See, e.g., Wolin, *Walter Benjamin*, 7; Witte, *Walter Benjamin*, 28–29; Gary Smith, "'Das Jüdische versteht sich immer von selbst': Walter Benjamins frühe Auseinandersetzung mit dem Judentum," *Deutsche Vierteljahrsschrift für Literatur und Geisteswissenschaft* 65, no. 2 (1991): 318–34; Schöttker and Wizisla, *Arendt und Benjamin*, 76; Sandro Pignotti, *Walter Benjamin—Judentum und Literatur: Tradition, Ursprung, Lehre mit einer kurzen Geschichte des Zionismus* (Freiburg, Germany: Rombach, 2009), 7; Brodersen, *Walter Benjamin*, 52; Steizinger, *Revolte*, 119; Guerra, *Judentum*, 56.
179. See, e.g., Aschheim, "German Jews," 31–44; Dieckhoff, *Mythos*, 8; Rabinbach, *In the Shadow*, 27.
180. Gershom Scholem, *The Story of a Friendship* (New York: New York Review of Books, 1981); Gary Smith, "Das Jüdische," 318–34; Pignotti, *Walter Benjamin*, 7; Brodersen, *Walter Benjamin*, 52.
181. Benjamin, *Correspondence*, 17.
182. "Ihre Persönlichkeit war im innern keineswegs vom Jüdischen bestimmt: sie propagieren Palestina und saufen deutsch," Benjamin, *Gesammelte Schriften*, vol. 2, 838.
183. See, e.g, Gershom Scholem, "Jugendbewegung, Judenarbeit und Blau-Weiß," *Blau-Weiß Blätter (Führernummer). Monatsschrift für Jüdisches Jugendwandern* 1, no. 2 (1917): 26–30; Gershom Scholem, "Jüdische Jugendbewegung," *Der Jude: Eine Monatsschrift* 1, no. 12 (1917): 822–25. During this period Scholem contributed mainly to Buber's *Der Jude* and the short-lived journal *Blau-Weisse Brille*.
184. Scholem, "Jüdische Jugendbewegung," 822.
185. Gershom Scholem, *From Berlin to Jerusalem: Memories of My Youth* (New York: Schocken, 1980), 166.
186. Ibid.
187. Scholem, "Jüdische Jugendbewegung," 824.
188. See Christoph Schmidt, "The Political Theology of Gershom Scholem," *Theory and Criticism* 6 (1995): 149–60 [Hebrew].

189. Benjamin, *Correspondence*, 92–94.
190. Walter Benjamin, *Briefe* (Frankfurt: Suhrkamp, 1966), 672.
191. Rose Sven-Erick, *Jewish Philosophical Politics in Germany, 1789–1848* (Waltham, MA: Brandeis University Press, 2014), 1.
192. Stephane Moses, *The Angle of History: Rosenzweig, Benjamin, Scholem* (Stanford, CA: Stanford University Press, 2009), 12.

Chapter 3

1. His annual radio lectures were published in Theodor W. Adorno, *Erziehung zur Mündigkeit: Vorträge und Gespräche mit Hellmut Becker 1959–1969* (Frankfurt: Suhrkamp, 1970) and later in English: Theodor Adorno, *Critical Models: Interventions and Catchwords*, trans. Henry W. Pickford (New York: Columbia University Press, 2005). For Adorno's extensive paper, see Theodor W. Adorno, "Theorie der Halbbildung" (1959), in *Gesammelte Schriften*, vol. 8 (Darmstadt, Germany: Wissenschaftliche Buchgesellschaft, 1998), 93–121; Theodor W. Adorno, "Theory of Pseudo-Culture," *Telos* 20, no. 95 (1993): 15–38. For Adorno's broad introductory courses from the winter semester of 1964–65 and the spring semester of 1965, see Theodor Adorno, *Metaphysics: Concept and Problems* (Malden, MA: Polity, 2000); Theodor Adorno, *History and Freedom* (Malden, MA: Polity, 2006). On the relation of Adorno's *Negative Dialektik* (Frankfurt: Suhrkamp, 1966) to his university courses, see Peter E. Gordon, *Adorno and Existence* (Cambridge, MA: Harvard University Press, 2016), 134.
2. Theodor Adorno, "Education after Auschwitz," in *Critical Models*, 191.
3. See, e.g., Theodor Adorno, "Philosophy and Teachers," in *Critical Models*, 19–36 (broadcast on December 7, 1961, by the radio services of Hessen under the title "Lehrer und Philosophie: Ansprache an Studenten") and Theodor Adorno, "The Meaning of Working through the Past," in *Critical Models*, 89–104 (broadcast on February 7, 1960, by the radio services of Hessen under the title "Was bedeutet: Aufarbeitung der Vergangenheit?"). See also Adorno, "Education after Auschwitz," 194–200.
4. Adorno, "Philosophy and Teachers," 19–36; Adorno, "Education after Auschwitz," 194–200. See also Daniel K. Cho, "Adorno on Education or, Can Critical Self-Reflection Prevent the Next Auschwitz?," *Historical Materialism* 17 (2009): 75; Helmut Schreier and Matthias Heyl, eds., *Never Again! The Holocaust's Challenge for Educators* (Hamburg: Krämer, 1997), 3–5.
5. See Theodor Adorno, *Minima Moralia: Reflections from Damaged Life*, trans. E. F. N. Jephcott (London: Verso, 1974), i; Theodor Adorno, *Minima Moralia: Reflexionen aus dem Beschädigten Leben* (Frankfurt: Suhrkamp, 1950), 1.
6. Adorno, *Metaphysics*, 4.
7. Ibid., 24.

8. Ibid., 24.
9. Ibid., 145.
10. Ibid., 3.
11. Ibid., 3.
12. Ibid., 98.
13. Ibid., 98. See also Gerhard Richter, *Thinking with Adorno: The Uncoercive Gaze* (New York: Fordham University Press, 2019), 46.
14. Adorno, *Metaphysics*, 88. Emphasis in original.
15. Ibid.
16. Ibid., 51.
17. See also the point made in Hent de Vries, *Minimal Theologies: Critiques of Secular Reason in Adorno and Levinas* (Baltimore: Johns Hopkins University Press, 2005), 57.
18. Adorno, *Metaphysics*, 101. See also Theodor Adorno, *Negative Dialectics* (New York: Continuum, 1973), 361.
19. See Adorno's letter from March 14, 1967, in Theodor W. Adorno and Gershom Scholem,*"Der liebe Gott wohnt im Detail": Briefwechsel 1939–1969*, ed. Asaf Angermann (Berlin: Suhrkamp, 2015), 407–16 ("Die Intention einer Rettung der Metaphysik ist tatsächlich in der 'Negative Dialektik' die zentrale").
20. Adorno, *Metaphysics*, 101. For the concept of "civilizational break," see Dan Diner, ed., *Zivilisationsbruch: Denken nach Auschwitz* (Frankfurt: Fischer Taschenbuch, 1988); Dan Diner, ed., *Beyond the Conceivable: Studies on Germany, Nazism, and the Holocaust* (Berkeley: University of California Press, 2000).
21. Adorno, *Metaphysics*, 127.
22. Adorno, "Critique," in *Critical Models*, 281–88.
23. Ibid.
24. Ibid., 281.
25. Adorno, *Metaphysics*, 19. Emphasis in original.
26. See Adorno, "Meaning of Working through the Past," 98. See also Adorno, "Why Still Philosophy?," in *Critical Models*, 11.
27. Adorno, *Metaphysics*, 144.
28. Carl Schmitt, *Political Theology: Four Chapters on the Concept of Sovereignty* (Chicago: University of Chicago Press, 2005), 36.
29. See, e.g., Philipp von Wussow, *Leo Strauss and the Politics of Culture* (Albany: State University of New York Press, 2021); Peter E. Gordon, "The Concept of the Apolitical: German Jewish Thought and Weimar Political Theology," *Social Research* 74, no. 3 (2007): 855–78; Leora Batnitzky, "Leo Strauss and the 'Theologico-Political Predicament,'" in *The Cambridge Companion to Leo Strauss*, ed. Steve B. Smith (Cambridge: Cambridge University Press, 2009), 41–62; Facundo Vega, "On the Tragedy of the Modern Condition: The 'Theologico-Political Problem' in Carl Schmitt, Leo Strauss, and Hannah Arendt," *The European Legacy* 22, no. 6 (2017): 697–728.

30. See the discussion in Christoph Schmidt and Bernhard Greiner, eds., *Arche Noach: Die Idee der Kultur im deutschjüdischen Diskurs* (Freiburg, Germany: Rombach, 2000), 1–15.

31. See the point made by Paul Mendes-Flohr, " 'To Brush History against the Grain': The Eschatology of the Frankfurt School and Ernst Bloch," *Journal of the American Academy of Religion* 51, no. 4 (1983): 631–50.

32. Adorno, *Metaphysics*, 88.

33. Ibid., 88–89. According to Adorno, this also differentiates Aristotle's metaphysics from Plato's doctrine of ideas. See Adorno, *Metaphysics*, 18, 85.

34. Ibid., 77.

35. Ibid., 77–78.

36. See, e.g., Yotam Hotam, "Gnosis and Modernity: A Postwar German Intellectual Debate on Secularisation, Religion and 'Overcoming' the Past," *Totalitarian Movements and Political Religions* 8, no. 3–4 (2007): 591–608; Yotam Hotam, *Modern Gnosis and Zionism: The Crisis of Culture, Life Philosophy and National Jewish Thought* (London: Routledge, 2013); Willem Styfhals, *No Spiritual Investment in the World: Gnosticism and Postwar German Philosophy* (New York: Cornell University Press, 2019).

37. Adorno, *Metaphysics*, 122.

38. Eric Voegelin, *The New Science of Politics* (Chicago: University of Chicago Press, 1952).

39. Hans Jonas, "Gnosticism and Modern Nihilism," *Social Research* 19 (1952): 430–52.

40. Ibid.

41. Ibid.

42. Hans Blumenberg, *The Legitimacy of the Modern Age* (Cambridge, MA: MIT Press, 1966).

43. Blumenberg, *Legitimacy*, 138; Hotam, "Gnosis and Modernity," 591–608.

44. Ernst Bloch, *The Spirit of Utopia* (Stanford, CA: Stanford University Press, 2000), 279–82; Jacob Taubes, *Gnosis und Politik* (Munich: W. Fink, 1984); Gershom Scholem, *Jewish Gnosticism, Merkabah Mysticism, and Talmudic Tradition* (New York: Jewish Theological Seminary of America, 1960). See also Christoph Schmidt, "The Leviathan Crucified: A Critical Introduction to Jacob Taubes' 'The Leviathan as Mortal God,' " *Political Theology* 19, no. 3 (2018): 172–92; Elliot R. Wolfson, *Poetic Thinking* (Leiden: Brill, 2015), 189; Benjamin M. Korstvedt, *Listening for Utopia in Ernst Bloch's Musical Philosophy* (Cambridge: Cambridge University Press, 2010), 32.

45. Gershom Scholem, *The Messianic Idea in Judaism and Other Essays in Jewish Spirituality* (New York: Schocken, 1971), 133. Here Scholem refers specifically to Hans Jonas's *Gnosis und Spätantiker Geist*.

46. See Angermann, *Briefwechsel*, 9–12.

47. Adorno, *History and Freedom*, 59.

48. G. W. F. Hegel, "The Spirit of Christianity and Its Fate," in G. W. F. Hegel, *Early Theological Writings*, trans. T. M. Knox (Chicago: University of Chicago Press, 1948), 182–301.

49. Adorno, "Progress," 59.

50. Karl Loewith, *Meaning in History* (Chicago: University of Chicago Press, 1949).

51. Adorno, *Metaphysics*, 95.

52. Ibid., 117.

53. Adorno, *History and Freedom*, 147.

54. Ibid., 147–48.

55. Adorno, *Minima Moralia*, 154.

56. Ibid., 152.

57. Adorno, *Negative Dialectics*, 361.

58. Theodor Adorno, *The Culture Industry: Selected Essays on Mass Culture* (New York: Routledge, 1991), 5.

59. Adorno, *History and Freedom*, 69.

60. Ibid., 135.

61. Ibid., 76–78.

62. Ibid., 135.

63. Adorno, "Halbbildung," 93–121.

64. See, e.g., Sharon Jessop, "Education for Citizenship and 'Ethical Life': An Exploration of the Hegelian Concepts of *Bildung* and *Sittlichkeit*," *Journal of Philosophy of Education* 46, no. 2 (2012): 287–302; Heinz Sünker, *Politics, Bildung and Social Studies: Perspectives for a Democratic Society* (Rotterdam: Sense, 2006); Christiane Thompson, "The Non-Transparency of the Self and the Ethical Value of *Bildung*," *Journal of Philosophy of Education* 39, no. 3 (2005): 519–34; Walter Bauer, "Introduction," *Educational Philosophy and Theory* 35, no. 2 (2003): 133–37; Fritz Ringer, "*Bildung*: The Social and Ideological Context of the German Historical Tradition," *History of European Ideas* 10, no. 2 (1989): 193–202; David Sorkin, "Wilhelm von Humboldt: The Theory and Practice of Self-Formation (*Bildung*), 1791–1810," *Journal of the History of Ideas* 44 (1983): 55–74; Heinz-Joachim Heydron, *Über den Widerspruch von Bildung und Herrschaft* (Frankfurt: Europäische Verlagsanstalt, 1970).

65. Wilhelm von Humboldt, *The Sphere and Duties of Government* (London: John Chapman, 1854), 11. See also Wilhelm von Humboldt, *Ideen zu einem Versuch die Gränzen der Wirksamkeit des Staats zu bestimmen* (Breslau: Verlag von Eduard Trewendt, 1851), 9: "Die Wahre Zweck des Menschen . . . ist die höchste und proportionirlichste Bildung seiner Kräfte zu einem Ganzen."

66. Bauer, "Introduction," 134.

67. Humboldt, *Sphere*, 18.

68. Aschheim, "German Jews beyond *Bildung* and Liberalism: The Jewish Radical Revival in the Weimar Republic," in *The German-Jewish Dialogue Recon-*

sidered: A Symposium in Honor of George L. Mosse, ed. Klaus L. Berghahn (New York: Peter Lang, 1996), 31–44.

69. Ringer, "*Bildung*," 199. On the centrality of progress, see also Adorno, "Halbbildung," 97; Bauer, "Introduction," 134; Jessop, "Education for Citizenship," 287.

70. Klaus Prange, "Bildung: A Paradigm Regained?," *European Educational Research Journal* 3, no. 2 (2004): 508.

71. Otto Brunner, Werner Conze, and Reinhart Koselleck, *Geschichtliche Grundbegriffe: Lexikon zur politisch-sozialen Sprache in Deutschland* (Stuttgart: Klett-Cotta, 1984), 210; Bauer, "Introduction," 134–35; Yotam Hotam, "*Bildung*: Liberal Education and Its Devout Origins," *Journal of the Philosophy of Education* 54, no. 3 (2019): 619–32.

72. Hotam, "*Bildung*," 619–32.

73. Gotthold Ephraim Lessing, "The Education of the Human Race," in *Lessing's Theological Writings*, ed. Henry Chadwick (Stanford, CA: Stanford University Press, 1956), 83. In 1932 Adorno taught Lessing's theory of education in a seminar together with Paul Tillich. See Adorno, *History and Freedom*, xv.

74. "[Bildung] ist zu sozialisierter Halbbildung geworden, der Allgegenwart des entfremdeten Geistes." Adorno, "Halbbildung," 93. I slightly amended the English translation to better reflect the educational aspect of *Bildung*.

75. Ibid., 94.

76. Ibid., 105.

77. This is a slightly amended translation of Adorno, "Pseudo-Culture," 19. See also the German original: "Der Traum der Bildung, Freiheit vom Diktat der Mittel, der sturen und kargen Nützlichkeit, wird verfälscht zur Apologie der Welt, die nach jenem Diktat eingerichtet ist," in Adorno, "Halbbildung," 98.

78. Adorno, "Halbbildung," 104.

79. Max Horkheimer, *Critical Theory* (New York: Seabury, 1982), 244. See also Max Horkheimer, "Die Emanzipation des Menschen aus versklavenden Verhältnissen," in Max Horkheimer, *Kritische Theorie* (Frankfurt: S. Fischer Verlag, 1982), 194.

80. Theodor W. Adorno and Max Horkheimer, *Dialectic of Enlightenment* (New York: Herder & Herder, 1972), 162.

81. This is a slightly amended translation of Adorno, "Pseudo-Culture," 32, which refers to the German passage "Halbbildung hat das geheime Königreich zu dem aller gemacht." See Adorno, "Halbbildung," 113.

82. Georg Lukács, "Reification and the Consciousness of the Proletariat," in Georg Lukács, *History and Class Consciousness* (Cambridge, MA: MIT Press, 1971), 83–122; Adorno, "Education after Auschwitz," 194–200.

83. Brian O'Connor, ed., *The Adorno Reader* (Malden, MA: Blackwell, 2000), 13.

84. Ibid., 14.

85. Adorno, *Culture Industry*, 68.

86. Adorno, "Halbbildung," 115. I slightly adjusted the original English translation of a "permanent short circuit."
87. *Metropolis*, directed by Fritz Lang (Germany: UFA, 1928).
88. Theodor Adorno, *Kierkegaard: Construction of the Aesthetic* (Minneapolis: University of Minnesota Press, 1989), 131.
89. Hotam, *Modern Gnosis*, 32–41.
90. Sigmund Freud, *Civilization and Its Discontents* (New York: W. W. Norton, 1961), 34. See also Adorno, "Education after Auschwitz," 191.
91. Adorno, "Education after Auschwitz," 191.
92. Angermann, *Briefwechsel*, 83–84, 408–9; Peter Gordon, "The Odd Couple," *The Nation*, June 9, 2016. https://www.thenation.com/article/the-odd-couple/.
93. Immanuel Kant, "An Answer to the Question: What Is Enlightenment?," in *Practical Philosophy*, ed. Mary J. Gregor (Cambridge: Cambridge University Press, 1996), 22.
94. Adorno, *Culture Industry*, 100.
95. Ibid., 64.
96. Theodor Adorno, "Reason and Revelation," in *Critical Models*, 139. The lecture "Offenbarund oder autonome Vernunft" was broadcast by Wesdeutscher Rundfunk on November 20, 1957.
97. Adorno, *Culture Industry*, 98–99.
98. Adorno and Horkheimer, *Dialectic of Enlightenment*, 21.
99. Martin Heidegger, "The Question Concerning Technology," in Martin Heidegger, *The Question Concerning Technology, and Other Essays*, trans. William Lovitt (New York: Garland, 1977), 3–35. Originally published as "Die Frage nach Technik," in Martin Heidegger, *Vorträge und Aufsätze*, vol. 7 (Frankfurt: Vittorio Klostermann, 1954), 5–36.
100. Terence Holden, "Adorno and Arendt: Transitional Regimes of Historicity," *New German Critique* 46, no. 1 (2019): 41–70.
101. Adorno, *Culture Industry*, 18.
102. See also Adorno's personal reflections on the "guilt" of "one who escaped by accident" and was consequently "spared," in Adorno, *Negative Dialectics*, 363.
103. For a critique of Adorno's universalization of Auschwitz, see Ernesto Laclau, *Emancipation(s)* (London: Verso, 1996), 23–24.
104. Adorno, "Meaning of Working through the Past," in *Critical Models*, 92. For Adorno the reluctance to "throw any wrenches into the machinery" ("Sand ins Getrieb") characterizes "the desire to get on with things" in postwar Germany.
105. Adorno, "Education after Auschwitz," 192; Adorno, "Why Still Philosophy?," 102.
106. Theodor Adorno, "Gloss on Personality," in *Critical Models*, 164.
107. Mendes-Flohr, "To Brush History," 634–35. On negativity as "nonidentity," see also Eric S. Nelson, *Levinas, Adorno, and the Ethics of the Material Other* (Albany: State University of New York Press, 2020), 4–5.

108. Peter E. Gordon, *Migrants in the Profane* (New Haven, CT: Yale University Press, 2020), 146.

109. Adorno, "Gloss on Personality," 164. The public lecture "Persönlichkeit: Höchstes Glück der Erdenkinder?" was broadcast by the Westdeutscher Rundfunk on January 2, 1966.

110. Theodor Adorno, "Gloss on Personality," 164. See also Adorno, "Meaning of Working through the Past," 101.

111. Adorno, "Why Still Philosophy?," 7.

112. Adorno, "Philosophy and Teachers," 21.

113. Adorno, "Why Still Philosophy?," 9.

114. Ibid., 9.

115. Ibid., 5–6. See also Axel Honneth, *Pathologies of Reason: On the Legacy of Critical Theory* (New York: Columbia University Press, 2009), 26–27; Wolfson, *Poetic*, 182.

116. Adorno, "Why Still Philosophy?," 7.

117. Adorno, "Education after Auschwitz," 192; Adorno, "Why Still Philosophy?," 102.

118. Adorno, *History and Freedom*, 96.

119. Adorno, *Negative Dialectics*, 320.

120. Adorno, "Why Still Philosophy?," 10.

121. Adorno, *History and Freedom*, 135.

122. Adorno, "Resignation," in *Critical Models*, 292.

123. See a similar argument made by Kathy J. Kiloh, "Adorno's Materialist Ethic of Love," in *A Companion to Adorno*, ed. Peter E. Gordon, Espen Hammer, and Max Pensky (Hoboken, NJ: Wiley, 2020), 601.

124. Adorno, *Metaphysics*, 126.

125. Adorno, "Philosophy and Teachers," 28.

126. Adorno, "Education after Auschwitz," 200.

127. Ibid., 202–3.

128. Ibid., 200–201.

129. Ibid., 202.

130. Ibid., 202.

131. Theodor W. Adorno, "On Kierkegaard's Doctrine of Love," *Zeitschrift fur Sozialforschung* 8, no. 3 (1939): 413–29.

132. Theodor Adorno, *Kierkegaard: Construction of the Aesthetic*, trans. Robert Hullot-Kentor (Minneapolis: University of Minnesota Press, 1962). On Kierkegaard's importance for Adorno, see, e.g., Asaf Angermann, *Beschädigte Ironie: Kierkegaard, Adorno und die negative Dialektik kritischer Subjektivität* (Berlin: De Gruyter, 2014); Gordon, *Adorno and Existence*, 160.

133. Adorno, "On Kierkegaard's," 413.

134. Gordon, *Adorno and Existence*, 31.

135. For agape as a "motif," see Anders Nygern, *Agape and Eros* (Philadelphia: Westminster, 1953), 61–81.

136. Adorno, "On Kierkegaard's," 424.
137. Ibid.
138. Gordon, *Adorno and Existence*, 31.
139. David Sherman, *Sartre and Adorno: The Dialectics of Subjectivity* (Albany: State University of New York Press, 2007), 35.
140. Adorno, "Why Still Philosophy?," 7.
141. Kiloh, "Adorno's Materialist Ethics," 608.
142. Adorno, "On Kierkegaard's," 425.
143. Ibid., 424.
144. Ibid., 414.
145. See also the point made by Marcia Morgan, "Reading Kierkegaard," in *A Companion to Adorno*, ed. Peter E. Gordon, Espen Hammer, and Max Pensky (Hoboken, NJ: Wiley, 2020), 38.
146. Adorno, "On Kierkegaard's," 421.
147. See also Angermann, *Ironie*, 127–29, and Gordon, *Adorno and Existence*, 25. Both authors rightly point out that Adorno's critique of Kierkegaard's retreat to an "interior" realm within the subject is already a central argument in his *Kierkegaard: Construction of the Aesthetic*.
148. Adorno, "On Kierkegaard's," 415.
149. Ibid.
150. Ibid., 416–17.
151. Ibid., 427–28; Sherman, *Sartre*, 34.
152. Adorno, "On Kierkegaard's," 420.
153. Ibid., 421.
154. Ibid.
155. Adorno, "Education after Auschwitz," 202.
156. Ibid., 202.
157. Nygern, *Agape and Eros*, 61–81.
158. See the opening statement in Emmanuel Levinas, *Time and the Other and Additional Essays* (Pittsburgh: Duquesne University Press, 1987), 42. For a similar point, see Nelson, *Levinas*, 2. I thank Cedric Cohen Skalli for pointing me to this aspect of Levinas's philosophy.
159. Adorno, "Why Still Philosophy?," 5–6.
160. Lars Rensmann and Samir Gandesha, eds., *Arendt and Adorno: Political and Philosophical Investigations* (Stanford, CA: Stanford University Press, 2012).
161. Gordon, *Adorno and Existence*, 181. On Adorno's inverse theology, see, e.g., Christopher Craig Brittain, *Adorno and Theology* (London: T&T Clark, 2010), 83–113.
162. Wolfson, *Poetic*, 180. See also Josh Cohen, *Interrupting Auschwitz: Art, Religion, Philosophy* (London: Continuum, 2005), 33.
163. Wolfson, *Poetic*, 181–82.
164. Ibid., 184. See also Christoph Schmidt, "The Return of the Dead Souls: The German Students' Movement and the Holocaust," *Journal of Modern Jewish Studies* 13, no. 1 (2014): 75–86.

165. Wolfson, *Poetic*, 186.
166. Adorno, *Minima Moralia*, 247.
167. Adorno, *History and Freedom*, 89–90.
168. Ibid., 90–91.
169. Adorno, *Metaphysics*, 138.
170. Ibid.; Adorno, *History and Freedom*, 138.
171. Adorno, *Metaphysics*, 121.
172. Theodor Adorno and Herbert Marcuse, "Correspondence on the Student Revolution," *New Left Review* 1, no. 233 (1999): 123–36.
173. See his letter to Marcuse dated May 5, 1969, written a couple of weeks after the students' so-called *Busenaktion* had disrupted Adorno's classroom lecture on April 22, 1969, leaving him weary and in need of a vacation (from which he never returned). Adorno, "Correspondence," 127. Cited also in Gordon, *Adorno and Existence*, 181.
174. Isaiah Berlin, "Two Concepts of Liberty," in Isaiah Berlin, *Four Essays on Liberty* (Oxford: Oxford University Press, 1969), 118–72.
175. Adorno, *Metaphysics*, 138.
176. See, e.g., Elizabeth A. Pritchard, "*Bilderverbot* meets Body in Theodor W. Adorno's Inverse Theology," *Harvard Theological Review*, no. 95 (2002): 291–318; Alexander Garcia Düttmann, *The Memory of Thought: An Essay on Heidegger and Adorno* (New York: Bloomsbury, 2002), 58–61; Schmidt, "Return," 75–86.
177. Adorno, *Negative Dialectics*, 207. See also Schmidt, "Return," 75–86; Christoph Schmidt, "The Return of the Katechon: Giorgio Agamben contra Erik Peterson," *Journal of Religion* 94, no. 2 (2014): 182–203; Cohen, *Interrupting Auschwitz*, 33; Rebecca Comay, "Materialist Mutations of the Bilderverbot," in *The Discursive Construction of Sight in the History of Philosophy*, ed. Michael Levin (Cambridge, MA: MIT Press, 1997), 337–38.
178. Adorno, *Negative Dialectics*, 207.
179. See Max Weber, "Science as a Vocation," in Max Weber, *The Vocation Lectures* (Indianapolis, IN: Hackett), 30–31.
180. Adorno, *Metaphysics*, 143.
181. For Adorno's concept of "melancholic science," see Adorno, *Minima Moralia*, i.

Chapter 4

1. Dana Villa, ed., *The Cambridge Companion to Hannah Arendt* (Cambridge: Cambridge University Press, 2000), 5. The collection of political writings published in the 1960s include Hannah Arendt, *On Revolution* (New York: Viking, 1963); Hannah Arendt, *Men in Dark Times* (New York: Harcourt, Brace & World, 1968); Hannah Arendt, *Between Past and Future* (New York: Viking,

1961/1968); Hannah Arendt, *On Violence* (New York: Harcourt Brace Jovanovich, 1969); Hannah Arendt, *Crises of the Republic* (New York: Harcourt Brace, 1969).

2. Arendt, *Between*, 124.

3. See also Gerhard Richter, *Thinking with Adorno: The Uncoercive Gaze* (New York: Fordham University Press, 2019), 50.

4. Arendt, *Between*, 124.

5. Ibid., 13, 25.

6. Mircea Eliade, *The Sacred and the Profane: The Nature of Religion* (New York: Harcourt, 1987), 68–69. See also David J. Wolken, "Thinking in the Gap: Hannah Arendt and the Prospects for a Postsecular Philosophy of Education," in *Keywords in Radical Philosophy and Education: Common Concepts for Contemporary Movements*, ed. Derek R. Ford (Leiden: Brill/Sense, 2019), 317–27.

7. A. Dirk Moses, "*Das römische Gespräch* in a New Key: Hannah Arendt, Genocide, and the Defense of Republican Civilization," *Journal of Modern History* 85, no. 4 (2013): 871.

8. Ibid.

9. Dean Hammer, "Hannah Arendt and Roman Political Thought: The Practice of Theory," *Political Theory* 30, no. 1 (2002): 124–49. See also Moses, "*Das römische*," 874; Jacques Taminiaux, "Athens and Rome," in Villa, *Cambridge Companion*, 170–71. On the importance of Greek philosophy for Arendt, see, e.g., Noel O'Sullivan, "Hannah Arendt: Hellenic Nostalgia and Industrial Society," in *Contemporary Political Philosophers*, ed. Anthony de Crespigny and Kenneth Minogue (New York: Dodd, Mead, 1975); Margaret Canovan, *Hannah Arendt: A Reinterpretation of Her Political Thought* (Cambridge: Cambridge University Press, 1992); Maurizio Passerin d'Entrèves, *The Political Philosophy of Hannah Arendt* (New York: Routledge, 1994); John McGowan, *Hannah Arendt: An Introduction* (Minneapolis: University of Minnesota Press, 1998); Dana Villa, ed., *Politics, Philosophy, Terror: Essays on the Thought of Hannah Arendt* (Princeton, NJ: Princeton University Press, 1999); Patricia Bowen-Moore, *Hannah Arendt's Philosophy of Natality* (New York: St. Martin's, 1989); Seyla Benhabib, *The Reluctant Modernism of Hannah Arendt* (London: Sage, 1996).

10. Samuel Moyn, "Hannah Arendt on the Secular," *New German Critique* 35, no. 3 (105) (2008): 71–96. See also Douglas Klusmeyer, "Hannah Arendt's Case for Federalism," *Journal of Federalism* 40, no. 1 (2009): 31–58; Miguel Vatter, "Roman Civil Religion and the Question of Jewish Politics in Arendt," *Philosophy Today* 62, no. 2 (2018): 573–606.

11. See Paul Franks, "Sinai since Spinoza: Reflections on Revelation in Modern Jewish Thought," in *The Significance of Sinai: Traditions about Sinai and Divine Revelation in Judaism and Christianity*, ed. George J. Brooke, Hindy Najman, and Loren T. Stuckenbruck (Leiden: Brill, 2008), 333–54.

12. See, e.g., Villa, *Cambridge Companion*, 1; Christopher Irwin, "Reading Hannah Arendt as a Biblical Thinker," *Sophia* 54, no. 4 (2015): 545–61; Steve

Buckler, *Hannah Arendt and Political Theory: Challenging the Tradition* (Edinburgh: Edinburgh University Press, 2011), 2.

13. Irwin, "Reading," 546–54. See also Rafael Zawisza, "Thank God We Are Creatures: Hannah Arendt's Cryptotheology," *Religions* 9, no. 11 (2018): 117–40; Roy T. Tsao, "Arendt's Augustine," in *Politics in Dark Times: Encounters with Hannah Arendt*, ed. Seyla Benhabib (Cambridge: Cambridge University Press, 2010), 39–57; Tatjana Noemi Tömmel, "Vita Passiva: Love in Arendt's Denktagebuch," in *Artifacts of Thinking: Reading Hannah Arendt's Denktagebuch*, ed. Roger Berkowitz and Ian Storey (New York: Fordham University Press 2017), 107; Canovan, *Hannah Arendt*, 8; Stephan Kampowski, *Arendt, Augustine, and the New Beginning: The Action Theory and Moral Thought of Hannah Arendt in the Light of Her Dissertation on St. Augustine* (Grand Rapids, MI: William B. Eerdmans, 2008), 6; Helen Banner, "Existential Failure and Success: Augustinianism in Oakeshott and Arendt," *Intellectual History Review* 21, no. 2 (2011): 171.

14. Hannah Arendt, *Der Liebesbegriff bei Augustin* (Berlin: J. Springer, 1929). In the late 1950s Arendt received a translated manuscript that she continued to rework and rewrite during the 1960s. See, e.g., the editors' notes in Hannah Arendt, *Love and St. Augustine* (Chicago: University of Chicago Press, 1996), 118–19; Tsao, "Arendt's Augustine," 41; Kampowski, *Arendt*, 13–16. Jaspers wrote a letter to Arendt dated January 25, 1966, stating that in her reworked versions "you are now able to say better what you back then already meant." See Lotte Köhler and Hans Saner, *Hannah Arendt/Karl Jaspers Correspondence 1926–1969* (New York: Harcourt Brace Jovanovich, 1992), 661. The final English version of Arendt's work was published posthumously (by University of Chicago Press in 1996, as cited above).

15. Arendt, *Love*, 123.

16. Arendt, *Between*, 73.

17. Arendt, *Love*, 6, 21, 28–31, 38.

18. Arendt, *Between*, 126.

19. Ibid., 127. Ernst Kantorowicz, *The King's Two Bodies: A Study in Medieval Political Theology* (Princeton, NJ: Princeton University Press, 1957).

20. Adolf von Harnack, *Marcion: Das Evagelium vom fremden Gott* (Leipzig: J. C. Hinrische Buchhandlung, 1924).

21. Arendt, *Love*, 8. See also the point made by Patrick Boyle, "Elusive Neighborliness," in *Amor Mundi: Explorations in the Faith and Thought of Hannah Arendt*, ed. James W. Bernauer (Dordrecht, Netherlands: Martinus Nijhoff, 1987), 84–85.

22. Arendt, *Love*, 22.

23. Ibid., 22.

24. Ibid., 20–21.

25. Ibid., 40.

26. Ibid., 7.

27. See also the editors' note in ibid., xvii.
28. Ibid., 42.
29. Ibid., 38–39.
30. Ibid., 39.
31. Ibid., 39.
32. Philip Schaff, ed., *Augustine's "The City of God" and Christian Doctrine* (New York: Christian Literature, 1890), 220.
33. Arendt, *Love*, 17.
34. Ibid., 50–51.
35. Ibid., 18.
36. Anders Nygren, *Eros and Agape* (London: Westminster, 1953), 49–81.
37. Arendt, *Love*, 21.
38. Ibid., 31.
39. Ibid., 49. See also Kampowski, *Arendt*, 73; Eric Gregory, "Augustine and Arendt on Love: New Dimensions in the Religion and Liberalism Debate," *Annual of the Society of Christian Ethics* 21, no. 20 (2001): 156.
40. Arendt, *Love*, 43.
41. Ibid., 58–59. According to Arendt, the Latin word *agere* encapsulated this everlasting process.
42. Tsao, "Arendt's Augustine," 39–57.
43. Arendt, *Love*, 112.
44. See also Gregory, "Augustine," 165.
45. See, e.g., Hannah Arendt, *The Human Condition* (Chicago: University of Chicago Press, 1958), 52.
46. Hannah Arendt, *The Jew as Pariah: Jewish Identity and Politics in the Modern Age* (New York: Grove, 1978), 241.
47. Arendt, *Love*, 122.
48. Schaff, "City of God," 166.
49. Ibid., 166.
50. Ibid., 168.
51. Ibid., 169.
52. Ibid., 170.
53. See Facundo Vega, "On the Tragedy of the Modern Condition: The 'Theologico-Political Problem' in Carl Schmitt, Leo Strauss, and Hannah Arendt," *The European Legacy* 22, no. 6 (2017): 697–728.
54. Schaff, "City of God," 170.
55. Ibid., 177.
56. Ibid., 180.
57. Ibid., 186.
58. Ibid., 200.
59. Ibid., 200.
60. Arendt, *Love*, 39.

61. Hannah Arendt, "Jewish History Revised," *Jewish Frontier*, March 1948, 38. Seealso Elizabeth Young-Bruehl, *Hannah Arendt: For Love of the World* (Binghamton, NY: Vail-Ballou, 1982), 161–63; Irwin, "Reading," 548–49. See also the analysis offered in Judith Bulter, *Parting Ways: Jewishness and the Critique of Zionism* (New York: Columbia University Press, 2013), 114–50.

62. See, e.g., Arendt, *Pariah*, 98; Arendt, "Jewish History Revised," 30–38; on Benjamin, see, e.g., Hannah Arendt, ed., *Illuminations* (New York: Harcourt, Brace & World, 1968), 255–66.

63. Richard J. Bernstein, *Hannah Arendt and the Jewish Question* (Cambridge, UK: Polity, 1966), 10.

64. See, e.g., Hannah Arendt, *The Last Interview and Other Conversations* (New York: Melville, 2013), 28; Bernstein, *Hannah Arendt*, 11.

65. Arendt, *Pariah*, 77.

66. Arendt, *Between*, 125.

67. See Feldman's introduction in Arendt, *Pariah*, 17. See a similar argument in Natan Sznaider, *Jewish Memory and the Cosmopolitan Order* (Cambridge, UK: Polity, 2011), 26.

68. Arendt, *Between*, 18.

69. Arendt, *Love*, 124.

70. Hannah Arendt, "Understanding and Politics," *Partisan Review* 20, no. 4 (1953): 390.

71. See also d'Entrèves, *Political Philosophy*, 28–35.

72. Arendt, *Between*, 15.

73. See also Richter, *Thinking*, 42; Boyle, "Elusive," 81.

74. Antonia Grunenberg, "Arendt, Heidegger, Jaspers: Thinking Through the Breach in Tradition," *Social Research* 74, no. 4 (2007): 1003–28; Banner, "Existential," 176; Hans-Jörg Sigwart, *The Wandering Thought of Hannah Arendt* (London: Macmillan, 2016), 121; Rebecca Dew, *Hannah Arendt: Between Ideologies* (Cham, Switzerland: Palgrave Macmillan, 2020), 81–107; Lewis P. Hinchman and Sandra K. Hinchman, "Existentialism Politicized: Arendt's Debt to Jaspers," in *Hannah Arendt: Critical Essays*, ed. Lewis P. Hinchman and Sandra K. Hinchman (Albany: State University of New York Press, 1994), 143–78; Young-Bruehl, *Hannah Arendt*, 651–63; Kampowski, *Arendt*, 1–2.

75. In the first footnote of chapter 6 of *The Human Condition* Arendt already underlines how, by the seventeenth century, an explicit turn against tradition was fully displayed in Western scientific thought. Arendt, *Human Condition*, 249.

76. Arendt, *Between*, 94.

77. Hannah Arendt, *Lectures on Kant's Political Philosophy* (Chicago: University of Chicago Press, 1989), 39–42.

78. Susan Neiman, "Theodicy in Jerusalem," in *Hannah Arendt in Jerusalem*, ed. Steven E. Aschheim (Berkeley: University of California Press, 2001), 72.

79. Arendt, *Between*, 264.

80. Ibid., 11–13. See also Vivian Liska, *Giorgio Agambens Leerer Messianismus: Hannah Arendt, Walter Benjamin, Franz Kafka* (Vienna: Schlebrügge. Editor, 2008), 26–27. On the centrality of Arendt's "spatial construct," see also Rodrigo Cordero, "It Happens 'In-Between': On the Spatial Birth of Politics in Arendt's *On Revolution*," *European Journal of Cultural and Political Sociology* 1, no. 3 (2014): 249–65. Her reference to the gap as "this small non-time-space" in the "very heart of time" may be best served, arguably, if read with an adjustment of the hyphenation, as a non-time space.

81. Arendt, *Love*, 14.
82. Ibid., 15.
83. Ibid.,15.
84. Ibid., 28.
85. Arendt, *Between*, 11.
86. Arendt, *Men*, 195.
87. Ibid., 203.
88. Ibid., 193, 200. See also Richter, *Adorno*, 43.
89. Arendt, *Men*, 193.
90. Ibid., 193.
91. Ibid., 206.
92. Ibid., 204.
93. Ibid., 198.
94. Ibid., 194.
95. Ibid.
96. Arendt, *Between*, 31. Emphasis in original.
97. Ibid., 39.
98. Ibid.
99. Ibid., 27–28, 55.
100. Ibid., 22.
101. Ibid., 17. See also Arendt, *Human Condition*, 40.
102. Arendt, *Between*, 52.
103. Ibid., 129–32.
104. See also Trevor Tchir, *Hannah Arendt's Theory of Political Action: Daimonic Disclosure of the "Who"* (New York: Palgrave Macmillan, 2017); John Kiess, *Hannah Arendt and Theology* (London: T&T Clark, 2016).
105. Arendt, *Last Interview*, 28.
106. Hannah Arendt, "What is Existenz Philosophy?," *Partisan Review* 13, no. 1 (1946): 34–56. Cited also in Arendt, *Love*, 117. See also the point made in Buckler, *Arendt*, 9. Arendt suggests a clear distinction between action (*praxis*), which characterizes the public sphere, and fabrication (*poiesis*), which relates to those activities that the Romans, in following the Greeks, thought to be restricted to the private, social sphere of the household, having to do with the satisfaction of our material needs. See Arendt, *Human Condition*, 22–27; Franco Palazzi,

"'Reflections on Little Rock' and Reflective Judgment," *Philosophical Papers* 46, no. 3 (2017): 389–441.

107. Arendt, *Between*, 11, 25.

108. Ibid., 94.

109. Arendt, *Human Condition*, 36.

110. Emmanuel Levinas, *Time and the Other and Additional Essays* (Pittsburgh: Duquesne University Press, 1987), 40–41. See also Liska, *Giorgio Agambens*, 26.

111. Arendt, *On Violence*, 52, 91.

112. Karl Jaspers, *The Origin and Goal of History* (New Haven, CT: Yale University Press, 1953), 2; Taran Kang, "The Problem of History in Hannah Arendt," *Journal of the History of Ideas* 74, no. 1 (2013): 149–50. See also Jaspers's own three-part division in his magnum opus Karl Jaspers, *Philosophie 3 Bände (I. Philosophische Weltorientierung. II. Existenzerhellung. III. Metaphysik)* (Berlin: Springer, 1932).

113. Arendt, *On Revolution*, 66.

114. Arendt, *Between*, 94.

115. Ibid., 122–23.

116. Arendt, *On Revolution*, 214. For Heidegger's terminology, see Martin Heidegger, *Poetry, Language, Thought* (New York: Harper Perennial, 2001), 17; Kang, "Problem of History," 47.

117. Arendt, *Between*, 104. See also Dean Hammer, "Authoring within History: The Legacy of Roman Politics in Hannah Arendt," *Classical Receptions Journal* 7, no. 1 (2015): 129–39.

118. Arendt, *Between*, 111.

119. Ibid., 97.

120. Ibid., 264.

121. Ibid., 122–23.

122. Ibid., 259.

123. Ibid. 91–92.

124. Ibid.

125. Hannah Arendt, *The Burden of Our Time* (London: Secker & Warburg, 1951), 436.

126. Arendt, *Between*, 148.

127. Hannah Arendt, "The Legitimacy of Violence as a Political Act?," in *Dissent, Power, and Confrontation*, ed. Alexander Klein (New York: McGraw-Hill, 1967), 97–133; Ilya Winham, "Rereading Hannah Arendt's 'What Is Freedom?': Freedom as a Phenomenon of Political Virtuosity," *Theoria: A Journal of Social and Political Theory* 59, no. 131 (2012): 90.

128. See also Mavis Louise Biss, "Arendt and the Theological Significance of Natality," *Philosophy Compass* 7, no. 11 (2012): 762–71.

129. See Maurice Blanchot, *The Gaze of Orpheus* (Barrytown, NY: Station Hill, 1995), 55. Cited in Elliot R. Wolfson, *Poetic Thinking* (Leiden: Brill, 2015), 128. Wolfson rightly points out, however, that "the instant of death" is no more than "the mirror image of the instant of the beginning" and that the opposite of both can be either the eternal or timelessness. See Wolfson, *Poetic*, 139.

130. Arendt, *Human Condition*, 178. See also Biss, "Arendt," 762.

131. See, e.g., Chad Kautzer, "Political Violence and Race: A Critique of Hannah Arendt," *CLCWeb: Comparative Literature and Culture* 21, no. 3 (2019), https://doi.org/10.7771/1481-4374.3551.

132. Arendt, *Between*, 92–93.

133. Ibid.

134. Ibid., 123. For further reading on the fact that authority is bound by the law, see Arendt, *Between*, 97–98.

135. Giorgio Agamben, "On the Limits of Violence," *Diacritics*, 39, no. 4 (2009): 108–9.

136. See, e.g., Moyn, "Arendt," 71–96; Peter E. Gordon, "The Concept of the Apolitical: German Jewish Thought and Weimar Political Theology," *Social Research* 74, no. 3 (2007): 855–78.

137. Anna Jurkevics, "Hannah Arendt Reads Carl Schmitt's *The Nomos of the Earth*: A Dialogue on Law and Geopolitics from the Margins," *European Journal of Political Theory* 16, no. 3 (2017): 345–66. See also Carl Schmitt, *Political Theology: Four Chapters on the Concept of Sovereignty* (Cambridge, MA: MIT Press, 1985); Carl Schmitt, *Theorie des Partisanen: Zwischenbemerkung zum Begriff des Politischen* (Berlin: Duncker & Humblot, 1963).

138. See Gordon, "Concept," 855–78.

139. See the point also made by Vatter, "Roman," 573.

140. See Gordon, "Concept," 855–78.

141. Schmitt, *Political Theology*, 37.

142. Arendt, *Between*, 141.

143. Arendt, *On Revolution*, 2; Buckler, *Arendt*, 104.

144. Arendt, *Between*, 141.

145. Arendt, *Last Interview*, 112. See also Arendt, *On Revolution*, 199.

146. Arendt, *Between*, 94.

147. Arendt, *On Revolution*, 30–31. See also Hannah Arendt, *Denktagebuch, 1950–1973* (Munich: Piper, 2002), 71–72; Moses, "Das römische," 886. For Arendt's reading of Strauss, see Keedus Liisi, *The Crisis of German Historicism: The Early Political Thought of Hannah Arendt and Leo Strauss* (Cambridge: Cambridge University Press, 2015), 5. On Strauss, see also Eugene R. Sheppard, *Leo Strauss and the Politics of Exile: The Making of a Political Philosopher* (Lebanon, NH: Brandeis University Press, 2006); Philipp von Wussow, *Leo Strauss and the Politics of Culture* (Albany: State University of New York Press, 2021).

148. See Arendt, *Between*, 138.
149. Arendt, *On Revolution*, 31.
150. Ibid., 225.
151. Canovan, *Hannah Arendt*, 202.
152. Moyn, "Arendt," 71–96.
153. Arendt, *On Revolution*, 36–37. See also Gershom Scholem, *Dvarim Be'go* (Tel Aviv: Am Oved, 1976), 157 [Hebrew].
154. Irving Louis Horowitz, *Hannah Arendt: Radical Conservative* (New Brunswick, NJ: Transaction, 2012), 28. See also Martin Jay, "Hannah Arendt: Opposing Views," *Partisan Review* 45, no. 3 (1978): 353; George Kateb, *Politics, Conscience, Evil* (Totowa, NJ.: Rowman & Allenheld, 1984), 28–44; Kimberley F. Curtis, "Aesthetic Foundations of Democratic Politics in the Work of Hannah Arendt," in *Hannah Arendt and the Meaning of Politics*, ed. Craig Calhoun and John McGowan (Minneapolis: University of Minnesota Press, 1997), 29; Liisi, *Crisis*, 135–60.
155. Peter Baehr and Gordon C. Wells, "Debating Totalitarianism: An Exchange of Letters between Hannah Arendt and Eric Voegelin," *History and Theory* 51, no. 3 (2012): 379.
156. Arendt, *Between*, 175.
157. Bruno Latour, *We Have Never Been Modern* (Cambridge, MA: Harvard University Press, 1991).
158. Christoph Schmidt, *Der häretische Imperativ: Überlegungen zur theologischen Dialektik der Kulturwisssenschaft in Deutschland* (Tübingen, Germany: Max Niemeyer Verlag, 2000), 1–10.
159. Hannah Arendt, "Religion and the Intellectuals: A Symposium," *Partisan Review* 17 (1950): 113–16. Also cited in Arendt, *Love*, 141. Arendt refers particularly to the intertwining of philosophy and religion in the works of Spinoza, Descartes, and Heidegger.
160. Stephane Moses, *The Angel of History: Rosenzweig, Benjamin, Scholem* (Stanford, CA: Stanford University Press, 2009), 108–9. See also Wolfson, *Poetic*, 169. Moses adopts the term "revolutionary energy" from Benjamin's *The Arcades Project* (Cambridge, MA: Harvard University Press, 1999), 488. Benjamin cites Henri Focillon, *Vie des formes* (Paris: Presses Universitaires de France, 1934), 12 ("l'énergie révolutionnaire des inventeurs").
161. Arendt, *On Revolution*, 284. See also Buckler, *Arendt*, 122–23.
162. Arendt, *On Revolution*, 184–88. See also Buckler, *Arendt*, 115.
163. Arendt, *On Revolution*, 31.
164. Ibid., 184.
165. Elliot R. Wolfson, "Patriarchy and the Motherhood of God in Zoharic Kabbalah and Meister Eckhart," in *Envisioning Judaism: Studies in Honor of Peter Schäfer on the Occasion of His Seventieth Birthday*, vol. 2, ed. Ra'anan S. Bourstan et al. (Tubingen, Germany: Mohr Siebeck, 2013), 1063.

166. Arendt, *Denktagebuch*, 208, in which Arendt writes that "every beginning is holy." See also in Peter Trawny, "Verstehen und Urteilen: Hannah Arendts Interpretation der Kantischen 'Urteilskraft' als politisch-ethische Hermeneutik," *Zeitschrift für philosophische Forschung* 60, no. 2 (2006): 273; Trömmer, "Vita Passiva," 106-23.

167. Arendt, *Between*, 10-15. See also Liska, *Giorgio Agambens*, 38.

168. Arendt, *Between*, 173-96; Hannah Arendt, "Reflections on Little Rock," *Dissent* 6, no. 1 (Winter 1959): 45-56. See also Evelyn Temme, *Von der Bildung des Politischen zur politischen Bildung: Politikdidaktische Theorien mit Hannah Arendt Weitergedacht* (Frankfurt: Peter Lang, 2014), 253-57.

169. Arendt, *Men*, 5-6. See also Cordero, "It Happens," 151.

170. Arendt, *Between*, 65.

171. Karl Loewith, *Meaning in History* (Chicago: University of Chicago Press, 1949). See also Galili Shahar und Felix Steilen, eds., *Karl Löwith: Welt, Geschichte und Deutung* (Göttingen: Wallstein Verlag, 2019).

172. Julia Kristeva, *Female Genius: Life, Madness, Words—Hannah Arendt, Melanie Klein, Gabrielle Colette; A Trilogy*, vol. 1 (New York: Columbia University Press, 2001).

173. Hannah Arendt, *Essays in Understanding* (New York: Schocken, 1945), 134. See also Bernstein, *Hannah Arendt*, 137.

174. Hannah Arendt, *Eichmann in Jerusalem: A Report on the Banality of Evil* (New York: Viking, 1963).

175. Dan Diner, "Hannah Arendt Reconsidered: On the Banal and the Evil in Her Holocaust Narrative," *New German Critique*, no. 71 (1997): 177.

176. Jerome Kohn, "Evil and Plurality: Hannah Arendt's Way to *The Life of the Mind*, I," in *Hannah Arendt: Twenty Years Later*, ed. Jerome Kohn and Larry May (Cambridge, MA: MIT Press, 1997), 155. The author cites Arendt's letter to Kenneth Thompson of the Rockefeller Foundation from 1969. See also Villa, *Cambridge Companion*, 58.

177. Immanuel Kant, *Religion within the Limits of Reason Alone* (New York: Harper & Brothers, 1960). See also Trawny, "Verstehen," 270. On Arendt's debt to Kant, see in particular Dew, *Hannah Arendt*, 53-79.

178. Benhabib, *Reluctant Modernism*, 186-87; Seyla Benhabib, "Arendt and Adorno: The Elusiveness of the Particular and the Benjaminian Moment," in *Arendt and Adorno: Political and Philosophical Investigations*, ed. Lars Rensmann and Samir Gandesha (Stanford, CA: Stanford University Press, 2012), 40. See also Terence Holden, "Adorno and Arendt: Evil, Modernity and the Underside of Theodicy," *Sophia* 58, no. 2 (2017): 3-5.

179. Arendt, *Origins*, 433.

180. Arendt, *Human Condition*, 241.

181. Leibniz's engagement with the problem of evil was central to his first and last publications, *The Philosopher's Confessions* from 1672 and *Theodicy* from

1709. See, e.g., Mary Morris and George Henry Radcliffe Parkinson, eds., *Leibniz: Philosophical Writings* (London: J. M. Dent & Sons, 1973).

182. George Cotkin, "Illuminating Evil: Hannah Arendt and Moral History," *Modern Intellectual History* 4, no. 3 (2007): 463-90.

183. Arendt, *Eichmann*, 287-88. Except for the title of the book, the term "banality" appears in only one other passage. See Arendt, *Eichmann*, 252.

184. Arendt, *Correspondence*, 62. See also Bernstein, *Hannah Arendt*, 148; Elhanan Yakira, "Hannah Arendt, the Holocaust, and Zionism: A Story of a Failure," *Israeli Studies* 11, no. 3 (2006): 31-61.

185. Arendt, *Correspondence*, 62.

186. Carol Brightman, ed., *Between Friends: The Correspondence of Hannah Arendt and Mary McCarthy 1949-1975* (New York: Harcourt, Brace, 1995), 148.

187. Interview with Joachim Fest, November 9, 1964, in Arendt, *Last Interview*, 48.

188. See Jaspers's letter to Arendt dated October 22, 1963, in Arendt, *Correspondence*, 525.

189. See Arendt, *Pariah*, 240-41.

190. Michal Ben-Naftali, *The Visitation of Hannah Arendt* (Berlin: De Gruyter, 2020), 13.

191. Agata Bielik-Robson, "'The God of Myth Is Not Dead': Modernity and Its Cryptotheologies: A Jewish Perspective," in *The Making of Modern German Thought*, ed. Willem Styfhals and Stephane Symons (Albany: State University of New York Press, 2019), 52.

Epilogue

1. Jürgen Habermas, "Notes on a Post-Secular Society," *New Perspectives Quarterly* 25, no. 4 (2008): 13. See also Jürgen Habermas and Joseph Ratzinger, *Dialektik der Säkularisierung: Über Vernunft und Religion* (Freiburg, Germany: Herder, 2005).

2. Charles Taylor, *A Secular Age* (Cambridge, MA.: Harvard University Press, 2007), 534-35.

3. Brian Turner, *The New Blackwell Companion to the Sociology of Religion* (Oxford: Wiley-Blackwell, 2010), 652; Max Weber, "Science as a Vocation," in *From Max Weber: Essays in Sociology*, ed. H. H. Gerth and C. Wright Mills (New York: Oxford University Press, 1946), 129-56. See also Jose Casanova, *Public Religions in the Modern World* (Chicago: University of Chicago Press, 1994).

4. Salvoj Žižek and John Milbank, *The Monstrosity of Christ: Paradox or Dialectic?* (Cambridge, MA: MIT Press, 2009), 4; Hent de Vries, ed., *Religion beyond a Concept: The Future of the Religious Past* (New York: Fordham University Press), xiii.

5. See also Agata Bielik-Robson, "The Post-Secular Turn: Enlightenment, Tradition, Revolution," *Eidos: A Journal for Philosophy of Culture* 3, no. 9 (2019): 57–83.

6. On the concept of "visitation," see Emmanuel Levinas, "The Trace of the Other," in *Deconstruction in Context: Literature and Philosophy*, ed. Mark C. Taylor (Chicago: University of Chicago Press, 1986), 345–59.

7. Hent de Vries, *Minimal Theologies: Critiques of Secular Reason in Adorno and Levinas* (Baltimore: Johns Hopkins University Press, 2005), 50.

8. Bruno Latour, "Why Has Critique Run Out of Steam? From Matters of Fact to Matters of Concern," *Critical Inquiry* 30, no. 2 (2004): 225–48; Jacques Rancière, *Aesthetics and Its Discontents* (Cambridge, UK: Polity, 2009); Rita Felski, *The Limits of Critique* (Chicago: University of Chicago Press, 2015); Elizabeth S. Anker and Rita Felski, eds., *Critique and Postcritique* (Durham, NC: Duke University Press, 2017).

9. Rita Felski, *Uses of Literature* (Oxford: Blackwell, 2008), 22.

10. The term "hermeneutics of suspicion" was suggested by Paul Ricour, *Freud and Philosophy: An Essay on Interpretation* (New Haven, CT: Yale University Press, 1970), 35. See also Felski, *Limits*, 1.

11. Bielik-Robson, "Post-Secular," 57–66.

12. Eric L. Santner, *On the Psychotheology of Everyday Life: Reflections on Freud and Rosenzweig* (Chicago: University of Chicago Press, 2001), 146.

13. Bielik-Robson, "Post-Secular," 59.

14. See, e.g., Ronald Inglehart and Wayne E. Baker, "Modernization, Cultural Change, and the Persistence of Traditional Values," *American Sociological Review* 65, no. 1 (2000): 19–51; Yaacov Yadgar, *Secularism and Religion in Jewish-Israeli Politics: Traditionists and Modernity* (London: Routledge, 2010).

15. Hans-Georg Gadamer, *Truth and Method* (New York: Continuum, 2003), 309, 358–62; Andrew Bowie, "Gadamer and Romanticism," in *Gadamer's Repercussions: Reconsidering Philosophical Hermeneutics*, ed. Bruce Krajewski (Berkeley: University of California Press, 2004), 69; Theodor Kisiel, "The Happening of Tradition: The Hermeneutics of Gadamer and Heidegger," *Man and World* 2 (1969): 358–85.

16. David Biale, *Not in Heaven: The Tradition of Jewish Secular Thought* (Princeton, NJ: Princeton University Press, 2011).

17. Paul North, *The Yield: Kafka's Atheological Reformation* (Stanford, CA: Stanford University Press, 2015), 1.

18. Judith Butler, *Parting Ways: Jewishness and the Critique of Zionism* (New York: Columbia University Press, 2014), 122.

19. Rose Sven Erick, *Jewish Philosophical Politics in Germany 1789–1848* (Waltham, MA: Brandeis University Press, 2014), 1.

20. Paul Franks, "Jewish Philosophy after Kant: The Legacy of Salomon Maimon," in *The Cambridge Companion to Modern Jewish Philosophy*, ed. Michael

L. Morgan and Peter Eli Gordon (Cambridge: Cambridge University Press, 2007), 53–79.

21. Jürgen Habermas, "The German Idealism of the Jewish Philosophers," in Jürgen Habermas, *Philosophical-Political Profiles* (Cambridge, MA: MIT Press, 1983), 42; Peter E. Gordon, *Migrants in the Profane: Critical Theory and the Question of Secularization* (New Haven, CT: Yale University Press, 2020), 17.

22. Peter E. Gordon, *Rosenzweig and Heidegger: Between Judaism and German Philosophy* (Berkeley: University of California Press, 2003), 3; Paul Mendes-Flohr, *Divided Passions: Jewish Intellectuals and the Experience of Modernity* (Detroit: Wayne State University Press, 1991), 28.

23. The point is emphasized by Agata Bielik-Robson, *Jewish Cryptotheologies of Late Modernity: Philosophical Marranos* (London: Routledge, 2014), 63, citing from Max Horkheimer, "Die Sehnsucht nach dem ganz Anderen (Gespräch mit Helmut Gumnior 1970)," in *Gesammelte Schriften in 19 Bände*, vol. 7, 385–404.

24. Gordon, *Migrants*, 147.

25. Habermas, "Notes," 28.

26. Talal Asad, *Formations of the Secular: Christianity, Islam, Modernity* (Stanford, CA: Stanford University Press, 2003), 181.

27. Ibid., 2. See also James Arthur, Liam Gearon, and Alan Sears, *Education, Politics and Religion: Reconciling the Civil and the Sacred in Education* (London: Routledge, 2010), 98; Ayman K. Agbaria and Muhanad Mustafa, "The Case of Palestinian Civil Society in Israel: Islam, Civil Society, and Educational Activism," *Critical Studies in Education* 55, no. 1 (2014): 44–57.

28. See a similar argument in Ronny Miron, *The Angel of Jewish History: The Image of the Jewish Past in the Twentieth Century* (Brighton, MA: Academic Studies Press, 2014), xiii–xvi.

29. Bielik-Robson, "Post-Secular," 58.

Bibliography

Abraham, Hilda C., and Ernst L. Freud, eds. *A Psycho-Analytic Dialogue: The Letters of Sigmund Freud and Karl Abraham, 1907–1926*. London: Hogarth, 1965.
Adorno, Theodor W. *Critical Models: Interventions and Catchwords*. New York: Columbia University Press, 2005.
———. *The Culture Industry: Selected Essays on Mass Culture*. New York: Routledge, 1991.
———. *Erziehung zur Mündigkeit: Vorträge und Gespräche mit Hellmut Becker 1959–1969*. Frankfurt: Suhrkamp, 1970.
———. *History and Freedom*. Malden, MA: Polity, 2006.
———. *Kierkegaard: Construction of the Aesthetic*. Minneapolis: University of Minnesota Press, 1989.
———. "Lehrer und Philosophie." *Neue Sammlung* 2 (1962): 101–14.
———. *Metaphysics: Concept and Problems*. Malden, MA: Polity, 2000.
———. *Minima Moralia: Reflections from Damaged Life*. London: Verso, 1974.
———. *Minima Moralia: Reflexionen aus dem beschädigten Leben*. Frankfurt: Suhrkamp, 1950.
———. *Negative Dialectics*. New York: Continuum, 1973.
———. "On Kierkegaard's Doctrine of Love." *Zeitschrift für Sozialforschung* 8, no. 3 (1939): 413–29.
———. "Theorie der Halbbildung." In *Gesammelte Schriften*, vol. 8, edited by Rolf Tiedemann, 93–121. Darmstadt, Germany: Wissenschaftliche Buchgesellschaft, 1998.
———. "Theory of Pseudo-Culture." *Telos*, no. 20 (1993): 15–38.
Adorno, Theodor W., and Herbert Marcuse. "Correspondence on the Student Revolution." *New Left Review 1, no. 233 (1999)*: 123–36.
Adriaansen, Robbert-Jan. *The Rhythm of Eternity: The German Youth Movement and the Experience of the Past 1900–1933*. New York: Berghahn, 2015.
Agamben, Giorgio. "On the Limits of Violence." *Diacritics* 39, no. 4 (2009): 103–11.

Agbaria, Ayman K., and Mustafa Muhanad. "The Case of Palestinian Civil Society in Israel: Islam, Civil Society, and Educational Activism." *Critical Studies in Education* 55, no. 1 (2014): 44–57.
Alter, Robert. *Necessary Angels: Tradition and Modernity in Kafka, Benjamin, and Scholem.* Cambridge, MA: Harvard University Press, 1991.
Andrew, Benjamin, and Peter Osborne, eds. *Walter Benjamin's Philosophy: Destruction and Experience.* London: Routledge, 1994.
Angermann, Asaf. *Beschädigte Ironie: Kierkegaard, Adorno und die negative Dialektik kritischer Subjektivität.* Berlin: De Gruyter, 2014.
———, ed. *Der liebe Gott wohnt im Detail: Theodor W. Adorno, Gershom Scholem Briefwechsel 1939–1969.* Berlin: Suhrkamp, 2015.
Anker, Elizabeth S., and Rita Felski, eds. *Critique and Postcritique.* Durham, NC: Duke University Press, 2017.
Anzieu, Didier, *Freud's Self-Analysis.* London: Hogarth, 1986.
Arendt, Hannah. *Between Past and Future.* New York: Viking, 1968.
———. *The Burden of Our Time.* London: Secker & Warburg, 1951.
———. *Crises of the Republic.* New York: Harcourt, 1969.
———. *Denktagebuch, 1950–1973.* Munich: Piper, 2002.
———. *Eichmann in Jerusalem: A Report on the Banality of Evil.* New York: Viking, 1963.
———. *Essays in Understanding.* New York: Schocken, 1945.
———. *The Human Condition.* Chicago: University of Chicago Press, 1958.
———. *The Jew as Pariah: Jewish Identity and Politics in the Modern Age.* New York: Grove, 1978.
———. "Jewish History Revised." *Jewish Frontier*, March 1948, 34–38.
———. *The Last Interview and Other Conversations.* New York: Melville House, 2013.
———. "The Legitimacy of Violence as a Political Act?" In *Dissent, Power, and Confrontation*, edited by A. Klein, 97–133. New York: McGraw-Hill, 1967.
———. *Lectures on Kant's Political Philosophy.* Chicago: University of Chicago Press, 1989.
———. *Der Liebesbegriff bei Augustin: Versuch einer philosophischen Interpretation.* Berlin: Springer, 1929.
———. *Love and St. Augustine.* Chicago: University of Chicago Press, 1996.
———. *Men in Dark Times.* New York: Harcourt Brace Jovanovich, 1968.
———. *On Revolution.* New York: Viking, 1963.
———. *On Violence.* New York: Harcourt Brace Jovanovich, 1969.
———. *The Origins of Totalitarianism.* Cleveland: World, 1958.
———. "Religion and the Intellectuals: A Symposium." *Partisan Review* 17 (1950): 113–16.
———. "Understanding and Politics." *Partisan Review* 20, no. 4 (1953): 377–92.

———. "What is Existenz Philosophy?" *Partisan Review* 8, no. 1 (1946): 34–56.
Arndt, David. *Arendt on the Political*. Cambridge: Cambridge University Press, 2019.
Arthur, James, Liam Gearon, and Alan Sears. *Education, Politics and Religion: Reconciling the Civil and the Sacred in Education*. London: Routledge, 2010.
Asad, Talal. *Formations of the Secular: Christianity, Islam, Modernity*. Stanford, CA: Stanford University Press, 2003.
———. *Genealogies of Religion: Discipline and Reasons of Power in Christianity and Islam*. Baltimore: Johns Hopkins University Press, 1993.
Asad, Talal, Wendy Brown, Judith Butler, and Saba Mahmood. *Is Critique Secular? Blasphemy, Injury, and Free Speech*. Berkeley: University of California Press, 2009.
Aschheim, Steven E. *At the Edge of Liberalism: Junctions of European, German, and Jewish History*. New York: Palgrave Macmillan, 2012.
———. *Beyond the Borders: The German-Jewish Legacy Abroad*. Princeton, NJ: Princeton University Press, 2008.
———. "German Jews beyond *Bildung* and Liberalism: The Jewish Radical Revival in the Weimar Republic." In *The German-Jewish Dialogue Reconsidered: A Symposium in Honor of George L. Mosse*, edited by Klaus L. Berghahn, 31–44. New York: Peter Lang, 1996.
Aschheim, Steven E., and Vivian Liska, eds. *The German-Jewish Experience Revisited*. Berlin: De Gruyter, 2015.
Assmann, Jan. *Moses the Egyptian: The Memory of Egypt in Western Monotheism*. Cambridge, MA: Harvard University Press, 1997.
The Babylonian Talmud. https://halakhah.com/indexrst.html
The Babylonian Talmud. Jerusalem: Israel Institute for Talmudic Publications, 1983. [Hebrew]
Baeck, Leo. *The Essence of Judaism*. London: Macmillan, 1936.
Baehr, Peter, and Gordon C. Wells. "Debating Totalitarianism: An Exchange of Letters between Hannah Arendt and Eric Voegelin." *History and Theory* 51, no. 3 (2012): 364–80.
Bakan, David. *Sigmund Freud and the Jewish Mystical Tradition*. New York: Schocken, 1965.
Banner, Helen. "Existential Failure and Success: Augustinianism in Oakeshott and Arendt." *Intellectual History Review* 21, no. 2 (2011): 171–94.
Bates, David W. "Enemies and Friends: Arendt on the Imperial Republic at War." *History of European Ideas*, no. 36 (2010): 112–24.
Batnitzky, Leora. "Leo Strauss and the 'Theologico-Political Predicament.'" In *The Cambridge Companion to Leo Strauss*, edited by Steve B. Smith, 41–62. Cambridge: Cambridge University Press, 2009.
Bauer, Walter. "Introduction." *Educational Philosophy and Theory* 35, no. 2 (2003): 133–37.

Benhabib, Seyla. "Arendt and Adorno: The Elusiveness of the Particular and the Benjaminian Moment." In *Arendt and Adorno: Political and Philosophical Investigations*, edited by Lars Rensmann and Samir Gandesha, 31–55. Stanford, CA: Stanford University Press, 2012.

———. *Critique, Norm, and Utopia*. New York: Columbia University Press, 1987.

———. *Politics in Dark Times: Encounters with Hannah Arendt*. Cambridge: Cambridge University Press, 2010.

———. *The Reluctant Modernism of Hannah Arendt*. London: Sage, 1996.

Benjamin, Walter. *The Arcades Project*. Cambridge, MA: Harvard University Press, 1999.

———. *Berliner Chronik*. Stuttgart: Suhrkamp, 1970.

———. *Briefe*, edited by Theodor Adorno and Gershom Scholem. Frankfurt: Suhrkamp, 1966.

———. *The Correspondence of Walter Benjamin*. Chicago: University of Chicago Press, 1994.

———. *Early Writings (1910–1917)*. Cambridge, MA: Belknap Press of Harvard University Press, 2011.

———. *Gesammelte Schriften*, edited by von Rolf Tiedemann and Hermann Schweppenhäuser. Frankfurt: Suhrkamp, 1991.

———. *Illuminations*, edited by Hannah Arendt. New York: Harcourt Brace Jovanovich, 1968.

———. *Selected Writings*. Vol. 1. *1913–1926*. Cambridge, MA: Belknap Press of Harvard University Press, 1996.

Ben-Naftali, Michal. *The Visitation of Hannah Arendt*. Berlin: De Gruyter, 2020.

Benyamini, Itzhak. *A Critical Theology of Genesis: The Non-Absolute God*. New York: Palgrave Macmillan, 2016.

Benyamini, Itzhak, and Yotam Hotam. "An Outline for Critical Theology from an Israeli Jewish Perspective." *Journal of Modern Jewish Studies* 14, no. 2 (2015): 333–39.

Bergson, Henri. *Le Rire: Essai sur la signification du comique*. Paris: Quadrige, 1900.

Berke, Joseph H. *The Hidden Freud: His Hassidic Roots*. New York: Karnac Books, 2015.

Berkowitz, Roger, and Ilan Storey, eds. *Artifacts of Thinking: Reading Hannah Arendt's Denktagebuch*. New York: Fordham University Press, 2017.

Berlin, Isaiah. "Two Concepts of Liberty." In Isaiah Berlin, *Four Essays on Liberty*, 118–72. Oxford: Oxford University Press, 1969.

Bernstein, Richard J. *Hannah Arendt and the Jewish Question*. Cambridge, UK: Polity, 1996.

Biale, David. *Gershom Scholem: Kabbalah and Counter-History*. Cambridge, MA: Harvard University Press, 1982.

———. *Not in the Heavens: The Tradition of Jewish Secular Thought*. Princeton, NJ: Princeton University Press, 2011.

Bielik-Robson, Agata. "'The God of Myth Is Not Dead': Modernity and Its Cryptotheologies, a Jewish Perspective." In *Genealogies of the Secular: The Making of Modern German Thought*, edited by Willem Styfhals and Stephane Symons, 51–80. Albany: State University of New York Press, 2019.
———. *Jewish Cryptotheologies of Late Modernity: Philosophical Marranos*. London: Routledge, 2014.
———. "The Post-Secular Turn: Enlightenment, Tradition, Revolution." *Eidos: A Journal for Philosophy of Culture* 3, no. 9 (2019): 57–83.
Biemann, Asher D. *Dreaming of Michelangelo: Jewish Variations on a Modern Theme*. Stanford, CA: Stanford University Press, 2012.
Biss, Mavis Louise. "Arendt and the Theological Significance of Natality." *Philosophy Compass* 7, no. 11 (2012): 762–71.
Blanchot, Maurice. *The Gaze of Orpheus*. Barrytown, NY: Station Hill, 1995.
Blanton, Smiley. *Diary of My Analysis with Freud*. New York: Hawthorn Books, 1971.
Bloch, Ernst. *The Spirit of Utopia*. Stanford, CA: Stanford University Press, 2000.
Bloom, Harold. *Ruin the Sacred Truths: Poetry and Belief from the Bible to the Present*. Cambridge, MA: Harvard University Press, 1987.
Blüher, Hans. *Wandervogel: Geschichte einer Jugendbewegung*. Berlin: Bernhard Weise Buchhandlung, 1912.
Blumenberg, Hans. *Lebenszeit und Weltzeit*. Frankfurt: Suhrkamp, 1986.
———. *The Legitimacy of the Modern Age*. Cambridge, MA: MIT Press, 1966.
Böhme, Harmut. "Das Verewigen und das Veralten der Jugend." In *Jugend: Psychologie-Literatur-Geschichte. Festschrift für Carl Pietzcker*, edited by Michael Bogdal Klaus, Gutjahr Ortrud, and Joachim Pfeiffer, 25–38. Würzburg, Germany: Königshausen & Neumann, 2011.
Bonaparte, Maria, Anna Freud, and Ernst Kris, eds. *Aus den Anfängen der Psychoanalyse*. London: Imago, 1950.
Borrow, William. *The Crisis of Reason: European Thought 1848–1914*. New Haven, CT: Yale University Press, 2000.
Bowen-Moore, Patricia. *Hannah Arendt's Philosophy of Natality*. New York: St. Martin's, 1989.
Bowie, Andrew. "Gadamer and Romanticism." In *Gadamer's Repercussions: Reconsidering Philosophical Hermeneutics*, edited by Bruce Krajewski, 55–81. Berkeley: University of California Press, 2004.
Boyle, Patrick. "Elusive Neighborliness." In *Amor Mundi: Explorations in the Faith and Thought of Hannah Arendt*, edited by James W. Bernauer, 81–113. Dordrecht, Netherlands: Martinus Nijhoff, 1987.
Braun, Helmuth F. *Sigmund Freud: "Ein gottloser Jude": Entdecker des Unbewussten*. Berlin: Hentrich & Hentrich, 2006.
Braune, Joan. *Erich Fromm's Revolutionary Hope: A Prophetic Messianism as a Critical Theory of the Future*. Leiden: Brill, 2014.

Breier, Karl-Heinz. *Hannah Arendt interkulturell gelesen.* Nordhausen, Germany: Bautz, 2007.
Brightman, Carol, ed. *Between Friends: The Correspondence of Hannah Arendt and Mary McCarthy 1949–1975.* New York: Harcourt, Brace, 1995.
Brill, Abraham Arden. "Freud's Theory of Wit." *Journal of Abnormal Psychology* 6, no. 4 (1911): 279–316.
Brodersen, Momme. *Walter Benjamin: A Biography.* London: Verso, 1990.
Brome, Vincent. *Freud and His Disciples.* London: Caliban, 1984.
Brumlik, Micha. "Verborgene Tradition und messianisches Licht: Arendt, Adorno und ihr Judentum." In *Arendt und Adorno,* edited by Dirk Auer, Lars Rensmann, and Julia Schulye Wessel, 74–93. Frankfurt: Suhrkamp, 2003.
Brunkhorst, Hauke. *Hannah Arendt.* Munich: Beck, 1999.
Brunner Otto, Werner Conze, and Reinhart Koselleck. *Geschichtliche Grundbegriffe: Lexikon zur politisch-sozialen Sprache in Deutschland.* Stuttgart: Klett-Cotta, 1984.
Buber, Martin. *Daniel: Gespräche von der Verwirklichung.* Leipzig: Insel Verlag, 1913.
Buckler, Steve. *Hannah Arendt and Political Theory: Challenging the Tradition.* Edinburgh: Edinburgh University Press, 2011.
Buck-Morss, Susan. *The Origin of Negative Dialectics: Theodor W. Adorno, Walter Benjamin, and the Frankfurt Institute.* New York: Free Press, 1977.
Butler, Judith. *Parting Ways: Jewishness and the Critique of Zionism.* New York: Columbia University Press, 2013.
Büttmer, Hermann. *Meister Eckharts Schriften und Predigten.* Leipzig: E. Diedrichs, 1903.
Byrd, Dustin J., ed. *The Critique of Religion and Religion's Critique: On Dialectical Religiology.* Leiden: Brill, 2020.
Calhoun, Craig, and John McGowan, eds. *Hannah Arendt and the Meaning of Politics.* Minneapolis: University of Minnesota Press, 1997.
Canovan, Margaret. *Hannah Arendt: A Reinterpretation of Her Political Thought.* Cambridge: Cambridge University Press, 1992.
Casanova, Jose. *Public Religions in the Modern World.* Chicago: University of Chicago Press, 1994.
Caygill, Howard. "Non-Messianic Political Theology in Benjamin's 'On the Concept of History.'" In *Walter Benjamin and History,* edited by Andrew Benjamin, 215–26. New York: Continuum, 2005.
Chacón, Rodrigo. "Hannah Arendt in Weimar: Beyond the Theological-Political Predicament?" In *The Weimar Moment: Liberalism, Political Theology, and Law,* edited by Leonard V. Kaplan and Rudy Koshar, 73–107. Plymouth, MA: Lexington Books, 2012.
Cho, Daniel K. "Adorno on Education or, Can Critical Self-Reflection Prevent the Next Auschwitz?" *Historical Materialism,* no. 17 (2009): 74–97.
Clark, Ronald W. *Freud: The Man and the Cause.* New York: Random House, 1980.

Cohen, Josh. *Interrupting Auschwitz: Art, Religion, Philosophy*. London: Continuum, 2005.
Collins, Ashok. "Towards a Saturated Faith: Jean-Luc Marion and Jean-Luc Nancy on the Possibility of Belief after Deconstruction." *Sophia* 54 (2015): 321–41.
Comay, Rebecca. "Materialist Mutations of the *Bilderverbot*." In *The Discursive Construction of Sight in the History of Philosophy*, edited by Michael Levin, 337–78. Cambridge, MA: MIT Press, 1997.
Cordero, Rodrigo. "It Happens 'In-Between': On the Spatial Birth of Politics in Arendt's *On Revolution*." *European Journal of Cultural and Political Sociology* 1, no. 3 (2014): 249–65.
Cotkin, George. "Illuminating Evil: Hannah Arendt and Moral History." *Modern Intellectual History* 4, no. 3 (2007): 463–90.
Cover, Robert M. "Nomos and Narrative." In *Narrative, Violence, and the Law: The Essays of Robert Cover*, edited by Martha Minow, Michael Ryan, and Austin Sarat, 95–172. Ann Arbor: University of Michigan Press, 1993.
———. "The Supreme Court 1982 Term—Forward: Nomos and Narrative." *Harvard Law Review* 97, no. 4 (1983–84): 1–68.
Cowan, Bainard. "Walter Benjamin's Theory of Allegory." *New German Critique*, no. 22 (1985): 109–22.
Craig, Brittain Christopher. *Adorno and Theology*. London: T&T Clark, 2010.
Curtis, Kimberley F. "Aesthetic Foundations of Democratic Politics in the Work of Hannah Arendt." In *Hannah Arendt and the Meaning of Politics*, edited by Craig Calhoun and John McGowan, 27–52. Minneapolis: University of Minnesota Press, 1997.
d'Entrèves, Maurizio Passerin. *The Political Philosophy of Hannah Arendt*. New York: Routledge, 1994.
de Certeau, Michel. *The Writings of History*. New York: Columbia University Press, 1988.
de Vries, Hent. *Minimal Theologies: Critiques of Secular Reason in Adorno and Levinas*. Baltimore: Johns Hopkins University Press, 2005.
———, ed. *Religion beyond a Concept: The Future of the Religious Past*. New York: Fordham University Press, 2008.
Degenhardt, Ingeborg. *Studien zum Wandel des Eckhartbildes*. Leiden: Brill, 1967.
Deuber-Mankowsky, Astrid. *Der frühe Walter Benjamin und Hermann Cohen: Jüdische Werte, kritische Philosophie, vergängliche Erfahrung*. Berlin: Verlag Vorwerk 8, 2000.
Dew, Rebecca. *Hannah Arendt: Between Ideologies*. Cham, Switzerland: Palgrave Macmillan, 2020.
Dickinson, Colby, and Stephane Symons, eds. *Walter Benjamin and Theology: Perspectives in Continental Philosophy*. New York: Fordham University Press, 2016.

Dieckhoff, Reiner. *Mythos und Moderne: Über die verborgene Mystik in den Schriften Walter Benjamins*. Cologne: Janus, 1987.
Diller, Jerry Victor. *Freud's Jewish Identity: A Case Study in the Impact of Ethnicity*. London: Associated University Presses, 1991.
Diner, Dan. *Beyond the Conceivable: Studies on Germany, Nazism, and the Holocaust*. Berkeley: University of California Press, 2000.
———. "Hannah Arendt Reconsidered: On the Banal and the Evil in Her Holocaust Narrative." *New German Critique*, no. 71 (1997): 177–90.
———, ed. *Zivilisationsbruch: Denken nach Auschwitz*. Frankfurt: Fischer Taschenbuch, 1988.
Dolar, Mladen. "Freud and the Political." *Unbound* 15, no. 4 (2008): 15–29.
Draper, Hal. *The Complete Poems of Heinrich Heine: A Modern English Version*. Oxford: Oxford University Press, 1982.
Düttmann, Alexander Garcia. *The Memory of Thought: An Essay on Heidegger and Adorno*. New York: Bloomsbury, 2002.
Eagleton, Terry. *Walter Benjamin: Or, Towards a Revolutionary Criticism*. London: Verso, 1981.
Eckhart, Meister. *The Complete Mystical Works of Meister Eckhart*. New York: Herder & Herder, 2009.
Edel, Edmund. *Der Witz der Juden*. Berlin: L. Lamm, 1909.
Eiland, Howard, and Michael W. Jennings. *Walter Benjamin: A Critical Life*. Cambridge, MA: Belknap Press of Harvard University Press, 2014.
Eliade, Mircea. *The Sacred and the Profane: The Nature of Religion*. Orlando, FL: Harcourt, 1987.
Felski, Rita. *The Limits of Critique*. Chicago: University of Chicago Press, 2015.
Fenves, Peter. *The Messianic Reduction: Walter Benjamin and the Shape of Time*. Stanford, CA: Stanford University Press, 2010.
Fischer, Kuno. *Über den Witz*. Heidelberg: Carl Winter's Universitätsbuchhandlung, 1889.
Focillon Henri. *Vie des formes*. Paris: Presses Universitaires de France, 1934.
Ford, Derek R., ed. *Keywords in Radical Philosophy and Education: Common Concepts for Contemporary Movements*. Leiden: Brill/Sense, 2019.
Foucault, Michel. "Préface a la transgression." *Critique*, no. 195–96 (1963): 751–69.
———. "Preface to Transgression." In Michel Foucault, *Language, Counter-Memory, Practice: Selected Essays and Interviews*, edited by Donald F. Bouchar, 29–52. Ithaca, NY: Cornell University Press, 1977.
———. "What Is Critique?" In *What Is Enlightenment? Eighteenth-Century Answers and Twentieth-Century Questions*, edited by James Schmidt, 382–98. Berkeley: University of California Press, 1996.
Franks, Paul. "Divided by Common Sense: Mendelssohn and Jacobi on Reason and Inferential Justification." In *Moses Mendelssohn's Metaphysics and Aesthetics:13* (Studies in German Idealism, vol. 13), edited by Reinier Munk, 203–15. New York: Springer, 2011.

---. "From World-Soul to Universal Organism: Maimon's Hypothesis and Schelling's Physicalization of a Platonic-Kabbalistic Concept." In *Schelling's Philosophy: Freedom, Nature, and Systematicity*, edited by Anthony G. Bruno, 71–92. Oxford: Oxford University Press, 2020.
---. "Jewish Philosophy after Kant: The Legacy of Salomon Maimon." In *The Cambridge Companion to Modern Jewish Philosophy*, edited by Michael L. Morgan and Peter Eli Gordon, 53–79. Cambridge: Cambridge University Press, 2007.
---. "Sinai since Spinoza: Reflections on Revelation in Modern Jewish Thought." In *The Significance of Sinai: Traditions about Sinai and Divine Revelation in Judaism and Christianity*, edited by George J. Brooke, Hindy Najman, and Loren T. Stuckenbruck, 333–54. Leiden: Brill, 2008.
Freeman, Erika. *Insights: Conversations with Theodor Reik*. Englewood Cliffs, NJ: Prentice-Hall, 1971.
Freud, Sigmund. *Aus den Anfängen der Psychoanalyse: Briefe an Wilhelm Fliess, Abhandlugen und Notizen aus den Jahren 1887–1902*. London: Imago, 1950.
---. *An Autobiographical Study*. London: Hogarth, 1948.
---. *Civilization and Its Discontents*. New York: W. W. Norton, 1961.
---. "Humor." *International Journal of Psychoanalysis* 9, no. 1 (1927): 161–66.
---. *The Interpretation of Dreams*. New York: Basic Books, 1955.
---. *Jokes and Their Relation to the Unconscious*. New York: W. W. Norton, 1960.
---. *Der Mann Moses und die Monotheistische Religion: Drei Abhandlungen*. Amsterdam: Verlag Allert de Lange, 1939.
---. "Der *Moses* des Michelangelo." *Imago* 3, no. 1 (1914): 15–36.
---. "The Moses of Michelangelo." In Sigmund Freud, *The Standard Edition of the Complete Psychological Works of Sigmund Freud*, vol. 13, 209–38. London: Hogarth, 1955.
---. *The Origins of Psycho-Analysis: Letters to Wilhelm Fliess, Drafts and Notes, 1887–1902*, edited by Marie Bonaparte, Anna Freud, and Ernst Kris. New York: Basic Books, 1954.
---. *Psychopathology of Everyday Life*. New York: W. W. Norton, 1960.
---. *Three Essays on the Theory of Sexuality*. London: Imago, 1949.
---. *Totem und Tabu: Einige Übereinstimmungen im Seelenleben der Wilden und der Neurotiker*. Leipzig: Hugo Heller & CIE, 1913.
---. *Der Witz und seine Beziehung zum Unbewußten*. Leipzig: Franz Deuticke, 1905.
---. "Die Zukunf einer Illusion." In Sigmund Freud, *Gesammelte Werke*, vol. 14, 325–80. Frankfurt: Fischer, 1946.
---. "Zwangshandlungen und Religionsübungen." *Zeitschrift für Religionspsychologie* 1, no. 1 (1907): 127–39.
Friedlander, Eli. *Walter Benjamin: A Philosophical Portrait*. Cambridge, MA: Harvard University Press, 2012.

Frisby, David. *Fragments of Modernity: Theories of Modernity in the Work of Simmel, Kracauer and Benjamin*. Cambridge, UK: Polity, 1985.
Gadamer, Hans-Georg. *Truth and Method*. New York: Continuum, 2003.
Galili, Shahar. "The Sacred and the Unfamiliar: Gershom Scholem and the Anxieties of the New Hebrew." *Germanic Review* 83, no. 4 (2008): 299–320.
Galili, Shahar, und Felix Steilen, eds. *Karl Löwith: Welt, Geschichte und Deutung*. Göttingen, Germany: Wallstein Verlag, 2019.
Gay, Peter. *Freud: A Life of Our Time*. New York: W. W. Norton, 1988.
———. *Freud, Jews and Other Germans: Masters and Victims in Modernist Culture*. New York: Oxford University Press, 1978.
———. *A Godless Jew: Freud, Atheism, and the Making of Psychoanalysis*. New Haven, CT: Yale University Press, 1987.
Gilman, Sander, L. "Jewish Jokes: Sigmund Freud and the Hidden Language of the Jews." *Psychoanalysis and Contemporary Thought* 7, no. 4 (1984): 591–614.
Glazova, Anna, and Paul North, eds. *Messianic Thought outside Theology*. New York: Fordham University Press, 2014.
Goebel, Rolf J. "Einschreibungen der Trauer: Schrift, Bild und Musik in Walter Benjamins Sonetten auf Christoph Friedrich Heinle." *Weimarer Beiträge: Zeitschrift für Literaturwissenschaft, Ästhetik und Kulturwissenschaften* 59, no. 1 (2013): 65–78.
Gordon, Peter E. *Adorno and Existence*. Cambridge, MA: Harvard University Press, 2016.
———. "The Concept of the Apolitical: German Jewish Thought and Weimar Political Theology." *Social Research* 74, no. 3 (2007): 855–78.
———. *Migrants into the Profane: Critical Theory and the Question of Secularization*. New Haven, CT: Yale University Press, 2020.
———. "The Odd Couple." *The Nation*, June 9, 2016. https://www.thenation.com/article/the-odd-couple/
———. *Rosenzweig and Heidegger: Between Judaism and German Philosophy*. Berkeley: University of California Press, 2003.
Görling, Reinhold. "Die Sonette an Heinle." In *Benjamin Handbuch: Leben, Werk, Wirkung*, edited by B. Lindner, 585–91. Stuttgart: J. B. Metzler, 2011.
Grainer, Bernhard, and Christoph Schmidt, eds. *Arche Noah: Die Idee der "Kultur" im Deutsch-Jüdischen Diskurs*. Freiburg, Germany: Rombach Verlag, 2001.
Gregory, Eric. "Augustine and Arendt on Love: New Dimensions in the Religion and Liberalism Debate." *Annual of the Society of Christian Ethics*, no. 21 (2001): 155–72.
Gresser, Moshe. *Dual Allegiance: Freud as a Modern Jew*. Albany: State University of New York Press, 1994.
Grollman, Earl A. *Judaism in Sigmund Freud's World*. New York: Bloch, 1965.
Grunenberg, Antonia. "Arendt, Heidegger, Jaspers: Thinking Through the Breach in Tradition." *Social Research* 74, no. 4 (2007): 1003–28.

Guerra, Gabriele. *Judentum zwischen Anarchie und Theokratie: Eine religionspolitische Diskussion am Beispiel der Begegnung zwischen Walter Benjamin und Gershom Scholem.* Bielefeld, Germany: Aisthesis Verlag, 2007.
Gutkind, Erich. *Siderische Geburt: Seraphische Wanderung vom Tode der Welt zur Taufe der Tat.* Berlin: Schuster & Loeffler, 1914.
Habermas, Jürgen. "The German Idealism of the Jewish Philosophers." In *Philosophical-Political Profiles*, edited by Jürgen Habermas, 21–44. Cambridge, MA: MIT Press, 1983.
———. "Notes on a Post-Secular Society." *New Perspectives Quarterly* 25, no. 4 (2008): 17–29.
Habermas, Jürgen, and Joseph Ratzinger. *Dialektik der Säkularisierung: Über Vernunft und Religion.* Freiburg, Germany: Herder, 2005.
Hammer, Dean. "Authoring within History: The Legacy of Roman Politics in Hannah Arendt." *Classical Receptions Journal* 7, no. 1 (2015): 129–39.
———. "Hannah Arendt and Roman Political Thought: The Practice of Theory." *Political Theory* 30, no. 1 (2002): 124–49.
Hegel, G. W. F. "The Spirit of Christianity and Its Fate." In G. W. F. Hegel, *Early Theological Writings*, 182–301. Chicago: University of Chicago Press, 1948.
Heidegger, Martin. "Die Frage nach Technik." In Martin Heidegger, *Vorträge und Aufsätze*, vol. 7, 5–36. Frankfurt: Vittorio Klostermann, 1954.
———. *Poetry, Language, Thought.* New York: Harper Perennial, 2001.
———. "The Question Concerning Technology." In Martin Heidegger, *The Question Concerning Technology, and Other Essays*, 3–35. New York: Garland, 1977.
Heine, Heinrich. *Romanzero.* Hamburg: Hoffmann und Campe, 1852.
Heins, Volker. "Saying Things That Hurt: Adorno as Educator." *Thesis Eleven* 11, no. 1 (2012): 68–82.
Heller, Sharon. *Freud A to Z.* Hoboken, NJ: Wiley, 2005.
Hering, James. "Judaism and the Contingency of Religious Law in Kant's Religion within the Boundaries of Mere Reason." *Journal of Religious Ethics* 48, no. 1 (2020): 74–100.
Herzog, Rudolf. *Heil Hitler, Das Schwein ist Tot: Lachen unter Hitler—Komik und Humor im Dritten Reich.* Frankfurt: Eichborn, 2006.
Heydron, Heinz-Joachim. *Über den Widerspruch von Bildung und Herrschaft.* Frankfurt: Europäische Verlagsanstalt, 1970.
Hillach, Ansgar. "Ein neu entdecktes Lebensgesetz der Jugend: Wynekens Führergeist im Denken des jungen Benjamin." In *Global Benjamin: Internationaler Benjamin-Kongress 1992*, vol. 2., edited by K. Garber and L. Rehm, 873–90. Munich: Wilhelm Fink Verlag, 1999.
Hinchman, Lewis P., and Hinchman, Sandra K. *Hannah Arendt: Critical Essays.* Albany: State University of New York Press, 1994.
Holden, Terence. "Adorno and Arendt: Evil, Modernity and the Underside of Theodicy." *Sophia* 58, no. 2 (2019): 197–224.

———. "Adorno and Arendt: Transitional Regimes of Historicity." *New German Critique* 46, no. 1 (2019): 41–70.
Honneth, Axel. *Pathologies of Reason: On the Legacy of Critical Theory*. New York: Columbia University Press, 2009.
Horkheimer, Max. *Critical Theory*. New York: Seabury, 1982.
———. *Kritische Theorie*. Frankfurt: S. Fischer Verlag, 1982.
———. "Die Sehnsucht nach dem ganz Anderen (Gespräch mit Helmut Gumnior 1970)." In Max Horkheimer, *Gesammelte Schriften in 19 Bände*, vol. 7, edited by A. Schmidt, 385–404. Frankfurt: S. Fischer Verlag, 1970.
Horkheimer, Max, and Theodor Adorno. *The Dialectics of Enlightenment*. New York: Continuum, 1993.
Horowitz, Irving Louis. *Hannah Arendt: Radical Conservative*. New York: Routledge, 2012.
Hotam, Yotam, ed. *Deutsch-Jüdische Jugendliche im Zeitalter der Jugend*. Göttingen, Germany: V&R Unipress, 2009.
———. "Gnosis and Modernity: A Postwar German Intellectual Debate on Secularisation, Religion and 'Overcoming' the Past." *Totalitarian Movements and Political Religions* 8, no. 3–4 (2007): 591–608.
———. *Modern Gnosis and Zionism: The Crisis of Culture, Life Philosophy and National Jewish Thought*. London: Routledge, 2013.
Hutton, Christopher. "Freud and the Family Drama of Yiddish." In *Studies in Yiddish Linguistics*, edited by Paul Wexler, 9–22. Tübingen, Germany: Max Niemeyer, 1990.
Idel, Moshe. "Transfer of Categories: The German-Jewish Experience and Beyond." In *The German-Jewish Experience Revisited*, edited by Steven E. Aschheim and Vivian Liska, 25–26. Berlin: De Gruyter, 2015.
Inglehart, Ronald, and Wayne E. Baker. "Modernization, Cultural Change, and the Persistence of Traditional Values." *American Sociological Review* 65, no. 1 (2000): 19–51.
Irwin, Christopher. "Reading Hannah Arendt as a Biblical Thinker." *Sophia* 54, no. 4 (2015): 545–61.
Jacobson, Eric. *Metaphysics of the Profane*. New York: Columbia University Press, 2003.
Jansen, Harry. "In Search of New Times: Temporality in the Enlightenment and Counter-Enlightenment." *History and Theory* 55, no. 1 (2016): 66–90.
Janz, Peter. "Die Faszination der Jugend durch Rituale und sakrale Symbole: Mit Anmerkungen zu Fidus, Hess, Hoffmannsthal und George." In *"Mit uns zieht die neue Zeit": Der Mythos Jugend*, edited by Thomas Koebner, Peter Rolf-Janz, and Frank Trommler, 62–82. Frankfurt: Suhrkamp, 1985.
Jaspers, Karl. *The Origin and Goal of History*. New Haven, CT: Yale University Press, 1953.
———. *Philosophie 3 Bände (I. Philosophische Weltorientierung. II. Existenzerhellung. III. Metaphysik)*. Berlin: Springer, 1932.

Jay, Martin. "Hannah Arendt: Opposing Views." *Partisan Review* 45, no. 3 (1978): 348–80.
Jennings, Michael W. *Dialectical Images: Walter Benjamin's Theory of Literary Criticism*. Ithaca, NY: Cornell University Press, 1987.
———. "Walter Benjamin, Siegfried Kracauer, and Weimar Criticism." In *Weimar Thought: A Constant Legacy*, edited by Peter E. Gordon and John P. McCormick, 203–19. Princeton, NJ: Princeton University Press, 2013.
The Jerusalem Talmud. Jerusalem: Israel Institute for Talmudic Publications, 1988. [Hebrew]
Jessop, Sharon. "Education for Citizenship and 'Ethical Life' and Exploration of the Hegelian Concepts of *Bildung* and *Sittlichkeit*." *Journal of Philosophy of Education* 46, no. 2 (2012): 287–302.
Jonas, Hans. "The Concept of God after Auschwitz: A Jewish Voice." *Journal of Religion* 67, no. 1 (1987): 1–13.
———. "Gnosticism and Modern Nihilism." *Social Research*, no. 19 (1952): 430–52.
Jones, Ernest. *The Life and Work of Sigmund Freud*. New York: Basic Books, 1953.
Joskowicz, Ari, and Ethan Katz, eds. *Secularism in Question: Jews and Judaism in Modern Times*. Philadelphia: University of Pennsylvania Press, 2016.
Jung, Carl Gustav. *Answer to Job*. Princeton, NJ: Princeton University Press, 1969.
Jurkevics, Anna. "Hannah Arendt Reads Carl Schmitt's *The Nomos of the Earth*: A Dialogue on Law and Geopolitics from the Margins." *European Journal of Political Theory* 16, no. 3 (2017): 345–66.
Kahane, Reuven. *The Origins of Postmodern Youth: Informal Youth Movements in a Comparative Perspective*. Berlin: De Gruyter, 1997.
Kampowski, Stephan. *Arendt, Augustine, and the New Beginning: The Action Theory and Moral Thought of Hannah Arendt in the Light of Her Dissertation on St. Augustine*. Grand Rapids, MI: William B. Eerdmans, 2008.
Kang, Taran. "The Problem of History in Hannah Arendt." *Journal of the History of Ideas* 74, no. 1 (2013): 139–60.
Kant, Immanuel. "An Answer to the Question: What Is Enlightenment?" In Immanuel Kant, *Practical Philosophy*, edited by M. J. Gregor, 1–22. Cambridge: Cambridge University Press, 1996.
———. *The Conflict of the Faculties*. Lincoln: University of Nebraska Press, 1979.
———. *Critique of Judgement*. Oxford: Oxford University Press, 2008.
———. *Critique of Pure Reason*. Cambridge: Cambridge University Press, 1998.
———. *Kritik der Reinen Vernunft*. Hamburg: Felix Meiner Verlag, 1998.
———. *Religion within the Limits of Reason Alone*. Indianapolis, IN: Hackett.
———. "What Real Progress Has Metaphysics Made in Germany since the Time of Leibniz and Wolff?" In *Theoretical Philosophy after 1781*, edited by H. Allison and P. Heath, 337–424. Cambridge: Cambridge University Press, 2002.
Kantorowicz, Ernst. *The King's Two Bodies: A Study in Medieval Political Theology*. Princeton, NJ: Princeton University Press, 1957.

Kanzer, Mark, and Jules Glenn, eds. *Freud and His Self-Analysis*. New York: Jason Aronson, 1979.
Kara Ivanov-Kaniel, Ruth. *Birth in Kabbalah and Psychoanalysis*. Berlin: De Gruyter, 2022.
Kateb, George. *Politics, Conscience, Evil*. Totowa, NJ: Rowman & Allanheld, 1984.
Katzoff, Binyamin. "The Relationship between Tosefta and Yerushalmi of *Berachot*." PhD diss., Bar-Ilan University, 1994. [Hebrew]
Kautzer, Chad. "Political Violence and Race: A Critique of Hannah Arendt." *CLCWeb: Comparative Literature and Culture* 21, no. 3 (2019). https://doi.org/10.7771/1481-4374.3551
Keedus, Liisi. *The Crisis of German Historicism: The Early Political Thought of Hannah Arendt and Leo Strauss*. Cambridge: Cambridge University Press, 2015.
Khatib, Sami R. *"Theleologie ohne Endzweck": Walter Benjamins Ent-stellung des Messianischen*. Marburg, Germany: Tectum Verlag, 2013.
Kiess, John. *Hannah Arendt and Theology*. New York: T&T Clark, 2016.
Kiloh, J. Kathy. "Adorno's Materialist Ethic of Love." In *A Companion to Adorno*, edited by Peter E. Gordon, Espen Hammer, and Max Pensky, 601–13. Hoboken, NJ: Wiley, 2020.
Kirchner, Sascha. *Walter Benjamin und das Wiener Judentum zwischen 1900 und 1938*. Würzburg, Germany: Königshausen & Neumann, 2009.
Kisiel, Theodor. "The Happening of Tradition: The Hermeneutics of Gadamer and Heidegger." *Man and World*, no. 2 (1969): 358–85.
Klusmeyer, Douglas. "Hannah Arendt's Case for Federalism." *Journal of Federalism* 40, no. 1 (2009): 31–58.
Kohlenbach, Margarete. *Walter Benjamin: Self-Reference and Religiosity*. New York: Palgrave Macmillan, 2002.
Köhler, Lotte, and Saner, Hans. *Hannah Arendt/Karl Jaspers Correspondence 1926–1969*. New York: Harcourt Brace Jovanovich, 1992.
Kohn, Jerome. "Evil and Plurality: Hannah Arendt's Way to *The Life of the Mind*." In *Hannah Arendt: Twenty Years Later*, edited by Jerome Kohn and Larry May, 147–78. Cambridge: MIT Press, 1997.
Kopper, Joachim. *Die Metaphysik Meister Eckharts*. Saarbrücken, Germany: West-Ost, 1955.
Korstvedt, Benjamin M. *Listening for Utopia in Ernst Bloch's Musical Philosophy*. Cambridge: Cambridge University Press, 2010.
Koselleck, Reinhart. *Critique and Crisis: Enlightenment and the Pathogenesis of Modern Society*. Hamburg: Berg, 1988.
Kristeva, Julia. *Female Genius: Life, Madness, Words—Hannah Arendt, Melanie Klein*. New York: Columbia University Press, 2001.
Krüll, Marianna. *Freud and His Father*. New York: W. W. Norton, 1986.
Laclau, Ernesto. *Emancipation(s)*. London: Verso, 1996.

Lalonde, Marc P. *From Critical Theology to a Critical Theory of Religion: Essays in Contemporary Religious Thought*. London: Peter Lang, 2010.
———, ed. *The Promise of Critical Theology: Essays in Honor of Charles Davis*. Waterloo, ON: Wilfrid Laurier University Press, 1995.
Landauer, Gustav. *Meister Eckharts mystische Schriften*. Berlin: Karl Sehnabel, 1903.
Laqueur, Walter. *Young Germany: A History of the German Youth Movement*. London: Routledge, 1962.
Largier, Niklaus. *Bibliographie zu Meister Eckahrt*. Fribourg, Switzerland: Universitätsverlag, 1989.
Last Stone, Suzanne. "In Pursuit of the Counter-Text: The Turn to the Jewish Legal Model in Contemporary American Legal Theory." *Harvard Law Review* 106, no. 4 (1993): 813–89.
Latour, Bruno. *We Have Never Been Modern*. Cambridge, MA: Harvard University Press, 1991.
———. "Why Has Critique Run Out of Steam? From Matters of Fact to Matters of Concern." *Critical Inquiry* 30, no. 2 (2004): 225–48.
Lazier, Benjamin. *God Interrupted: Heresy and the European Imagination between the World Wars*. Princeton, NJ: Princeton University Press, 2008.
Lessing, Gotthold Ephraim. "The Education of the Human Race." In Gotthold Ephraim Lessing, *Lessing's Theological Writings*, edited by Henry Chadwick. Stanford, CA: Stanford University Press, 1956.
Levinas, Immanuel. *Time and the Other and Additional Essays*. Edited and translated by Richard A. Cohen. Pittsburgh: Duquesne University Press, 1987.
———. "The Trace of the Other." In *Deconstruction in Context: Literature and Philosophy*, edited by Mark C. Taylor, 345–59. Chicago: University of Chicago Press, 1986.
Levine, Michael G. *A Weak Messianic Power: Figures of a Time to Come in Benjamin, Derrida, and Celan*. New York: Fordham University Press, 2014.
Lipps, Theodor. *Komik und Humor: Eine psychologisch-ästhetische Untersuchung*. Hamburg: Verlag von Leopold Voss, 1898.
Liska, Vivian. *German-Jewish Thought and Its Afterlife: A Tenuous Legacy*. Bloomington: Indiana University Press, 2017.
———. *Giorgio Agambens leerer Messianismus: Hannah Arendt, Walter Benjamin, Franz Kafka*. Vienna: Schlebrügge.Editor, 2008.
Loewith, Karl. *Meaning in History*. Chicago: University of Chicago Press, 1949.
Löwy, Michael. *Redemption and Utopia: Jewish Libertarian Thought in Central Europe: A Study in Elective Affinity*. London: Athlone, 1992.
Lukács, Georg. "Reification and the Consciousness of the Proletariat." In George Lukács, *History and Class Consciousness*, 83–222. Cambridge, MA: MIT Press, 1971.
———. *Die Seele und die Formen: Essays*. Berlin: E. Fleischel, 1911.

Major, Rene, and Chantal Talagrand. *Freud: The Unconscious and World Affairs.* New York: Routledge, 2018.
Mannheim, Karl. "The Problem of Generations." In Karl Mannheim, *Essays on the Sociology of Knowledge*, 276–322. New York: Oxford University Press, 1952.
Marcia, Morgan. "Reading Kierkegaard." In *A Companion to Adorno*, edited by Peter E. Gordon, Espen Hammer, and Max Pensky, 35–50. Hoboken, NJ: Wiley, 2020.
Marshall, David. *The Weimar Origins of Rhetorical Inquiry.* Chicago: University of Chicago Press, 2020.
McCole, John. *Walter Benjamin and the Antinomies of Tradition.* Ithaca, NY: Cornell University Press, 1993.
McFarland, James. *Constellation: Friedrich Nietzsche and Walter Benjamin in the Now-Time of History.* New York: Fordham University Press, 2013.
McGowan, John. *Hannah Arendt: An Introduction.* Minneapolis: University of Minnesota Press, 1998.
Mehlman, Jeffrey. "How to Read Freud on Jokes: The Critic as *Schadchen*." *New Literary History* 6, no. 2 (1975): 439–61.
Mendes-Flohr, Paul. *Divided Passions: Jewish Intellectuals and the Experience of Modernity.* Detroit: Wayne State University Press, 1991.
———. "Jewish Thought and Philosophy: Modern Thought." *Encyclopedia of Religion.* 2nd ed., 4899–4910. New York: Gale, 2005.
———. *Martin Buber: A Life of Faith and Dissent.* New Haven, CT: Yale University Press, 2019.
———. "To Brush History against the Grain: The Eschatology of the Frankfurt School and Ernst Bloch." *Journal of the American Academy of Religion* 51, no. 4 (1983): 631–50.
Menninghaus, Winfried. *Walter Benjamin: Theorie der Sprachmagie.* Frankfurt: Suhrkamp, 1980.
Miron, Ronny. *The Angel of Jewish History: The Image of the Jewish Past in the Twentieth Century.* Brighton, MA: Academic Studies Press, 2014.
The Mishnah: A New Integrated Translation and Commentary. https://www.emishnah.com/index1.html
Morris, Leslie. *The Translated Jews: German-Jewish Culture outside the Margins.* Evanston, IL: Northwestern University Press, 2018.
Morris, Mary, and George H. R. Parkinson, eds. *Leibniz: Philosophical Writings.* London: J. M. Dent & Sons, 1973.
Moses, A. Dirk. "*Das römische Gespräch* in a New Key: Hannah Arendt, Genocide, and the Defense of Republican Civilization." *Journal of Modern History* 85, no. 4 (2013): 867–913.
———. "Genocide and Modernity." In *The Historiography of Genocide*, edited by Dan Stone, 156–93. Houndmills, UK: Palgrave Macmillan, 2008.
Moses, Stephane. *The Angel of History: Rosenzweig, Benjamin, Scholem.* Stanford, CA: Stanford University Press, 2009.

Mosse, George L. *The Culture of Western Europe: The Nineteenth and Twentieth Centuries*. Boulder, CO: Westview, 1988.

———. *German Jews beyond Judaism*. Bloomington, IN: Hebrew Union College Press, 1985.

———. *Nationalism and Sexuality*. New York: H. Fertig, 1985.

Moyn, Samuel. "Amos Funkenstein on the Theological Origins of Historicism." *Journal of the History of Ideas*, 64, no. 4 (2003): 639–57.

———. "Hannah Arendt on the Secular." *New German Critique* 35, no. 3 (2008): 71–96.

Musch, Sebastian. *Jewish Encounters with Buddhism in German Culture: Between Moses and Buddha, 1890–1940*. Cham, Switzerland: Palgrave Macmillan, 2019.

Nancy, Jean-Luc. *Dis-Enclosure: The Deconstruction of Christianity*. New York: Fordham University Press, 2008.

Neiman, Susan. *Evil in Modern Thought: An Alternative History of Philosophy*. Princeton, NJ: Princeton University Press, 2002.

———. "Theodicy in Jerusalem." In *Hannah Arendt in Jerusalem*, edited by Steven E. Aschheim, 65–92. Berkeley: University of California Press, 2001.

Nelson, Eric S. *Levinas, Adorno, and the Ethics of the Material Other*. Albany: State University of New York Press, 2020.

North, Paul. *The Yield: Kafka's Atheological Reformation*. Stanford, CA: Stanford University Press, 2015.

Nur, Ofer. *Eros and Tragedy: Jewish Male Fantasies and the Masculine Evolution of Zionism*. Brighton, MA: Academic Studies Press, 2014.

Nygern, Anders. *Agape and Eros*. Philadelphia: Westminster, 1953.

O'Connor, Brian, ed. *The Adorno Reader*. Malden, MA: Blackwell, 2000.

O'Sullivan, Noel. "Hannah Arendt: Hellenic Nostalgia and Industrial Society." In *Contemporary Political Philosophers*, edited by Anthony de Crespigny and Kenneth Minogue, 228–51. New York: Dodd, Mead, 1975.

Oring, Elliott. "Jokes and Their Relation to Sigmund Freud." *Western Folklore* 43, no. 1 (1984): 37–48.

———. *The Jokes of Sigmund Freud: A Study in Humor and Jewish Identity*. Philadelphia: University of Pennsylvania Press, 1984.

Owens, Patricia. *Between War and Politics: International Relations and the Thought of Hannah Arendt*. Oxford: Oxford University Press, 2007.

Palmquist, Stephen R. "Kant's 'Appropriation' of Lampe's God." *Harvard Theological Review* 85, no. 1 (1992): 85–108.

———. *Kant's Critical Religion*. Burlington, VT: Ashgate, 2000.

Parson, William. *Freud and Augustine in Dialogue: Psychoanalysis, Mysticism, and the Culture of Modern Spirituality*. Charlottesville: University of Virginia Press, 2013.

Pfeiffer, Franz. *Deutsche Mystiker des vierzehnten Jahrunderts: Meister Eckhart*. Leipzig: G. J. Göschensche Verlagshandlung, 1857.

Pignotti, Sandro. *Walter Benjamin—Judentum und Literatur: Tradition, Ursprung, Lehre mit einer kurzen Geschichte des Zionismus*. Freiburg, Germany: Rombach, 2009.

Prange, Klaus. "*Bildung*: A Paradigm Regained?" *European Educational Research Journal* 3, no. 2 (2004): 501–9.

Pritchard, Elizabeth A. "*Bilderverbot* Meets Body in Theodor W. Adorno's Inverse Theology." *Harvard Theological Review* 95, no. 3 (2002): 291–318.

Puner, Helen Walker. *Freud: His Life and His Mind*. New York: Howell, Soskin, 1947.

Rabinbach, Anson. *In the Shadow of Catastrophe: German Intellectuals between Apocalypse and Enlightenment*. Princeton, NJ: Princeton University Press, 1997.

Rancière, Jacques. *Aesthetics and Its Discontents*. Cambridge, MA: Polity, 2009.

Raschke, Carl A. *Critical Theology: Introducing an Agenda for an Age of Global Crisis*. Downers Grove, IL: Intervarsity, 2016.

Rensmann, Lars, and Gandesha Samir, eds. *Arendt and Adorno: Political and Philosophical Investigations*. Stanford, CA: Stanford University Press, 2012.

Rice, Emanuel. *Freud and Moses: The Long Journey Home*. Albany: State University of New York Press, 1990.

Richter, Gerhard. *Thinking with Adorno: The Uncoercive Gaze*. New York: Fordham University Press, 1919.

Ringer, Fritz. "Bildung: The Social and Ideological Context of the German Historical Tradition." *History of European Ideas* 10, no. 2 (1989): 193–202.

Rosine, Kelz. *The Non-Sovereign Self, Responsibility, and Otherness: Hannah Arendt, Judith Butler, and Stanley Cavell on Moral Philosophy and Political Agency*. London: Palgrave Macmillan, 2016.

Rrenban, Monad. *Wild, Unforgettable Philosophy: In Early Works of Walter Benjamin*. Lanham, MD: Lexington Books, 2005.

Rüegg, Walter. "Jugend und Gesellschaft um 1900." In *Kulturkritik und Jugendkultur*, edited by Walter Rüegg, 47–59. Frankfurt: Verlag Vittorio Klostermann, 1974.

Rürup, Miriam, and Simone Lässig, eds. *German-Jewish Space and Spatiality in Modern History*. New York: Berghahn Books, 2017.

Santner, Eric L. *On the Psychotheology of Everyday Life: Reflections on Freud and Rosenzweig*. Chicago: University of Chicago Press, 2001.

Schaff, Philip, ed. *Augustine's "The City of God" and Christian Doctrine*. New York: Christian Literature, 1890.

Scharf, Orr. *Thinking in Translation: Scriptures and Redemption in the Thought of Franz Rosenzweig*. Berlin: De Gruyter, 2019.

Schmidt, Christoph. *Die Apokalypse des Subjekts: Ästhetische Subjektivität und politische Theologie bei Hugo Ball*. Bielefeld, Germany: Aisthesis, 2003.

———. "'Es gibt Vernichtung': Anmerkungen zu Jakob Taubes' *Die Politische Theologie des Paulus*." In Christoph Schmidt, *Die theopolitische Stunde: Zwölf Perspektiven auf das eschatologische Problem der Moderne*, 269–302. Paderborn, Germany: Wilhelm Fink Verlag, 2009.

---. "Gershom Scholem's Political Theology." In *God Will Not Stand Still: Jewish Modernity and Political Theology*, edited by Christoph Schmidt and Eli Schonfeld, 122-33. Jerusalem: Van Leer Institute, 2009. [Hebrew]

---. *Der häretische Imperativ: Überlegungen zur theologischen Dialektik der Kulturwisssenschaft in Deutschland*. Tübingen, Germany: Max Niemeyer Verlag, 2000.

---. "The Israel of the Spirit: The German Student Movement of the 1960s and Its Attitude to the Holocaust." *Dapim: Journal of Holocaust Research* 24, no. 1 (2010): 269-318. [Hebrew]

---. "Kairos and Culture: Some Remarks on the Formation of the Cultural Sciences in Germany and the Emergence of a Jewish Political Theology." In *Arche Noah: Die Idee der "Kultur" im deutsch-jüdischen Diskurs*, edited by Bernhard Greiner and Christoph Schmidt, 321-46. Freiburg, Germany: Rombach, 2002.

---. "The Leviathan Crucified: A Critical Introduction to Jacob Taubes' 'The Leviathan as Mortal God.'" *Political Theology* 19, no. 3 (2018): 172-92.

---. "The Political Theology of Gershom Scholem." *Theory and Criticism*, no. 6 (1995): 149-60. [Hebrew]

---. "The Return of the Dead Souls: The German Students' Movement and the Holocaust." *Journal of Modern Jewish Studies* 13, no. 1 (2014): 75-86.

---. "The Return of the Katechon: Giorgio Agamben contra Erik Peterson." *Journal of Religion* 94, no. 2 (2014): 182-203.

Schmidt, Christoph, and Bernd Greiner, eds. *Arche Noach: Die Idee der Kultur im deutschjüdischen Diskurs*. Freiburg, Germany: Rombach, 2000.

Schmitt, Carl. *Political Theology: Four Chapters on the Concept of Sovereignty*. Cambridge, MA: MIT Press, 1985.

---. *Theorie des Partisanen: Zwischenbemerkung zum Begriff des Politischen*. Berlin: Duncker & Humblot, 1963.

Scholem, Gershom. "Confession on the Subject of Our Language (1926)." In *Acts of Religion*, edited by Jacques Derrida, 226-27. New York: Routledge, 2002.

---. *Dvarim Be'go*. Tel Aviv: Am Oved, 1976. [Hebrew]

---. *From Berlin to Jerusalem: Memories of My Youth*. New York: Schocken, 1980.

---. *Jewish Gnosticism, Merkabah Mysticism, and Talmudic Tradition*. New York: Jewish Theological Seminary of America, 1960.

---. "Jugendbewegung, Judenarbeit und Blau-Weiß." *Blau-Weiß Blätter (Führernummer): Monatsschrift für Jüdisches Jugendwandern* 1, no. 2 (1917): 26-30.

---. *The Messianic Idea in Judaism: And Other Essays in Jewish Spirituality*. New York: Schocken, 1971.

---. *The Story of a Friendship*. New York: New York Review of Books, 1981.

---. *Tagebücher*. Vol. 2. Frankfurt: Suhrkamp, 1999.

---, ed. *Walter Benjamin and Gershom Scholem: Briefwechsel*. Frankfurt: Suhrkamp, 1980.

———. *Walter Benjamin: Die Geschichte einer Freundschaft*. Frankfurt: Suhrkamp, 1981.
Schorske, Karl. *Fin-de-Siecle Vienna: Politics and Culture*. New York: Knopf, 1980.
Schöttker, Detlev, and Erdmut Wizisla. *Arendt und Benjamin: Texte, Briefe, Dokumente*. Frankfurt: Suhrkamp, 2006.
Schreier, Helmut, and Heyl Matthias, eds. *Never Again! The Holocaust's Challenge for Educators*. Hamburg: Krämer, 1997.
Schur, Max. *Freud: Living and Dying*. New York: International Universities Press, 1972.
Schüssler, Fiorenza Elisabeth. "Feminist Theology as a Critical Theology of Liberation." *Theological Studies* 36, no. 4 (1975): 605–26.
Schwartz, Yossef. "Gustav Landauer and Gerhard Scholem: Anarchy and Utopia." In *Gustav Landauer: Anarchist and Jew*, edited by Paul Mendes-Flohr and Anya Mali, 172–90. Berlin: De Gruyter, 2015.
———. "Martin Buber and Gustav Landauer: The Politicization of the Mystical." In *Martin Buber: Neue Perspektiven/New Perspectives*, edited by Michael Zank, 205–19. Tübingen, Germany: Mohr Siebeck, 2006.
Sharvit, Gilad, and Karen S. Feldman, eds. *Freud and Monotheism: Moses and the Violent Origins of Religion*. New York: Fordham University Press, 2018.
Sheppard, Eugene R. *Leo Strauss and the Politics of Exile: The Making of a Political Philosopher*. Lebanon, NH: Brandeis University Press, 2006.
Sherman, David. *Sartre and Adorno: The Dialectics of Subjectivity*. Albany: State University of New York Press, 2007.
Sigwart, Hans-Jörg. *The Wandering Thought of Hannah Arendt*. London: Macmillan, 2016.
Simon, Ernst. "Sigmund Freud, the Jew." *Leo Baeck Institute Year Book*, no. 2 (1957): 270–305.
Smith, Gary. "'Das Jüdische versteht sich immer von selbst': Walter Benjamins frühe Auseinandersetzung mit dem Judentum." *Deutsche Vierteljahrsschrift für Literatur und Geisteswissenschaft* 65, no. 2 (1991): 318–34.
Sorkin, David. *The Religious Enlightenment: Protestants, Jews, and Catholics from London to Vienna*. Princeton, NJ: Princeton University Press, 2008.
———. "Wilhelm von Humboldt: The Theory and Practice of Self-Formation (*Bildung*), 1791–1810." *Journal of the History of Ideas*, no. 44 (1983): 55–74.
Spector, Scott. *German Modernism without Jews? German-Jewish Subjects and Histories*. Bloomington: Indiana University Press, 2017.
Spengler, Oswald. *Der Untergang des Abendlandes: Umrisse einer Morphologie der Weltgeschichte*. Munich: Beck, 1922.
Sperber, Daniel. "A Dictionary of Greek and Latin Legal Terms in Rabbinic Literature." PhD diss., Bar-Ilan University, 1984. [Hebrew]
Stachura, Peter D. *The German Youth Movement 1900–1945*. New York: Macmillan, 1981.

Steizinger, Johannes. *Revolte, Eros und Sprache*. Berlin: Kulturverlag Kadmos, 2013.
———. "Zwischen emanzipatorischem Appell und melancholischem Verstummen Walter Benjamins Jugendschriften." In *Benjamin-Studien*, edited by D. Weidner and S. Weigel, 223–38. Munich: Wilhem Fink Verlag, 2011.
Stoff, Heiko. *Ewige Jugend: Konzepte der Verjüngung vom späten 19. Jahrhundert bis ins Dritten Reich*. Cologne: Böhlau Verlag, 2004.
Strauss, Leo. "Reason and Revelation." In *Leo Strauss and the Theologico-Political Problem*, edited by Heinrich Meier, 141–80. Cambridge: Cambridge University Press, 2016.
Styfhals, Willem. *No Spiritual Investment in the World: Gnosticism and Postwar German Philosophy*. Ithaca, NY: Cornell University Press, 2019.
Styfhals, Willem, and Stephane Symons, eds. *Genealogies of the Secular: The Making of Modern German Thought*. Albany: State University of New York Press, 2019.
Sünker, Heinz. *Politics, Bildung and Social Studies: Perspectives for a Democratic Society*. Rotterdam: Sense, 2006.
Sven-Erick, Rose. *Jewish Philosophical Politics in Germany, 1789–1848*. Waltham, MA: Brandeis University Press, 2014.
Symons, Stéphane. *Walter Benjamin: Presence of Mind, Failure to Comprehend*. Leiden: Brill, 2013.
Sznaider, Natan. *Jewish Memory and the Cosmopolitan Order*. Cambridge, MA: Polity Press, 2011.
Talmudic Encyclopedia. Vol. 3. Jerusalem: Talmudic Encyclopedia, 1951. [Hebrew]
Taubes, Jacob. *Gnosis und Politik*. Munich: W. Fink, 1984.
Taylor, Charles. *A Secular Age*. Cambridge, MA: Harvard University Press, 2007.
Tchir, Trevor. *Hannah Arendt's Theory of Political Action: Daimonic Disclosure of the "Who."* New York: Palgrave Macmillan, 2017.
Temme, Evelyn. *Von der Bildung des Politischen zur politischen Bildung: Politikdidaktische Theorien mit Hannah Arendt Weitergedacht*. Frankfurt: Peter Lang, 2014.
Thompson, Christiane. "The Non-Transparency of the Self and the Ethical Value of *Bildung*." *Journal of Philosophy of Education* 39, no. 3 (2005): 519–34.
Toller, Ernst. *I Was a German: The Autobiography of Ernst Toller*. New York: William Morrow, 1934.
Tömmel, Tatjana Noemy. "Vita Passiva: Love in Arendt's Denktagebuch." In *Artifacts of Thinking: Reading Hannah Arendt's Denktagebuch*, edited by Roger Berkowitz and Ilan Storey, 106–13. New York: Fordham University Press, 2017.
Trabitzsch, Michael. *Walter Benjamin—Moderne, Messianismus, Politik: Über die Liebe zum Gegenstand*. Berlin: Verlag der Beeken, 1985.
Trawny, Peter. "Verstehen und Urteilen: Hannah Arendts Interpretation der Kantischen 'Urteilskraft' als politisch-ethische Hermeneutik." *Zeitschrift für philosophische Forschung* 60, no. 2 (2006): 269–89.

Trommler, Frank. "Mission ohne Ziel: Über den Kult der Jugend im modernen Deutschland." In *"Mit uns zieht die neue Zeit": Der Mythos Jugend*, edited by Thomas Koebner, Rolf-Peter Janz, and Frank Trommler, 14–49. Frankfurt: Suhrkamp, 1985.

Tsao, Roy T. "Arendt's Augustine." In *Politics in Dark Times: Encounters with Hannah Arendt*, edited by Seyla Benhabib, 39–57. Cambridge: Cambridge University Press, 2010.

Turner, Brian. *The New Blackwell Companion to the Sociology of Religion*. Oxford: Wiley-Blackwell, 2010.

Tzur Mahalel, Anat. *Reading Freud's Patients: Memoir, Narrative and the Analysand*. New York: Routledge, 2020.

Vatter, Miguel. "Roman Civil Religion and the Question of Jewish Politics in Arendt." *Philosophy Today* 62, no. 2 (2018): 573–606.

Vega, Facundo. "On the Tragedy of the Modern Condition: The 'Theologico-Political Problem' in Carl Schmitt, Leo Strauss, and Hannah Arendt." *The European Legacy* 22, no. 6 (2017): 697–728.

Villa, Dana R., ed. *The Cambridge Companion to Hannah Arendt*. Cambridge: Cambridge University Press, 2000.

———. *Politics, Philosophy, Terror: Essays on the Thought of Hannah Arendt*. Princeton, NJ: Princeton University Press, 1999.

———. *Socratic Citizenship*. Princeton, NJ: Princeton University Press, 2001.

Vitz, Paul C. *Sigmund Freud's Christian Unconscious*. New York: Guilford, 1988.

Voegelin, Eric. *The New Science of Politics*. Chicago: University of Chicago Press, 1952.

von Harnack, Adolf. *What Is Christianity?* New York/London: G. P. Putnam's Sons/Williams & Norgate, 1902.

———. *Marcion: Das Evangelium vom Fremden Gott*. Leipzig: J. C. Hinrisch'sche Buchhandlung, 1924.

von Humboldt, Wilhelm. *Ideen zu einem Versuch die Gränzen der Wirksamkeit des Staats zu bestimmen*. Breslau: Verlag von Eduard Trewendt, 1851.

———. *The Sphere and Duties of Government*. London: John Chapman, 1854.

von Wussow, Philipp. *Leo Strauss and the Politics of Culture*. Albany: State University of New York Press, 2021.

Wallach, Kerry. *Passing Illusion: Jewish Visibility in Weimar Germany*. Ann Arbor: University of Michigan Press, 2017.

Weber, Max. "Science as a Vocation." In *From Max Weber: Essays in Sociology*, edited by H. H. Gerth and C. Wright Mills, 129–56. New York: Oxford University Press, 1946.

Weddekind, Frank. *Frühlings Erwachen*. Stuttgart: Reclam, 1991.

Wetters, Kirk. *Demonic History: From Goethe to the Present*. Evanston, IL: Northwestern University Press, 2014.

Wexler, Philip. *Mystical Interactions: Sociology, Jewish Mysticism and Education.* Los Angeles: Cherub, 2007.
Whitebook, Joel. *Freud: An Intellectual Biography.* Cambridge: Cambridge University Press, 2017.
Winham, Ilya. "Rereading Hannah Arendt's 'What Is Freedom?': Freedom as a Phenomenon of Political Virtuosity." *Theoria: A Journal of Social and Political Theory* 59, no. 131 (2012): 84–106.
Wisse, Ruth R. *No Joke: Making Jewish Humor.* Princeton, NJ: Princeton University Press, 2013.
Wistrich, Robert S. "The Jewish Identity of Sigmund Freud." *Jewish Quarterly* 34, no. 3 (1987): 47–55.
Witte, Bernd. *Walter Benjamin: An Intellectual Biography.* Detroit: Wayne State University Press, 1991.
Wizisla, Erdmut. "Fritz Heinle war Dichter: Walter Benjamin und sein Jugendfreund." In *Was nie geschrieben wurde, lesen: Frankfurter Benjamin-Vorträge (1988–1991)*, edited by Lorenz Jäger and Thomas Regehly, 115–31. Bielefeld, Germany: Aisthesis, 1992.

———. "'Krise und Kritik' (1930/31): Walter Benjamin und das Zeitschriftenprojekt." In *Aber ein Sturm weht vom Paradiese her: Texte zu Walter Benjamin*, edited by Michael Opitz and Wizisla Erdmut, 270–302. Leipzig: Reclam, 1992.

Wohlfarth, Irvin. "On Some Jewish Motifs in Benjamin." In *The Problems of Modernity: Adorno and Benjamin*, edited by Andrew Benjamin, 157–216. London: Routledge, 1989.
Wolfson, Elliot R. "Patriarchy and the Motherhood of God in Zoharic Kabbalah and Meister Eckhart." In *Envisioning Judaism: Studies in Honor of Peter Schäfer on the Occasion of His Seventieth Birthday*, vol. 2, edited by Ra'anan S. Bourstan, Klaus Hermann, Reimund Leicht, Annette Yoshiko Reid, and Giuseppe Veltri, 1049–88. Tübingen, Germany: Mohr Siebeck, 2013.

———. *Poetic Thinking*, Leiden: Brill, 2015.

———. "Theolatry and the Making-Present of the Nonrepresentable." *Journal of Jewish Thought and Philosophy* 25, no. 1 (2017): 5–35.

Wolin, Richard. *Heidegger's Children: Hannah Arendt, Karl Löwith, Hans Jonas, and Herbert Marcuse.* Princeton, NJ: Princeton University Press, 2001.

———. *Walter Benjamin: An Aesthetic of Redemption.* New York: Columbia University Press, 1982.

Wolken, David J. "Thinking in the Gap: Hannah Arendt and the Prospects for a Postsecular Philosophy of Education." In *Keywords in Radical Philosophy and Education: Common Concepts for Contemporary Movements*, edited by Derek R. Ford, 317–27. Leiden: Brill/Sense, 2019.
Yadgar, Yaacov. *Secularism and Religion in Jewish-Israeli Politics: Traditionists and Modernity.* London: Routledge, 2010.

Yakira, Elhanan. "Hannah Arendt, the Holocaust, and Zionism: A Story of a Failure." *Israeli Studies* 11, no. 3 (2006): 31–61.

Yerushalmi, Yossef Haim. *Freud's Moses: Judaism Terminable and Interminable*. New Haven, CT: Yale University Press, 1993.

Young-Bruehl, Elisabeth. *Hannah Arendt: For Love of the World*. Binghamton, NY: Vail-Ballou, 1982.

Zawisza, Rafael. "Thank God We Are Creatures: Hannah Arendt's Cryptotheology." *Religions* 9, no. 11 (2018): 117–40.

Žižek, Salvoj. *Metastases of Enjoyment: Six Essays on Woman and Causality*. London: Verso, 1994.

Žižek, Salvoj, and John Milbank. *The Monstrosity of Christ: Paradox or Dialectic?* Cambridge, MA: MIT Press, 2009.

Index

Abraham, Karl, 42
absolute, the, 111, 112, 115, 119–22
absolute evil, 108, 156–59
Adorno, Theodor. *See also specific topics*
   Arendt and, 8–9, 12, 108, 118, 120, 137, 139, 141, 142, 149–50, 153–55, 165
   barbarism and, 108
   Bilderverbot and, 111, 122
   Carl Schmitt and, 94, 149–50
   on Christianity, 96
   on coldness, 104, 117, 121
   correspondence with Marcuse, 121
   critical self-reflection and, 108–13, 118, 119, 164
   on critique, 90, 92–95, 109, 114, 137, 154
   deliverance and, 101, 122–23
   democracy and, 93
   dialectic of secularization, 110. *See also under* secularization
   on dualism, 96, 98
   on education, 10, 61, 89, 90, 93, 101, 103–5, 109–12, 119–21, 154, 164
   eschatology and, 99, 101, 119
   freedom and, 94, 101, 103
   on "fruitless waiting," 142–43
   German student movement and, 121
   God and, 96, 112, 117
   Holocaust and, 107–8. *See also* "after Auschwitz"
   Kierkegaard and, 114–18, 120, 132, 164
   on love, 113–18, 120, 132
   as Marxist, 8–9
   materialism and, 121, 122
   metaphysics and, 90–93, 95, 100, 113, 120, 122–23, 154
   migration into the profane, 110
   mysticism and, 154
   negative theology, 111, 142
   on personality, 110
   on philosophy, 110–11, 113
   reification and, 104–6, 114, 115, 117
   on "reified consciousness," 104, 109, 113
   sabotage and, 108–13
   on the secular, 154
   soteriology, cosmology, and, 95, 99, 100, 120, 121
   symbolism and, 105, 106
   on technology, 106, 107, 113
   unity/oneness/identity and, 98–99, 101, 110, 112

Adorno, Theodor *(continued)*
  and the world in which we live, 94, 118, 122–23
  writings, 9, 12, 113
    Minima Moralia, 100, 119
    Negative Dialectics, 12, 89, 93
    "On Kierkegaard's Doctrine of Love," 114
    postwar, 10, 89–90, 92–93, 95, 105, 106, 109–10, 142, 154, 160
    „Theorie der Halbbildung," 12, 89, 101
  Zionism and, 8
"after Auschwitz" (Adorno), 12, 89–94. *See also* "Education after Auschwitz"
Agamben, Giorgio, 82, 148, 152
agape, 114, 118, 129, 131. *See also* Christian love
allegories, mystical
  Benjamin's, 63, 64, 66–69, 80, 154. *See also* "Metaphysics of Youth"
  Eckhart's, 63–66
American Revolution, 150, 151, 153
anarchism, 83
annihilation, 105, 107–8
anti-Semitism, 18, 19, 32–33, 43, 105
Aquinas, Thomas, 7
Arendt, Hannah, 135, 150. *See also specific topics*
  Adorno and, 8–9, 12, 108, 118, 120, 137, 139, 141, 142, 149–50, 153–55, 165
  "apolitical" stance, 135, 144
  Augustine and, 14, 65, 128–34, 136, 138, 140, 141, 145
  authority and, 126, 128–29, 145–49
  on banality of evil, 156–59
  on Benjamin, 81, 83–84, 120, 137, 141–42
  Benjamin contrasted with, 154
  characterizations of, 8, 128
  on Christianity, 128, 132, 144, 155, 162
  on crisis of modernity, 126, 136, 138–40, 143
  on critique, 137, 138
  foundation and, 128, 138, 139, 145, 147–51
  on gap, 139–40
  Gershom Scholem and, 8–9, 83, 132, 141, 158
  God and, 129, 132, 133, 141, 144, 146, 157
  Heidegger and, 138, 145–47
  Jewishness, Judaism, and, 8, 83–84, 125, 128, 132, 135, 136, 165
  Kant and, 138, 155–58
  Karl Jaspers and, 138, 145, 158, 159
  on language and naming, 61–62, 141–42
  on love, 118, 129–33
  on modernity, 135–38, 141, 143, 147, 152, 155, 157, 159
  philosophy and, 127, 142, 143, 155
  Plato and, 61, 143, 144, 146
  political theory, 136, 147, 149
  on power, 146, 148, 156–59
  on revelation, 127, 138, 143, 145, 154
  on revolutions, 150, 151, 153
  Roman thought and, 127, 128, 132, 134–38, 143–48, 152, 154–55
  secularization and, 8, 153–56, 159, 162
  theology and, 164–65
    political, 144–47, 149–51, 155
    tripartite, 14, 133–38, 142–43
  time and, 65, 137–40
  on "togetherness of men," 144–45, 149
  on totalitarianism, 10, 30, 126, 156
  on tradition, 9, 10, 81, 124–33, 135–39, 142–45, 151, 153, 154, 159

on traditional concepts, 137–39,
  141, 142, 147, 159–60
traditionalism and, 141, 150, 151,
  165
truth and, 143, 145, 150, 164
on violence, 147–48
and the world in which we live,
  144, 145, 157, 164–65, 167
writings
  Between Past and Future, 137–
    40
  The Burden of Our Time, 147,
    156
  dissertation, 128, 129, 140
  Eichmann in Jerusalem, 156, 158
  On Violence, 82, 148
  The Origins of Totalitarianism,
    147, 156, 158
  political, 9, 10, 126, 138, 142,
    156, 164, 165
  postwar, 125, 126, 139, 142, 154,
    156, 160
Aristotle, 95, 96, 100
Asad, Talal, 2, 68, 81, 167
assimilation of Jews, 84–85
augmentation, 126, 127
Augustine of Hippo, 129, 144
  Arendt and, 14, 65, 128–34, 136,
    138, 140, 141, 145
  on desire, 129–31
  God and, 129–31, 133–34
  on love, 14, 129–32
  modernity and, 14, 136, 138
  Plato and, 130. *See also*
    Neoplatonism
  revelation, truth, and, 145
  on three kinds of theology, 133–34
  on time, 140
  tripartite theology and, 14, 133,
    134, 136
  Varro and, 133, 134
Augustinian gap, 140

Auschwitz, 93, 107–8. *See also* "after
  Auschwitz"; "Education after
  Auschwitz"
authority, 83, 94, 146, 149
  Adorno and, 94, 110
  Arendt on, 126, 128–29, 145–49
  Benjamin on, 81, 83, 85, 86
  definition and nature of, 146
  foundation and, 145–47
  higher principle of, 81, 86–87
  Machiavelli and, 150, 153
  metaphysical, 110
  resistance to, 94
  Romans and, 126, 128–29, 145,
    146, 148
  tradition and, 86, 126, 128, 145–47
  youth and, 81
awakening, 72
  Benjamin on, 67, 71, 76, 78, 80,
    154
  Eckhart on, 64, 65, 71
  God and, 64, 65, 80, 154

Baeck, Leo, 84
banality of evil, 156–59
barbarism, 108, 135
Ben-Naftali, Michal, 159
Benhabib, Seyla, 7, 156
Benjamin, Walter. *See also specific
  topics*
  Adorno and, 8–9, 91, 102, 103, 120,
    141
  Arendt contrasted with, 154
  Arendt on, 81, 83–84, 120, 137,
    141–42
  on authority, 81, 83, 85, 86
  on awakening, 67, 71, 76, 78, 80,
    154
  on critique, 55, 74–81, 84, 86–87
  Eckhart and, 63, 66, 69–71, 73, 78
  enslavement and, 67, 75, 76
  freedom and, 59, 61, 75

Benjamin, Walter *(continued)*
    Freud and, 74, 76, 77, 81, 86
    Gershom Scholem and, 8-9, 58, 62, 67, 72, 83, 85, 86, 141
    gnosis and, 63, 96
    history and, 58-60
    Judaism and, 83-84
    Kingdom of God, 60, 61, 104
    liberation and, 74-76
    Martin Buber and, 58, 61, 83
    materialism and, 9, 120
    materiality and, 75-76
    on meaning, 68-69
    messianism and, 9, 59-60, 72, 73, 80, 83, 86, 120
    mystical allegories, 63, 64, 66-69, 80, 154. See also "Metaphysics of Youth"
    mysticism and, 55, 68, 75-79, 81, 84, 86, 95, 154, 164
    nothingness and, 72-74, 83, 86-87, 164
    Plato and, 60-62
    power and, 79, 81-83
    purity and, 62, 70, 72, 74-76, 79, 81, 82, 84, 91
    reason and, 71, 74
    revelation and, 61, 72, 76, 79, 80, 141, 154
    on silence, 68
    on spiritual core, 58-59, 66, 75, 76, 84, 85
    theory of language, 61-62, 68-69, 142
    traditionalism, 141
    true criticism and, 73-87
    and unity with the divine, 66-67, 80
    on violence, 79, 81-83, 148
    and the world in which we live, 80, 164
    writings, 58, 60, 73
        "Critique of Violence," 79, 81-82, 148
        "Metaphysics of Youth," 66-73, 78, 80
        "On Language as Such and on the Language of Man," 61
        "The Life of the Students," 59, 60, 62
    youth and, 10, 59, 61, 62. See also "Metaphysics of Youth"; youth: age of transcendence and, 58-63, 66
    Zionism and, 85, 86
Bergson, Henri, 37
Berlin, Isaiah, 121
Bernstein, Richard, 135
Biale, David, 165
Bible, 40-41, 61-62, 131. See also Jesus Christ; Moses
biblical prohibition of making images. See *Bilderverbot*
Bielik-Robson, Agata, 51
Bilderverbot, 111, 122
Bildung, 89, 102. See also "self-formation"
    Adorno on, 101-3
birth. See also natality
    mystical notion of, 154. See also awakening
blasphemy, 22, 121
Bloch, Ernst, 98
Bloom, Harold, 43
Blumenberg, Hans
    on discourse of legitimation, 2
    gnosis, gnosticism, and, 97, 98, 157
    The Legitimacy of the Modern Age, 97-98
    on life-time (*Lebenszeit*) and world-time (*Weltzeit*), 70
body, spirit, and soul. See tripartite theology
break. See gap

brevity
  Freud on, 30, 34
  wit and, 30–35, 37, 38
Brumlik, Micha, 8
Buber, Martin, 58, 61, 83
Buck-Morss, Susan, 80
Butler, Judith, 165

Canovan, Margaret, 151
caritas, 129, 130
cathectic energy, 37
Catholic Church, 128–29
censors, 36, 46
  jokes and, 27, 28, 30, 34, 36, 39
  moral/ethical, 30, 34
Christian love. *See also* agape
  Augustine on, 129, 132. *See also* Augustine of Hippo: on love
  Kierkegaard's, 115, 116. *See also* Kierkegaard, Søren: doctrine of love
Christianity, 96. *See also specific topics*
  Arendt on, 128, 132, 144, 155, 162
  modernity and, 98, 99, 114, 135, 152, 155
  Plato and, 60, 130, 144
Christianization of modernity, 155. *See also* modernity: Christianity and
"church" of psychoanalysis, 43
coldness, Adorno on, 104, 117, 121
concepts, 137. *See also* traditional concepts
condensation, 31, 32, 35
confusion
  creative, 139
  jokes and, 27–28
conservatism, 151
  Arendt and, 151
  revolutions and, 151
  tradition and, 151, 165
Constitution, U.S., 150

conversation
  Benjamin on, 68, 69
  gender and, 68, 69
  silence and, 68
cosmology, soteriology, and Adorno, 95, 99, 100, 120, 121
Cover, Robert M., 26–27, 50
"creative word of God," 61
crisis of modernity, 125, 136, 143, 144
  Arendt on, 126, 136, 138–40, 143
critical approach, 1, 31, 74, 77, 100
critical path, 5–9
critical practice, 90
critical self-reflection (in education). *See also* love supreme
  Adorno and, 108–13, 118, 119, 164
  love and, 113
  messianic passion, 119–23
  sabotage, 108–13
critical theological predicament, 4, 95, 142
critical theology
  vs. critique of theology, 4
  Kierkegaard's, 114–15, 117
  political theology and, 149–52
critical theory, 8, 113–14, 166–67
  Adorno and, 13, 114
  Max Horkheimer on, 77, 166
  theology and, 13, 164
critical thinking, 3, 100–102
  Adorno and, 90, 95, 96
  Benjamin on, 74
  philosophy and, 110
  theology and, 90, 95–96, 100, 110, 166
criticism, true. *See* true criticism
critique, 137. *See also specific topics*
  definitions and meanings, 46, 75, 94, 109, 114, 137
  freedom and, 45, 46, 77, 103
  nature of, 92
  objective, 5

critique of theology, 4–5, 73–80, 95–101. *See also* critique; shortcuts
   Adorno's, 95–96, 98–101, 105, 106, 116, 119
   Arendt's, 126, 137–42, 152, 154, 156, 163, 164
   Benjamin's, 55–58, 73–81, 84–87, 142
   characterization of, 4–5
   critique as handmaid of theology, 7, 77
   Freud's, 23, 44–53. *See also* Freud, Sigmund: on religion
critique of violence, Arendt's, 147–48
"Critique of Violence" (Benjamin), 79, 81–82, 148
Cuddihy, John Murray, 29
Culture Industry, 107

de Certeau, Michel, 10, 26, 27
de Vries, Hent, 161
decisionism, 94
defense mechanisms. *See* censors; *specific defense mechanisms*
Degenhardt, Ingeborg, 63
deliverance
   Adorno and, 101, 122–23
   Benjamin and, 76
   Freud and, 19–20, 22
   youth and, 75, 76
democracy, 93, 166, 167
"demonic love," 116
"demonic," the, 117, 157–59
demons, 79
desire(s). *See also* eros
   Arendt and, 129–31
   Augustine on, 129–31
   Benjamin on, 60, 67
   Freud on, 33, 34, 46, 48
   God and, 130–31
   love and, 130–31
   sexuality and, 33, 34, 48, 67

dialectics. *See also* dualism; negative dialectics
   Hegel's, 99, 100
   of secularization, 110, 152–55
discharge of mental energy, 34, 37, 43–47
displacement, 31–32
divine, the. *See also* God
   unity/oneness/identity with, 51–53, 66–67, 80, 99–101, 110, 112
divine violence, 82, 83. *See also* nonviolence
dreams
   Freud on, 18–19, 23, 25, 32, 35, 43
   jokes and, 23, 25, 32, 35
dreamwork (*Traumarbeit*), 23, 32
dualism, 78, 96. *See also* dialectics
   Adorno on, 96, 98
   Eckhart and, 65, 70
   evil and, 97, 100, 116, 157, 158
   modernity and, 98

Eckhart, Meister
   on awakening, 64, 65, 71
   Benjamin and, 63, 66, 69–71, 73, 78
   characterizations of, 64
   on gender, 65, 69
   impact, 63–64
   mysticism and, 63–66, 69, 72, 78
   overview, 63–64
   on widow, 64, 65, 69
   writings, 63, 64, 69, 78
   youth and, 63–66, 71–73, 78
"economy in psychical expenditure," 24
education. *See also* critical self-reflection; *specific topics*
   Adorno on, 10, 61, 89, 90, 93, 101, 103–5, 109–12, 119–21, 154, 164
   democratic, 93
   fake, 103, 104, 110
   false vs. true, 60
   transcendence and, 60, 61

"Education after Auschwitz"
(Adorno), 113, 117. *See also*
Adorno, Theodor
educational ideals, 101–4
Eichmann, Adolf, 158, 159
Eleazar ben Shammua, 41
Eliade, Mircea, 127
emancipation, human, 26, 77. *See also*
liberation
emergency, state of, 28–29, 150
emptiness, 66, 70. *See also*
nothingness
energy. *See* mental energy
enlightenment. *See* awakening
Enlightenment, 1, 2, 5, 7, 74, 101, 102
enslavement, 100, 103, 107
 Benjamin and, 67, 75, 76
 critique and, 100, 106, 112
 liberation from, 76, 77, 94, 114, 164
enslaving circumstances, 75, 77, 100, 103, 164
 Kierkegaard on love and, 114, 120
entrapment
 Adorno on, 13, 100–109, 114
 Benjamin and, 74, 75
 of critique, 101
 and education (from *Bildung* to *Halbbildung*), 101–5
 love and, 114
eros, 129, 131
 Benjamin on, 60, 61
eschatology, 99
 Adorno and, 99, 101, 119
 Hegel and, 99, 119
Essence of Judaism, The (Baeck), 84
eternal laws
 Eckhart on, 65
 Freud on, 19, 21, 27, 29, 44, 45, 50
 jokes and, 27, 29, 44, 45, 52
eternal life of the soul, 65
eternal now, 62, 65

eternal within the world, 44, 50, 81, 164
ethics, 41, 73. *See also Minima Moralia*
 Kant, reason, and, 6, 7
 liberal, 102
evil. *See also* "demonic"
 absolute/radical, 108, 156–59
 Adorno and, 108, 116, 118
 Arendt on, 132, 156–59
 banal, 156–59
 definitions, 156
 gnosis and, 97, 116, 157, 158
 Kant and, 156–58
 the problem of, 156–60
evil power, Arendt on, 157–59
exception, state of, 94
exile, 83–84, 120
existentialism
 Adorno and, 110, 115
 gnosis and, 97
 Hans Jonas and, 97
 Heidegger and, 97, 110, 115
 meaning and, 97, 98
expectation(s)
 messianic, 119, 122
 tension of constant, 73

Fiddler on the Roof, 125
fingerprints of a dynamic spirit, 9–15
"forever young," 57, 66
Foucault, Michel, 1
 vs. Freud, 49, 51, 52
 jokes and, 49
 Kant and, 5
 modernity and, 48–49
 Preface to Transgression, 47–50
 secularization and, 50, 51
 theology and, 49–52
foundation
 Arendt and, 128, 138, 139, 145, 147–51
 defined, 145

founding, sacred, 126, 145
Franks, Paul, 6, 7, 165–66
freedom, 71–72, 75, 83, 101–3, 151. *See also* liberation
  Adorno and, 94, 101, 103
  Arendt on, 147, 148
  Benjamin and, 59, 61, 75
  critique and, 45, 46, 77, 103
  foundation, natality, and, 147–49
  God and, 79
  jokes and, 30, 45
  Kant on, 46, 75, 106–7
  purity, liberation, and, 72, 75–76
French Revolution, 150, 153
Freud, Sigmund, 106. *See also* law; *specific topics*
  anti-Semitism and, 18, 19, 43
  Arendt and, 154, 165
  Benjamin and, 74, 76, 77, 81, 86
  Catholic Rome and, 19, 128
  Catholic Vienna and, 19
  collection of Jewish stories, 17, 18
  on critique, 18–19, 25–26, 77, 137
  on critique of law, 18, 21, 23, 26–27, 29, 35, 38, 44, 46
  death of, 43
  death of his father, 17
  deliverance and, 19–20, 22
  on desires, 33, 34, 46, 48
  on dreams, 18–19, 23, 25, 32, 35, 43
  on eternal laws, 19, 21, 27, 29, 44, 45, 50
  eternal within the world and, 44, 50, 81, 164
  vs. Foucault, 49, 51, 52
  Heinrich Heine and, 24, 31
  Jewishness, Judaism, and, 8, 9, 11, 18, 21–23, 29, 40, 43–44, 52–53
  on laughter, 37, 76
  letters to Wilhelm Fliess, 17, 19
  on *Moses* (Michelangelo), 20–23, 27, 39, 44, 46, 49, 50, 128
  as "old-school" liberal, 52, 53
  personal life, 17–19
  reason and, 27, 30, 52
  on religion, 8, 44. *See also* critique of theology: Freud's
  resistance and, 24, 26, 34–35, 39, 45, 53
  secularization and, 50, 51, 84
  self-analysis, 17, 19
  short circuits and, 37, 53, 104–5
  on shortcuts, 39, 40, 42, 44–46
  on shortcutting character of jokes, 38, 40, 42, 44
  social critique and, 10–11, 18, 23, 25–28, 32, 38, 40, 42, 45–46
  subversion and, 22–24, 26–30, 34, 35, 39, 44, 53, 118–19
  transgression and, 11, 18, 20, 22, 23, 39, 40, 44, 45, 47, 49–52, 104
  and unity with the divine, 51–53
  writings, 18. *See also specific writings*
friend–foe dichotomy, 149
"fruitless waiting" (Adorno), 142–43

Gadamer, Hans-Georg, 165
gap, 139–40
Garden of Eden, 61
gender
  conversation and, 68, 69
  Eckhart on, 65, 69
Genesis, 61–62
"genius," 68, 69, 134
German Youth Movement, 57, 58
gnosis
  Adorno and, 96, 98–100, 112–13, 116, 121
  Arendt and, 157, 158
  Benjamin and, 63, 96
  "demonic love" and, 116
  Eric Voegelin and, 97, 157
  evil and, 97, 116, 157, 158

existentialism and, 97
Gershom Scholem and, 97, 98, 158
Hans Blumenberg and, 97, 98, 157
Hans Jonas and, 97
Hegel and, 99–100
Jaspers and, 158
messianism and, 98, 121, 158
modernity and, 97, 98, 157
overcoming, 97, 116, 157
gnostic dualism, 78, 96–99, 116, 158, 159
gnostic theology, 96–98
God, 80. *See also* divine
  absence of. *See* widow
  Adorno and, 96, 112, 117
  Arendt and, 129, 132, 133, 141, 144, 146, 157
  Augustine and, 129–31, 133–34
  and awakening, 64, 65, 80, 154
  death of, 48–49
  evil and, 157
  images of, 111, 122. *See also* idolatry
  love of, 115–17, 129–32
  Machiavelli and, 150, 153
  word of, 61, 142
"Godless Jew," 52
godlikeness of man (*imago Dei*), 102
Golden Rule. *See* "love thy neighbor"
Gordon, Peter Eli, 8, 110, 116, 150, 166
Grainer, Bernhard, 78
Greek concepts, 129, 143, 146–47
Greek origins of critique, 90, 92
Greek philosophy, 90, 127

Habermas, Jürgen, 161, 166
Halbbildung (pseudoculture/pseudo-education)
  Adorno on, 12, 89, 101, 103, 109, 120
  transformation of *Bildung* into, 103, 109, 110, 120

Hamlet (Shakespeare), 30, 34
Harnack, Adolf von, 78, 84, 129, 132
Hegel, Georg Wilhelm Friedrich, 100, 155
  Adorno and, 95–96, 98–100, 106, 112, 114, 119
  Benjamin and, 71
  Christianity and, 99
  dialectics, 99, 100
  on progress, 98–99
  redemption and, 99, 119
Heidegger, Martin, 70, 107
  Arendt and, 138, 145–47
  existentialism and, 97, 110, 115
  gnosis and, 97
  "jargon of authenticity," 115
Heine, Heinrich, 5, 135
  on deathbed, 31
  Freud and, 24, 31
  Reisebilder, 24
  wit and, 24–27, 31, 36
Herzog, Rudolf, 30
"hidden tradition," 135–36, 152
history, Adorno's concept of, 95, 106
holding onto an unholdable object, 110, 112, 119, 154
  Adorno and, 110–13, 119, 154
  Arendt and, 154
  redemption, messianism, and, 86, 119
Holocaust, 93. *See also* Auschwitz; Nazism
  aftermath. *See* "after Auschwitz"
Horkheimer, Max, 164
  Adorno and, 107, 114
  on critical theory, 77, 166
  on enslaving circumstances, 77, 103
  on Judaism, 166
  on realm of immanence, 164
humor. *See* jokes; laughter; wit
"Humor" (Freud), 39
Hutton, Christopher, 29

id, Freud on jokes and the, 39
idealism, German, 121. See also
    Eckhart, Meister
ideals, 53, 109, 110
    educational, 101–4
identity. See unity
idolatry, 21, 106. See also Bilderverbot
imago Dei (godlikeness of man), 102
immanence
    realm of, 164
    transcendence and, 63, 100, 108, 121
immanentization, 51, 81, 160
"incarnated" time, 71
inverse theology, 118
Israel, 132. See also Zionism

Jaspers, Karl, 138, 145, 158–59
    Arendt and, 138, 145, 158–59
    on evil, 158–59
Jesus Christ
    Eckhart on, 64–65
    redemption and, 99, 108
Jewish jokes, 17, 29, 32–33. See also jokes
Jewish spirit, 83–85
"joke-work" (Witzarbeit)
    dreamwork and, 23, 32
    Freud and, 34, 39
    nature of, 52
jokes. See also shortcutting character of jokes; wit
    dreams and, 23, 25, 32, 35
    eternal laws and, 27, 29, 44, 45, 52
    Freud's definition of, 38
    and liberation, 26, 30, 35
    meaning of, 29
    obscenity and, 32–35
    pleasure and, 23–24, 32–38
    subversion and, 23–30, 34–36, 39, 44
    tendentious, 32, 33, 35
    transgression and, 38, 39, 44, 49, 50

Jokes and Their Relation to the Unconscious (Freud), 9, 18, 23–25, 30, 31, 55
    Adorno and, 104–5
    dreams and, 32
    overview, 17–18
    principle of pleasure and, 34–35. See also pleasure
    and the Talmud, 42
    theology and, 10, 18, 23
Jonas, Hans, 6, 97
Jones, Ernest, 18, 23
Judah bar Ilai. See Yehuda bar Ma'arava
Judaism, 83–84, 165, 166. See also specific topics
    vs. Christianity, 44, 99
    essence of, 53, 84
    law and, 11, 21–23
    undefined, 53
Jung, Carl Gustav, 57

Kafka, Franz, 2, 154
Kant, Immanuel, 7
    Adorno and, 90, 106–7
    appeal to Jewish philosophers, 165–66
    Arendt and, 138, 155–58
    Benjamin and, 75, 77
    critique and, 5–7, 25, 46, 75, 77, 90, 106–7, 138
    evil and, 156–58
    on freedom, 46, 75, 106–7
    handmaid's tale and, 6–7, 77, 168
    human beings as machines and, 106–7
    metaphysics and, 6, 90
    reason and, 5–7, 25, 90
    on transcendental condition, 157
Kantorowicz, Ernst, 58, 129
kapandaria, 40–42
Kierkegaard, Søren, 117
    Adorno and, 114–18, 120, 132, 164
    Christianity and, 114, 116

critical theology, 114–15, 117
doctrine of love, 114–18, 120, 132
reification and, 114, 115, 117
resistance and, 114, 117–20
Kingdom of God, 60, 61, 104
Klages, Ludwig, 58, 105
Kohlenbach, Margarete, 80

Landauer, Gustav, 64, 83
language, 68
Arendt on naming and, 61–62, 141–42
Benjamin's theory of, 61–62, 68–69, 142
humor and, 29, 76
laughter, 37–40, 76
Freud on, 37, 76
lawgiver(s)
deeply significant stories, 17–23
Freud, lawgiving, and, 10, 18, 21–23, 27, 40, 42–44, 46, 49–51
a mechanism of social critique, 23–30
Moses as, 20–23, 27, 46, 49–50
lawmaking, 82
laws/the law. *See also* wit and law
ambiguity of laws, 79
Freud and, 18, 19, 23, 26, 27, 49, 51, 76, 154, 164. *See also under* Freud, Sigmund; lawgiver(s); wit and law
Judaism and, 11, 21–23
meanings and notions of "law," 6, 18, 19, 23, 26, 51
resisting, 34, 38–40, 45. *See also* political resistance
Robert Cover on, 26, 27, 50
shortcuts and, 39–40, 42–45
social critique and critique of law, 26, 27
transgression of, 11, 23, 38–40, 42–45, 49, 51, 52, 79, 104, 105

Legitimacy of the Modern Age (Blumenberg), 97. *See also* Blumenberg, Hans
legitimation, 50, 149
discourse of, 2
legitimization, 49
Leibniz, Gottfried Wilhelm, 157
Lessing, Gotthold Ephraim, 102
liberation, 70, 74, 75, 77, 78. *See also* freedom
Benjamin and, 74–76
critique and, 7, 13, 46, 75
from enslavement, 76, 77, 94, 114, 164
Freud and, 35, 46
jokes and, 26, 30, 35
Max Horkheimer on, 77
notions and conceptions of, 75, 77
pleasure and, 35
purity and, 72, 75–76
by reason, 121
youth and, 74, 75
Loewith, Karl, 99, 155
love, 120. *See also* Christian love
Adorno on, 113–18, 120, 132
Arendt on, 118, 129–33
Augustine on, 14, 129–32
Augustine's tripartite hierarchy of, 129, 130, 133, 134, 144
defined, 131
forms of, 130
of God, 115–17, 129–32
Greek concepts of, 129. *See also* agape; eros
Kierkegaard's doctrine of, 114–18, 120, 132
tradition and, 129–31
love supreme, 113–19
"love thy neighbor," 116, 117, 129–31

Machiavelli, 150, 153
Mannheim, Karl, 57

Marcion of Sinope, 78
Marcuse, Herbert, 121
Marx, Karl, 143
materialism, 56
   Adorno and, 121, 122
   Benjamin and, 9, 120
   types of, 121
materiality, Benjamin and, 75–76
meaning, 68
   Arendt and, 154–55
   Benjamin on, 68, 69
   existentialism and, 97, 98
   loss/absence of, 70
   source of, 68–70
Meaning in History (Loewith), 155
Mendes-Flohr, Paul, 109–10, 166
mental energy, 34
   discharge of, 34, 37, 43–47
   saving of, 24, 35, 37, 38. *See also* brevity; subversion
messianic expectations, 119, 122
"messianic halt," 148
messianic moment, 80, 82, 84
messianic passion, 119–23
messianic potential, 83, 120
messianic time, 73, 120
messianism, 167
   Adorno and, 119–23
   Arendt and, 135, 158
   Benjamin and, 9, 59–60, 72, 73, 80, 83, 86, 120
   Elliot Wolfson and, 119, 120, 122
   Gershom Scholem and, 9, 86, 158
   gnosis and, 98, 121, 158
   Jewish, 86, 98, 120, 122, 158
   materialism and, 120–22
   nature of, 73, 121
   types of, 120, 122
metaphysical quest for youth, 86
metaphysics
   Adorno and, 90–93, 95, 100, 113, 120, 122–23, 154
   Aristotle's, 96, 100
   Christianity and, 96, 98
   critique and, 90–92, 99
   defined, 90
   Hegel's dialectics and, 99, 100
   and the Holocaust, 92–93
   Kant and, 6, 90
   modernity and, 93
   reason and, 91, 92
   secularization and, 91
   theology and, 91–93, 95, 96, 98
   transcendence and, 100, 159
"Metaphysics of Youth" (Benjamin), 66–73, 78, 80
Metropolis (film), 105–6
Michelangelo. *See Moses*
Minima Moralia (Adorno), 100, 119. *See also* Adorno, Theodor
Mishnah, 40–42
Miteinandersein, 145
modernity. *See also* crisis of modernity
   Adorno and, 93, 95, 98, 99
   Arendt on, 135–38, 141, 143, 147, 152, 155, 157, 159
   Augustine and, 14, 136, 138
   Benjamin and, 86, 141
   Christianity and, 98, 99, 114, 135, 152, 155
   Eric Voegelin's revolt against, 97
   Foucault and, 48–49
   gnosis, gnosticism, and, 97, 98, 157
   Hans Blumenberg and, 97–98, 157
   metaphysics and, 93
   myth and, 86
   Roman religion and, 135–38, 143, 144, 155
   roots of, 155
   secularization and, 86, 152, 155
   transgression in, 48–49
   tripartite critique of
      critical and political theology, 149–52
      a critique of theology, 137–42

philosophy, myth, and politics, 142–49
youth and, 56–57
Moloch, 105–7
morality. *See* ethics
moratorium (sociology), 62–63
Moses (Michelangelo), 22, 23, 49–50
   Freud on, 20–23, 27, 39, 44, 46, 49, 50, 128
   jokes and, 23, 44
Moses (Old Testament)
   Christianity and, 20–22, 39, 44, 49
   as lawgiver, 20–23, 27, 46, 49–50
   Paul the Apostle and, 21, 22
Moses, Dirk, 127
Moses and Monotheism (Freud), 20
"Moses of Michelangelo, The" (Freud), 20, 23. *See also Moses*
Mount Sinai, 127, 128
Moyn, Samuel, 128, 151
mystical allegories. *See* allegories
mysticism, 83
   Adorno on, 98, 121, 154
   Arendt and, 154
   Benjamin and, 55, 68, 75–79, 81, 84, 86, 95, 154, 164
   Christian, 51, 65, 121
   Eckhart and, 63–66, 69, 72, 78
   Foucault on, 51
   Freud and, 51, 53
   Gershom Scholem and, 98
   Jewish, 65
   nothingness and, 66, 72, 76, 83, 86–87
   secularization and, 51, 80–81
   youth and, 66–68, 164
"myth and modernity" (Benjamin), 86
mythical theology, 132–34
mythical thinking, 91

naming, 61, 62
   Arendt on, 61–62, 141–42
   Benjamin on, 62

natality
   Arendt and, 147
   Roman theology and, 147–49
nationalism, 121, 193
natural theology, 132, 133, 143, 144
Nazism, 30, 93, 156, 158. *See also* Auschwitz
negative dialectics, 120
Negative Dialectics (Adorno), 12, 89, 93
negative theology, 111, 115, 122
negativity, 109–10
   Adorno on, 109–11, 122, 154. *See also Negative Dialectics*
Neoplatonism, 121, 129
new order of the world (*novus ordo seclorum*), 148, 152, 164
nihil, 66, 72, 154
nihilism, 97
nihility, 77
nomos. *See also* normative universe
   earthbound, 50, 149
   Robert Cover on, 26, 50
nonidentity, 110, 112
nonviolence, divine, 82–83, 148
normative dimension, 7, 25–26
normative universe, 26, 27. *See also* nomos
norms. *See* social norms
North, Paul, 68
nothingness, 77, 164
   Benjamin and, 72–74, 83, 86–87, 164
   mysticism and, 66, 72, 76, 83, 86–87
   notions of, 66, 72
   youth and, 66, 72–74, 83
"nothingness of revelation," 72, 164
novus ordo seclorum (new order of the world), 148, 152, 164
"now," 62, 65, 140
Nygren, Anders, 131

obscenity
　aggression and, 32, 33
　jokes and, 32–35
O'Connor, Brian, 104
oneness. *See* unity
Oring, Elliott, 18, 28
"other"
　alien, 112
　Kant on guidance of an, 5, 46

Paul the Apostle
　Augustine and, 129, 131
　on love, 131
　Marcion of Sinope and, 78
　Moses and, 21, 22
personality, 110
phenomenology, German, 136
philosophy, 110–11. *See also specific topics*
　Adorno on, 110–11, 113
　Arendt and, 127, 142, 143, 155
"Philosophy and Teachers" (Adorno), 113
Plato, 130, 143, 146. *See also* Neoplatonism
　Arendt and, 61, 143, 144, 146
　Benjamin and, 60–62
　Christianity and, 60, 130, 144
　on grades of the soul in universal nature, 134
pleasure
　jokes and, 23–24, 32–38
　principle of, 34–37
political, the. *See also specific topics*
　power and, 81, 82
　vs. the "pure divine," 82
　violence, nonviolence, and, 82, 148. *See also* violence
political concepts, 137, 145–47
political emergency, 150
political imagination, secularization and, 80–87

political resistance, 59, 81, 93, 94. *See also* laws/the law: resisting
political theological predicament, 4, 8
political theology, 132, 133
　Adorno and, 94, 121
　Benjamin and, 83, 86
　Carl Schmitt's, 94, 149
　critical theology and, 149–52
　and critique of theology, 4
　Gershom Scholem and, 85, 86
　origin of the term, 133
　Roman, 144–47, 150
　youth and, 85
political theory of Arendt, 136, 147, 149
postcritique approach, 163
postsecular world/postsecular society, 162, 163
power
　Arendt on, 146, 148, 156–59
　authority and, 146, 148. *See also* authority
　Benjamin and, 79, 81–83
　evil, 157–59
　of the sovereign, 84
profanation, 41, 42, 45, 48
profane, migration into the, 110
profane sexual acts, 47, 48
progress, 53, 59
　Bildung and, 102. *See also Bildung*
　Hegel's idea of, 98–99
pseudo-education. *See Halbbildung*
psychoanalysis, 17, 18. *See also* Freud, Sigmund
　spiritual component in, 43
　Talmud and, 42
"pure concept" of thought, 96
pure concepts, 74–75
pure criticism, theology as, 79
pure essence, 62, 74–76
pure inwardness, 116, 132
pure power, 82

pure spiritual singularity, 72
"pure" substance, 91
pure time, 70
pure (and immediate) violence, 82
purification, critique and, 5, 25
purifying concepts of fallacies., 5
purity
    Benjamin and, 62, 70, 72, 74–76, 79, 81, 82, 84, 91
    critique and, 75–77
    freedom, liberation, and, 72, 75–76
    youth and, 59, 70, 72, 75, 76, 84

rabbinic literature, 40–42, 44, 45, 47, 51
radical evil, 156–59
radical youth, 58
reason
    Benjamin and, 71, 74
    categories of, 6, 91, 92
    censorship of, 27, 39. See also censors
    critique and, 1, 5, 25, 79, 90, 121
    ethics and, 6, 7
    Freud and, 27, 30, 52
    jokes and, 25, 27, 30, 39
    Kant and, 5–7, 25, 90
    metaphysics and, 91, 92
    modernity and, 98
    secular, 166, 167
    theology and, 5, 6, 91
redemption
    Adorno and, 99, 112, 119–21
    Benjamin's notion of nothingness and, 72–73
    Hegel and, 99, 119
    messianism, blasphemy, and, 121
    modernity and, 98, 99
redemptive mission, 112
reflection, power of, 113, 118
reification (of human beings)
    Adorno and, 104–6, 114, 115, 117
    defined, 104
    Kierkegaard and, 114, 115, 117
"reified consciousness" (Adorno), 104, 109, 113
repression. See censors
resistance, 33, 38–39, 112. See also political resistance; social norms
    Adorno and, 94, 117, 118, 120
    critique and, 93, 114
    Freud and, 24, 26, 34–35, 39, 45, 53
    jokes and, 24–26, 30, 38, 39, 45
    Kierkegaard and, 114, 117–20
    to the law, 34, 38–40, 45
    love and, 114, 115, 117–20
    pleasure and, 34–35
    shortcuts as, 38, 45
resurrection, 71, 122, 123
revelation, 6
    Arendt on, 127, 138, 143, 145, 154
    Benjamin and, 61, 72, 76, 79, 80, 141, 154
    critique and, 1, 76, 80, 139
    moment of, 61, 126, 154
    nothingness of, 72, 164
    reason and, 79
    Roman concept of, 139, 145, 149
    secular, 80, 102
"revelation coming to the individual man" (Lessing), 102
revolution(s), 82, 150–51, 153
    Arendt on, 150, 151, 153
    definitions and meanings of the term, 151, 153
    modern, 150, 151, 153
Roman political theology, 144–47, 150
Roman religion and modernity, 135–38, 143, 144, 155
Roman tripartite theology. See tripartite theology
Romans and Roman thought
    Arendt and, 127, 128, 132, 134–38, 143–48, 152, 154–55

Romans and Roman thought (continued)
  authority and, 126, 128–29, 145, 146, 148
  combination of Roman and Jewish sources, 128, 135
romanticism, German, 67, 68

sabotage, 108–13
"sacred founding," 126, 145. *See also* foundation
sacred violence, 82. *See also* nonviolence
sacrifice, 105. *See also* self-sacrifice
Santner, Eric L., 8, 43
  Freud and, 11, 43, 50, 164
Schmidt, Christoph, 51, 78, 94
Schmitt, Carl, 94, 149, 150
  Adorno and, 94, 149–50
  Arendt and, 149–50
Scholem, Gershom, 106
  Adorno and, 8–9, 93, 106
  Arendt and, 8–9, 83, 132, 141, 158
  Benjamin and, 8–9, 58, 62, 67, 72, 83, 85, 86, 141
  gnosis and, 97, 98, 158
  Karl Jaspers and, 158–59
  on "love of Israel" ("Ahabat Israel"), 132
  messianism and, 9, 86, 158
  on "nothingness of revelation," 72, 164
  political theology and, 85, 86
  theory of youth, 85–86
  Zionism and, 8, 85, 86
secular, the, 163. *See also* secularization
  Adorno's concept of, 154
  Benjamin's concept of, 81
  and the religious, 1, 81, 161–63
secular banality, 158
secular reason, 166, 167

secularization. *See also specific topics*
  Adorno and, 91, 94, 99, 102, 106, 108, 119, 122, 155, 167
  Arendt and, 8, 153–56, 159, 162
  dialectics of, 110, 152–55. *See also* secular: and the religious
  Freud and, 50, 51, 84
  meanings and notions of, 91, 102, 152
  modernity and, 86, 152, 155
  and political imagination, 80–87
  of religion, 51
  of revelation, 102. *See also* revelation
  of theology, 154. *See also* theological concepts: reconceptualization of
  transgression and, 50
secularized theological concepts, 94. *See also* theological concepts
secular-religious continuum, 162–63, 167
"self-formation," 60, 101, 155. *See also* Bildung
self-love. *See* Kierkegaard, Søren: doctrine of love
self-reflection. *See* critical self-reflection
self-sacrifice, 82, 106, 115
sexuality. *See also* desire(s); eros
  Freud's theory of, 18, 33, 51
  jokes and, 9, 18, 32, 33
  modernity and, 48
  religion and, 47, 48, 51
  sin, taboo, and, 47, 48
Shechinah, 73
short circuit (*Kurzschluss*), 38
  Adorno on, 104
  Freud and, 37, 53, 104–5
  jokes and, 37, 38, 104–5
shortcuts
  Freud on, 39, 40, 42, 44–46

Judaism and, 40–42, 45
and the law, 39–40, 42–45
notion of, 38, 45
prohibitions against, 40–42
transgression and, 38–40, 43, 45
shortcutting character of jokes, 38–40
Foucault on, 49
Freud on, 38, 40, 42, 44
silence, Benjamin on, 68
Sinai, Mount, 127, 128
social norms, resistance to, 24–26, 38, 59, 74. See also resistance
"Socrates" (Benjamin), 60
Sorkin, David, 7
soteriology, cosmology, and Adorno, 99, 100, 120, 121
soul, 65
body, spirit, and. See tripartite theology
grades of the soul in universal nature, 134
silent conversation in the, 68
sovereign, the, 94
sovereign violence, 83
Spinoza, Baruch, 60, 100, 128
spirit, 59
body, soul, and. See tripartite theology
Jewish, 83–85
spiritual core, Benjamin on, 58–59, 66, 75, 76, 84, 85
Star Trek, 108
state of emergency, 28–29, 150
state of exception (Ausnahmezustand), 94
Strauss, Leo, 5–6
subversion, 118–19
Freud and, 22–24, 26–30, 34, 35, 39, 44, 53, 118–19
jokes and, 23–30, 34–36, 39, 44
nature of, 24

Talmud, 41, 42, 76
Taubes, Jacob, 98
Taylor, Charles, 161
technology
Adorno on, 106, 107, 113
theology and, 106
temporality. See also time
theology and, 127
tendentious jokes, 32, 33, 35
theocratic anarchism, 83
theodicy
Arendt and, 157, 159
defined, 157
dualism, evil, and, 157
secularization of, 159
theologia tripartita. See tripartite theology
theological conceptions, translation of, 89–101
theological concepts, 167
of God, 6
reconceptualization of, 8, 112, 140, 144, 154. See also theological conceptions
Adorno and, 13, 14, 91, 92, 95, 102, 112, 117, 139, 154, 164
Arendt and, 14, 140, 141, 143–46, 151–52, 164–65
Benjamin and, 141, 164
Kierkegaard and, 117, 118
Roman political, 145–47
theological thinking, 4–5, 91, 92
theology. See also critique of theology; specific topics
holding onto an unholdable, 111, 113. See also holding onto an unholdable object
kinds of, 133–34
notion of, 6
purpose of, 165
time. See also temporality
Arendt and, 65, 137–40

time *(continued)*
  Augustine on, 140
  emptiness of, 70
  pure, 70
"togetherness of men," 144–45, 149
totalitarianism, Arendt on, 10, 30, 126, 156. *See also under* Arendt, Hannah: writings
tradition
  Arendt on, 9, 10, 81, 124–33, 135–39, 142–45, 151, 153, 154, 159
  Augustine on, 131
  authority and, 86, 126, 128, 145–47
  definitions and notions of, 126, 127, 129, 139, 145
  etymology of the term, 126
  "hidden," 135–36, 152
  love and, 129–31
  tripartite theology and, 133. *See also* tripartite theology
"Tradition" (song), 125
traditional concepts, 159–60
  Arendt on, 137–39, 141, 142, 147, 159–60
  critique and, 137–39, 141
traditionalism, 150
  Arendt and, 141, 150, 151, 165
  Benjamin's, 141
transcendence
  Adorno and, 90, 99, 106, 160
  Arendt and, 159, 160
  Benjamin's theory of youth and, 58–63, 66
  divinity, eternity, and, 58–63
  immanence and, 63, 100, 108, 121
  nature of, 61
  radical, 154, 158, 159
transgression
  of borders, 18, 20
  critique and, 39, 52
  definitions and meanings, 38, 48–49
  Foucault and, 47–50, 52
  Freud and, 11, 18, 20, 22, 23, 39, 40, 44, 45, 47, 49–52, 104
  jokes and, 38, 39, 44, 49, 50
  of laws, 11, 23, 38–40, 42–45, 49, 51, 52, 79, 104, 105
  in modernity, 48–49
  religion, theology, and, 11, 23, 40–42, 44, 45, 47–49, 51
  sexual, 48
  shortcuts and, 38–45
translation, 62, 91
tripartite theology (*theologia tripartita*), 133–36, 142–43
  Arendt and, 14, 133–38, 142–43
  Augustine and, 14, 133, 134, 136
true criticism
  Benjamin and, 73–87
  critique of theology, 73–80
  secularization and political imagination, 80–87
truth, 111, 137, 143
  Arendt and, 143, 145, 150, 164
  hidden, 29, 52, 103
  revelation and, 143, 145

unity, 112
  with the divine, 51–53, 66–67, 80, 99–101, 108, 110, 112
  of opposites, 72
universities, the "perversion" of, 60
unmoved mover (Aristotle), 96

Varro, Marcus Terentius, 133, 134
Villa, Dana, 10, 126
violence, 31. *See also* critique of violence
  Arendt on, 147–48
  Benjamin on, 79, 81–83, 148
  Freud on jokes and, 32, 33
  power, authority, and, 148
  theology and, 144
  types of, 82, 83, 148

Voegelin, Eric, 97, 152
vulgar materialism, 121
vulgarization. *See also* obscenity
    of messianism, 121

Weber, Max, 122, 135, 161
Wetters, Kirk, 79
widow (Eckhart), 64, 65, 69
wit. *See also* jokes; laughter
    Benjamin on, 76
    brevity and, 30–35, 37, 38
    Freud on. See *Jokes and Their Relation to the Unconscious*; laughter; wit and law
    principle of pleasure, 34–38
    translation of the term, 11, 18, 30
wit and law, 26, 39–40
    eternal laws and jokes, 27, 29, 44, 45, 52
    Freud and, 36, 39, 44, 45, 52, 55, 84, 105. *See also* critique of theology: Freud's
"word of God," 61, 142
wordlessness, Arendt and, 143, 144
world in which we live, 161–66
    Adorno and, 94, 118, 122–23
    Arendt and, 144, 145, 157, 164–65, 167
    Benjamin and, 80, 164
    Robert Cover, the law, and, 26

Wyneken, Gustav, 58

Yehuda bar Ma'arava, 40
Yerushalmi, Yossef Haim, 8, 43
Yiddish, 29
Yom Kippur, 33, 43
youth
    age of
        Benjamin on, 57–59. *See also* Benjamin, Walter: youth and
        rebellion and quest, 55–58
        transcendence, divinity, and eternity, 58–63
    definitions and meanings, 55, 57, 59
    Eckhart and, 63–66, 71–73, 78
    metaphysical quest for, 86
    metaphysics of, 66–73
    mystical allegories, 63–73
    "Young man, I tell you, stand up!," 64
    mysticism and, 66–68, 164
    nature of, 59, 62, 73, 84, 85
    nothingness and, 66, 72–74, 83
    political theology and, 85
    purity and, 59, 70, 72, 75, 76, 84

Zionism, 85–86
    Benjamin and, 85, 86
    Gershom Scholem and, 8, 85, 86
Žižek, Salvoj, 161

www.ingramcontent.com/pod-product-compliance
Lightning Source LLC
Chambersburg PA
CBHW020645230426
43665CB00008B/319